A Dreamer and a Visionary

Liverpool Science Fiction Texts and Studies

General Editor DAVID SEED

Series Advisers
I. F. Clarke, Edward James, Patrick Parrinder and Brian Stableford

Robert Crossley *Olaf Stapledon: Speaking for the Future*

David Seed (ed.) *Anticipations: Essays on Early Science Fiction and its Precursors*

Jane L. Donawerth and Carol A. Kolmerten (eds) *Utopian and Science Fiction by Women: Worlds of Difference*

Brian W. Aldiss *The Detached Retina: Aspects of SF and Fantasy*

Carol Farley Kessler *Charlotte Perkins Gilman: Her Progress Toward Utopia, with Selected Writings*

Patrick Parrinder *Shadows of the Future: H. G. Wells, Science Fiction and Prophecy*

I. F. Clarke (ed.) *The Tale of the Next Great War, 1871–1914: Fictions of Future Warfare and of Battles Still-to-come*

Joseph Conrad and Ford Modox Ford (Foreword by George Hay, Introduction by David Seed) *The Inheritors*

Qingyun Wu *Female Rule in Chinese and English Literary Utopias*

John Clute *Look at the Evidence: Essays and Reviews*

Roger Luckhurst *'The Angle Between Two Walls': The Fiction of J. G. Ballard*

Franz Rottensteiner (ed.) *View from Another Shore: European Science Fiction*

Val Gough and Jill Rudd (eds) *A Very Different Story: Studies in the Fiction of Charlotte Perkins Gilman*

Gary Westfahl *The Mechanics of Wonder: the Creation of the Idea of Science Fiction*

Jeanne Cortiel *Demand My Writing: Joanna Russ/Feminism/Science Fiction*

Mike Ashley *The Time Machines: The Story of the Science-Fiction Pulp Magazines from the Beginning to 1950, The History of the Science-Fiction Magazine, Volume I*

Patrick Parrinder (ed.) *Learning from Other Worlds: Estrangement, Cognition and the Politics of Science Fiction and Utopia*

Warren Rochelle *Communities of the Heart: The Rhetoric of Myth in the Fiction of Ursula K. Le Guin*

S. T. Joshi *A Dreamer and a Visionary: H. P. Lovecraft in his Time*

A Dreamer and a Visionary

H. P. Lovecraft in his Time

S. T. JOSHI

LIVERPOOL UNIVERSITY PRESS

First published 2001 by
Liverpool University Press
4 Cambridge Street
Liverpool
L69 7ZU

British Library Cataloguing-in-Publication Data
A British Library CIP record is available.

ISBN 0 85323 936 3 cased
ISBN 0 85323 946 0 paperback

Typeset in Meridien by
Koinonia, Bury, Lancashire
Printed in Great Britain by
Bell and Bain Ltd, Glasgow

Contents

To David E. Schultz

… from earliest childhood I have been a dreamer and a visionary.
—H. P. Lovecraft, 'The Tomb'

Preface

I do not believe that much needs to be said here regarding the scope and overall purpose of this volume. I have sought to trace, in some detail, the life of Howard Phillips Lovecraft, to supply some account of his major writings, and to give at least an outline of the philosophical thought that structures his work and in accordance with which he led his life. All these features have been treated in more detail elsewhere, but readers may find their fusion in this work of some benefit.

I have been involved in the study of Lovecraft for two and a half decades, and in that interim have incurred more debts of gratitude from colleagues than I could possibly repay or even record. When I first began to take a scholarly interest in Lovecraft, I was guided by Dirk W. Mosig, J. Vernon Shea, and George T. Wetzel; other colleagues such as R. Boerem, Kenneth W. Faig, Jr, Richard L. Tierney, Scott Connors, Matthew H. Onderdonk, Peter Cannon, and David E. Schultz also helped me considerably. Marc A. Michaud's Necronomicon Press offered me abundant opportunities to expand my interests into realms I might otherwise not have pursued.

Much of my work on Lovecraft has of course been done at the John Hay Library of Brown University, the largest repository of Lovecraft material in the world. Its assistant librarian, John H. Stanley, has been of invaluable assistance in countless ways, as have such other librarians there as Jennifer B. Lee and Jean Rainwater. I have also done much work at the Rhode Island Historical Society, the Providence Public Library, the New York Public Library, the New York University Library, the Columbia University Library, and elsewhere.

The entire manuscript of this book has been read by Kenneth W. Faig, Jr, and Steven J. Mariconda, both of whom (but Faig in particular) offered a great many useful suggestions. Other facts, large and small, have been supplied by Donald R. Burleson, Stefan Dziemianowicz, Perry M. Grayson, T. E. D. Klein, Dan Lorraine,

Donovan K. Loucks, M. Eileen McNamara, M.D., Marc A. Michaud, Sam Moskowitz, Robert M. Price, David E. Schultz, A. Langley Searles, and Richard D. Squires.

A Note on Sources

Because of the ready availability of most of Lovecraft's work, I have not seen the need to cite editions of his tales, essays, and poems in this book, or indeed to supply a bibliography at all. Works by Lovecraft are chiefly cited from the editions listed below; full bibliographical information on works about Lovecraft is given in the notes.

Lovecraft's juvenile fiction and poetry (1897–1905) is contained in my edition of *Juvenilia* (1984). The juvenile nonfiction (scientific periodicals and treatises) has not been published, but most of it can be found in the John Hay Library of Brown University.

The following four volumes, edited by me, contain the great majority of Lovecraft's stories and revisions:

> *The Dunwich Horror and Others* (1984)
> *At the Mountains of Madness and Other Novels* (1985)
> *Dagon and Other Macabre Tales* (1986)
> *The Horror in the Museum and Other Revisions* (1989)

The remaining fiction is contained in my edition of Lovecraft's *Miscellaneous Writings* (1995). Lovecraft's poetry is contained in my edition of *The Ancient Track: Complete Poetical Works* (2001).

Lovecraft's essays are not very readily available, but a large selection is contained in *Miscellaneous Writings*. There are many editions published by Necronomicon Press of select bodies of his work, of which note can be made of the following:

> *The Conservative: Complete* (1976)
> *Writings in* The United Amateur (1976)
> *The Californian* (1977)
> *Uncollected Prose and Poetry* (1978–82; 3 vols)
> *In Defence of Dagon* (1985)
> *Autobiographical Writings* (1992)

Other editions containing essays are August Derleth's various miscellany volumes, *Marginalia* (1944), *Something about Cats and Other Pieces* (1949), *The Shuttered Room and Other Pieces* (1959), and *The*

Dark Brotherhood and Other Pieces (1966), as well as L. Sprague de Camp's edition of *To Quebec and the Stars* (1976).

Because of the large quantity of Lovecraft's letters and the valuable information they contain, I have been careful to cite these documents very specifically. The primary source for Lovecraft's letters remains *Selected Letters* (1965–76; 5 vols; abbreviated as SL), even if many of the letters are abridged. This edition was itself founded upon an immense quantity of transcripts prepared by Arkham House over the years, and in many cases these transcripts contain fuller versions of the letters. I have abbreviated citations from these transcripts as AHT. Another substantial volume is *Lord of a Visible World: An Autobiography in Letters* (2000), edited by David E. Schultz and myself, and containing many of the autobiographical letters from which I have drawn so heavily in this book.

The manuscripts of many of Lovecraft's letters are available at the John Hay Library of Brown University, the primary repository of works by and about Lovecraft. Lovecraft's letters to August Derleth, and some other relevant documents, are at the State Historical Society of Wisconsin in Madison.

CHAPTER ONE
Unmixed English Gentry

Only an intermittently diligent genealogist, Howard Phillips Lovecraft was able to discover little about the paternal side of his ancestry beyond the notes collected by his great-aunt Sarah Allgood. Subsequent genealogical research has failed to verify much of this information, especially regarding the Lovecrafts prior to their coming to America in the early nineteenth century. According to the Allgood notes, the Lovecraft or Lovecroft name does not appear any earlier than 1450, when various heraldic charts reveal Lovecrofts in Devonshire near the Teign. Lovecraft's own direct line does not emerge until 1560, with John Lovecraft.

The paternal line becomes of immediate interest only with Thomas Lovecraft (1745–1826), who apparently lived such a dissolute life that he was forced in 1823 to sell the ancestral estate, Minster Hall near Newton Abbot. According to Lovecraft (or the notes he was consulting), Thomas Lovecraft's sixth child, Joseph S. Lovecraft, decided in 1827 to emigrate, taking his wife Mary Fulford and their six children, John Full, William, Joseph, Jr, George, Aaron, and Mary, to Ontario, Canada. Finding no prospects there, he drifted down to the area around Rochester, New York, where he was established by at least 1831 as a cooper and carpenter.

Lovecraft's paternal grandfather was George Lovecraft, who was probably born in 1818 or 1819.[1] In 1839 he married Helen Allgood (1821–81) and lived much of his life in Rochester as a harness maker. Of his five children, two died in infancy; the other three were Emma Jane (1847–1925), Winfield Scott (1853–1898), and Mary Louise (1855–1916). Winfield married Sarah Susan Phillips and begat Howard Phillips Lovecraft.

Lovecraft appears to have been much more industrious in tracking down his maternal ancestry, but again his conclusions are not always to be trusted. At various points in his life he traced his maternal line either to the Rev. George Phillips (d. 1644), who in 1630 left England on the *Arbella* and settled in Watertown, Massachusetts, or to Michael Phillips (1630?–86) of Newport, Rhode Island. Whatever the case, Asaph Phillips (1764–1829), probably Michael's great-great-grandson, headed inland and settled around 1788 in Foster, in the west-central part of the state near the Connecticut border. Asaph and his wife Esther Whipple had eight children, all of whom, incredibly, survived to adulthood. The sixth child, Jeremiah Phillips (1800–48), built a water-powered grist mill on the Moosup River in Foster and was killed on 20 November 1848 when his flowing greatcoat got caught in the machinery, dragging him into it. As Jeremiah's wife Roby Rathbun Phillips had died earlier in 1848, their four children were left as orphans. They were Susan, James, Whipple, and Abbie. Whipple Van Buren Phillips (1833–1904) is Lovecraft's maternal grandfather.

Whipple attended the East Greenwich Academy (then called The Providence Conference Seminary), probably prior to the death of his father Jeremiah. In 1852 he went to live with his uncle James Phillips (1794–1878) in Delavan, Illinois, a temperance town his relatives had founded; he returned the next year to Foster because the climate did not suit him. He married his first cousin, Robie Alzada Place (1827–1896),[2] on 27 January 1856, settling in a homestead in Foster built by Robie's father Stephen Place. Their first child, Lillian Delora (1856–1932), was born less than three months later. There were four other children: Sarah Susan (1857–1921), Emeline (1859–65), Edwin Everett (1864–1918), and Annie Emeline (1866–1941). Lovecraft's mother Sarah Susan was born, as her own mother had been, at the Place homestead.

In 1855 Whipple purchased a general store in Foster and ran it for at least two years; he then presumably sold the store and its goods, probably at a substantial profit, thereby commencing his career as entrepreneur and land speculator. At that time he moved a few miles south of Foster to the town of Coffin's Corner, where he built 'a mill, a house, an assembly hall, and several cottages for employees';[3] since he had purchased all the land there, he renamed the town Greene (in honour of the Rhode Island Revolutionary War hero Nathanael Greene). It is remarkable to think of a twenty-four-year-old essentially owning an entire small town, but Whipple was clearly a bold and dynamic businessman, one who would gain and lose several fortunes in his crowded life.

One particular financial collapse, in 1870, led to the selling of the Place homestead in Foster and a move to Providence. Whipple settled initially on the West Side of Providence—the western shore of the Providence River, site of the present business district—since his business offices were in this general area. In connection with his various businesses he travelled widely in Europe, particularly France (he attended the Paris Exposition of 1878), England, and Italy.

By this time Whipple Phillips was clearly a man of substantial means, and, aside from building the house at 194 Angell Street in 1880–81, he undertook what was to be his most ambitious business enterprise: the establishment of the Owyhee Land and Irrigation Company in Owyhee County in the southwest corner of Idaho, 'which had for its object the damming of the Snake River & the irrigation of the surrounding farming & fruit-growing region'.[4] Kenneth W. Faig, Jr, has performed a remarkable feat of excavation in supplying the details of his enterprise, and I can do no better than to summarize his findings.[5]

The company was incorporated in Providence as the Snake River Company as early as 1884, with Whipple as president and his nephew Jeremiah W. Phillips as secretary and treasurer. Initially the company dealt in land and livestock, but shortly thereafter Whipple shifted his attention to the building of a dam—not over the Snake River, as Lovecraft erroneously believed, but over its tributary, the Bruneau River.

Work on the dam began in the autumn of 1887 and was completed by early 1890. Whipple purchased a ferry in 1887 and established a town near the ferry on the Snake River, naming it Grand View. He also built a Grand View Hotel, to be managed by his son Edwin. At this point disaster struck. On 5 March 1890, the dam was completely washed out by high waters, and the $70,000 spent in constructing it was lost. A new dam was begun in the summer of 1891 and completed by February 1893.

Whipple was, of course, by no means permanently at the site; indeed, he appears to have visited it only occasionally. We shall see that, when he was not in Idaho, he was spending considerable time and effort (especially after April 1893) raising his then only grand-child, Howard Phillips Lovecraft.

The Owyhee Land and Irrigation Company suffered some sort of financial difficulties around 1900, and on 12 March 1901 the company was sold at a sheriff's sale in Silver City. Whipple Phillips was one of five purchasers, but the total property value of the company had been assessed on 25 May 1900 at only $9430. The final blow came in early 1904, when the dam was wiped out again. Lovecraft states that this second disaster 'virtually wiped the

Phillips family out financially & hastened my grandfather's death—age 70, of apoplexy'.[6] Whipple Phillips died on 28 March 1904; after his death three other individuals bought out his interest in the Owyhee Land and Irrigation Company and renamed it the Grand View Irrigation Company, Ltd.

It is clear that the Owyhee project was Whipple's principal business concern during his later years, although no doubt he had other interests in Providence and elsewhere, as his wide travels suggest. He did, however, certainly lose a good deal of money in the Idaho venture. Nevertheless, the picture that emerges of Whipple Phillips is that of an abundantly capable businessman—bold, innovative, and perhaps a little reckless—but also a man of wide culture and one who took great concern in the financial, intellectual, and personal well-being of his extended family.

Lovecraft's elder aunt, Lillian Delora Clark, attended the Wheaton Female Seminary (now Wheaton College) in Norton, Massachusetts, for at least the period 1871–73. Lovecraft states that she 'also attended the State Normal School, and was for some time a teacher',[7] but her attendance at the Normal School has not been confirmed. Lovecraft was proud of the artistic skills of both his aunt and his mother, and claimed that Lillian has 'had canvases hung in exhibitions at the Providence Art Club'.[8]

Lovecraft speaks little of his uncle, Edwin Everett Phillips, and does not seem to have been close to him. Edwin briefly assisted his father in his Idaho enterprise, but he returned to Providence in 1889 and attempted—not very successfully, it appears—to go into business for himself. In 1894 he married Martha Helen Mathews; at some point they were divorced, then remarried in 1903. Throughout his life Edwin held various odd jobs, and at some point established the Edwin E. Phillips Refrigeration Company. His one significant involvement with Lovecraft and his mother was, as we shall see, an unfortunate one.

Annie Emeline Phillips, Lovecraft's younger aunt, was nine years younger than Susie. Lovecraft remarks that she 'was yet a very young lady when I first began to observe events about me. She was rather a favourite in the younger social set, & brought the principal touch of gayety to a rather conservative household.'[9] I know nothing about her education.

We can finally turn our attention to Sarah Susan Phillips, born on 17 October 1857. Regrettably little is known about her early years. Lovecraft states that she, like Lillian, attended Wheaton

Female Seminary, but her attendance can be confirmed only for the school year 1871–72. From this period up to the time of her marriage in 1889 the record is blank. Clara Hess, a friend of the Lovecrafts, gives a description of Susie, probably dating from the late 1890s: 'She was very pretty and attractive, with a beautiful and unusually white complexion—got, it is said, by eating arsenic, although whether there was any truth to this story I do not know. She was an intensely nervous person.'[10] Elsewhere Hess remarks: 'She had a peculiarly shaped nose which rather fascinated me, as it gave her a very inquiring expression. Howard looked very much like her.'[11]

What little we know of Winfield Scott Lovecraft prior to his marriage derives from research recently conducted by Richard D. Squires of the Wallace Library at the Rochester Institute of Technology.[12] Winfield was born on 26 October 1853, probably at the home of George and Helen Lovecraft at 42 Marshall Street in Rochester. George Lovecraft was at the time a 'traveling agent' for the Ellwanger & Barry Nursery, a major business in Rochester. The family attended services at the Grace Episcopal (now St Paul's) Church. These facts may be of some relevance to Winfield, since he was himself a salesman and was married at St Paul's Episcopal Church in Boston, even though his bride was a Baptist.

From 1871 to 1873 Winfield was employed as a blacksmith for the James Cunningham & Son carriage factory, Rochester's largest employer for many years. During this time he boarded with another uncle, John Full Lovecraft, in a home on Marshall Street. By 1874 all traces of Winfield Scott Lovecraft disappear from the records in Rochester.

Lovecraft stated on several occasions that his father was educated at a military school, but the location of this military school has not been traced; Winfield clearly did not attend West Point, as a check of its registry of graduates establishes. It is possible that it may not have been a formal military academy (of which there were very few at the time) but a school that emphasized military training. In any event, it is likely to have been local—somewhere in New York State, perhaps close to the Rochester area.

At some point Winfield moved to New York City, as this is given as his place of residence on his marriage certificate. He probably roomed there with his cousin, Frederick A. Lovecraft (1850–93). It is believed that he became employed by Gorham & Co., Silversmiths, of Providence, then one of the major business concerns in the city. The evidence for this employment does not derive from any statement by Lovecraft, but from a remark by Lovecraft's wife Sonia in her 1948 memoir.[13] It is not clear how and when Winfield began work for Gorham (assuming that he actually did so), and why, even if he was working as a travelling salesman, he was listed as a resident of New York City at the time of his marriage on 12 June 1889.

Equally a mystery is how he met Sarah Susan Phillips and how they fell in love. Susie certainly does not appear to have been a 'society girl' like her sister Annie, and Winfield was not a door-to-door salesman, so that he is not likely to have met her in this way; nor, if he had, would the social mores of the time have allowed them to fraternize. The Phillipses were, after all, part of the Providence aristocracy.

The fact that the wedding ceremony took place at St Paul's Episcopal Church in Boston may or may not be noteworthy. We have already seen that Winfield's family was Episcopal; and, although there were many Episcopal churches in Providence where the ceremony could have taken place, the fact that Winfield planned to settle his family in the Boston area may have made St Paul's a logical site. Indeed, it might have been odd for a member of the Phillips family of Providence, so associated with the Baptist faith, to have been married in a local Episcopal church. I discount the possibility, therefore, that the marriage was somehow not approved by Susie's parents, for which no true evidence exists. Although she was thirty-one at the time of the marriage, Susie was the first of Whipple Phillips's daughters to be married; as she was still living under his roof, it is not likely that he would have allowed her to marry someone of whom he did not approve.

Lovecraft, so keen on racial purity, was fond of declaring that his 'ancestry was that of unmixed English gentry';[14] and if one can include a Welsh (Morris) strain on his paternal side and an Irish (Casey) strain on his maternal, then the statement can pass. His maternal line is, indeed, far more distinguished than his paternal, and we find Rathbones, Mathewsons, Whipples, Places, Wilcoxes, Hazards, and other old New England lines behind Susie Lovecraft and her father Whipple Van Buren Phillips. What we do not find—as Lovecraft frequently bemoaned—is much in the way of intellectual, artistic, or imaginative distinction. But if Lovecraft himself failed to inherit the business acumen of Whipple Phillips, he did somehow acquire the literary gifts that have resulted in a subsidiary fascination with his mother, father, grandfather, and the other members of his near and distant ancestry.

CHAPTER TWO

A Genuine Pagan (1890–97)

In April 1636 Roger Williams left the Massachusetts-Bay colony and headed south, settling first on the east bank of the Seekonk River and later, when Massachusetts asserted territorial rights to this region, on the west bank. He named this site Providence. Williams's immediate reason for seeking new territory was, of course, religious freedom: his own Baptist beliefs did not sit well with the Puritan theocracy of the Massachusetts-Bay. The religious separatism present at the very birth of Rhode Island left a permanent legacy of political, economic, and social separatism in the state.

Although Roger Williams had negotiated with the Indians for his plot of land at Providence, the native population of Rhode Island did not fare so well thereafter. King Philip's War (1675–76) was devastating to both sides, but particularly to the Indians (Narragansetts, Wampanoags, Sakonnets, and Niantics), who were nearly wiped out, their pitiful remnants huddled together on a virtual reservation near Charlestown. The rebuilding of the white settlements that had been destroyed in Providence and elsewhere was slow but certain; from now on it would not be religious freedom or Indian warfare that would concern the white colonists, but economic development. In the eighteenth century the four Brown brothers (John, Joseph, Nicholas, and Moses) would be among the leading entrepreneurs in the Colonies. It is, however, a stain on Rhode Island's record that it was one of the leading slave-trading states both before and just after the Revolution, its many merchant vessels (some of them privateers) carting away hundreds of thousands of slaves, mostly from the West Indies. Relatively few ended up actually in Rhode Island; most that did so worked on large plantations in the southern part of the state.

Much to the chagrin of Lovecraft's Tory sentiments, Rhode Island was a spearhead of the Revolution, and people here were more united in favour of independence than in the other colonies. Stephen Hopkins, provincial governor of Rhode Island for much of the period between 1755 and 1768, was one of the signers of the

Declaration of Independence. Separatist to the end, however, Rhode Island refused to send delegates to the Constitutional Convention and was the last of the thirteen colonies to ratify the Federal Constitution.

Roger Williams had founded the Baptist church in Rhode Island—the first in America—in 1638. For more than two centuries the state remained largely Baptist, but other sects came in over time. There were Quakers, Congregationalists, Unitarians, Episcopalians, Methodists, and other, smaller groups. A colony of Jews had been present since the seventeenth century, but their numbers were small and they were careful to assimilate with the Yankees. Roman Catholics began to be prominent only in the middle nineteenth century. Their numbers were augmented by successive waves of immigration: French Canadians during the Civil War (establishing themselves especially in the town of Woonsocket in the northeast corner of the state), Italians after 1890 (settling in the Federal Hill area of Providence's West Side), Portuguese shortly thereafter. It is disturbing, but sadly not surprising, to note the increasing social exclusiveness and scorn of foreigners developing among the old-time Yankees throughout the nineteenth century. The Know-Nothing Party, with its anti-foreign and anti-Catholic bias, dominated the state during the 1850s. Rhode Island remained politically conservative into the 1930s, and Lovecraft's entire family voted Republican throughout his lifetime. If Lovecraft voted at all, he also voted Republican almost uniformly until 1932. The state's leading paper, the *Providence Journal*, remains conservative to this day even though the state has been largely Democratic since the 1930s.

Newport, on the southern end of Aquidneck Island, gained early ascendancy in what became Rhode Island, and Providence did not overtake it until after the Revolutionary war. By 1890 Providence was the only city of any significant size in the state: its population was 132,146, making it the twenty-third largest city in the nation. Its principal topographic features are its seven hills and the Providence River, which divides at Fox Point and splits into the Seekonk River on the east and the Moshassuck River on the west. Between these two rivers is the East Side, the oldest and most exclusive part of the city, especially the lofty eminence of College Hill, which rises steeply on the east bank of the Moshassuck. The area west of the Moshassuck is the West Side—the downtown area and a newer residential district. To the north lies the suburb of

Pawtucket, to the northwest North Providence, to the southwest Cranston, and to the east—on the other side of the Seekonk—the suburbs of Seekonk and East Providence.

Brown University—founded in 1764 (as King's College) under Baptist auspices—lords it on the pinnacle of College Hill, and has lately been gobbling up more and more of the surrounding colonial area. This is the oldest part of the city in terms of the structures still surviving, although nothing dates before the middle of the eighteenth century. Lovecraft would have been heartened by the tremendous restoration of the colonial houses on College Hill in the 1950s and onward, conducted under the auspices of the Providence Preservation Society. The restoration has caused Benefit Street in particular to be regarded as the finest mile of colonial architecture in the United States.

To the east of College Hill is a spacious array of residences dating no earlier than the middle nineteenth century but impressively built and with well-kept grounds and gardens. This, rather than the colonial area, is the true home of the Providence aristocracy and plutocracy. At the eastern edge of this area, running alongside the Seekonk River, is Blackstone Boulevard, whose luxurious homes are still the haven of old Yankee money. At the northern end of Blackstone Boulevard is Butler Hospital for the Insane, opened in 1847. Juxtaposed to Butler Hospital on its north side is the vast expanse of Swan Point Cemetery—not perhaps quite as lavishly landscaped as Mt Auburn in Boston but one of the most topographically beautiful cemeteries in the country.

Howard Phillips Lovecraft was born at 9 a.m.[1] on 20 August 1890, at 194 (renumbered 454 in 1895–96) Angell Street on what was then the eastern edge of the East Side of Providence. The sequence and details of the family's travels and residences in the period 1890–93 are very confused. It appears that Winfield and Susie Lovecraft took up residence in Dorchester, Massachusetts (a suburb of Boston), as soon as they married on 12 June 1889. They came to Providence late in Susie's pregnancy, then presumably moved back to Dorchester a few weeks or months after Howard was born, then moved to the Auburndale area (also in the Boston metropolitan zone) in 1892. There may even have been other temporary residences in the area. Lovecraft states in 1934:

> My first memories are of the summer of 1892—just before
> my second birthday. We were then vacationing in Dudley,

> Mass., & I recall the house with its frightful attic water-tank
> & my rocking-horses at the head of the stairs. I recall also the
> plank walks laid to facilitate walking in rainy weather—& a
> wooded ravine, & a boy with a small rifle who let me pull
> the trigger while my mother held me.[2]

Dudley is in the west-central portion of Massachusetts. In Auburndale the Lovecrafts stayed at least briefly with the poet Louise
Imogen Guiney and her mother. Letters from Guiney to F. H. Day,
dating to May, June, and July 1892, have been thought to allude to
the Lovecrafts; however, recent research by Kenneth W. Faig, Jr,
reveals that the persons in question were some German visitors.
Lovecraft himself states that 'we stayed [at the Guineys'] during the
winter of 1892–93',[3] and in the absence of contrary evidence we
are compelled to accept this testimony.

Lovecraft says that Guiney (1861–1920) 'had been educated in
Providence, where she met my mother years before'.[4] There is
some little mystery around this. Guiney was indeed educated at the
Academy of the Sacred Heart at 736 Smith Street in the Elmhurst
section of Providence, attending the school from the year it opened
in 1872 until 1879; but Susie, as we have seen, attended the
Wheaton Seminary in Norton, Massachusetts, for at least the period
1871–72. Although Guiney scholar Henry G. Fairbanks asserts that
the Sacred Heart accepted Protestants as well as Catholics,[5] I think
it is unlikely that Susie was actually sent there. Nevertheless, one
must assume that Susie and Guiney somehow became acquainted
during this time. It is possible that Lovecraft exaggerated the degree
of his mother's acquaintance with Guiney; or perhaps his mother
herself did so to her son. She may have stressed the Guiney connection once she saw Lovecraft developing into a writer himself.

Lovecraft's memories of Auburndale—especially of the Guiney
residence—are numerous and clear:

> I distinctly recall the quiet, shady suburb as I saw it in 1892
> … Miss Guiney kept a most extraordinary collection of St.
> Bernard dogs, all named after authors and poets. A shaggy
> gentleman by the classic name of Brontë was my particular
> favourite & companion, being ever in attendance on my
> chariot as my mother wheeled that vehicle through the
> streets & avenues. Brontë would permit me to place my fist
> in his mouth without biting me, & would snarl protectingly
> if any stranger approached me.[6]

Another memory Lovecraft had was the tableau of a railway bridge in the city:

> I can see myself as a child of $2^1/_2$ on the railway bridge at Auburndale, Mass., looking across and downward at the business part of the town, and feeling the imminence of some wonder which I could neither describe nor fully conceive—and there has never been a subsequent hour of my life when kindred sensations have been absent.[7]

His first literary stirrings can be dated to this period:

> At the age of two I was a rapid talker, familiar with the alphabet from my blocks & picture-books, & ... absolutely *metre-mad*! I could not read, but would repeat any poem of simple sort with unfaltering cadence. Mother Goose was my principal classic, & Miss Guiney would continually make me repeat parts of it; not that my rendition was necessarily notable, but because my age lent uniqueness to the performance.[8]

Guiney herself seems to have taken to the infant; she would repeatedly ask, 'Whom do you love?' to which Lovecraft would pipe back: 'Louise Imogen Guiney!'[9]

Lovecraft had a brief encounter with a distinguished friend of Guiney's, Oliver Wendell Holmes—one of many fleeting brushes with established writers he would have throughout his life: 'Oliver Wendell Holmes came not infrequently to this [Guiney's] menage, and on one occasion (unremembered by the passenger) is said to have ridden the future *Weird Tales* disciple on his venerable knee.'[10] Holmes (1809–94) was at this time very old, and was indeed a close friend of Guiney; no doubt he failed to remember for very long his meeting with the future master of weird fiction.

Lovecraft's early residences and travels were, of course, dictated by his father's business. The latter's medical record lists him as a 'Commercial Traveller', and Lovecraft frequently affirms that his father's commercial interests kept him and his family in the Boston area during the period 1890–93. There is little reason to doubt Lovecraft when he says that 'my image of him is but vague':[11] Winfield lived with his family for only the first two and a half years of Lovecraft's life, and perhaps less than that if his business trips took him very far afield for long periods of time.

The illness that struck Winfield Scott Lovecraft in April 1893 and forced him to remain in Butler Hospital in Providence until his death in July 1898 is worth examining in detail. The Butler Hospital medical record reads as follows:

> For a year past he has shown obscure symptoms of mental disease—doing and saying strange things at times; has, also, grown pale and thin in flesh. He continued his business, however, until Apr. 21, when he broke down completely while stopping in Chicago. He rushed from his room shouting that a chambermaid had insulted him, and that certain men were outraging his wife in the room above. He was extremely noisy and violent for two days, but was finally quieted by free use of the bromides, which made his removal here possible. We can get no history of specific disease.

Upon Winfield's death in 1898, the medical record diagnosed him as having 'General Paralysis'; his death certificate listed the cause of death as 'general paresis'. In 1898 (and, for that matter, today) these terms were virtually synonymous. What was not then known —and would not be known until 1911—was the connection between general paresis and syphilis. Although general paresis was a kind of catch-all term for a variety of ailments, M. Eileen McNamara, M.D., studying Winfield's medical record, has concluded that the probability of Winfield's having tertiary syphilis is very strong. Winfield displayed nearly all the symptoms of tertiary syphilis as identified by Hinsie and Campbell in their *Psychiatric Dictionary* (4th ed., 1970):

> (1) simple dementia, the most common type, with deterioration of intellect, affect and social behavior; (2) paranoid form, with persecutory delusions; (3) expansive or manic form, with delusions of grandiosity; or (4) depressive form, often with absurd nihilistic delusions.[12]

The medical record clearly bears out at least the first three of these symptoms: (1) on 28 April 1893 'the patient ... broke out violently this morning—rushed up and down the ward shouting and attacked watchman'; (2) 29 April 1893: 'says three men—one a negro—in the room above trying to do violence to his wife'; 15 May 1893: 'believes his food is poisoned'; 25 June 1893: 'looks upon the officers and attendants as enemies and accuses them of stealing his clothing, watch, bonds, &c.'; (3) under the heading 'Mental Condition': 'boasts of his many friends; his business success, his family, and above all his great strength—asking writer to see how perfectly his muscles are developed'. For the fourth symptom—depression—the record is not sufficiently detailed to make a conjecture.

If, then, it is admitted that Winfield had syphilis, the question is how he contracted it. At this point, of course, we can only indulge in conjecture. McNamara reminds us that the 'latent period between inoculation and the development of tertiary syphilis is ten to twenty years', so that Winfield 'might have been infected as early as eighteen or as late as twenty-eight, well before his marriage at age thirty-five'.[13] It is, unfortunately, exactly this period of Winfield's life about which nothing is known. It is difficult to doubt that Winfield contracted syphilis either from a prostitute or from some other sex partner prior to his marriage, either while attending the military academy or during his stint as a 'Commercial Traveller', if indeed that began so early as the age of twenty-eight. (The conjecture that Lovecraft himself might have had congenital syphilis is disproved by the fact that the Wassermann test he was given during his own final illness was negative.)

The course of Winfield's illness makes horrifying reading. After the first several months the entries become quite sporadic, sometimes as many as six months passing before a notation is made. Occasionally there are signs of improvement; sometimes Winfield seems to be failing, and toward the end of 1895 it was thought that he had only days to live. A few times he was permitted to go about the ward or take some air in the yard. His condition began to decline markedly by the spring of 1898. By May he had developed constipation and required an enema every three days. On 12 July he had a temperature of 103° and a pulse of 106, with frequent convulsions. On 18 July he 'passe[d] from one convulsion into another' and was pronounced dead the next day.

The trauma experienced by Susie Lovecraft over this excruciating period of five years—with doctors ignorant of how to treat Winfield's illness, and with periods of false hope where the patient seems to recover only to lapse into more serious physical and mental deterioration—can only be imagined. When Susie herself was admitted to Butler Hospital in 1919, her doctor, F. J. Farnell, 'found disorder had been evidenced for fifteen years; that in all, abnormality had existed at least twenty-six years'.[14] It is no accident that the onset of her 'abnormality' dates to 1893.

The critical issue, of course, is what—if anything—Lovecraft himself knew of the nature and extent of his father's illness. He was two years and eight months old when his father was committed, and seven years and eleven months old when his father died. If he was already reciting poetry at two and a half, he must at least have been aware that something peculiar had happened—why else would he and his mother have moved suddenly back from Auburndale to the maternal home in Providence?

It is obvious from Lovecraft's remarks that he was intentionally kept in the dark about the specific nature of his father's illness. One wonders, indeed, whether Susie herself knew all its particulars. Lovecraft's first known statement on the matter occurs in a letter of 1915: 'In 1893 my father was seized with a complete paralytic stroke, due to insomnia and an overstrained nervous system, which took him to the hospital for the remaining five years of his life. He was never afterward conscious.'[15] It need hardly be said at this point that nearly every part of this utterance is false. When Lovecraft refers to a 'complete paralytic stroke', either he is remembering some deliberate falsehood he was told (i.e., that his father was paralysed), or he has misconstrued the medical term 'General Paralysis' or some account of it that he heard. The medical record does confirm that Winfield was overworked ('Has been actively engaged in business for several years and for the last two years has worked very hard'), and no doubt Lovecraft was told this also; and the remark about Winfield not being conscious may have been the excuse he was given for not visiting his father in the hospital.

One matter of importance is whether Lovecraft ever saw his father in Butler Hospital. He never says explicitly that he did not, but his late statement that 'I was never in a hospital till 1924'[16] certainly suggests that he himself believed (or claimed to others) that he never did so. Recently there has been speculation that Lovecraft did indeed visit his father in the hospital; but there is absolutely no documentary evidence of this. I believe that this speculation is an inference from the fact that on two occasions—29 August 1893 and 29 May 1894—Winfield was taken out into the 'yard' and the 'airing-court'; but there is no reason to believe that the three- or four-year-old Lovecraft, or his mother, or anyone at all, visited him at this or any other time.

Perhaps more important than all these matters is the image and tokens of his father which Lovecraft retained in maturity. Remarking that 'In America, the Lovecraft line made some effort to keep from becoming nasally Yankeeised', he continues: 'my father was constantly warned not to fall into Americanisms of speech and provincial vulgarities of dress and mannerisms—so much so that he was generally regarded as an Englishman despite his birth in Rochester, N.Y. I can just recall his extremely precise and cultivated British voice.'[17] We need look no further for the source of Lovecraft's own Anglophilia—his pride in the British Empire, his use of British spelling variants, and his desire for close cultural and political ties between the United States and England. At about the age of six, 'when my grandfather told me of the American Revolution, I shocked everyone by adopting a dissenting view … Grover Cleveland was grandpa's ruler, but Her Majesty, Victoria, Queen of Great Britain & Ireland & Empress of India commanded my allegiance. "God Save the Queen!" was a stock phrase of mine.'[18] It would be going too far to suggest that Lovecraft's father actually induced his son to take the British side in the American revolution; but it is clear that the maternal side of his family, proud Yankees as they were, did not share that view. Winfield Townley Scott reports that a 'friend of the family' referred to Winfield as a 'pompous Englishman'.[19] This appears to be Ella Sweeney, a schoolteacher who knew the Lovecrafts from as early as their 1892 vacation in Dudley. Even individuals beyond Lovecraft's immediate family appear to have found Winfield's English bearing a little trying.

It is poignant to hear Lovecraft tell of his one genuine memory of his father:

> I can just remember my father—an immaculate figure in black coat & vest & grey striped trousers. I had a childish habit of slapping him on the knees & shouting 'Papa, you look just like a young man!' I don't know where I picked that phrase up; but I was vain & self-conscious, & given to repeating things which I saw tickled my elders.[20]

This litany of his father's clothing—'his immaculate black morning-coat and vest, ascot tie, and striped grey trousers'—is found in an earlier letter, and Lovecraft adds touchingly: 'I have myself worn some of his old ascots and wing collars, left all too immaculate by his early illness and death.'[21]

Winfield Scott Lovecraft was buried on 21 July 1898 in the Phillips plot in Swan Point Cemetery, Providence. There is every reason to believe that young Howard attended this service. The mere fact that he was buried here is (as Kenneth W. Faig has noted)[22] a testimony to Whipple Phillips's generosity of heart, and perhaps even an indication that Whipple paid for Winfield's medical expenses; Winfield's estate was valued at $10,000 upon his death, and it is unlikely that it could have been so great if it had been used for full-time hospital costs for more than five years.

The immediate effect of the hospitalization of Winfield Scott Lovecraft was to bring the two-and-a-half-year-old Howard more closely than ever under the influence of his mother, his two aunts (both of whom, as yet unmarried, were still residing at 454 Angell Street), his grandmother Robie, and especially his grandfather Whipple. Naturally, his mother's influence was at the outset the dominant one.

For his part, Whipple Van Buren Phillips proved to be an entirely satisfactory replacement for the father Lovecraft never knew. Lovecraft's simple statement that at this time 'my beloved grand-father ... became the centre of my entire universe'[23] is all we need to know. Whipple cured his grandson of his fear of the dark by daring him at the age of five to walk through a sequence of dark rooms at 454 Angell Street; he showed Lovecraft the art objects he brought from his travels to Europe; he wrote him letters when travelling on business; and he even recounted extemporaneous weird tales to the boy.

And so, with Whipple virtually taking the place of his father, Howard and his mother seemed to lead a normal enough life; indeed, with Whipple's finances still robust, Lovecraft had an idyllic and actually rather spoiled early childhood.

He appears to have begun reading at the age of four, and one of his earliest books appears to have been Grimm's *Fairy Tales*. The next year, he discovered a seminal book in his aesthetic development: the *Arabian Nights*. The book's effect upon Lovecraft was immediate and pronounced:

> how many dream-Arabs have the *Arabian Nights* bred! I ought to know, since at the age of 5 I was one of them! I had not then encountered Graeco-Roman myth, but found in Lang's *Arabian Nights* a gateway to glittering vistas of wonder and freedom. It was then that I invented for myself the name of Abdul Alhazred, and made my mother take me to all the Oriental curio shops and fit me up an Arabian corner in my room.[24]

Elsewhere, however, Lovecraft provides a different (and probably more accurate) account of the coining of the name Abdul Alhazred: 'I can't quite recall where I did get *Abdul Alhazred*. There is a dim recollection which associates it with a certain elder—the family lawyer, as it happens, but I can't remember whether I asked him to make up an Arabic name for me, or whether I merely asked him to criticise a choice I had otherwise made.'[25] The family lawyer was Albert A. Baker, who would be Lovecraft's legal guardian until 1911. His coinage (if indeed it was his) was a singularly infelicitous one from the point of view of Arabic grammar, since the result is a reduplicated article (Abd*ul Al*hazred). In any event, the name stuck.

The *Arabian Nights* may not have definitively steered Lovecraft toward the realm of weird fiction, but it certainly did not impede his progress in that direction. Although only a relatively small proportion of tales are actually supernatural, there are abundant accounts of crypts, tombs, caves, deserted cities, and other elements that would form significant features in Lovecraft's imaginative landscape.

What might have finally stacked the deck in favour of the weird for Lovecraft was his unexpected discovery of an edition of Coleridge's *Rime of the Ancient Mariner* illustrated by Gustave Doré, which he stumbled upon at the house of a friend of his family's at the age of six. Here is the impression the poem, and the pictures, made upon a young Lovecraft:

> Fancy ... the discovery of a great atlas-sized gift-book leaning against the mantel & having on the cover gilt letters reading 'With Illustrations by Gustave Doré'. The title didn't matter—for didn't I know the dark, supernal magic of the Doré pictures in our Dante & Milton at home? I open the book—& behold a hellish picture of a corpse-ship with ragged sails under a waning moon! I turn a page ... God! A spectral, half-transparent ship on whose deck a corpse & a skeleton play at dice! By this time I am flat on the bearskin rug & ready to thumb through the whole book ... of which I've never heard before ... A sea full of rotting serpents, & death-fires dancing in the black air ... troops of angels & daemons ... crazed, dying, distorted forms ... dead men rising in their putrescence & lifelessly manning the dank rigging of a fate-doomed barque ...[26]

Who could resist such a spell? However, if the *Ancient Mariner* was
the principal *literary* influence in the early development of Lovecraft's taste for the weird, a searing personal event may have been
as significant: the death, on 26 January 1896, of his maternal
grandmother, Robie Alzada Place Phillips.

It was, perhaps, not so much the loss of a family member—to
whom Lovecraft does not appear to have been especially close—as
its effect upon the remaining members of the family that so affected
the young boy:

> the death of my grandmother plunged the household into a
> gloom from which it never fully recovered. The black attire
> of my mother & aunts terrified & repelled me to such an
> extent that I would surreptitiously pin bits of bright cloth or
> paper to their skirts for sheer relief. They had to make a
> careful survey of their attire before receiving callers or going
> out!

Seriocomically as Lovecraft narrates these events, twenty years
after the fact, it is evident that they left a profound impression upon
him. The aftermath was quite literally nightmarish:

> And then it was that my former high spirits received their
> damper. I began to have nightmares of the most hideous
> description, peopled with *things* which I called 'night-
> gaunts'—a compound word of my own coinage. I used to
> draw them after waking (perhaps the idea of these figures
> came from an edition de luxe of *Paradise Lost* with
> illustrations by Doré, which I discovered one day in the east
> parlor). In dreams they were wont to whirl me through
> space at a sickening rate of speed, the while fretting &
> impelling me with their detestable tridents. It is fully fifteen
> years—aye, more—since I have seen a 'night-gaunt', but
> even now, when half asleep & drifting vaguely along over a
> sea of childhood thoughts, I feel a thrill of fear ... &
> instinctively *struggle to keep awake*. That was my own prayer
> back in '96—each night—to *keep awake* & ward off the night-
> gaunts![27]

And so begins Lovecraft's career as one of the great dreamers—or,
to coin a term that must be coined for the phenomenon,
nightmarers—of literary history. Even though it would be another
ten years from the writing of this letter, and hence a full thirty years

after these dreams, that he would utilize the night-gaunts in his work, it is already evident that his boyhood dreams contain many conceptual and imagistic kernels of his mature tales: the cosmic backdrop; the utterly outré nature of his malignant entities (in a late letter he describes them as 'black, lean, rubbery things with bared, barbed tails, bat-wings, and *no faces at all*'[28]), so different from conventional demons, vampires, or ghosts; and the helpless passivity of the protagonist-victim, at the mercy of forces infinitely more powerful than himself. It would, of course, take a long time for Lovecraft to evolve his theory and practice of weird fiction; but, with dreams like these at such an early age, his career as a writer of horror tales comes to seem like an inevitable destiny.

Lovecraft's family—in particular his mother—must, however, have been concerned for his physical and psychological health at the onset of his dreams, and at what may have been a general pattern of gloomy or depressed behaviour. Lovecraft speaks frequently in later years of a trip to western Rhode Island taken in 1896, and it seems likely that this trip to ancestral lands was, at least in part, an attempt by his family to rid him of his nightmares and his general malaise.

In conformity with his carefree and rather unsupervised childhood, Lovecraft was allowed ready access to the 'windowless third-story trunk-room'[29] at 454 Angell Street, where the family's collection of eighteenth-century volumes—then considered outdated and of no contemporary relevance—was stored. Lovecraft took to them eagerly, particularly the volumes of poetry and belleslettres. This eighteenth-century predilection led indirectly to a literary and philosophical interest of still greater importance: classical antiquity. At the age of six Lovecraft read Hawthorne's *Wonder-Book* (1852) and *Tanglewood Tales* (1853), and professed himself 'enraptured by the Hellenic myths even in their Teutonised form' ('A Confession of Unfaith'). From Hawthorne Lovecraft naturally graduated to Thomas Bulfinch's imperishable retelling of Graeco-Roman myths, *The Age of Fable* (1855).

Lovecraft finally came upon the ancients themselves around this time, doing so in a way that felicitously united his burgeoning love of classical myth with his already existing fondness for eighteenth-century prosody. His grandfather's library had an edition of 'Garth's Ovid'—that gorgeous 1717 translation of the *Metamorphoses* assembled by Sir Samuel Garth, and including contributions from such poets as Dryden, Congreve, Pope, Addison, and Gay. It is not surprising that 'The even decasyllabic rhythm seemed to strike some responsive chord in my brain, and I forthwith became wedded to that measure.'[30]

Whipple Phillips also assisted in fostering Lovecraft's love of Rome: 'He had loved to muse amidst the ruins of the ancient city, & had brought from Italy a wealth of mosaics, ... paintings, & other objets d'art whose theme was more often classically Roman than Italian. He always wore a pair of mosaics in his cuffs for buttons— one a view of the Coliseum (so *tiny* yet so *faithful*); the other of the Forum.'[31] The downstairs parlour of 454 Angell Street had a life-size Roman bust on a gilded pedestal. No doubt all this was part of the reason why Lovecraft always preferred the culture of Rome to that of Greece, although other philosophical, aesthetic, and tempera-mental factors eventually entered into it.

In the short term the effect of reading Hawthorne, Bulfinch, and Garth's Ovid was that 'My Bagdad name and affiliations dis-appeared at once, for the magic of silks and colours faded before that of fragrant templed groves, faun-peopled meadows in the twilight, and the blue, beckoning Mediterranean' ('A Confession of Unfaith'). A more important result is that Lovecraft became a writer.

Lovecraft dates the commencement of his writing to the age of six, remarking: 'My attempts at versification, of which I made the first at the age of six, now took on a crude, internally rhyming ballad metre, and I sang of the exploits of Gods and Heroes.'[32] In context this appears to suggest that Lovecraft had begun to write verse prior to his discovery of classical antiquity, but that his fascination with the ancient world impelled him toward renewed poetic composi-tion, this time on classical themes. None of this pre-classical verse survives, and the first poetical work we do have is the 'second edition' of 'The Poem of Ulysses; or, The Odyssey: Written for Young People'. This elaborate little book is dated to 8 November 1897 in the preface, and we have to believe that the 'first edition' dated to earlier in the year, prior to Lovecraft's seventh birthday on 20 August 1897.

On the copyright page Lovecraft writes: 'Acknowledgements are due to Popes Odyssey and Bulfinch's Mythology and Harpers Half Hour Series.' Then, helpfully, 'Homer first writ the poem.' I have not been able to ascertain what the book in Harper's Half Hour Series is; in 'A Confession of Unfaith' Lovecraft describes it as a 'tiny book in the private library of my elder aunt' (i.e., Lillian D. Phillips). It is rather remarkable to think that Lovecraft had already read the whole of Pope's *Odyssey* by the age of seven; but it becomes immediately obvious that in his eighty-eight-line poem he could not possibly have been dependent upon Pope's fourteen-thousand-line translation either metrically or even in terms of the story line. Here is how Lovecraft's poem begins:

> The nighte was darke! O readers, Hark!
> And see Ulysses' fleet!
> From trumpets sound back homeward bound
> He hopes his spouse to greet

This is certainly not Pope; rather, the metre is clearly adapted from Coleridge's *Ancient Mariner*. In 1926 Lovecraft remarked that 'My 6-year-old "verse" was pretty bad, and I had recited enough poetry to know that it was so'; what helped him to improve his prosody was a very careful study of Abner Alden's *The Reader* (1797), which he declares 'was so utterly and absolutely the very thing I had been looking for, that I attacked it with almost savage violence'.[33] After a month or so, he produced 'The Poem of Ulysses'.

If nothing else, the work is a remarkable example of concision: in eighty-eight lines Lovecraft has compressed the twelve-thousand lines of Homer's *Odyssey*. Lovecraft achieves this compression by deftly omitting relatively inessential portions of the story—in particular, the entire first four books (the Adventures of Telemachos) and, perhaps surprisingly, book eleven (the descent into Hades)—and, more importantly, by retelling the entire story in *chronological sequence*, from Odysseus's sailing from Troy to his final return home to Ithaca, rather than in the elaborately convoluted way in which Homer's Odysseus narrates his adventures.

According to various catalogues of works found at the rear of Lovecraft's juvenile writings, Lovecraft wrote similar paraphrases of the *Iliad* and *Aeneid*, as well as items called 'Mythology for the Young' (perhaps a paraphrase of some of Bulfinch) and 'An Old Egyptian Myth Prepared Specially for Small Children' (again possibly drawn from Bulfinch, as chapter 34 of *The Age of Fable* discusses some Egyptian myths, especially that of Isis and Osiris).

Classical antiquity was, however, more than a literary experience for Lovecraft; it was both a personal and even a quasi-religious one. In 1897–99 he pored over the classical relics of the museum of the Rhode Island School of Design (the college situated at the foot of College Hill, mostly along Benefit Street), and shortly afterward became familiar with other classical art museums in Providence and Boston. The result was an infatuation with the classical world and then a kind of religious epiphany. Let Lovecraft tell it in his own inimitable way:

> When about seven or eight I was a genuine pagan, so intoxicated with the beauty of Greece that I acquired a half-sincere belief in the old gods and Nature-spirits. I have in literal truth built altars to Pan, Apollo, Diana, and Athena, and have watched for dryads and satyrs in the woods and fields at dusk. Once I firmly thought I beheld some of these sylvan creatures dancing under autumnal oaks; a kind of 'religious experience' as true in its way as the subjective ecstasies of any Christian. If a Christian tell me he has *felt* the reality of his Jesus or Jahveh, I can reply that I have *seen* the hoofed Pan and the sisters of the Hesperian Phaëthusa. ('A Confession of Unfaith')

This certainly puts the lie to Bulfinch, who solemnly declared at the very beginning of *The Age of Fable*: 'The religions of ancient Greece and Rome are extinct. The so-called divinities of Olympus have not a single worshipper among living men.'

In writing the above passage Lovecraft was clearly wishing to show that his scepticism and anticlericalism were of very early origin; but he may be guilty of some exaggeration. Earlier in this essay he reports that 'I was instructed in the legends of the Bible and of Saint Nicholas at the age of about two, and gave to both a passive acceptance not especially distinguished either for its critical keenness or its enthusiastic comprehension'. He then declares that just before the age of five he was told that Santa Claus does not exist, and that he thereupon countered with the query as to 'why God is not equally a myth'. 'Not long afterwards', he continues, he was placed in a Sunday school at the First Baptist Church, but became so pestiferous an iconoclast that he was allowed to discontinue attendance. Elsewhere, however, he declares that this incident occurred at the age of twelve. When we examine Lovecraft's philosophical development, the likelihood is that the Sunday school incident indeed took place at the age of twelve, and not at five.

By the age of seven Lovecraft had already begun to read, begun to write poetry and prose nonfiction, and gained what would prove to

be a lifelong love of England and of the past. But his imaginative
appetite was not complete; for he claims that in the winter of 1896
yet another interest emerged: the theatre. The first play he saw was
'one of Denman Thompson's minor efforts',[34] *The Sunshine of
Paradise Alley*, which featured a slum scene that fascinated him.
Shortly thereafter he was enjoying the 'well-made' plays of Henry
Arthur Jones and Arthur Wing Pinero; but the next year his taste
was improved by seeing his first Shakespearian play, *Cymbeline*, at
the Providence Opera House. He set up a little toy theatre in his
room, hand-painted the scenery, and played *Cymbeline* for weeks.
Lovecraft's interest in drama continued sporadically for at least the
next fifteen to twenty years; around 1910 he saw Robert Mantell's
company perform *King John* in Providence, with the young Fritz
Leiber, Sr, as Faulconbridge. Lovecraft was also a very early
enthusiast of film, and throughout his life we will find selected
films influencing some of his most significant writing.

From the age of three onward—while his father was slowly
deteriorating both physically and mentally in Butler Hospital—the
young Howard Phillips Lovecraft was encountering one intellectual
and imaginative stimulus after the other: first the colonial
antiquities of Providence, then Grimm's *Fairy Tales*, then the
Arabian Nights, then Coleridge's *Ancient Mariner*, then eighteenth-
century belles-lettres, then the theatre and Shakespeare, and finally
Hawthorne, Bulfinch, and the classical world. It is a remarkable
sequence, and many of these stimuli would be of lifelong duration.
But there remained one further influence that would definitively
turn Lovecraft into the man and writer we know: 'Then I struck
EDGAR ALLAN POE!! It was my downfall, and at the age of eight I
saw the blue firmament of Argos and Sicily darkened by the
miasmal exhalations of the tomb!'[35]

CHAPTER THREE

Black Woods and Unfathomed Caves (1898–1902)

Lovecraft dates his first work of prose fiction to 1897,[1] and elsewhere identifies it as 'The Noble Eavesdropper', about which all we know is that it concerned 'a boy who overheard some horrible conclave of subterranean beings in a cave'.[2] As the work does not survive, it would be idle to point to any literary sources for it; but the influence of the *Arabian Nights* (the cave of Ali Baba and other stories involving caves) might be conjectured. A still more likely source, perhaps, would be his grandfather Whipple, the only member of his family who appears to have enjoyed the weird. As Lovecraft states in a late letter:

> I never heard *oral* weird tales except from my grandfather—who, observing my tastes in reading, used to devise all sorts of impromptu original yarns about black woods, unfathomed caves, winged horrors (like the 'night-gaunts' of my dreams, about which I used to tell him), old witches with sinister cauldrons, & 'deep, low, moaning sounds'. He obviously drew most of his imagery from the early gothic romances—Radcliffe, Lewis, Maturin, &c.—which he seemed to like better than Poe or other later fantaisistes.[3]

Here are some of the components (unfathomed caves, deep, low, moaning sounds) of the imagery of 'The Noble Eavesdropper'. But Lovecraft admits that this is the only tale he wrote prior to his reading of Poe.

Poe was, by the turn of the century, slowly gaining a place of eminence in American literature, although he still had to face posthumous attacks by Henry James and others. His championing by Baudelaire, Mallarmé, and other European writers had slowly impelled reconsideration of his work by English and American critics.

I do not know which edition of Poe was read by the eight-year-old Lovecraft; it must have been some school edition. It is, in fact, a little difficult to discern any clear-cut Poe influence in the first several of Lovecraft's surviving juvenile stories—'The Little Glass Bottle', 'The Secret Cave; or, John Lees Adventure', 'The Mystery of the Grave-yard; or, A Dead Man's Revenge', and 'The Mysterious Ship'. None of these early stories is dated, with the exception of 'The Mysterious Ship' (clearly dated to 1902), but they must have been written during the period 1898–1902, perhaps more toward the earlier than the later end of that spectrum. Perhaps the only tale of genuine interest is 'The Mystery of the Grave-yard'—which contains not only a subtitle ('or, "A Dead Man's Revenge"') but a sub-subtitle ('A Detective story'). This is the longest of Lovecraft's juvenile stories, and at the end of the autograph manuscript he has noted (obviously at a much later date): 'Evidently written in late 1898 or early 1899'. The fact that it is labelled a detective story should not lead us to think it is influenced by Poe's 'The Murders in the Rue Morgue' or any of his other detective stories, although no doubt Lovecraft read them. Even the most cursory glance at this wild, histrionic, and rather engaging story should allow us to point to its predominant source: the dime novel.

The first dime novel was published in 1860, when the firm later known as Beadle & Adams reprinted, in a 128-page paper-covered volume 6 by 4 inches in dimensions, a novel by Ann Sophia Winterbotham Stephens. The fact that it was a reprint was critical, for it allowed the firm to claim that here was a 'dollar book for a dime'.[4] Beadle & Adams was the leading publisher of dime novels until it folded in 1898, having been driven out of business by the bold and innovative publishing practices of Street & Smith, which entered the dime novel market in 1889.

It should not be assumed that dime novels were merely action thrillers, although many of them were; there were westerns (Deadwood Dick from Beadle & Adams; Diamond Dick from Street & Smith), detective or espionage stories (Nick Carter from Street & Smith; Old King Brady from Frank Tousey), tales of high school and college life (Frank Merriwell from Street & Smith), and even pious tales of moral uprightness (Horatio Alger, Jr, wrote prolifically for Street & Smith in the 1890s). Their principal features were their price, their format (paper covers, 128 pages or less), and, in general, their action-packed narrative style. The leading dime novel series were, of course, priced at 10 cents, although there was a wide array of smaller books, called 'nickel libraries', at 5 cents aimed at younger readers.

It is one of the great paradoxes of Lovecraft's entire literary career that he could, on the one hand, absorb the highest aesthetic fruits of Western culture—Greek and Latin literature, Shakespeare, the poetry of Keats and Shelley—and at the same time go slumming in the cheapest dregs of popular fiction. Throughout his life Lovecraft vigorously defended the *literary* value of the weird tale (unlike some modern critics who misguidedly vaunt both the good and the bad, the aesthetically polished and the mechanically hackneyed, as representative of 'popular culture'—as if there is any merit to what masses of half-literate people like to read), and he adamantly, and rightly, refused to consider the weird work found in dime novels and pulp magazines as genuine literature; but this did not prevent him from voraciously lapping up these lesser products. Lovecraft knew that he was reading trash, but he read it anyway.

Among the dime novel series Lovecraft admits to reading were *Pluck and Luck* (Tousey, 1898f.), *Brave and Bold* (Street & Smith, 1903f.), Frank Reade (Tousey, 1892–98, 1903f.), *Jesse James Stories* (Street & Smith, 1901f.), Nick Carter (Street & Smith, 1886f.), and Old King Brady (featured first in the *New York Detective Library* (Tousey, 1885–99), then, along with his son Young King Brady, in *Secret Service* (1899–1912)).

Old King Brady may be the most interesting of the lot for our purposes, since the hero of 'The Mystery of the Grave-yard' is one King John, described as 'a famous western detective'. Old King Brady was not a western character, but he was a detective. Moreover, Beadle had a series detective, Prince John (written by Joseph E. Badger, Jr), in the early 1890s. I do not know whether King John—even in terms of his name—is some sort of fusion of Old King Brady and Prince John, but he is certainly a dime novel detective.

And 'The Mystery of the Grave-yard' is a miniature dime novel, pure and simple. The action is nothing if not fast-paced. In twelve relatively short chapters (some as little as fifty words in length) we read a lurid story involving kidnapping, a trap-door in a tomb, and other flamboyant details. King John not only solves the mystery but ends up marrying the kidnapped woman.

'The Mysterious Ship' is the latest of the surviving juvenilia, and by far the most disappointing. This story—consisting of nine very brief chapters, some as short as twenty-five words and none longer than seventy-five words—is so dry and clipped that it led L. Sprague de Camp to think it 'an outline rather than a story'.[5] This seems unlikely given the elaborate 'publishing' procedures Lovecraft has undertaken for this work. In the first place, we here encounter Lovecraft's first surviving *typescript*, a text of twelve pages enclosed in a little booklet. This could not have been typed on the 1906 Remington that served Lovecraft for the rest of his life, but must have been some similar behemoth belonging to his grandfather or perhaps even his father. Moreover, there is a sort of gauze cloth cover with a drawing of a ship in pen on it, and another drawing of a ship on the back cover. The imprint on the title page is 'The Royal Press. 1902'. It is obvious that Lovecraft is aiming for a sort of dramatic terseness in this narrative; but the result is mere confusion as to what exactly happens.

Aside from discovering Poe and giving his fledgling fictional career a boost, Lovecraft also found himself in 1898 fascinated with science. This is the third component of what he once described as his tripartite nature: love of the strange and fantastic, love of the ancient and permanent, and love of abstract truth and scientific logic.[6] It is perhaps not unusual that it would be the last to emerge in his young mind, and it is still remarkable that it emerged so early and was embraced so vigorously. Lovecraft first came upon a section devoted to 'Philosophical and Scientific Instruments' at the back of Webster's Dictionary, and very shortly thereafter he had a full-fledged chemistry set and was deep in experimentation. As with his enthusiasm for the *Arabian Nights*, his chemical tastes led his family to indulge the boy in whatever tools he needed. The first book he read on the subject was *The Young Chemist* (1876) by John Howard Appleton, a professor of chemistry at Brown University and a friend of the family.

The immediate result of the discovery of science was a spate of literary work. Lovecraft began *The Scientific Gazette* on 4 March 1899. This first issue—a single sheet—still survives; it contains an amusing report: 'There was a great explosion in the Providence Laboratory this afternoon. While experimenting some potassium blew up causing great damage to everyone.' Incredibly, this magazine was initially a *daily*, but 'it soon degenerated into a weekly'.[7] No subsequent issues survive until the New Issue Vol. I, No. 1 (12 May 1902), and I shall postpone discussion of it until the next chapter.

Lovecraft also wrote a number of short chemical treatises. There was a six-volume series with the general title *Chemistry*, of which four volumes survive: *Chemistry* (10 cents); *Chemistry, Magic, & Electricity* (5 cents); *Chemistry III* (5 cents); and *Chemistry IV* (15 cents). These volumes discuss such things as argon, gunpowder, a carbon cell battery, gases, acids, tellurium, lithium, explosives, 'explosive experiments', and the like. There is also a small work called *A Good Anaesthetic* (5 cents). Judging by the handwriting, these works probably all date to around 1899. Non-extant works include *Iron Working* (5 cents), *Acids* (5 cents), *Explosives* (5 cents), and *Static Electricity* (10 cents).

It appears that Lovecraft's early scientific interests engendered some practical experimentation, if the following account—related to W. Paul Cook by one of Lovecraft's neighbours—dates to this period. It is one of the most delightful and celebrated anecdotes about Lovecraft that has come down to us. Let Cook tell it in his own inimitable way:

> That section [of Providence, in which Lovecraft lived] was then open fields, rather swampy here and there, with very few houses. One day this neighbor, Mrs. Winslow Church, noticed that someone had started a grass fire that had burned over quite an area and was approaching her property. She went out to investigate and found the little Lovecraft boy. She scolded him for setting such a big fire and maybe endangering other peoples' property. He said very positively, 'I wasn't setting a *big* fire. I wanted to make a fire one foot by one foot.' That is the little story in the words in which it came to me. It means little except that it shows a passion for exactitude (in keeping with him as we knew him later)—but it is a story of Lovecraft.[8]

This anecdote is, as I say, not dated; but the mention of 'open fields' suggests that it occurred while Lovecraft was at 454 Angell Street, since the area was already being built up during his early teenage years.

Another rather anomalous discovery Lovecraft made at this time was anatomy—or, rather, the specific facts of anatomy relating to sex. Here is his account of it:

> In the matter of the justly celebrated 'facts of life' I didn't wait for oral information, but exhausted the entire subject in the medical section of the family library (to which I had access, although I wasn't especially loquacious about this

side of my reading) when I was 8 years old—through Quain's Anatomy (fully illustrated & diagrammed), Dunglison's Physiology, &c. &c. This was because of curiosity & perplexity concerning the strange reticences & embarrassments of adult speech, & the oddly inexplicable allusions & situations in standard literature. The result was the very opposite of what parents generally fear—for instead of giving me an abnormal & precocious interest in sex (as *unsatisfied* curiosity might have done), it virtually killed my interest in the subject. The whole matter was reduced to prosaic mechanism—a mechanism which I rather despised or at least thought non-glamourous because of its purely animal nature & separation from such things as intellect & beauty—& all the drama was taken out of it.[9]

This is an intensely interesting statement. First, when Lovecraft says that he did not wait for 'oral information', he is suggesting (perhaps without even knowing it) that his mother would certainly not have told him the 'facts of life'—at least not at the age of eight, and perhaps not at any age. Even his grandfather might not have done so. It is remarkable to note that Lovecraft was already so keenly aware of the 'strange reticences & embarrassments of adult speech' at this time that he sensed something was not being told him; at least up to the age of eight, and perhaps beyond, he was a solitary child who largely spent time in the company of adults. And as one who was already a prolific reader (and a reader of material rarely given to the very young), he may have become early aware of anomalies in some of his books also. And as for his declaration that his knowledge of the matter killed his interest in sex: this is certainly the impression Lovecraft consistently conveyed to his friends, correspondents, and even his wife. He does not seem to have had any romantic involvements in high school or at any time prior to about 1918 (and even this one is a matter of inference). It took three years for Sonia Greene to convince Lovecraft to marry her; the impetus was clearly on her side. There has been much speculation on Lovecraft's sex life, but I do not believe there are sufficient grounds for much of an opinion beyond the testimony given by Lovecraft himself—and his wife.

In any event, Lovecraft's initial enthusiasm for chemistry and physiology would lead to further interests in geography, geology, astronomy, anthropology, psychology, and other sciences that he would study over a lifetime. He may have remained a layman in all these branches of knowledge, but his absorption of many of them—especially astronomy—was prodigious for a literary man; and they helped to lay strong foundations for his philosophical thought, and would provide the backbone for some of his most powerful works of fiction.

Lovecraft reports that he began learning Latin around 1898.[10] Elsewhere he says that 'My grandfather had previously [i.e., previous to his entering school] taught me a great deal of Latin',[11] which suggests that he had begun the study of Latin prior to his attendance at the Slater Avenue School in the fall of 1898. It was natural for a boy so enthralled with the classical world to learn Latin, although to have begun it so early—and, evidently, to have mastered it in a few years, without much formal instruction—was a notable feat even at a time when knowledge of Latin was far commoner than it is now.

We will find that the poetry of Virgil, Horace, and Juvenal left a lasting impression upon Lovecraft, and that the Epicurean philosophy embodied in Lucretius was a central influence in his early thought. One remarkable instance of the classical influence on Lovecraft's juvenile writing is the piece entitled 'Ovid's Metamorphoses'.

This 116-line work is nothing less than a literal pentameter verse translation of the first eighty-eight lines of Ovid's *Metamorphoses*. The date of composition of this piece is, unfortunately, in doubt; but, by consulting the various catalogues of works found in his other juvenile works, one may infer that it dates to the period 1900–02.

The first thing to note about this translation is how different it is from Dryden's (he translated the first book of the *Metamorphoses* in 'Garth's Ovid'). Lovecraft attempts a far more literal, line-for-line translation, adhering as closely to the Latin as he can. Lovecraft has two subdivisions in his essay, with the headings 'The Creation of the World' (ll. 5–84) and 'The Creation of Man' (ll. 85–116). There are, admittedly, similar divisions and headings in Dryden, but his first one ('The Golden Age') appears just where Lovecraft's poem leaves off.

There is one more remarkable thing about 'Ovid's Metamorphoses', and that is the possibility that it may be a fragment. The autograph manuscript covers five sheets, and the text proceeds to the very bottom of the fifth sheet. Could Lovecraft have translated more of Ovid's text, and could this portion have been lost? I think the probability is strong: this item, priced at 25 cents, is currently not much longer than 'The Poem of Ulysses', priced at 5 cents. Perhaps it is not unreasonable to think that Lovecraft might have translated the entire first book of Ovid (779 lines in Latin). The translation as it stands admittedly ends at a clear break in the Latin text, as at line 89 Ovid is about to begin the account of the four ages of man; but I still believe there was once more to this work than we have.

The year 1898 was certainly an eventful one for Lovecraft: he discovered Poe and science, and began learning Latin; he first began attendance at school; and he had his first nervous break-down. In a late letter he refers to it as a 'near-breakdown';[12] I have no idea what that means. Another 'near-breakdown' occurred in 1900. There certainly does not seem to have been anything physically wrong with the boy, and there is no record of his admission into a hospital. The history and nature of Lovecraft's early nervous condition are very vexed issues, largely because we have only his words on the matter, most of them written many years after the fact.

Lovecraft reports that 'I didn't inherit a very good set of nerves, since near relatives on both sides of my ancestry were prone to headaches, nerve-exhaustion, and breakdowns'. He goes on to cite the case of his grandfather (who had 'frightful blind headaches'), his mother (who 'could run him a close second'), and his father. Then he adds: 'My own headaches and nervous irritability and exhaustion-tendency began as early as my existence itself—I, too, was an early bottle baby with unexplained miseries and meagre nutriment-assimilative capacities.'[13] Early weaning was common practice at the turn of the century and for a long time thereafter; but Lovecraft's remark suggests that his weaning occurred even earlier than was the custom.

One remarkable admission Lovecraft made late in life was as follows: 'My own nervous state in childhood once produced a tendency inclining toward chorea, although not quite attaining that level. My face was full of unconscious & involuntary motions now & then—& the more I was urged to stop them, the more frequent they became.'[14] Lovecraft does not exactly date these chorea-like attacks, but context suggests that they occurred before the age of ten. All this led J. Vernon Shea to suspect that Lovecraft might actually have had chorea minor, a nervous ailment that 'manifests itself in uncontrollable facial tics and grimaces' but gradually dissipates by puberty.[15] Certainty on the matter is, of course, impossible, but I think the probability of this conjecture is strong. And although Lovecraft maintains in the above letter that 'in time the tendency died down' and that his entrance into high school 'caused me to reform', I shall have occasion to refer to possible recurrences of these chorea-like symptoms at various periods in Lovecraft's life, even into maturity.

If, then, it is true that Lovecraft suffered some sort of 'near-breakdown' in 1898, it seems very likely that the death of his father on 19 July 1898 had much to do with it. The effect on his mother can only be imagined. It may be well, then, to summarize the relations between Lovecraft and his mother up to this time, as best we can piece them together.

There is no question but that his mother both spoiled Lovecraft and was overprotective of him. This latter trait appears to have developed even before Winfield's hospitalization in 1893. Winfield Townley Scott tells the following story:

> On their summer vacations at Dudley, Massachusetts ...,
> Mrs. Lovecraft refused to eat her dinner in the dining room,
> not to leave her sleeping son alone for an hour one floor
> above. When a diminutive teacher-friend, Miss Ella Sweeney,
> took the rather rangy youngster to walk, holding his hand,
> she was enjoined by Howard's mother to stoop a little lest
> she pull the boy's arm from its socket. When Howard
> pedaled his tricycle along Angell Street, his mother trooped
> beside him, a guarding hand upon his shoulder.[16]

Lovecraft admits that 'My array of toys, books, and other youthful pleasures was virtually unlimited'[17] at this time; whatever he wanted, he seems to have got.

At this point it may be well to mention a remarkable bit of testimony provided by Lovecraft's wife. In her 1948 memoir Sonia H. Davis states the following:

> It was ... at that time the fashion for mothers to start 'hope-
> chests' for their daughters even before they were born, so
> that when Mrs. Winfield Scott Lovecraft was expecting her
> first child she had hoped it would be a girl; nor was this
> curtailed at the birth of her boy. So this hope-chest was
> gradually growing; some day to be given to Howard's wife ...

> As a baby Howard looked like a beautiful little girl. He had, at the tender age of three years, a head of flaxen curls of which any girl would have been proud ... These he wore until he was about six. When at last he protested and wanted them cut off, his mother had taken him to the barber's and cried bitterly as the 'cruel' shears separated them from his head.[18]

I suppose one must accept this statement for the most part, although I think rather too much has been made of it—and also of the apparent fact that Susie dressed her son in frocks at an early age. The celebrated 1892 photograph of Lovecraft and his parents shows him with the curls and the frock, as does another picture probably taken around the same time.[19] Lovecraft remarks on the curls himself, saying that it was this 'golden mane' that partly led Louise Imogen Guiney to name him 'Little Sunshine'.[20] But another photograph of Lovecraft, probably taken at the age of seven or eight,[21] shows him as a perfectly normal boy with short hair and boy's attire. In fact, it cannot be ascertained when Susie ceased to dress Lovecraft in frocks; but even if she had persisted up to the age of four, it would not have been especially unusual.

There are two other pieces of evidence one can adduce here, although their purport is not entirely clear. R. H. Barlow, in his jottings about Lovecraft (mostly taken down in 1934 but some made evidently later), writes: 'Mrs. Gamwell's stories of how HPL for a while insisted "I'm a little girl."'[22] Annie Gamwell could not have made this observation later than early 1897, as that was when she married and moved out of 454 Angell Street; and the context of Barlow's remark (he adds the detail of how Lovecraft would spout Tennyson from the table-top) could date the event to as early as 1893. Then there is a letter from Whipple Phillips to Lovecraft, dated 19 June 1894: 'I will tell you more about what I have seen when I get home if you are a good boy and *wear trousers*.'[23] Whipple has underscored the last two words. The implication is, I suppose, that Lovecraft at this time was not fond of wearing trousers.

In spite of the above, I see little evidence of gender confusion in Lovecraft's later life; if anything, he displayed quick and unwavering prejudice against 'sissies' and homosexuals. Susie may have wanted a girl, and may have attempted to preserve the illusion for a few years, but Lovecraft even in youth was headstrong and made it evident that he was a boy with a boy's normal interests. It was, after all, he who wanted his flowing curls cut off at the age of six.

In addition to being oversolicitous of her son, Susie also attempted to mould him in ways which he found either irritating or repugnant. Around 1898 she tried to enrol him in a children's dancing class; Lovecraft 'abhorred the thought' and, fresh from an initial study of Latin, responded with a line from Cicero: *'Nemo fere saltat sobrius, nisi forte insanit!'* ('Scarcely any sober person dances, unless by chance he is insane').[24] Evidently Lovecraft had developed a certain skill in getting his own way, for—like his initial Sunday school attendance (probably the previous year), which he was allowed to forgo—he evidently escaped the dancing lessons. But what he did not escape were violin lessons, which lasted a full two years, between the ages of seven and nine.

These lessons were, however, initially at his own insistence:

> My rhythmic tendencies led me into a love of melody, and I was forever whistling & humming in defiance of convention & good breeding. I was so exact in time & tune, & showed such a semi-professional precision & flourish in my crude attempts, that my plea for a violin was granted when I was seven years of age, & I was placed under the instruction of the best violin teacher for children in the city—Mrs. Wilhelm Nauck. For two years I made such progress that Mrs. Nauck was enthusiastic, & declared that I should adopt music as a career—BUT, all this time the tedium of practising had been wearing shockingly on my always sensitive nervous system. My 'career' extended until 1899, its summit being a public recital at which I played a solo from Mozart before an audience of considerable size. Soon after that, my ambition & taste alike collapsed like a house of cards ... I began to detest classical music, because it had meant so much painful labour to me; & I positively *loathed* the violin! Our physician, knowing my temperament, advised an immediate discontinuance of music lessons, which speedily ensued.[25]

One would like to date Lovecraft's second 'near-breakdown' to the termination of these lessons, but he clearly asserts that the first occurred in 1898 and the second in 1900. In any event, Lovecraft manifestly continued to be under considerable nervous strain—a situation in part relieved and in part augmented by his first attempt at school attendance, from which he was withdrawn after a year's term (1898–99). Indeed, his casual remark in 1929 that 'I spent the summer of 1899 with my mother'[26] in Westminster, Massachusetts, must lead one to speculate on the purpose of such a trip, and to wonder whether health reasons were a factor. I am inclined to connect the trip with the trauma of his first year of school and also of his violin lessons, which probably ended in the summer of 1899.

From all that has gone before it will be evident that Lovecraft led a comparatively solitary young childhood, with only his adult family members as his companions. Many of his childhood activities—reading, writing, scientific work, practising music, even attending the theatre—are primarily or exclusively solitary, and we do not hear much about any boyhood friends until his entrance into grade school. All his letters discussing his childhood stress his relative isolation and loneliness:

> You will notice that I have made no reference to childish friends & playmates—I had none! The children I knew disliked me, & I disliked them. I was used to adult company & conversation, & despite the fact that I felt shamefully dull beside my elders, I had nothing in common with the infant train. Their romping & shouting puzzled me. I hated mere play & dancing about—in my relaxations I always desired *plot*.[27]

One confirmation of this comes from the recollections of Lovecraft's second cousin Ethel M. Phillips (1888–1987), later Mrs Ethel Phillips Morrish. Ethel, two years older than Lovecraft, was living with her parents Jeremiah W. Phillips (the son of Whipple's brother James Wheaton Phillips) and his wife Abby in various suburbs of Providence during the 1890s, and was sent over to play with young Howard. She confessed in an interview conducted in 1977 that she did not much care for her cousin, finding him eccentric and aloof. She was particularly vexed because Lovecraft did not know how a swing worked. But she does have a delightful image of Lovecraft, at about the age of four, turning the pages of some monstrously huge book in a very solemn and adult manner.[28]

Lovecraft provides one remarkable glimpse of some of the solitary games he played as a young boy:

> My favourite toys were *very small* ones, which would permit of their arrangement in widely extensive scenes. My mode of play was to devote an entire table-top to a scene, which I would proceed to develop as a broad landscape ... helped by occasional trays of earth or clay. I had all sorts of *toy villages*

with small wooden or cardboard houses, & by combining several of them would often construct *cities* of considerable extent & intricacy ... Toy trees—of which I had an infinite number—were used with varying effect to form parts of the landscape . . . even *forests* (or the suggested edges of forests). Certain kinds of blocks made walls & hedges, & I also used blocks in constructing large public buildings ... My people were mainly of the lead-soldier type & magnitude—frankly too large for the buildings which they presumably tenanted, but as small as I could get. I accepted some as they were, but had my mother modify many in costume with the aid of knife & paint-brush. Much piquancy was added to my scenes by special toy buildings like windmills, castles, &c.

But there was more to it than just a static landscape; with his inveterate feel for plot, and his already developing sense of time, history, and pageantry, Lovecraft would actually act out historical scenarios with his miniature cities. He adds significantly: 'Horror-plots were frequent, though (oddly enough) I never attempted to construct fantastic or extra-terrestrial scenes. I was too much of an innate realist to care for fantasy in its purest form.'[29] Lovecraft does not give an explicit date for the commencement of this fascinating exercise, but I suspect it dates to his seventh or eighth birthday.

Although Lovecraft may have been solitary, he was by no means devoted merely to indoor activities. The year 1900 saw the commencement of his career as bicyclist, something he would keep up for more than a decade. Late in life he claimed that he was a 'veritable bike-centaur' at this time.[30]

Lovecraft's attendance at the Slater Avenue School (formerly located at the northeast corner of Slater Avenue and University Avenue, where St Dunstan's Prep School now stands) changed all this, at least to some degree. He entered the for the first time in 1898, at the 'highest grade of primary school'[31] (presumably the fourth or fifth grade), but apparently withdrew at the end of the term in 1899.

Lovecraft does not seem to have returned to Slater Avenue until the 1902–03 school year. During the interim he was, as before, left to satisfy his intellectual curiosity in his own way: his family could hardly have failed to see that the boy was naturally bookish and did not need much incentive to investigate any subject that caught his fancy.

Lovecraft states that he discovered W. Frank Russell's *The Frozen Pirate* (1887), a lurid and histrionic novel about Antarctica, at the age of eight or nine, and that it impelled him to write some weird tales based on the same theme. It seems likely that this novel— along, perhaps, with the scarcely less histrionic but more artistically finished *Narrative of Arthur Gordon Pym* by Edgar Allan Poe— helped to inspire Lovecraft's interest in geography, particularly the Antarctic, an interest that led not merely to several works of fiction both early and late but several works of nonfiction as well.

Lovecraft on various occasions states that his interest in Antarctica began either in 1900 or in 1902. I am inclined to accept the earlier date, for in an early letter he goes on to say: 'The Borchgrevink expedition, which had just made a new record in South Polar achievement, greatly stimulated this study.'[32] The Norwegian Carsten Egeberg Borchgrevink's great achievement was to have established the first camp on actual Antarctic soil. He had sailed from England in August 1898, established the camp in February 1899, stayed all through the long Antarctic night (May– July 1899), walked on the Ross Ice Shelf on 19 February 1900, and returned to England in the summer of 1900.

It is not surprising that Lovecraft's interest would have been aroused by the Borchgrevink expedition, for this was the first important Antarctic voyage since the 1840s. It is also for this reason that two of the three lost treatises on Antarctic exploration which Lovecraft wrote around this time—*Voyages of Capt. Ross, R.N.* (1902), *Wilkes's Explorations* (1902), and *Antarctic Atlas* (1903)[33]—discuss those 1840s expeditions: there were no others in recent memory that he could have written about. In fact, I am wondering whether the dates of writing supplied (in 1936) by Lovecraft are entirely accurate: I would like to date them to an even earlier period, say 1900. The first two of these treatises must have treated the nearly simultaneous expeditions of the American Charles Wilkes (1838– 40), who named the continent, and the Englishman James Clark Ross (1839–41), for whom the Ross Ice Shelf is named.

It would seem odd for Lovecraft not to have chosen to write up the expeditions by Borchgrevink and also Robert Scott (1901–02), so fresh as they would have been in his mind, rather than the expeditions of the 1840s, some of whose discoveries had been superseded by the work of these later explorers. His correspondent C. L. Moore actually saw a copy of *Wilkes's Explorations* in late 1936,[34] although it was not found among his papers after his death a few months later. *Antarctic Atlas* must have been an interesting work, and presumably consisted largely of a map of the continent; but so little exploration of the land mass had been done by this time that large parts of it were still unknown and unnamed.

Lovecraft reports in 'A Confession of Unfaith' that 'my pompous "book" called *Poemata Minora*, written when I was eleven, was dedicated "To the Gods, Heroes, and Ideals of the Ancients", and harped in disillusioned, world-weary tones on the sorrow of the pagan robbed of his antique pantheon'. *Poemata Minora, Volume II* is Lovecraft's most finished and aesthetically satisfying juvenile work. The five poems bear comparison with any of his later verse, although this is an indication not so much of the merit of these early poems as of the mediocrity of his later ones.

The poems in *Poemata Minora* reveal considerable originality, and few can be traced to any specific works of classical poetry. Lovecraft was endlessly fond of citing the fourth and final stanza of 'Ode to Selene or Diana' as prototypical of his disharmony with the modern age:

> Take heed, *Diana*, of my humble plea.
> Convey me where my happiness may last.
> Draw me against the tide of time's rough sea
> And let my spirit rest amid the past.

Poemata Minora, Volume II is a pleasing little product, fully worth the 25 cents Lovecraft was charging. Volume I is likely to have been equally substantial, as an ad in Volume II offers it for 25 cents also. But this was, for the time being, the final product of Lovecraft's classicism. Although he would continue to draw upon the ancients for aesthetic and even philosophical inspiration, a new interest would for a time eclipse all others and impel an overhauling of his entire world view. For it was in the winter of 1902–03 that Lovecraft discovered astronomy.

CHAPTER FOUR
What of Unknown Africa?
(1902–1908)

The most poignant sensations of my existence are those of 1896, when I discovered the Hellenic world, and of 1902, when I discovered the myriad suns and worlds of infinite space. Sometimes I think the latter event the greater, for the grandeur of that growing conception of the universe still excites a thrill hardly to be duplicated. I made of astronomy my principal scientific study, obtaining larger and larger telescopes, collecting astronomical books to the number of 61, and writing copiously on the subject in the form of special and monthly articles in the local press. ('A Confession of Unfaith')

This remark, made around 1921, is a sufficient indication of the degree to which the discovery of astronomy affected Lovecraft's entire world view. I shall pursue the philosophical ramifications of his astronomical studies later; here it is worth examining how he came upon the science and what immediate literary products it engendered. In the winter of 1902 Lovecraft was attending the Slater Avenue School, but his statements lead one to believe that he stumbled upon astronomy largely of his own accord. The majority of his astronomy volumes were inherited from his maternal grandmother Robie Phillips's collection; some of these are rather old and elementary school manuals dating to the 1870s or 1880s. These books are too old to have been used at Slater Avenue or at Hope Street High School (Lovecraft did not, in any event, take astronomy courses at Hope Street, even though they were offered), and some at least must have come from Robie's library.

As with so many of his other early interests, Lovecraft's family was very obliging in supply the materials necessary for his pursuit of astronomy. He acquired three successive telescopes, the last being a Bardon 3-inch from Montgomery Ward, costing $50.00. He still had this telescope in 1936. His new enthusiasm led quickly to writing—in this case, to an unprecedented quantity of writing. He does not seem to have commenced astronomical writing until the late summer of 1903, but when he did, he did so with gusto.

Among the treatises Lovecraft produced around this time is 'The Science Library', a nine-volume series probably written in 1903 or 1904, mostly dealing with the moon and planets. He also began issuing several different periodicals, including *Astronomy* and *The Monthly Almanack*; a good many of these were reproduced using a process called the hectograph (or hektograph). This was a sheet of gelatin in a pan rendered hard by glycerine. A master page is prepared either in written form by the use of special hectograph inks or in typed form using hectograph typewriter ribbon; artwork of all sorts could also be drawn upon it. The surface of the pan would then be moistened and the master page pressed down upon it; this page would then be removed and sheets of paper would be pressed upon the gelatin surface, which had now picked up whatever writing or art had been on the master. The surface would be good for up to fifty copies, at which time the impression would begin to fade. Different colours could also be used.[1] Lovecraft must have had more than one such pan, since no more than one page could be hectographed in a day, as the inks must be given time to settle to the bottom. Although the hectograph was a relatively inexpensive reproductive process, the sheer quantity of work Lovecraft was running off must have come to no small expense— inks, carbon paper, gelatin, pans, and the like. No doubt his mother and grandfather were happy to foot the bill, given the precocity and enthusiasm Lovecraft must have exhibited.

We can now finally come to the most significant of Lovecraft's astronomical periodicals, *The Rhode Island Journal of Astronomy*. Even Lovecraft, with his seemingly boundless energy, must have had difficulty writing his other juvenile treatises and periodicals while the weekly deadline of the *Rhode Island Journal* continually impended. The journal was issued first weekly, then monthly; the following issues (a total of sixty-nine) survive:

> 2 August 1903–31 January 1904 (Volume I)
> 16 April 1905–12 November 1905 (Volume III).
> January 1906–April 1907.

There are also two anomalously late issues, January and February 1909. Lovecraft states that the journal 'was printed in editions of 15 to 25 on the hectograph'.[2] At the moment I wish to study only the issues of 1903–04.

An average issue would contain a number of different columns, features, and charts, along with news notes, advertisements (for works by Lovecraft, for items from his collection, and for outside merchants or friends), and fillers. They make wholly entertaining reading. A number of serials ran successively over several issues.

The issue for 1 November 1903 makes an interesting announcement: 'The Ladd Observatory Visited by a Correspondent Last Night.' The correspondent, of course, is Lovecraft. The Ladd Observatory, situated on Doyle Avenue off Hope Street, is a charming observatory operated by Brown University; the fact that a thirteen-year-old boy who was not even attending school at the time was allowed to use this facility is a testament to the degree of expertise Lovecraft had gained in astronomy, largely on his own. He states that 'The late Prof. Upton of Brown, a friend of the family, gave me the freedom of the college observatory, (Ladd Observatory) & I came & went there at will on my bicycle'.[3] Winslow Upton (1853–1914) was a respected astronomer whose *Star Atlas* (1896), and probably other volumes, Lovecraft owned. One wonders whether he was a friend of Dr Franklin Chase Clark, who had married Lovecraft's aunt Lillian in 1902.

Incredibly, while producing *The Rhode Island Journal of Astronomy* every Sunday, issuing other occasional weekly or monthly magazines, and writing separate treatises, Lovecraft resumed his chemical journal, *The Scientific Gazette*. As I have mentioned, after the first issue (4 March 1899) we have no issue until 12 May 1902; after this there are no more issues for more than a year, but by the issue of 16 August 1903 Lovecraft was ready to resume this journal as a weekly, doing so quite regularly until 31 January 1904, with sundry extra issues. Counting the issues for 1899 and 1902, there are a total of thirty-two surviving numbers. No doubt this was printed on the hectograph like the *Rhode Island Journal* (the very earliest issues, of 1899 and following, were printed in an 'edition' of 'one copy for family circulation'[4]). The journal strayed from its chemical focus pretty early on in the 1903 sequence, discussing such matters as Venus's rotation, how to construct a camera obscura, perpetual motion, telescopes (a series taken over from the *Rhode Island Journal* and later to return there), microscopy, and the like.

These scientific interests also manifested themselves in fictional composition. Lovecraft admits to being a 'Verne enthusiast' and that 'many of my tales showed the literary influence of the immortal Jules'. He goes on to say: 'I wrote one story about that side of the moon which is forever turned away from us—using, for fictional purposes, the Hansen theory that air and water still exist there as the result of an abnormal centre of gravity in the moon.'[5] This would presumably qualify, if it survived, as Lovecraft's first authentic tale of science fiction.

I have mentioned that Lovecraft was writing most of these scientific treatises and journals while not in school. He attended the Slater Avenue school in 1898–99, but was then withdrawn; he resumed schooling there for the 1902–03 school year, and was withdrawn again. He adds that 'In 1903–04 I had private tutors'.[6] We know of one such tutor, A. P. May, although Lovecraft did not have a very high opinion of him. There is an unwontedly sarcastic ad for this person in the 3 January 1904 issue of the *Rhode Island Journal*, proclaiming May as a '10th rate Private Tutor' who is offering 'Low Grade Instruction at High Rates'; the ad concludes: 'HIRE ME. I CAN'T DO THE WORK BUT I NEED THE MONEY.' Perhaps May was teaching Lovecraft things he already knew. In any case, it is not surprising that the flood of scientific periodicals began during the summer of 1903, when he probably had much time to himself.

Lovecraft observes that, when he resumed school attendance in 1902, his attitude was very different from what it had been in 1898: he had learnt in the interim that childhood was customarily regarded as a sort of golden age, and so he resolutely set about ensuring that this would be the case. Actually, he did not need much encouragement; for it was in this year at Slater Avenue that he developed two of his earliest but strongest friendships—with Chester and Harold Munroe, who lived about four blocks away from him. Other friends were Ronald Upham, Stuart Coleman (who had known Lovecraft from his earlier Slater Avenue session), and Kenneth Tanner.

Lovecraft remarked in 1935: 'Chester Pierce Munroe & I claimed the proud joint distinction of being the worst boys in Slater Ave. School … We were not so actively destructive as merely antinomian in an arrogant & sardonic way—the protest of individuality against capricious, arbitrary, & excessively detailed authority.'[7] This disregard of rules came to the fore during the graduation ceremony for Lovecraft's class in June 1903. He was asked to make a speech for the occasion—which may or may not suggest that he was the valedictorian and therefore ranked first in his class—but had initially refused to do so; then, while the ceremony was actually in progress, he changed his mind. Approaching Abbie Hathaway, the school principal, he announced boldly that he wished to make the speech after all, and she acquiesced and duly had him announced. Lovecraft had, however, in the interim written a hasty biography of Sir William Herschel, the astronomer; and as he mounted the podium he declaimed it in 'my best Georgian mode of speech'. He adds that, though the beginning of the speech 'elicited smiles, rather than attention' from the adults in the audience, he nevertheless received a round of applause at the end.[8]

But school was the least significant of Lovecraft's and his friends' concerns; they were primarily interested—as boys of that age, however precocious, are—in playing. And play they did. This was the heyday of the Providence Detective Agency, which featured Lovecraft and his pals carrying 'handcuffs' (of twine), tape measure, tin badge, and even (for Lovecraft) a real revolver—presumably not loaded. Lovecraft did some actual detective writing at this time: 'I used to write detective stories very often, the works of A. Conan Doyle being my model so far as plot was concerned', he writes in 1916, and then goes on to describe one such work about 'twin brothers—one murders the other, but conceals the body, and tries to *live the life of both* … This, I think, antedates my 11th year.'[9] If Lovecraft is accurate in the dating of this tale, it would predate 'The Mysterious Ship', and sounds rather more entertaining than that specimen.

Among the enthusiasms which Lovecraft and his boyhood friends shared was railroads. The coachman at 454 Angell Street had built a summer-house for the boy Lovecraft when he was about five. Lovecraft deemed this building 'The Engine House' and himself built 'a splendid engine … by mounting a sort of queer boiler on a tiny express-waggon'. Then, when the coachmen left (probably around 1900) and the stable was vacated of its horses and carriage, the stable itself became his playground, with 'its immense carriage room, its neat-looking "office", and its vast upstairs, with the colossal (almost scareful) expanse of the grain loft, and the little three-room apartment where the coachmen and his wife had lived'.[10]

Some odd literary works were produced as a result of this interest in railroads. First there is a single issue of a magazine called *The Railroad Review* (December 1901), a three-page item full of Lovecraft's usual profusion of illustrations. Much more interesting is a 106-line poem dated to 1901 whose title on the cover reads: *An Account in Verse of the Marvellous Adventures of H. Lovecraft, Esq. Whilst*

Travelling on the W. & B. Branch of the N.Y.N.H. & H.R.R. in Jany. 1901 in One of Those Most Modern of Devices, to Wit: An Electric Train. It bears an alternative title in its interior: 'H. Lovecraft's Attempted Journey betwixt Providence & Fall River on the N.Y.N.H. & H.R.R.'

This poem is notable for being the first—and, as it happens, one of the best—instances of Lovecraft's *humorous* verse. A little historical background for this piece is useful. The New York, New Haven, and Hartford Railroad (N.Y.N.H. & H.R.R.) had by 1893 become the principal operator of all railroads in the state of Rhode Island. The first electric street cars in Providence had begun running in 1892, and the extension of this service to the outlying localities of Warren, Bristol (the W. & B. Branch), and Fall River appears to have occurred in 1900. With his fascination for railroads, Lovecraft not surprisingly became one of the first patrons of the new service; and the result is a delightfully witty poem on a very modern theme.

In discussing Lovecraft's boyhood pastimes it is impossible to pass over the Blackstone Military Band. Lovecraft's violin lessons may have been a disaster, but this was something altogether different. Here's how he tells it:

> When, at the age of 11, I was a member of the Blackstone Military Band, (whose youthful members were all virtuosi on what was called the 'zobo'—a brass horn with a membrane at one end, which would transform humming to a delightfully brassy impressiveness!) my almost unique ability to keep time was rewarded by my promotion to the post of drummer. That was a difficult thing, insomuch as I was also a star zobo soloist; but the obstacle was surmounted by the discovery of a small papier-mache zobo at the toy store, which I could grip with my teeth without using my hands. Thus my hands were free for drumming—whilst one foot worked a mechanical triangle-beater and the other worked the cymbals—or rather, a wire (adapted from a second triangle-beater) which crashed down on a single horizontal cymbal and made exactly the right cacophony ... Had jazz-bands been known at that remote aera, I would certainly have qualified as an ideal general-utility-man—capable of working rattles, cow-bells, and everything that two hands, two feet, and one mouth could handle.[11]

I don't think I can add much to this. The zobo appears to have been a sort of combined harmonica and kazoo.

All this may seem to give the impression that Lovecraft, in spite of his precociousness, his early health problems, his solitude as a very young boy, and his unsettled nervous condition, was evolving into an entirely 'normal' youth with vigorous teenage interests (except sports and girls, in which he never took any interest). He also seems to have been the leader of his 'gang' of boys. But how normal, really, was he? The later testimony of Stuart Coleman is striking: 'from the age of 8 to 18, I saw quite a bit of him as we went to schools together and I was many times at his home. I won't say I knew him "well" as I doubt if any of his contemporaries at that time did. He was definitely not a normal child and his companions were few.'[12]

Clara Hess, the same age as Lovecraft, supplies a telling and poignant memory of Lovecraft's devotion to astronomy around this time:

> Howard used to go out into the fields in back of my home to study the stars. One early fall evening several of the children in the vicinity assembled to watch him from a distance. Feeling sorry for his loneliness I went up to him and asked him about his telescope and was permitted to look through it. But his language was so technical that I could not understand it and I returned to my group and left him to his lonely study of the heavens.[13]

This is certainly touching, but one should not conclude that Lovecraft's 'loneliness' was inveterate or even that he necessarily found in it anything to regret: intellectual interests were always dominant in his temperament, and he was entirely willing to sacrifice conventional gregariousness for its sake.

But Lovecraft's days of innocence came to an abrupt end. Whipple Phillips' Owyhee Land and Irrigation Company had suffered another serious setback when a drainage ditch was washed out by floods in the spring of 1904; Whipple, now an old man of seventy, cracked under the strain, suffering a stroke and dying on 28 March 1904. This blow was bad enough, but there was still worse to come: because of the mismanagement of Whipple's estate after his death, relatively little was left of his property and funds; so Lovecraft and his mother were forced to move out of 454 Angell Street and occupy a smaller house at 598 Angell Street.

This was probably the most traumatic event Lovecraft experienced prior to the death of his mother in 1921. By 1904 he and his mother were living alone with his widowed grandfather, as both of his aunts and his uncle had married. With Whipple gone, it would have been both financially and practically absurd to have maintained the huge house at Angell and Elmgrove just for the two of them, and the residence at 598 Angell Street was no doubt chosen because of its propinquity. It was, however, a duplex (the address is 598–600 Angell Street), and Lovecraft and his mother occupied only the western side of the smallish house. One would imagine that these quarters—which Lovecraft describes as five rooms and an attic[14]—would, in literal terms, still be adequate for a boy and his mother; but psychologically the loss of his birthplace, to one so endowed with a sense of place, was shattering. To compound the tragedy, Lovecraft's beloved cat, Nigger-Man, disappeared sometime in 1904. This was the only pet Lovecraft ever owned in his life, in spite of his almost idolatrous adoration of the felidae. Nigger-Man's loss perhaps symbolised the loss of his birthplace as no other event could.

To see exactly what an impact the death of his grandfather, the loss of the family fortune (whatever of it was left by this time—Whipple had left an estate valued only at $25,000, of which $5000 went to Susie and $2500 to Lovecraft[15]), and the move from his birthplace had on the thirteen-year-old boy, we must read a remarkable letter of 1934:

> for the first time I knew what a congested, servantless home—with another family in the same house—was ... I felt that I had lost my entire adjustment to the cosmos—for what indeed was HPL without the remembered rooms & hallways & hangings & staircases & statuary & paintings ... & yard & walks & cherry-trees & fountain & ivy-grown arch & stable & gardens & all the rest? How could an old man of 14 (& I surely felt that way!) readjust his existence to a skimpy flat & new household programme & inferior outdoor setting in which almost nothing familiar remained? It seemed like a damned futile business to keep on living. No more tutors—high school next September which would probably be a devilish bore, since one couldn't be as free & easy in high school as one had been during brief snatches at the neighbourly Slater Ave. school ... Oh, hell! Why not slough off consciousness altogether?

Was Lovecraft actually contemplating suicide? It certainly seems so—and, incidentally, this seems virtually the *only* time in Lovecraft's entire life (idle speculation by later critics notwithstanding) when he seriously thought of self-extinction. What stopped him? Let us read on:

> And yet certain elements—notably scientific curiosity & a sense of world drama—held me back. Much in the universe baffled me, yet I knew I could pry the answers out of books if I lived & studied longer. Geology, for example. Just *how* did these ancient sediments & stratifications get crystallised & upheaved into granite peaks? Geography—just *what* would Scott & Shackleton & Borchgrevink find in the great white antarctic on their next expeditions … which I could—if I wished—live to see described? And as to history—as I contemplated an exit without further knowledge I became uncomfortably conscious of what I didn't know. Tantalising gaps existed everywhere. When did people stop speaking Latin & begin to talk Italian & Spanish & French? What on earth ever happened in the black Middle Ages in those parts of the world other than Britain & France (whose story I knew)? What of the vast gulfs of space outside all familiar lands—desert reaches hinted of by Sir John Mandeville & Marco Polo … Tartary, Thibet … What of unknown Africa?[16]

This is a defining moment in the life of H. P. Lovecraft. How prototypical that it was not family ties, religious beliefs, or even—so far as the evidence of the above letter indicates—the urge to write that kept him from suicide, but scientific curiosity. Lovecraft may never have finished high school, may never have attained a degree from Brown University, and may have been eternally ashamed of his lack of formal schooling; but he was one of the most prodigious autodidacts in modern history, and he continued not merely to add to his store of knowledge to the end of his life but to revise his world view in light of that knowledge. This, perhaps, is what we ought most to admire about him.

In the short term the dreaded commencement of high school proved—to both Lovecraft's and his family's surprise—a delight. Hope Street English and Classical High School, at the corner of Hope and Olney Streets (the building, opened in 1898, was on the southeast corner; the present building, on the southwest corner, was opened in 1938), was a good mile from Lovecraft's 598 Angell

Street home, but there was no closer public high school to which he could have gone. Lovecraft on the whole had a very nice time there:

> Knowing of my ungovernable temperament, & of my lawless conduct at Slater Avenue, most of my friends (if friends they may be called) predicted disaster for me, when my will should conflict with the authority of Hope Street's masculine teachers. But a disappointment of the happier sort occurred. The Hope Street preceptors quickly *understood* my disposition as 'Abbie' [i.e. Abbie Hathaway] never understood it; & by *removing all restraint*, made me apparently their comrade & equal; so that I ceased to think of discipline, but merely comported myself as a gentleman among gentlemen.[17]

Since there are no independent accounts of Lovecraft's high school years, we have to accept this statement at face value.

Things were not always entirely harmonious between Lovecraft and his teachers, however. He notes several occasions in which he had various academic disputes, the most celebrated of which was with a 'fat old lady English teacher' named Mrs Blake. On one occasion she felt that a paper handed in by Lovecraft sounded like something she had read in a newspaper or magazine, and pointedly questioned its originality. Lovecraft boldly admitted that he had copied it directly from a newspaper, and—'as the good soul's bewilderment became almost apoplectic'[18]—pulled out a clipping, 'Can the Moon Be Reached by Man? By H. P. Lovecraft'—an article he had published in the *Pawtuxet Valley Gleaner* for 12 October 1906. As in several of his Slater Avenue antics, Lovecraft gives the impression of a show-off and smart-alec, and it is perhaps not surprising that his teachers—unsuccessfully, at least as he recounts it—attempted now and again to put him in his place.

It is worth studying what courses Lovecraft actually took during his three years at Hope Street. His transcript survives, and it is full of interesting and suggestive information. The school year lasted for thirty-nine weeks, and most of the courses Lovecraft took covered an entire year; occasionally he took courses lasting only one term, either nineteen or twenty weeks. (In the following enumeration, classes are for thirty-nine weeks save where listed.) Numerical grades were issued; an 80 represented a Certificate grade, 70 a passing grade. During the 1904–05 year, Lovecraft received the following grades: Elementary Algebra (74), Botany

(85), English (77), Ancient History (82), and Latin (87). There is not much that is unusual here, except the surprisingly low grade Lovecraft received in English.

Lovecraft returned to Hope High in September 1905, but his transcript states that he left on 7 November of that year, not returning until 10 September 1906 (presumably the beginning of the 1906–07 school year). This is no doubt the period of his 'near-breakdown' of 1906. There is not much evidence as to the nature of this illness. It is surely peculiar that Lovecraft does *not* admit to a 'near-breakdown' in 1904; the 1906 breakdown does not appear to have been as serious as its two predecessors (1898 and 1900), even if it did mean his withdrawal from high school for nearly a year.

When Lovecraft returned for the 1906–07 school year he received high marks in English (90), Plane Geometry (92), and Physics (95), and good marks in several other subjects, including Drawing, Latin, and Greek. The ominous thing here is the continuing low marks for Algebra (75).

In his final year at Hope High (1907–08) Lovecraft took only the following: Intermediate Algebra (ten weeks) (85); Chemistry (95); Physics (95). Here the interesting thing is his retaking Algebra. Lovecraft himself remarks: 'The first year I barely passed in algebra, but was so little satisfied with what I had accomplished, that I voluntarily repeated the last half of the term.'[19] There is a slight inaccuracy here, since it was not the Elementary Algebra of his first year that he retook but the Intermediate Algebra of the second year; and he does seem to have finally achieved a better grade this time.

The transcript states that Lovecraft left on 10 June 1908, presumably at the end of the term, since he is recorded as having attended the full thirty-nine weeks of chemistry and physics. But he clearly did not receive a diploma, and indeed it is evident that he has only finished the eleventh grade—or perhaps not even that, since he anomalously took only two full courses during this third year. He would surely have required at least another full year of schooling to qualify for graduation.

Lovecraft, aside from finding the teachers more or less congenial, had the usual scrapes with his classmates. He had been called 'Lovey' at Slater Avenue, but by the time he became well-established at Hope Street he was nicknamed 'Professor' because of his published astronomical articles. He admits to having an 'ungovernable temper' and being 'decidedly pugnacious': 'Any affront—especially any reflection on my truthfulness or honour as an 18th century gentleman—roused in me a tremendous fury, & I would always start a fight if an immediate retraction were not furnished. Being of scant physical strength, I did not fare well in these encounters; though I would never ask for their termination.'[20]

The sense of foreboding Lovecraft mentions as preceding his grandfather's death is evident in his juvenile scientific work—or, rather, in the absence of such work. Both *The Rhode Island Journal of Astronomy* and *The Scientific Gazette* come to an abrupt end with the issues of 31 January 1904. Lovecraft states that both journals resumed as monthlies, the first in May 1904 and the second in August 1904, but that they were stopped after a few weeks;[21] these issues do not survive.

And yet, Lovecraft clearly retained his interest in chemistry and, even if he had given up chemical writing, continued conducting experiments in chemistry and obtaining new instruments. Among the latter were a spectroscope (which Lovecraft still owned in 1918) and a spinthariscope for the detection of radioactivity. He relates one 'physical memorial' of his chemical interests: 'the third finger of my right hand—whose palm side is permanently scarred by a mighty phosphorus burn sustained in 1907. At the time, the loss of the finger seemed likely, but the skill of my uncle [F. C. Clark]—a physician—saved it.'[22]

As for *The Rhode Island Journal of Astronomy*, the later issues (beginning on 16 April 1905) are not appreciably different from their predecessors. Lovecraft is now experimenting with using various colours in the magazine, the only result of which is that some of the issues are extremely difficult to read; by the issue of 14 May 1905 Lovecraft declares that no more colour will be used.

These issues provide some indication of who exactly was reading the magazine. The members of his own family had surely done so at the outset; now that only his mother remained in the house with him, perhaps Lovecraft now concentrated on selling copies (still priced at 1cent per copy, 25 cents for six months, and 50 cents for a year) to his friends and to relatives living in the vicinity. A startling 'Notice!!' in the issue of 8 October 1905 states: 'Subscribers residing outside of Providence will receive their papers in a bunch once a month by mail.' This notice would not have been necessary unless there were at least a handful of such subscribers. Perhaps one can suspect Lovecraft's aunt Annie, now living in Cambridge,

Massachusetts, with her husband; and there may have been other relatives.

Still more startling is a notice in the issue of 22 October 1905: 'Since we have started, others are constantly copying, there is a new paper just out that is a direct copy. PAY NO ATTENTION to these but to the GENUINE.' Lovecraft's schoolmates at Hope Street were evidently offering him the sincerest form of flattery, but Lovecraft did not appreciate it.

Lovecraft, then, was making a game effort to resume his normal life and writing after his grandfather's death and the move to 598 Angell Street. And perhaps his friends lent their assistance. The Providence Detective Agency was revived in 1905 or thereabouts, as well as the Blackstone Orchestra. *The Rhode Island Journal of Astronomy* for 16 April 1905 prints an ad listing H. P. Lovecraft and C. P. Munroe as the leaders ('Fine music cheap'). The ads continue to appear as late as October 1906. In January 1906 we learn of its 'New Repertoire—Tenor & Baritone Solos' as well as 'Phonograph Concerts'. Can it be that Lovecraft was actually attempting to sing? It certainly seems that way; consider a letter of 1918:

> Something over a decade ago I conceived the idea of displacing Sig. Caruso as the world's greatest lyric vocalist, and accordingly inflicted some weird and wondrous ululations upon a perfectly innocent Edison blank. My mother actually liked the results—mothers are not always unbiased critics—but I saw to it that an accident soon removed the incriminating evidence. Later I tried something less ambitious; a simple, touching, plaintive, ballad sort of thing a la John McCormack. This was a better success, but reminded me so much of the wail of a dying fox-terrier that I very carelessly happened to drop it soon after it was made.[23]

Since Lovecraft in a 1933 letter rattles off many of the hit songs of 1906, we can assume that these were the songs he both performed in public and recorded on the phonograph.

This period was also the heyday of the Great Meadow Country Clubhouse. Lovecraft and his pals would ride on bicycles along the Taunton Pike (now State Road 44) to the rural village of Rehoboth, about eight miles from Providence just across the state line into Massachusetts. Here they found a small wooden hut with stone chimney and built an addition to it—'larger than the hut itself'[24]— where they could conduct whatever games they fancied. The hut and chimney had been built by an old Civil War veteran named James Kay, who probably also assisted them in building the addition. When Lovecraft and Harold Munroe returned to this site in 1921, they found very little changed: 'Tables stood about as of yore, pictures we knew still adorned the walls with unbroken glass. Not an inch of tar paper was ripped off, & in the cement hearth we found still embedded the small pebbles we stamped in when it was new & wet—pebbles arranged to form the initials G. M. C. C.'[25] I saw those pebbles myself about twenty years ago, although on a more recent trip I found them almost entirely scattered. Now, of course, only the stone chimney remains, and even that is disintegrating. In its day it must have been an impressive sight.

Also at this time Lovecraft himself developed an interest in firearms. Recall that during the initial creation of the Providence Detective Agency he himself, unlike the other boys, sported a real revolver. Lovecraft evidently amassed a fairly impressive collection of rifles, revolvers, and other firearms: 'After 1904 I had a long succession of 22-calibre rifles, & became a fair shot till my eyes played hell with my accuracy.'[26] At this point Lovecraft seemed to lose interest, and he sold off most of his weapons.

Interestingly, Lovecraft began to guide Chester and Harold Munroe into more academic interests, enlisting them as assistants and even colleagues in some of his own intellectual work. The *Rhode Island Journal* for March 1906 states that a meteorological sub-station has been opened by Harold at his home at 66 Patterson Street. Three months later we hear of the establishment of a Providence Astronomical Society. At this time one of the Munroes assisted Lovecraft in giving a lecture on the sun at the East Side Historical Club by showing lantern slides. I do not imagine that this was anything but a group of Lovecraft's high school friends; we shall see later that they continued to meet in this fashion for several years.

Rather different was the lecture Lovecraft gave to the Boys' Club of the First Baptist Church on 25 January 1907.[27] This was clearly a formal organization, although I do not believe that Lovecraft was a member: if the contretemps with his Sunday school class (for which see below) dates to 1902, it is not likely that he would have been invited back any time soon. But the mere fact that he gave the lecture may indicate that he had achieved a certain celebrity as an astronomical authority; for he had already become widely published in the local papers by this time.

The death of Lovecraft's grandfather roughly coincided with the emergence of two new elderly male figures in his personal and intellectual life: his uncles, Dr Franklin Chase Clark (1847–1915) and Edward Francis Gamwell (1869–1936).

Lovecraft became acquainted with Gamwell in 1895, when the latter began courting his aunt Annie Emeline Phillips. Edward and Annie married on 3 January 1897, with the six-year-old Lovecraft serving as usher. Annie went to live with Edward in Cambridge, Massachusetts, where Edward was the city editor of the *Cambridge Chronicle* (1896–1901), then the *Cambridge Tribune* (1901–12), and then the *Boston Budget and Beacon* (1913–15). But Annie and Edward visited Providence frequently, especially after the birth on 23 April 1898 of Phillips Gamwell, Lovecraft's only first cousin on the maternal side. Gamwell taught Lovecraft to recite the Greek alphabet at the age of six, and Lovecraft even maintains that it was his uncle's extensive editorial capacities that incited him to start *The Rhode Island Journal of Astronomy*.[28]

Lovecraft was much closer to Dr Clark than to Gamwell, and indeed the former became after Whipple's death exactly the sort of father replacement Whipple himself had been. Franklin Chase Clark had received an A.B. from Brown University in 1869, as Edward F. Gamwell would in 1894, had attended Harvard Medical School in 1869–70 (where he is likely to have studied with Oliver Wendell Holmes), and had gone on to attain his M.D. at the College of Physicians and Surgeons in New York. He married Lillian Delora Phillips on 10 April 1902. Lovecraft does not mention being involved with the wedding, but he probably served in some capacity. One imagines that Lillian left 454 Angell Street at that time and moved in with her husband, who lived at 80 Olney Street.

In spite of Clark's scientific background, it was in the area of belles-lettres that he exerted the greatest influence on the young Lovecraft. Clark had translated Homer, Virgil, Lucretius, and Statius into English verse, and Lovecraft reports that he 'did much to correct & purify my faulty style',[29] specifically in verse but also in prose. We can perhaps see Clark's influence as early as the accomplished classical verses in *Poemata Minora, Volume II* (1902).

One hopes, however, that Clark did not have any influence on the only surviving poem by Lovecraft between *Poemata Minora* and the several poems written in 1912: 'De Triumpho Naturae: The Triumph of Nature over Northern Ignorance' (July 1905). This poem, dedicated to William Benjamin Smith, author of *The Color*

Line: A Brief in Behalf of the Unborn (1905), is the first explicitly racist document Lovecraft ever produced; but it was not to be the last. In twenty-four lines Lovecraft paraphrases several central arguments out of Smith's book: that the Civil War was a tragic mistake; that freeing blacks and granting them civil and political rights is folly; and that in so doing the abolitionists have actually ensured the extinction of the black race in America. How will that occur? The argument expressed in the poem is a little cryptic, and cannot be understood without recourse to Smith's book. Smith maintains that the inherent biological inferiority of blacks, their physiological and psychological weaknesses, will cause them to perish over time. This allows Smith to conclude that the blacks will simply wither and die. All that can be said in defence of 'De Triumpho Naturae' is that it is a little less virulent than Smith.

The whole issue of Lovecraft's racism is one I shall have to treat throughout this book. It is not likely that at the age of fifteen Lovecraft had formulated clear views on the matter of race, and his attitudes were surely influenced by his environment and upbringing. Recall Winfield Scott Lovecraft's hallucinations regarding a 'negro' who was molesting his wife; it is conceivable that he could have passed on his prejudice against blacks even to his two-year-old son. Lovecraft's most virulently prejudiced letters were written in the 1920s to his aunt Lillian, who in all likelihood shared his sentiments, as probably did most of the other members of his family.

Lovecraft himself supplies a highly illuminating account of his early views on the subject when he notes his reaction to entering Hope Street High School in 1904:

> But Hope Street is near enough to the 'North End' to have a considerable *Jewish* attendance. It was there that I formed my ineradicable aversion to the Semitic race. The Jews were brilliant in their classes—calculatingly and schemingly brilliant—but their ideals were sordid and their manners coarse. I became rather well known as an anti-Semite before I had been at Hope Street many days.[30]

Lovecraft appears to make that last utterance with some pride. This whole passage is considerably embarrassing to those who wish to exculpate Lovecraft on the ground that he never took any direct actions against the racial or ethnic groups he despised but merely confined his remarks to paper.

'De Triumpho Naturae' appears to be an isolated example of this ugly strain in Lovecraft's early thought and writing; in other regards he continued to pursue abstract intellectual endeavour. A more significant literary product of 1905—one for which Franklin Chase Clark probably provided impetus and guidance—was *A Manual of Roman Antiquities*. This work very likely gave Lovecraft much-needed practice in sustained prose composition; certainly his prose needed work, if 'The Mysterious Ship' was the best he could do in 1902. Something remarkable certainly seems to have happened in the three years subsequent to the writing of 'The Mysterious Ship', and it is highly unfortunate that we have no tales from this period. We accordingly find ourselves wholly unprepared for the surprising competence and maturity of the tale entitled 'The Beast in the Cave'.

The first draft of this tale was written prior to the move from 454 Angell Street in the spring of 1904, and the finished version dates to 21 April 1905. Lovecraft reports having spent 'days of boning at the library'[31] (i.e., the Providence Public Library) in researching the locale of the tale, Mammoth Cave in Kentucky. It would take Lovecraft quite some time to learn the wisdom of basing a tale's locale on first-hand, rather than second-hand, information.

'The Beast in the Cave' deals with a man who, lost in Mammoth Cave, comes upon a creature whom he initially takes to be an ape but who proves to be a man who has been lost in the cave for years. The tale is admirably well told and suspenseful, although not many will have failed to guess the conclusion. In spite of Lovecraft's later dismissal of it as 'ineffably pompous and Johnsonese',[32] 'The Beast in the Cave' is a remarkable story for a fourteen-year-old, and represents a quantum leap over the crudeness of 'The Mysterious Ship'. Lovecraft is right to declare that in it 'I first wrote a story worth reading'.[33]

'The Alchemist' (1908) is still more of an advance in style and technique. This tale recounts an ancient aristocratic family in France that appears to be afflicted with a curse whereby the eldest son in each generation dies before the age of thirty-two; but the true cause of the curse is the machinations of Charles Le Sorcier, a magician who has extended his life preternaturally in order to kill each eldest son.

This tale, much more than its predecessor, betrays the influence of Poe in the narrator's obsessive interest in his own psychological state; indeed, many details in the story make us think of Lovecraft's remark that he himself 'felt a kinship to Poe's gloomy heroes with their broken fortunes'.[34] Antoine, the narrator, is of a lofty and ancient line; but 'poverty but little above the level of dire want, together with a pride of name that forbids its alleviation by the pursuits of commercial life, have prevented the scions of our line from maintaining their estates in pristine splendour'. As a result, Antoine—an only child—spends his years alone, 'poring over the ancient tomes that filled the shadow-haunted library of the chateau, and in roaming without aim or purpose through the perpetual dusk of the spectral wood'; he is kept away from the 'peasant children' who dwell nearby. All this can be seen as a deliberately distorted, but still recognizable, reflection of Lovecraft's own childhood and upbringing.

The last page of the autograph manuscript of 'The Beast in the Cave' bears the following notation:

Tales of Terror
  I. The Beast in the Cave
By H. P. Lovecraft
  (Period—Modern)

It is interesting to note that Lovecraft was already at this time thinking of assembling a collection of his tales; we do not know what other tales, if any, were to make up the volume. The autograph manuscript of 'The Alchemist' does not survive, so we do not know whether it formed part of this volume; probably it did.

We have only hints of what further tales Lovecraft wrote in the next three years, for he declares that in 1908 he destroyed all but two of the stories he had been writing over the last five years.[35] Late in life Lovecraft discovered a composition book bearing the title of one lost story dating to 1905: 'Gone—But Whither?' He remarks wryly: 'I'll bet it was a hell-raiser! The title expresses the fate of the tale itself.'[36] Then there was something called 'The Picture' (1907), which in his Commonplace Book he describes as concerning a 'painting of ultimate horror'. Elsewhere he says of it:

I had a man in a Paris garret paint a mysterious canvas embodying the quintessential essence of all horror. He is found clawed & mangled one morning before his easel. The picture is destroyed, as in a titanic struggle—but in one corner of the frame a bit of canvas remains ... & on it the coroner finds to his horror the painted counterpart of the sort of claw which evidently killed the artist.[37]

There was also a story about a Roman settlement in America, although Lovecraft states that he never completed it.[38]

By 1908, the time of the fourth 'near-breakdown' of his young life, Lovecraft had decided that he was not a fiction-writer, and resolved instead to devote himself to science and belles-lettres. At that time, in spite of the promise shown by 'The Beast in the Cave' and 'The Alchemist', his decision would not have been entirely unwarranted. Lovecraft had by this time already amassed an impressive record of publications on science, and it would have been reasonable for him to have assumed that he would continue to pursue such a course and become a professional writer in this field.

Lovecraft first broke into true print with a letter (dated 27 May 1906) printed in the *Providence Sunday Journal* for 3 June; it concerns a point of astronomy. On 16 July 1906 Lovecraft wrote a letter to the *Scientific American* on the subject of finding planets in the solar system beyond Neptune. Much to his delight, it was published in the issue of 25 August 1906. Around this time, Lovecraft simultaneously began to write two astronomy columns for local papers, the *Pawtuxet Valley Gleaner* and the *Providence Tribune* (morning, evening, and Sunday editions). The *Gleaner* articles begin on 27 July 1906, and after a hiatus of a month progress weekly until the end of the year. The *Tribune* articles commence on 1 August 1906 and proceed monthly until 1 June 1908.

The *Pawtuxet Valley Gleaner* was a weekly based in Phenix, Rhode Island, a community now incorporated into the city of West Warwick, well to the west and south of Providence. Lovecraft describes it as a 'country paper' and states that it was 'more than willing to print & feature anything from Whipple V. Phillips' grandson'.[39] In this letter he maintains that 'During 1906, 1907, & 1908 I flooded the *Pawtuxet Valley Gleaner* with my prose articles'; but no issues subsequent to 28 December 1906 seem to survive. Evidence exists, however, that the paper did indeed continue at least through 1907, so it appears that we have lost a good many articles that Lovecraft published in it.

The *Gleaner* articles—many of them based upon corresponding articles or serials in the *Rhode Island Journal of Astronomy*—do more than merely provide information on the astronomical phenomena for the month; they are among the first of several attempts by Lovecraft over the years to educate the public on the fundamentals of astronomy. In the present instance, Lovecraft has chosen provocative queries about Mars, the moon, and the solar system which he believes (probably rightly) the public will find stimulating.

The articles for the *Providence Tribune* tend to be less interesting only because they rather mechanically deal with the purportedly noteworthy celestial phenomena of each month, becoming somewhat repetitive in the process. They are distinguished, however, for the fact that they are among the few occasions when illustrations by Lovecraft were published: of the twenty articles, sixteen were accompanied by hand-drawn star charts.

My feeling is that a purchase Lovecraft made at this time with his own money—a rebuilt 1906 Remington typewriter—was connected with these published astronomy articles. The typewriter was not used for preparing his hectographed scientific journals (for they remain handwritten to the very end) nor even, apparently, the fiction he was writing (no typescripts from this period survive), so that the preparation of the astronomy columns—the only things he was submitting to a publisher at this time—would be the only logical purpose for securing a typewriter. It was the only typewriter Lovecraft would ever own in his life.

Lovecraft also states that he wrote a lengthy treatise, *A Brief Course in Astronomy—Descriptive, Practical, and Observational; for Beginners and General Readers*, in 1906: 'it got as far as the typed and hand-illustrated stage (circa one hundred fifty pages), though no copy survives'.[40] It is clearly the most substantial scientific work he had ever written or ever would write.

The quotation from 'A Confession of Unfaith' with which I opened this chapter suggests how radically the study of astronomy affected Lovecraft's entire philosophical conception of the universe. Indeed, it is around the period of 1906 that we can definitively date Lovecraft's philosophical awakening. Previous to that there had been only his various conflicts with church authorities in Sunday school. His first attendance, if it truly dates to the age of seven, saw him taking sides with the Romans against the Christians, but only because of his fondness for Roman history and culture and not out of any specifically anticlerical bias. By the age of nine, as he declares, he was conducting a sort of experimental course in comparative religion, pretending to believe in various faiths to see whether they convinced him; evidently none did. This led to his final Sunday school encounter:

> How well I recall my tilts with Sunday-School teachers during my last period of compulsory attendance! I was 12 years of age, and the despair of the institution. None of the answers of my pious preceptors would satisfy me, and my demands that they cease taking things for granted quite upset them. Close reasoning was something new in their little world of Semitic mythology. At last I saw that they were hopelessly bound to unfounded dogmata and traditions, and thenceforward ceased to treat them seriously. Sunday-School became to me simply a place wherein to have a little harmless fun spoofing the pious mossbacks. My mother observed this, and no longer sought to enforce my attendance.[41]

These sessions presumably occurred at the First Baptist Church, where his mother was still on the rolls.

But years of astronomical study triggered the 'cosmicism' that would form so central a pillar of both his philosophical and his aesthetic thought:

> By my thirteenth birthday I was thoroughly impressed with man's impermanence and insignificance, and by my seventeenth, about which time I did some particularly detailed writing on the subject, I had formed in all essential particulars my present pessimistic cosmic views. The futility of all existence began to impress and oppress me; and my references to human progress, formerly hopeful, began to decline in enthusiasm. ('A Confession of Unfaith')

Having sloughed off any belief in deity as scientifically unjustified, Lovecraft was left with the awareness that humankind was (probably) alone in the universe—at least, we have no way to establish contact with extraterrestrial races—and that the *quantitative* insignificance of the planet and all its inhabitants, both spatially and temporally, carried with it the corollary of a *qualitative* insignificance.

A rather remarkable consequence of Lovecraft's philosophical interests was a reformist instinct that led him to attempt to educate the masses—or, at least, one member of them. Lovecraft came upon a Swedish boy, Arthur Fredlund, at the Providence Public Library, and brought him frequently to his home to foster his education. The degree to which Lovecraft took Fredlund under his wing is suggested by the fact that Fredlund (no doubt with

Lovecraft's aid) revived and become the editor of *The Scientific Gazette*, which had been defunct since September 1905. That Lovecraft would have allowed Fredlund to take over the earliest of his scientific periodicals must have meant that he saw great things in the boy. Eventually, however, Lovecraft uncovered unspecified 'qualities' in Fredlund that he did not like, so he abandoned him to his 'plebeian fate'.[42]

In 1908 Lovecraft stood at the threshold of adulthood: he was doing reasonably well at Hope Street High School, he had become prodigiously learned in chemistry, geography, astronomy, and meteorology, and he was accomplished in belles-lettres as a Latinist, poet, and fiction writer. He seemed destined for a career as an academician of some sort; perhaps he would be a sort of transatlantic version of those later Oxford dons who wrote detective stories, teaching astronomy at a university while writing horror tales in his spare time. In any event, the future for so precocious and accomplished a young man seemed assured.

What derailed that future—and what ensured that Lovecraft would never lead a 'normal' life—was his fourth 'near-breakdown', clearly the most serious of his life. In some ways he never recovered from it.

CHAPTER FIVE
Barbarian and Alien (1908–14)

Lovecraft is very reticent about the causes or sources of what we can only regard as a full-fledged nervous breakdown in the summer of 1908. Beyond the mere fact of its occurrence, we know little. Consider four statements, made from 1915 to 1935:

> In 1908 I should have entered Brown University, but the broken state of my health rendered the idea absurd. I was and am a prey to intense headaches, insomnia, and general nervous weakness which prevents my continuous application to any thing.[1]

> In 1908 I was about to enter Brown University, when my health completely gave way—causing the necessary abandonment of my college career.[2]

> after all, high-school was a mistake. I liked it, but the strain was too keen for my health, and I suffered a nervous collapse in 1908 immediately after graduating, which prevented altogether my attending college.[3]

> My health did not permit me to go to the university—indeed, the steady application to high-school gave me a sort of breakdown.[4]

In the first, second, and fourth of these statements Lovecraft is a little disingenuous: he implies that his entry into Brown University was a matter of course, but in fact he never graduated from high school, and certainly would have required at least another year of schooling before he could have done so. The third statement, which states that he actually did graduate, is one of the few instances I have found where Lovecraft plainly lies about himself.

Since we are generally left in the dark about the nature of this breakdown, we can work only on conjecture. We have two pieces of external evidence. One comes from Harry Brobst, who spoke to a woman who had gone to high school with Lovecraft:

She ... described these terrible tics that he had—he'd be sitting in his seat and he'd suddenly up and jump—I think they referred to them as seizures. The family took him out of high school, and then whatever education he got presumably was done by private tutors, whatever that meant.[5]

This certainly is a remarkable account, and suggests that Lovecraft's chorea minor (if that is what it was) had not entirely worn off even by this time. Brobst, a Ph.D. in psychology who was trained as a psychiatric nurse, considers the possibility of 'chorea-like symptoms' and also conjectures that a hysteroid seizure—a purely psychological ailment without any organic basis—may have been involved. Whether these seizures were the actual cause of his removal from high school is something that cannot now be settled.

The other piece of evidence comes from Harold W. Munro, who writes that Lovecraft had been climbing on a house under construction and had fallen, landing on his head.[6] Munro does not date this incident (which he himself did not see but only heard about), but he implicitly links it with Lovecraft's withdrawal from high school.

The breakdown—whether purely mental or nervous or a combination of mental and physical factors—was, clearly, something related to his schoolwork, the same sort of thing that may have caused his milder breakdown of 1906; although even 'steady application' in only three classes (all he was taking in his third year at Hope Street) would not seem sufficient to induce so severe a collapse. Note, however, what three courses he was taking: chemistry, physics, and algebra. He was receiving the highest marks in the first two; in algebra he was repeating a part of the course he had taken the previous year. My feeling, therefore, is that Lovecraft's relative failure to master algebra made him gradually awaken to the realization that he could never do serious professional work in either chemistry or astronomy, and that therefore a career in these two fields was an impossibility. This would have been a shattering conception, requiring a complete revaluation of his career goals. Consider this remark, made in 1931:

In studies I was not bad—except for mathematics, which repelled and exhausted me. I passed in these subjects—but just about that. Or rather, it was *algebra* which formed the bugbear. Geometry was not so bad. But the whole thing disappointed me bitterly, for I was then intending to pursue *astronomy* as a career, and of course advanced astronomy is simply a mass of mathematics. That was the first major set-back I ever received—the first time I was ever brought up short against a consciousness of my own limitations. It was clear to me that I hadn't brains enough to be an astronomer—and that was a pill I couldn't swallow with equanimity.[7]

Again, Lovecraft does not connect this with his breakdown of 1908, but I think the implication of a connection is strong. I repeat that this is a conjecture, but, until further evidence is forthcoming, it may be the best we have.

One more small piece of evidence comes from Lovecraft's wife, who reports that Lovecraft told her that his sexual instincts were at their greatest at the age of nineteen.[8] It is conceivable that sex frustration—for I do not imagine Lovecraft acted upon his urges at this time—may have been a contributory cause of his breakdown; but, for one whose sexuality was, in general, so sluggish as Love-craft's, I am not convinced that this was a significant factor.

As a result of this breakdown, Lovecraft virtually withdrew from the world, so that the period 1908–13 is a virtual blank in his life. It is the only time in his life when we do not have a significant amount of information on what he was doing from day to day, who his friends and associates were, and what he was writing. It is also the only time of his life when the term 'eccentric recluse'—which many have used with careless ignorance—can rightly be applied to him.

Lovecraft doggedly attempted to maintain his scientific interests, although it seems a little pathetic that he revived his juvenile periodicals, *The Scientific Gazette* and *The Rhode Island Journal of Astronomy*, in early 1909, the latter after two years', the former after four years' hiatus (not counting the apparently brief revival by Arthur Fredlund). The sole issue of the *Gazette* for this period (January 1909) has an interesting ad for the 'International Correspondence Schools' in Scranton, Pennsylvania, offering a complete course for $161.00. This is no doubt the correspondence course in chemistry that Lovecraft admits to taking 'for a time'.[9] As to where he learned of this organisation, I shall have more to say a little later. That Lovecraft's mother was willing to pay out the money for such a thing suggests that she was still allowing him freedom to pursue his interests; perhaps she thought this course might lead to a job, although that likelihood was surely remote. Once again, however, it was the more technical or tedious parts of the science that caused him difficulty: 'I found myself so wretched bored that I positively could not study for more than fifteen minutes without acquiring an excruciating headache which prostrated me completely for the rest of the day.'[10] One significant work did come out of this, however: *A Brief Course in Inorganic Chemistry*, written in 1910 and deemed by Lovecraft a 'bulky manuscript'.[11] This work, so far as I know, does not survive, and we know nothing of its contents.

Lovecraft did attempt a more ambitious astronomical project, but it was not designed for publication. This is an astronomical notebook, once in the possession of David H. Keller and later in the Grill-Binkin collection of Lovecraftiana. It bears the title 'Astronomical Observations Made by H. P. Lovecraft, 598 Angell St., Providence, R.I., U.S.A., Years 1909 / 1910 / 1911 / 1912 / 1913 / 1914 / 1915'. Keller[12] reports that the book contains at least one hundred pages of writing; page 99 has the following:

Principal Astronomical Work

1. To keep track of all celestial phenomena month by month, as positions of planets, phases of the moon, Sign of Sun, occultations, Meteor Showers, unusual pheno-mena (record) also new discoveries.
2. To keep up a working knowledge of the constellations and their seasons.
3. To observe all planets, etc. with a large telescope when they are favourably situated (at 7 h 30" in winter, abt. 9 h in summer, supplemented by morning observations)
4. To observe opera or field glass objects among the stars with a low power instruments, recording results.
5. To keep a careful record of each night's work.
6. To contribute a monthly astronomical article of about 7p. Ms. or 4p. Type to the Providence Evening News[13] (begun Jan. 1, 1914.)

This sounds like an impressive agenda, but Lovecraft did not maintain it consistently; in fact, Keller reports that for the years 1911 and 1913 there are no observations at all. Otherwise what we have are things like an eclipse of the moon on 3 June 1909, a 'lengthy description' of Halley's Comet on 26 May 1910, a partial eclipse of the moon on 11–12 March 1914, and a long discussion of Delavan's Comet on 16–17 September 1914. I have not been able to consult this document myself and am reliant on Keller's account of it; but it does not seem to offer much evidence that Lovecraft was doing anything either to relieve his reclusiveness or to find a useful position in the outside world.

Later in life Lovecraft knew that, in spite of his lack of university education, he should have received training in some sort of clerical or other white-collar position that would at least have allowed him to secure employment rather than moping about at home:

> I made the mistake in youth of not realising that literary endeavour does not always mean an income. I ought to have trained myself for some routine clerical work (like Charles Lamb's or Hawthorne's) affording a dependable stipend yet leaving my mind free enough for a certain amount of creative activity—but in the absence of immediate need I was too damned a fool to look ahead. I seemed to think that sufficient money for ordinary needs was something which everyone had as a matter of course—and if I ran short, I 'could always sell a story or poem or something'. Well—my calculations were inaccurate![14]

And so Lovecraft condemned himself to a life of ever-increasing poverty.

What was his mother doing in this entire situation? It is a little hard to say. Recall her own medical record at Butler Hospital (now destroyed) as quoted by Winfield Townley Scott: 'a woman of narrow interests who received, with a traumatic psychosis, an awareness of approaching bankruptcy'.[15] This assessment was made in 1919, but the condition must have been developing for years, at the very least since the death of Susie's own father, Whipple Phillips. Although she had high praise for her son ('a poet of the highest order'), Scott rightly conjectures: 'However she adored him, there may have been a subconscious criticism of Howard, so brilliant but so economically useless.' No doubt her disappointment with her son's inability to finish high school, go to college, and support himself did not help this situation any.

Lovecraft, in speaking of the steady economic decline of the family, notes 'several sharp jogs downward, as when an uncle lost a lot of dough for my mother and me in 1911'.[16] Faig is almost certainly correct in identifying this uncle as Susie's brother Edwin E. Phillips.[17] Edwin had difficulty even maintaining his own economic position, as his chequered employment record indicates. We do not, of course, know how Edwin lost money for Susie and Howard, but one suspects that it had something to do with bad investments, which not only failed to yield interest but also dissolved the capital.

The effect of all this on Susie, and on her view of her son, can only be conjectured. Consider the following disturbing anecdote related by Clara Hess, which I believe dates to around this time if not a little earlier:

> when she [Susie] moved into the little downstairs flat in the house on Angell Street around the corner from Butler Avenue I met her often on the Butler Avenue cars, and one day after many urgent invitations I went in to call upon her. She was considered then to be getting rather odd. My call was pleasant enough but the house had a strange and shutup air and the atmosphere seemed weird and Mrs. Lovecraft talked continuously of her unfortunate son who was so hideous that he hid from everyone and did not like to walk upon the streets where people could gaze at him.
>
> When I protested that she was exaggerating and that he should not feel that way, she looked at me with a rather pitiful look as though I did not understand about it. I remember that I was glad to get out in the fresh air and sunshine and that I did not repeat my visit.[18]

This is one of the most notorious pieces of evidence regarding Lovecraft and his mother, and I see no reason why we should not accept it. The reference to 'hideous' is presumably to his physical appearance, and this is why I want to date the anecdote to Lovecraft's late teens or early twenties: as a younger boy he is so normal-looking that no one—even a mother who was getting a little 'odd'—could have deemed him hideous; but by the age of eighteen or twenty he had perhaps reached his full height of five feet eleven inches, and had probably developed that long, prognathous jaw which he himself in later years considered a physical defect. Harold W. Munro notes that as early as his high school years Lovecraft was bothered by ingrown facial hairs; but when Munro speaks of 'mean red cuts' on Lovecraft's face he evidently believes these to have been the product of a dull razor. In fact, as Lovecraft attests, these cuts came from his using a needle and tweezers to pull out the ingrown hairs.[19] This recurring ailment—which did not subside until Lovecraft was well into his thirties—may also have negatively affected his perception of his appearance. As late as February 1921, only a few months before his mother's death, Lovecraft writes to his mother of a new suit that 'made me appear as nearly respectable as my face permits'.[20]

I am of course not trying to defend this remark by Lovecraft's mother—surely no mother ought ever to say such a thing about her son, no matter how ugly he in fact is—and it may also be that her comment has a somewhat broader implication. It has often been conjectured that she was transferring to her son the hatred and disgust she felt for her husband after he was stricken with syphilis, and I think this is very likely. Susie, of course, is not likely to have known the exact nature or causes of her husband's ailment—the doctors themselves did not do so—but she may have sensed that something relating to sex had afflicted him; and, now that her own son was developing into an adult male with burgeoning sexual instincts, she may have feared that he might turn out very much like her husband—especially if Lovecraft had at this time taken to wearing his father's clothing. In any case, I do not think we have any grounds to deny that she made the 'hideous' remark; Lovecraft himself once (and only once) admitted to his wife that his mother's attitude to him was (and this is his word) 'devastating',[21] and we need look no further for the reasons for that than this single comment.

Both Clara Hess and Harold W. Munro give evidence that Lovecraft did indeed avoid human contact in his post-high-school period. Hess writes: 'Sometimes I would see Howard when walking up Angell Street, but he would not speak and would stare ahead with his coat collar turned up and chin down.'[22] Munro states: 'Very much an introvert, he darted about like a sleuth, hunched over, always with books or papers clutched under his arm, peering straight ahead recognizing nobody.'[23]

We have the merest scraps of information as to what Lovecraft was actually doing during this entire period. One highly suggestive datum is his admission that he visited Moosup Valley, and specifically the Stephen Place house in Foster (birthplace of his mother and grandmother), in 1908. This visit can scarcely have been purely recreational. His mother accompanied him, as there is a photograph of her (probably taken by Lovecraft himself) standing in front of the house.[24] Once again it seems as if Lovecraft required some sort of renewal of ancestral ties to help him out of a difficult psychological trauma; but in this case the visit seems to have accomplished little.

The record for 1909 (aside from his astronomical observations and the correspondence courses) is entirely blank. For 1910 we know that he saw Halley's Comet, but probably not at Ladd Observatory. In 1918 he stated:

> I no more visit the Ladd Observatory or various other attractions of Brown University. Once I expected to utilise them as a regularly entered student, and some day perhaps control some of them as a faculty member. But having known them with this 'inside' attitude, I am today unwilling to visit them as a casual outsider and non-university barbarian and alien.[25]

This sense of alienation presumably began soon after his collapse in 1908, and he probably saw Halley's with his own telescope. He mentions that he missed seeing a bright comet earlier that year 'by being flat in bed with a hellish case of measles!'[26] Elsewhere he states that he lost 54 pounds during this bout with the measles and nearly died.[27] The year 1910 was, however, the period of his most frequent attendance of stage plays, and he reports seeing many Shakespeare productions at the Providence Opera House that year. He also visited Cambridge, Massachusetts—probably to see his aunt Annie Gamwell and his twelve-year-old cousin Phillips. He celebrated his twenty-first birthday—20 August 1911—by riding the electric trolley cars all day, going through the states of Connecticut and Massachusetts before coming home.

Did Lovecraft continue to associate with his boyhood friends? The evidence is a little ambiguous. No doubt he felt a certain sense of failure and defeat as he saw his high school friends marry, find jobs, and in general take on the responsibilities of adult life. But consider this remarkable testimony from Addison P. Munroe, whom Winfield Townley Scott interviewed:

> He lived but a few houses distant from our own home and was quite frequently over here with our sons. I remember that we had a room fixed up in our basement for the boys to use as a club room, which was a popular place with Howard. The club, so called, consisted of about a half-dozen of the neighborhood boys, around twenty years of age, and when they had a so-called 'banquet,' improvised and usually self-cooked, Howard was always the speaker of the evening and my boys always said he delivered addresses that were gems.[28]

This appears to be East Side Historical Club, still meeting even after the boys had graduated from high school. If Munroe is right about the boys' age, then these sessions would have occurred exactly at the time (1910) when Lovecraft was maintaining that he 'shunned all human society',[29] in particular his friends. Lovecraft, in fact, never lost touch with the Munroes, as a number of subsequent events will demonstrate; and Addison P. Munroe may well be right about both the nature and the date of these meetings.

Lovecraft gives a picture of his literary production during this 'empty' period:

> Chemical writing—plus a little historical and antiquarian research—filled my years of feebleness till about 1911, when I had a reaction toward literature. I then gave my prose style the greatest overhauling it has ever had; purging it at once of some vile journalese and some absurd Johnsonianism. Little by little I felt that I was forging the instrument I ought to have forged a decade ago—a decent style capable of expressing what I wished tosay. But I still wrote verse and persisted in the delusion that I was a poet.[30]

The curious thing about this is that we have very few examples of his expository prose between 'The Alchemist' (1908) and the beginning of his astronomy column for the *Providence Evening News* on 1 January 1914. What we do have are a series of poems presumably written 'about 1911' or sometime thereafter. Few of these are at all distinguished, but one is of consuming biographical interest: 'The Members of the Men's Club of the First Universalist Church of Providence, R.I., to Its President, About to Leave for Florida on Account of His Health'.

There is no clear way of dating this poem, and it may have been written as early as 1910 or as late as 1914; but what is remarkable about it is its mere existence, indicating that Lovecraft was a member of this men's club. The First Universalist Society, established in Providence since 1821, had a new church built in 1872 at the corner of Greene and Washington Streets, near the Providence Public Library; and this must have been where Lovecraft went when he participated in the men's club. I can only sense the hand of Lovecraft's mother in this entire enterprise: having failed on at least two occasions to inculcate standard Sunday school training in him as a boy, she perhaps felt that a less rigidly doctrinal church would be more to his liking. Actually, in all likelihood it was a means of preventing Lovecraft from becoming wholly withdrawn from society—in effect, of getting him out of the house every now and then.

The other poems written around this time similarly concern themselves with local affairs, and unfortunately their one clear thematic link is racism. 'Providence in 2000 A.D.' is Lovecraft's first published poem, appearing in the *Evening Bulletin* for 4 March 1912. It is actually quite funny, although much of the humour would not be very well received today. The parenthetical prose paragraph that prefaces the poem—'(It is announced in the *Providence Journal* that the Italians desire to alter the name of Atwell's Avenue to "Columbus Avenue")'—tells the whole story: Lovecraft ridicules the idea that the Italians of the Federal Hill area have any right to change the Yankee-bestowed name of the principal thoroughfare of their own district. (The street was never renamed.) The satire tells of an Englishman who, in the year 2000, returns to Rhode Island, the land of his forebears, and finds everything foreignized. The fact that the *Evening Bulletin* published this poem must mean that others aside from Lovecraft found it funny.

Other poems of this period are much nastier, but were not published at the time. 'New-England Fallen' (April 1912) is a wretched 152-line spasm speaking of some mythical time when hard-working, pious Anglo-Saxon yeomen established the dominant culture of New England only to have 'foreign boors' infiltrate the society and corrupt it from within:

> The village rings with ribald foreign cries;
> Around the wine-shops loaf with bleary eyes
> A vicious crew, that mock the name of 'man',
> Yet dare to call themselves 'American'.

This is surely close to the nadir of Lovecraft's poetic output—not only for the ignorant racism involved, but for its array of trite, hackneyed imagery and nauseating sentimentality in depicting the blissful life of the stolid yeoman farmer. Perhaps only the notorious 'On the Creation of Niggers' (1912) exceeds this specimen in vileness. Here is the entire poem:

> When, long ago, the Gods created Earth,
> In Jove's fair image Man was shap'd at birth.
> The beasts for lesser parts were next design'd;
> Yet were they too remote from humankind.

> To fill this gap, and join the rest to man,
> Th' Olympian host conceiv'd a clever plan.
> A beast they wrought, in semi-human figure,
> Fill'd it with vice, and call'd the thing a NIGGER.

No publication has been found for this poem. The text survives, however, in a hectographed copy, which suggests that Lovecraft may at least have passed this poem around to friends or family; it is likely that they approved—or at least did not object—to his sentiments.

A somewhat more innocuous poem is 'Quinsnicket Park', which Lovecraft dates to 1913. Quinsnicket Park (now called Lincoln Woods Park) is situated four miles north of Providence, and was one of Lovecraft's favourite sylvan retreats; throughout his life he would walk there and read or write in the open air. His 117-line paean to this rustic haven is trite, wooden, and mechanical.

We do not know much else about Lovecraft's specific activities during these years. It is likely that he sequestered himself in his study and read enormous quanitites of books, whether it be science or belles lettres; it was probably at this time that he laid the foundations for that later erudition in so many fields which astounded his colleagues. No doubt he continued to read weird fiction also.

One specific type of fiction we know Lovecraft read in great quantities was the work contained in the early Munsey magazines. It is a point of debate whether the various magazines founded by Frank A. Munsey are or are not to be considered pulp magazines; for our purposes it will suffice to say that they were significant forerunners of the pulp magazines and form a natural chain of continuity in popular magazine fiction from the dime and nickel novels of the later nineteenth century to the genuine pulps of the 1920s. As avid a dime novel reader as Lovecraft appears to have been, it is in no way surprising that he would ultimately find the Munsey magazines a compelling if guilty pleasure. What he did not know at the time was that they would radically transform his life and his career—largely, but not uniformly, for the better.

Lovecraft mentions an article in a Munsey magazine in one of his hectographed magazines in 1903. Whether he read them continuously from this point on his unclear; but there is no gainsaying his remark in the following letter to the *All-Story Weekly* for 7 March 1914:

Having read every number of your magazine since its beginning in January, 1905, I feel in some measure privileged to write a few words of approbation and criticism concerning its contents.

In the present age of vulgar taste and sordid realism it is a relief to peruse a publication such as *The All-Story*, which has ever been and still remains under the influence of the imaginative school of Poe and Verne.

The *All-Story* was a companion magazine to the *Argosy*, which Munsey had changed to an all-fiction magazine in October 1896. Lovecraft of course read the *Argosy* also, as we shall presently see, although perhaps not this early. Lovecraft in 1916 states a little sheepishly that 'In 1913 I had formed the reprehensible habit of picking up cheap magazines like *The Argosy* to divert my mind from the tedium of reality',[31] but it is now evident that this is, at the very least, an equivocation as far as the *All-Story* is concerned. One further bit of evidence is the fact that full-page advertisements for the International Correspondence Schools regularly appear in the *Argosy*, and it is very likely from this source that Lovecraft learned of this organization and used its services around 1909. He also read the *Popular Magazine* (Street & Smith's rival to the *Argosy*) about the period 1905–10.

What was the fascination of these magazines for Lovecraft? The letter quoted above supplies a part of the answer: they contained a significant amount of horror, fantasy, mystery, and science fiction—material that was already ceasing to appear in the standard 'slick' or literary magazines of the day. As Lovecraft states in 1932: 'In general ... the Munsey publications did more to publish weird fiction than any other magazine enterprise of the early 20th century.'[32] Elsewhere he remarks that he 'first began to notice'[33] the *Black Cat* (1895–1922) around 1904, and that that magazine and the *All-Story* 'were the first source of *contemporary* weird material I ever stumbled on'.[34]

The letter-column of the *Argosy*—entitled 'The Log-Book'—had been established only in the February 1911 issue, and letters were initially slow to come in; but by the end of the year many letters (identified only by the initials of the writer and his or her city of residence) were being published, with running commentary by the editor. Lovecraft's first published letter to the Munsey magazines appeared in the *Argosy* for November 1911.[35] His next letter, in the 8 February 1913 issue of the *All-Story Cavalier*, is a comment on

Irvin S. Cobb's magnificent tale of a half-man, half-fish hybrid, 'Fishhead'.

In the fall of that year Lovecraft's letter-writing campaign shifts back to the *Argosy*; but at the moment I wish to return to the letter of 1914 that I have already quoted, a letter of close to two thousand words, taking up nearly two full printed pages. It is a sort of grand summation of everything he liked in the magazine and an encapsulation of what he thought it stood for. One of the most notorious of its statements is its judgment as to the *Argosy*'s leading author: 'At or near the head of your list of writers Edgar Rice Burroughs undoubtedly stands.' Later in life Lovecraft seemed embarrassed at his juvenile (or not so juvenile: he was twenty-three when he wrote this letter) fondness for Burroughs, and he sought to distance himself from the creator of Tarzan.

In his letter Lovecraft goes on to praise many other writers, few of whom are of any note. What is remarkable is that the writers mentioned here (as well as in a later letter published in the *All-Story Cavalier Weekly* for 15 August 1914) did not even write weird fiction. This means that Lovecraft read each issue—sometimes 192 pages, sometimes 240 pages—from cover to cover, month after month or even (when it changed to a weekly) week after week. This is an appalling amount of popular fiction for anyone to read, and in fact it contravened the purpose of the magazines, whereby each member of the family would read only those stories or those types of stories that were of interest to him or her.

It is possible that the *All-Story* published this long letter in its issue of 7 March 1914 because Lovecraft himself had become, after a fashion, a sort of celebrity in the entire Munsey chain. This had come about in a very odd way. Lovecraft, reading everything the *Argosy* put in front of him, found some material less appealing to his fastidious taste than others. In particular, a popular *Argosy* writer of sentimental romances named Fred Jackson was blasted by Lovecraft in the issue for September 1913. Jackson had become an *Argosy* staple, and two of his short novels had appeared complete in recent issues.

The response to Lovecraft's letter is not likely to have been predicted either by Lovecraft or by Matthew White, Jr, editor of the *Argosy*. The November 1913 issue contained several more letters on Jackson, two of which specifically supported Jackson and attacked Lovecraft. The affair, however, might not have taken the peculiar turn it did had not the other letter, by John Russell of Tampa,

Florida, been written *in verse*. This is a whimsical four-stanza piece which begins:

> Does Mr. Lovecraft think it wise
> With such long words to criticize
> An author whom we greatly prize?
> That's Freddie Jackson.

Lovecraft was so taken with this squib that he decided to reply in kind. The January 1914 issue contained a verse epistle of his own in what he fancied was the manner of Pope's *Dunciad*. In fact, it is a very clever poem, and reveals that penchant for stinging satire which would be one of the few virtues of his poetic output. The manuscript of the poem is headed 'Ad Criticos' ('To [my] critics'); in it Lovecraft praises Russell for his cleverness and wit, and then proceeds to take his other enemies to task.

But before Lovecraft's verse letter was printed, he was ferociously assailed in the December 1913 issue. Some of the titles which the editor affixed to the letters give some idea of the outrage Lovecraft had provoked: 'Challenge to Lovecraft' (G. E. Bonner, Springfield, Ohio); 'Virginia *vs*. Providence' (Miss E. E. Blankenship, Richmond, Virginia); 'Elmira *vs*. Providence' (Elizabeth E. Loop, Elmira, New York); 'Bomb for Lovecraft' (F. W. Saunders, Coalgate, Oklahoma). Two letters did take Lovecraft's side, however.

In a second instalment of 'Ad Criticos' published in the February 1914 *Argosy* Lovecraft takes potshots at these new opponents. The tone of this poem is much sharper than that of its predecessor. In this issue Lovecraft begins to gather both friends and enemies— mostly the latter.

The controversy continued desultorily for the next several issues; but something strange now happens: no more replies by Lovecraft are published in the *Argosy* until October 1914. There are two further segments of 'Ad Criticos' in manuscript: did he not submit them for publication? or were they not accepted? The latter seems unlikely, since an editorial note at the end of 'Correction for Lovecraft' (a prose letter published in the March 1914 issue) declares: 'You are always welcome in the Log-Book.'

The controversy comes to an end in the October 1914 issue. An entire section of 'The Log-Book' bears the heading 'Fred Jackson, Pro and Con'; inevitably, the 'Jackson Boosters' outnumber the 'Jackson Knockers'. The most interesting item is a poem headed 'The Critics' Farewell' and bearing both Lovecraft's and Russell's names. They did not actually collaborate on the poem; rather, Lovecraft wrote the first part (headed 'The End of the Jackson War') and Russell wrote the second (headed 'Our Apology to E. M. W.'). Lovecraft's, naturally, is in heroic couplets, and Russell's is in very racy short and irregular anapaests. Lovecraft notes that this truce was made at the insistence of an editor at the *Argosy*, who 'intimated that the poet's war must soon end, since correspondents were complaining of the prominence of our verses in their beloved magazine'.[36]

It is worth reflecting on what the whole *Argosy/All-Story* battle over Fred Jackson meant to Lovecraft. In a sense we owe thanks to Mr Jackson for making the rest of Lovecraft's career possible, for there is no telling how long he would have continued to vegetate in the increasingly hothouse atmosphere of 598 Angell Street. Lovecraft had no job, was only toying with chemistry and astronomy, was living with a mother who was steadily losing her mental stability, was writing random undistinguished bits of verse about his native region, and was devouring the Munsey magazines but had no thought of contributing any fiction to them or to any other market. But Jackson's work so irritated him that he emerged from his hermitry at least to the extent of bombarding letters to the magazines in question. While it was John Russell who initiated the habit of writing in verse, Lovecraft found it in a golden opportunity to adapt his beloved Augustan satire against a very modern target.

The principal immediate benefit of the *Argosy* experience was, of course, his discovery of—or, rather, by—the world of amateur journalism. Edward F. Daas, then Official Editor of the United Amateur Press Association, noticed the poetic battle between Lovecraft and Russell and invited both to join the organization. Both did so, Lovecraft officially enrolling on 6 April 1914. In a few years he would be transformed both as a writer and as a human being.

CHAPTER SIX

A Renewed Will to Live (1914–17)

The world of amateur journalism which Lovecraft entered in April 1914 with wide-eyed curiosity was a peculiar if rather fascinating institution. The papers produced by the members exhibited the widest possible range in content, format, style, and quality; in general they were quite inferior to the 'little magazines' of their day but considerably superior (both in typography and in actual literary content) to the science fiction and fantasy 'fanzines' of a later period, although few were so focused on a single topic as the fanzines were. Amateur journalism as a formal institution began around 1866, with a short-lived society being formed by the publisher Charles Scribner and others around 1869. This society collapsed in 1874, but in 1876 the National Amateur Press Association (NAPA) definitively took form; it continues to exist today. In 1895 the United Amateur Press Association (UAPA) was formed by William H. Greenfield (at that time only fourteen years old) and others who (as Lovecraft believed) wished for an organization more devoted to serious intellectual endeavour; it was this branch that Lovecraft joined. There still exists an alumni association of amateur journalists, The Fossils, who continue to issue a paper, *The Fossil*, on an irregular basis.

It is a sad fact that no one aside from Lovecraft himself has ever emerged from amateurdom to general literary recognition. This is not to say that others do not deserve to do so: the poetry of Samuel Loveman and Rheinhart Kleiner, the fiction of Edith Miniter (much of it professionally published), and the critical work of Ernest A. Edkins, James F. Morton, and Edward H. Cole need fear no comparison with their analogues in the standard literature of the day. It is, unfortunately, unlikely that much of this work will ever be revived or even taken note of except in connection with Lovecraft himself.

It was not required that amateur journalists produce their own journals. Indeed, no more than a fraction of the members ever did so, and some of these papers were extremely irregular. In most cases members would send contributions directly to editors of existing amateur journals or to two 'Manuscript Bureaus', one for the eastern part of the country, one for the western part; the managers of these bureaus would then dole out the manuscripts to journals in need of material. Individuals with printing apparatus were greatly in demand; indeed, NAPA was originally an organization not for disinterested *littérateurs* to excel in the art of self-expression but for youthful printers to practise the art of typography.

The literature produced by members varied widely in both content and quality: poetry, essays, fiction, reviews, news items, polemics, and every other form of writing that can fit into a small compass. If it is generally true that most of this material is the work of tyros—'amateurs' in the pejorative sense—then it means only that amateur journalism was performing a sound if humble function as a proving-ground for writers. Some amateurs did in fact go on to publish professionally. And yet, Lovecraft was all too correct when, late in life, he summed up the general qualitative level of amateur work: 'God, what crap!'[1]

Each association held an annual convention—NAPA in early July, UAPA in late July—at which the officers for the next official year were elected. The chief offices were President, Vice-President, Treasurer, and Official Editor. Other offices—including the Department of Public Criticism—were filled by appointments by the President. With this elaborate hierarchy, it was no surprise that some members became only interested in attaining eminence in the organization by holding office, and that intensely bitter, personal, and vituperative election campaigns were held to ensure the victory of a given individual or faction. All this becomes particularly absurd when we realize how few individuals were involved in amateurdom at any given time. The November 1918 *United Amateur* lists only 247 active members; the November 1917 *National Amateur* lists 227 (many individuals belonged to both associations).

Amateur journalism was exactly the right thing for Lovecraft at this critical juncture in his life. For the next ten years he devoted himself with unflagging energy to the amateur cause, and for the rest of his life he maintained some contact with it. For someone so unworldly, so sequestered, and so diffident about his own abilities, the tiny world of amateur journalism was a place where he could shine. Lovecraft realised the beneficial effects of amateurdom when he wrote in 1921:

Amateur Journalism has provided me with the very world in which I live. Of a nervous and reserved temperament, and cursed with an aspiration which far exceeds my endowments, I am a typical misfit in the larger world of endeavour, and singularly unable to derive enjoyment from ordinary miscellaneous activities. In 1914, when the kindly hand of amateurdom was first extended to me, I was as close to the state of vegetation as any animal well can be ... With the advent of the United I obtained a renewed will to live; a renewed sense of existence as other than a superfluous weight; and found a sphere in which I could feel that my efforts were not wholly futile. For the first time I could imagine that my clumsy gropings after art were a little more than faint cries lost in the unlistening void. ('What Amateurdom and I Have Done for Each Other')

To this analysis there is really very little to add, although a modicum of detail is necessary to flesh out the picture and to pinpoint exactly how this transformation occurred. As for what Lovecraft did for amateurdom, that too is a long story, and one worth studying carefully.

In 1914, when Lovecraft entered amateur journalism, he found two schisms that were creating much bad blood and using up valuable energy. The first was, of course, the split between the National and United Amateur Press Associations, which had occurred when the latter was founded in 1895. Some members did indeed belong to both associations; Lovecraft, although labelling himself repeatedly and ostentatiously a loyal 'United man', joined the National himself as early as 1917, and would later serve as interim president.

The other split was one within the United itself. Lovecraft addresses this matter in two essays, 'The Pseudo-United' (*United Amateur*, May 1920) and 'A Matter of Uniteds' (*Bacon's Essays*, summer 1927). In 1912 occurred a hotly contested election at the UAPA convention in La Grande, Oregon; the result was that both of the two candidates for president, Helene E. Hoffman and Harry Shepherd, declared themselves the winner. In his various remarks Lovecraft never makes it clear that it was the Hoffman faction that refused to accept the verdict of the UAPA directors (who confirmed the election of Shepherd) and withdrew. Indeed, if all one knows of the controversy comes from Lovecraft, one would think it was the

Shepherd group that was the rebel organization; but in fact the amateur world to this day regards the Hoffman group as the rebels and the discontents, even though many acknowledge their literary and numerical superiority.

In any event, the Hoffman supporters established their own association, retaining the title United Amateur Press Association, while the group around Shepherd called itself the United Amateur Press Association of America. Lovecraft joined the former because he had been recruited by Edward F. Daas of that faction; probably he did not at the time even know of the existence of the other, as it was largely centred on Seattle, Washington. It is, however, somewhat ironic that what Lovecraft called the 'pseudo-United' actually outlasted his own United; the latter essentially collapsed from disorganization and apathy around 1926, while the other United carried on until 1939. But for all practical purposes it was a moribund association, and when Lovecraft was persuaded to resume amateur activity in the 1930s he saw no option but to work for the NAPA.

The United's split with the National was something Lovecraft vigorously supported and never wished to see healed. His contempt for the older group—which he fancied (perhaps rightly) to be a haven of old-timers resting on their laurels, men who looked back fondly to their lost youth as amateur printers and typographers, and politicians devoted to furthering their own causes and gaining transient and meaningless power in an insignificant arena—is unremitting. In 'Consolidation's Autopsy' (published in the *Lake Breeze* for April 1915 under the not very accurate pseudonym 'El Imparcial') he dynamites the position of those Nationalites who are seeking some sort of rapport with the United. Dismissing the National as 'an inactive Old Men's Home', he writes scornfully of their fostering the ideal of the 'small boy with a printing press'—a somewhat double-edged charge, since Lovecraft himself had been exactly that only a few years earlier. Indeed, perhaps the vehemence of his response rests precisely in his awareness that he himself had a somewhat arrested adolescence and was anomalously long in separating himself from boyhood interests.

As Lovecraft plunged into amateur activity, contributing essays and poems (later stories) to amateur journals, becoming involved in heated controversies, and in general taking stock of the little world he had stumbled upon, he gradually formulated a belief— one that he gained remarkably early and maintained to the end of his life—that amateur journalism was an ideal vehicle for the effecting of two important goals: first, abstract self-expression without thought of remuneration; and second, education, especially for those who had not had the benefit of formal schooling. The first became a cardinal tenet in Lovecraft's later aesthetic theory, and its development during his amateur period may be the most important contribution of amateur journalism to his literary outlook. It is not, of course, likely that amateurdom actually originated this idea in Lovecraft's mind; indeed, he would not have responded so vigorously to amateurdom if he had not already held this view of literature as an elegant diversion.

At the same time that Lovecraft was hailing the non-mercenary spirit of amateurdom, he was regarding the amateur world as a practice arena for professional publication. This is not a paradox because what he meant by 'professional publication' was not hackwork but publication in distinguished magazines or with reputed book publishers. In so doing one is not buckling down to produce insincere pseudo-literature simply for money but allowing the polished products of one's 'self-expression' to achieve a worthy audience.

The means to achieve these lofty goals in amateurdom was education. It is surely plausible to believe that Lovecraft's own failures in formal education caused him to espouse this goal as fervently as he did. Consider his statement in 'For What Does the United Stand?' (*United Amateur*, May 1920):

> The United aims to assist those whom other forms of literary influence cannot reach. The non-university man, the dwellers in different places, the recluse, the invalid, the very young, the elderly; all these are included within our scope. And beside our novices stand persons of mature cultivation and experience, ready to assist for the sheer joy of assisting. In no other society does wealth or previous learning count for so little ... It is an university, stripped of every artificiality and conventionality, and thrown open to all without distinction. Here may every man shine according to his genius, and here may the small as well as the great writer know the bliss of appreciation and the glory of recognised achievement.

This all sounds very well, but Lovecraft regarded it as axiomatic that he was one of the 'great' writers in this little realm, one of the 'persons of mature cultivation and experience' who would raise his lessers to whatever heights they could achieve. This was not arrogance on Lovecraft's part but plain truth; he really was one of the leading figures of amateurdom at this time, and his reputation has remained high in this small field. This ideal of amateurdom as a sort of informal university was something Lovecraft found compelling and attempted—ultimately in vain—to bring about.

Only a few months after he joined amateur journalism, Lovecraft obtained a forum whereby he could put many of his developing theories—particularly that of education—into practice. Around November 1914 he was appointed by President Dora M. Hepner to take over the chairmanship of the Department of Public Criticism. It was the first office Lovecraft held, and he made the most of it.

The office entailed Lovecraft's writing a lengthy article for the *United Amateur* criticizing in detail each and every amateur journal that was submitted for review. His first article appeared in the January 1915 issue, and over the next five years Lovecraft wrote at least sixteen more. These pieces must be read to gain some idea of his devotion to the amateur cause. Plodding and schoolmasterly as many of them are—painstakingly correcting every grammatical blunder, pointing out flaws in prosody, lapses in taste, and errors in fact—it is exactly the sort of criticism that the amateurs needed. It would have been futile to present a lofty dissection of the aesthetic substance of their work when many were struggling to achieve the barest minimum of grammatical correctness in prose and verse. Lovecraft is tireless in the patient, careful advice he gives: he always attempts to find some merit in the work under consideration, but never lets a technical flaw go by.

Naturally, Lovecraft had his biases. His greatest flaws as an official critic (at least in his early phase) are political and social prejudices and a relentless advocacy of 'Georgian' standards in prose and verse. Slang and colloquialism particularly offended him. Another frequent target was simplified spelling. We may find Lovecraft's comments on this subject somewhat heavy-handed—akin to using a sledgehammer to crack a nut—but simple spelling was being advocated by a number of distinguished critics and grammarians of the day. Lovecraft delivers a learned lecture on the history of the subject in 'The Simple Spelling Mania' (*United Co-operative*, December 1918).

The degree to which Lovecraft was devoted to the literary standards of the eighteenth century is no more evident than in 'The

Case for Classicism' (*United Co-operative*, June 1919), in which he takes to task one Professor Philip B. McDonald for belittling the relevance of classic authors in developing effective style and rhetoric. Although Lovecraft claims that 'It is not my purpose here to engage in any extensive battle of ancient and modern books, such as that fought in Saint-James's Library and veraciously chronicled by Dean Swift', such a battle of the books is exactly what Lovecraft conducts here: 'I cannot refrain from insisting on the permanent paramountcy of classical literature as opposed to the superficial productions of this disturbed and degenerate age.' As if this were not enough, Lovecraft continues:

> The literary genius of Greece and Rome, developed under peculiarly favourable circumstances, may fairly be said to have completed the art and science of expression. Unhurried and profound, the classical author achieved a standard of simplicity, moderation, and elegance of taste, which all succeeding time has been powerless to excel or even to equal.

This utterance is quite remarkable. To say that the ancients 'completed the art and science of expression' means that there is nothing left for subsequent writers to do but to imitate; and Lovecraft in fact goes on to say that 'those modern periods have been most cultivated, in which the models of antiquity have been most faithfully followed'. What Lovecraft ignores here is that even in the eighteenth century it was the adaptation of classical models to the contemporary world that produced the most viable literature of the period. The brilliance of Johnson's *London* or Pope's *Dunciad* stems not from their aping of the forms of Roman satire but from their application of these forms to vivify very modern concerns.

With attitudes like these, it is not surprising that Lovecraft was, throughout the course of his amateur career, forced to defend himself against those who felt that his criticism was both too harsh and misguided. Lovecraft addresses the issue in several essays, including 'Amateur Criticism' (*Conservative*, July 1918) and 'Lucubrations Lovecraftian' (*United Co-operative*, April 1921). The tone of this latter piece is particularly sharp precisely because he placed so much value in the Department of Public Criticism as a tool for the educational improvement of amateur writing. Lovecraft himself certainly felt so during the three terms he was Chairman of the department (1915–16, 1916–17, and 1918–19), and he very likely inculcated his views to the two other chairmen who served between 1915 and 1922 (Rheinhart Kleiner (1917–18) and Alfred Galpin (1919-22)), since both were close friends of his. The fact that both these individuals shared many of Lovecraft's strict views on the 'dignity of journalism' may have caused resentment from those members who did not.

Beginning some time in 1914 Lovecraft made an attempt to practise his educational ideal very close to home, by assisting in the formation of a Providence Amateur Press Club. The impetus for this club came from one Victor L. Basinet, who on the suggestion of Edward H. Cole (a Boston amateur journalist associated with the NAPA) formed an amateur press club amongst some working-class people in the 'North End' of Providence who were attending night classes at a local high school. Cole—who was very likely already in touch with Lovecraft—probably urged the group to gain assistance from the UAPA's only Rhode Island member; and Lovecraft, thinking that this attempt to 'uplift the masses' might succeed better than the incident with Arthur Fredlund eight years earlier, gave considerable assistance.

Most of the members were Irish; among them was a particularly feisty young man, about a year and a half older than Lovecraft, named John T. Dunn (1889–1983). The press club set about assembling an amateur journal, the *Providence Amateur*; the first issue (June 1915) appears to have been written entirely by Lovecraft and Dunn, although only three of the six pieces are signed. The second issue (February 1916) is more substantial, although the typographical accuracy is very poor. This issue contains contributions by a variety of members, including two poems by Lovecraft: 'To Charlie of the Comics' (unsigned) and 'The Bride of the Sea' (as by 'Lewis Theobald, Jr.'). In this issue Lovecraft is listed as Official Editor.

Dunn, interviewed by L. Sprague de Camp in 1975, provides some fascinating glimpses of Lovecraft's personal comportment at the meetings of the club:

> Dunn found Lovecraft … odd or even eccentric. At gatherings, Lovecraft sat stiffly staring forward, except when he turned his head towards someone who spoke to him. He spoke in a low monotone.
>
> 'He sat—he usually sat like that, looking straight ahead, see? Then he'd answer a question, and go back again,' said Father Dunn. 'I can see him now … and he looked straight

ahead; and ... he didn't emphasize things. He nodded sometimes to emphasize a word or an expression.

'I liked the fellow,' he continued. 'I didn't have anything against him at all, see? Only we did disagree; but I hope we disagreed like gentlemen, see?'

...

Lovecraft's voice was high-pitched but not what one would call shrill; Dunn said it was about like his own. Lovecraft had great self-control, never losing his temper no matter how heated the argument. 'He—ah—I never saw him show any temper, see? But when he wrote, he wrote very vigorously; there's no doubt about that, see ...? And he never got excited like I would get excited.'[2]

Dunn and Lovecraft certainly did have some epistolary fireworks, especially over the Irish question. Dunn later refused to register for the draft and was imprisoned for a time, but was released after the war.

Lovecraft washed his hands of the club shortly after the appearance of the second issue, although he continued to keep in touch with Dunn for another year or so. The club itself had definitely folded by the fall of 1916. So ended Lovecraft's second attempt to uplift the masses.

I have made reference to the *Conservative*. This was, of course, Lovecraft's own amateur journal, and the first periodical he edited since the demise of *The Rhode Island Journal of Astronomy* in February 1909. Although he was on the editorial board of several other amateur journals, the *Conservative* was the only one of which he was the sole editor. Thirteen issues appeared from 1915 to 1923, broken down as follows:

Volume I: April 1915, July 1915, October 1915, January 1916
Volume II: April 1916, July 1916, October 1916, January 1917
Volume III: July 1917
Volume IV: July 1918
Volume V: July 1919
No. 12: March 1923
No. 13: July 1923

The issues range from four to twenty-eight pages. The first three issues were written almost entirely by Lovecraft, but thereafter his contributions decline considerably except for occasional poems and—beginning with the October 1916 issue—a regular column of opinion entitled 'In the Editor's Study'.

It is clear that Lovecraft welcomed the prospect of editing his own paper rather than merely contributing random pieces to other amateur journals or appearing in the official organ. What this allowed him to do—aside from promoting his own vision of amateurdom as a haven for literary excellence and a tool for humanist education—was to express his own opinions fearlessly. He did just that. The 'Editorial' in the July 1915 issue contains his statement of editorial policy:

> That the arts of literature and literary criticism will receive prime attention from *The Conservative* seems very probable. The increasing use among us of slovenly prose and lame metre, supported and sustained by the light reviewers of the amateur press, demands an active opponent, even though a lone one, and the profound reverence of *The Conservative* for the polished writers of a more correct age, fits him for a task to which his mediocre talent might not otherwise recommend him.
>
> ...
>
> Outside the domain of pure literature, *The Conservative* will ever be found an enthusiastic champion of total abstinence and prohibition; of moderate, healthy militarism as contrasted with dangerous and unpatriotic peace-preaching; of Pan-Saxonism, or the domination by the English and kindred races over the lesser divisions of mankind; and of constitutional representative government, as opposed to the pernicious and contemptible false schemes of anarchy and socialism.

A mighty tall agenda. I have already touched on some of the controversies over literature in which Lovecraft engaged; his political debates—both in published works and in private correspondence—were no less vigorous, and I shall treat them later. We will find that some of Lovecraft's early opinions are quite repugnant, and many of them are uttered in a cocksure, dogmatic manner greatly in contrast with his later views. Nevertheless, it was evident to all amateurs that the editor of the *Conservative* was an intellectual force to be dealt with.

Lovecraft's official career in amateur journalism was augmented by his election in July 1915 as First Vice-President of the UAPA.

Part of his responsibility was to be the head of the Recruiting Committee, for which he wrote the pamphlet *United Amateur Press Association: Exponent of Amateur Journalism*. This, the second separate publication by Lovecraft (for the first, *The Crime of Crimes* (1915), see below), was issued in late 1915.

For the next term (1916–17) Lovecraft had no official function except Chairman of the Department of Public Criticism. He was, however, elected President at the UAPA convention in late July 1917. For the next five years he and his associates essentially controlled the UAPA, and the result really was a very significant raising of the literary tone. For a time it looked as if Lovecraft's goals for amateurdom would be grandly fulfilled.

During this whole period Lovecraft had recommenced the writing of monthly astronomy articles, this time for the *Providence Evening News*. The first one appears in the issue for 1 January 1914, and hence actually predates his entry into amateur journalism. I have no doubt that Lovecraft was paid for each of the fifty-three articles he published.

The *Evening News* articles become tedious and repetitious if read all at once, for they are in large part merely accounts of the notable celestial phenomena for the month: the phases of the moon, the constellations visible in the morning or evening sky, any eclipses, meteor showers, or other events of note, and the like. After a year, of course, many of the same phenomena will recur. Nevertheless, Lovecraft gradually loosens up a little and introduces other side-lights along the way. In particular, he becomes keen on explaining the origin of the Greek or Roman names for the constellations, and this naturally allows him to recount, sometimes at considerable length, the myths behind such names as Castor and Pollux, Argo Navis (recall his lost juvenile work, *The Argonauts*), and many others. His early reading of Bulfinch and other mythographers held in him good stead here.

In the fall of 1914, however, as Lovecraft was steadily writing article after article for the *News*, a rude interruption occurred. An article entitled 'Astrology and the European War' by one J. F. Hartmann appeared in the issue for 4 September 1914—only three days after Lovecraft's column for that month, and in the exact place in the newspaper (the centre of the last page) occupied by his column. Joachim Friedrich Hartmann (1848–1930) was, one imagines, of German ancestry, but was born in Pennsylvania. He came to Providence no later than 1912.[3] Hartmann's article begins resoundingly with an attack on the 'vulgar prejudice against the noble science of astrology by otherwise learned men' and goes on to transcribe certain predictions for the rest of the year. Given the state of international relations in Europe in 1914, the predictions are not especially remarkable: 'The influences operating in King George's horoscope are very unfavourable'; 'The kaiser is under very adverse directions, and danger both to health and person is indicated'; and so on.

This was just the sort of thing to make Lovecraft see red. He began with a straightforward but somewhat intemperate response entitled 'Science versus Charlatanry', published in the issue for 9 September. But Lovecraft had underestimated his foe. Hartmann responded with a direct rebuttal to Lovecraft's letter in the issue for 7 October, addressing Lovecraft's points sytematically and actually scoring a few telling blows. Three days later, on 10 October, a letter by Lovecraft appeared under the title 'The Falsity of Astrology'. This letter is still more intemperate than the first. While asserting that Hartmann had said little new in his response, Lovecraft's own letter does little to flesh out his argument.

But before Hartmann could respond to this latest attack, Lovecraft struck back in a different manner, adapting Jonathan Swift's attacks on the astrologer Partridge, written under the pseudonym Isaac Bickerstaffe. The result is a series of articles, as by 'Isaac Bickerstaffe, Jun.', mercilessly poking fun at Hartmann and astrology in general. Lovecraft does not follow Swift in exact particulars—Swift's *tour de force* had been to predict the death of Partridge, and then to follow it up with a very convincing account of Partridge's death, after which the poor devil had a very difficult time proving that he was still alive—but merely maintains that, by its own principles, astrology ought to be able to predict events far in the future rather than merely a year or so in advance. Accordingly, one of Lovecraft's articles concludes with a prediction of the earth's destruction on 26 February 4954. In spite of several game rebuttals by Hartmann (in which it becomes pitifully obvious that he has no idea that Bickerstaffe is Lovecraft), the satires did the trick and shut him up.

From May to February 1915 Lovecraft published a series of fourteen rather routine articles entitled 'Mysteries of the Heavens Revealed by Astronomy' in the *Asheville* (N.C.) *Gazette-News*, although part of the thirteenth and the fourteenth article have not come to light. This series claims to be a systematic and elementary treatise on all phases of astronomy for the complete novice. As such, 'Mysteries of the Heavens' is a good example of what Lovecraft might have done had he decided to become merely a popular science writer. Mildly interesting as the series is, it is good for the sake of literature that he did not so limit his horizons. The assignment was presumably arranged for Lovecraft by Chester Munroe, who had established himself in Asheville.

If Lovecraft's views on prose style were conservative and old-fashioned, in poetry they were still more so, both in precept and in practice. We have seen that his poetry of the early teens bears a self-consciously antiquated cast, and is in some ways *more* archaistic than even some of his juvenile verse, which (as in the 'Attempted Journey') at least features some contemporaneousness in subject.

The interesting thing is that, right from the beginning, Lovecraft was aware that his poetry had relatively little intrinsic merit aside from academic correctness in metre and rhyme. Writing in 1914 to Maurice W. Moe, a high-school English teacher and one of his earliest amateur colleagues, he stated in defence of his inveterate use of the heroic couplet: 'Take the form away, and nothing remains. I have no real poetic ability, and all that saves my verse from utter worthlessness is the care which I bestow on its metrical construction.'[4]

In 1929 Lovecraft articulated perhaps the soundest evaluation of his verse-writing career that it is possible to give:

> In my metrical novitiate I was, alas, a chronic & inveterate mimic; allowing my antiquarian tendencies to get the better of my abstract poetic feeling. As a result, the whole purpose of my writing soon became distorted—till at length I wrote only as a means of re-creating around me the atmosphere of my 18th century favourites. Self-expression as such sank out of sight, & my sole test of excellence was the degree with which I approached the style of Mr. Pope, Dr. Young, Mr. Thomson, Mr. Addison, Mr. Tickell, Mr. Parnell, Dr. Goldsmith, Dr. Johnson, & so on. My verse lost every vestige of original-ity & sincerity, its only core being to reproduce the typical forms & sentiments of the Georgian scene amidst which it was supposed to be produced. Language, vocabulary, ideas, imagery—everything succumbed to my own intense

> purpose of thinking & dreaming myself back into that world
> of periwigs & long s's which for some odd reason seemed to
> me the normal world.[5]

To this analysis very little need be added. What it demonstrates is
that Lovecraft utilized poetry not for *aesthetic* but for *psychological*
ends: as a means of tricking himself into believing that the
eighteenth century still existed—or, at least, that he was a product
of the eighteenth century who had somehow been transported into
an alien and repulsive era. And if the 'sole test of excellence' of
Lovecraft's verse was its success in duplicating the style of the great
Georgian poets, then it must flatly be declared that his poetry is a
resounding failure. He certainly manages to copy the mechanical
externals of eighteenth-century verse, but its vital essence
invariably escapes him.

Lovecraft's poetry falls into a number of groupings differentiated
generally by subject matter. The bulk of his verse must fall under
the broad rubric of occasional poetry; within this class there are
such things as poems to friends and associates, seasonal poems,
poems on amateur affairs, imitations of classical poetry (especially
Ovid's *Metamorphoses*), and other miscellaneous verse. There is, at
least up to about 1919, a large array of political or patriotic verse,
almost entirely worthless. There is also a small group of mediocre
philosophical or didactic verse. Satiric poetry bulks large in
Lovecraft's early period, and this is perhaps the most consistently
meritorious of his early metrical output. Weird verse does not
become extensive until 1917—the precise time when Lovecraft
resumed the writing of weird fiction—so shall be considered later.
These categories of course overlap: some of the satiric poetry is
directed toward colleagues or individuals in the amateur circle, or is
on political subjects.

Of the occasional poetry in general it is difficult to speak kindly.
In many instances one quite is literally at a loss to wonder what
Lovecraft was attempting to accomplish with such verse. These
poems appear frequently to have served merely as the equivalents
of letters. Indeed, Lovecraft once confessed that 'In youth I scarcely
did any letter-writing—thanking anybody for a present was so
much of an ordeal that I would rather have written a two-hundred-
fifty-line pastoral or a twenty-page treatise on the rings of Saturn'.[6]

Of the seasonal poems very little can be said. There are poems on
almost every month of the year, as well as each of the individual
seasons; but all are trite, mechanical, and quite without genuine

feeling. One heroic work—in more ways than one—that requires some consideration is 'Old Christmas' (*Tryout*, December 1918; written in late 1917), a 332-line monstrosity that is Lovecraft's single longest poem. Actually, if one can accept the premise of this poem—a re-creation of a typical Christmas night in the England of Queen Anne's time—then one can derive a certain enjoyment from its resolutely wholesome and cheerful couplets. The sheer geniality of the poem eventually wins one over if one can endure the antiquated diction.

Two facets of Lovecraft's poetry that must be passed over in merciful brevity are his classical imitations and his philosophical poetry. Lovecraft seemed endlessly fond of producing flaccid imitations of Ovid's *Metamorphoses*—his first poetic love, let us recall—including such things as 'Hylas and Myrrha: A Tale' (*Tryout*, May 1919), 'Myrrha and Strephon' (*Tryout*, July 1919), and several others. Of the early philosophical poetry, only a few are notable. 'Inspiration' (*Conservative*, October 1916) is a delicate two-stanza poem on literary inspiration coming to a writer at an unexpected moment. It is of importance largely because it is the very first piece of *professionally* published poetry by Lovecraft outside of local newspaper appearances: it was reprinted in the *National Magazine* of Boston in November 1916. Lovecraft had a number of poems printed in this magazine over the next several years.

As the years passed, it became evident to Lovecraft's readers in the amateur press (as it was always evident to Lovecraft himself) that in his poetry he was a self-consciously antiquated fossil with admirable technical skill but no real poetic feeling. Eventually Lovecraft began to poke fun at himself on this score, as in 'On the Death of a Rhyming Critic' (*Toledo Amateur*, July 1917) and 'The Dead Bookworm' (*United Amateur*, September 1919).

This brings us to Lovecraft's satiric poetry, which not only ranges over a very wide array of subject matter but is clearly the only facet of his poetry aside from his weird verse that is of any account. Kleiner made this point in 'A Note on Howard P. Lovecraft's Verse' (*United Amateur*, March 1919), the first critical article on Lovecraft:

> Many who cannot read his longer and more ambitious productions find Mr. Lovecraft's light or humorous verse decidedly refreshing. As a satirist along familiar lines, particularly those laid down by Butler, Swift and Pope, he is most himself—paradoxical as it seems. In reading his satires one cannot help but feel the zest with which the author has

composed them. They are admirable for the way in which they reveal the depth and intensity of Mr. Lovecraft's convictions, while the wit, irony, sarcasm and humour to be found in them serve as an indication of his powers as a controversialist. The almost relentless ferocity of his satires is constantly relieved by an attendant broad humour which has the merit of causing the reader to chuckle more than once in the perusal of some attack levelled against the particular person or policy which may have incurred Mr. Lovecraft's displeasure.

This analysis is exactly on target. Lovecraft himself remarked in 1921: 'Whatever merriment I have is always derived from the satirical principle.'[7]

Literary faults or literary modernism (much the same thing to Lovecraft at this time) are also the target of many satires. When Charles D. Isaacson in his amateur journal *In a Minor Key* championed Walt Whitman as the 'Greatest American Thinker', Lovecraft responded with a sizzling rebuttal in prose entitled 'In a Major Key' (*Conservative*, July 1915) in which he included an untitled poem on Whitman:

> Behold great *Whitman*, whose licentious line
> Delights the rake, and warms the souls of swine;
> Whose fever'd fancy shuns the measur'd place,
> And copies Ovid's filth without his grace.

And so on. Whitman was the perfect anathema for Lovecraft at this time, not only in his scornful abandonment of traditional metre but in his frank discussions of both homosexual and heterosexual sex.

Lovecraft's greatest poem in this regard is 'Amissa Minerva' (*Toledo Amateur*, May 1919). Steven J. Mariconda has written a thorough commentary on this poem, and has illuminated many of its distinctive features.[8] After supplying a highly encapsulated history of poetry from Homer to Swinburne, Lovecraft launches upon a systematic attack on modern poetry, mentioning Amy Lowell, Edgar Lee Masters, Carl Sandburg, and others by name. The subject matter of modern poetry offends Lovecraft ('Exempt from wit, each dullard pours his ink / In odes to bathtubs, or the kitchen sink') as much as its abandonment of traditional rhyme and metre.

Actually, Lovecraft's first exposure to poetic radicalism had occurred some years before. 'I have lately been amusing myself by a perusal of some of the "Imagism" nonsense of the day', he writes in August 1916.[9] 'As a species of pathological phenomena it is interesting.' This provides a sufficient indication of Lovecraft's attitude toward free verse in general and Imagism in particular. I am not sure what works Lovecraft read at this time; perhaps he read some of the three anthologies entitled *Some Imagist Poets*, which appeared between 1915 and 1917. He sums up his objections to modern poetry in 'The Vers Libre Epidemic' (*Conservative*, January 1917). Here Lovecraft distinguishes between two forms of radicalism, one of mere form, the other of thought and ideals. For the first, Lovecraft cites a fellow-amateur, Anne Tillery Renshaw, whom he admired greatly for her devotion to the amateur cause but whose poetic theories he found every opportunity to rebut. He frequently remarks that, for all the metrical novelty of her own poetry, it very often lapses in spite of itself into fairly orthodox forms. In 'Metrical Regularity' (*Conservative*, July 1915) Lovecraft paraphrases her theory ('the truly inspired bard must chant forth his feelings independently of form or language, permitting each changing impulse to alter the rhythm of his lay, and blindly resigning his reason to the "fine frenzy" of his mood') as expressed in an article in her amateur journal, *Ole Miss'*, for May 1915; to which Lovecraft makes the pointed response: 'The "language of the heart" must be clarified and made intelligible to other hearts, else its purport will forever be confined to its creator.' This single sentence could serve as an adequate indictment of the obscurantism of much twentieth-century poetry.

The second, more disturbing type of radicalism—of thought and ideals—is treated more harshly. In 'The Vers Libre Epidemic' this school is said to be represented by 'Amy Lowell at her worst': 'a motley horde of hysterical and half-witted rhapsodists whose basic principle is the recording of their momentary moods and psychopathic phenomena in whatever amorphous and meaningless phrases may come to their tongues or pens at the moment of inspirational (or epileptic) seizure'. This is fine polemic, but not very good reasoned argument. Lovecraft would carry on the battle against avant-garde poetry for the rest of his life, although one imagines that by the 1930s he was beginning to feel that the struggle was hopeless. But this did not alter his devotion to conservative poetry, although in his later arguments he modified his position considerably and advocated the view that poetry must speak straightforwardly, but elegantly and coherently, in the language of its own day.

Lovecraft frequently used pseudonyms for his contributions to the amateur press, especially for poetry. A total of about twenty pseudonyms have so far been identified. Only a few, however, were used with any regularity: Humphry Littlewit, Esq.; Henry Paget-Lowe; Ward Phillips; Edward Softly; and, most frequent of all, Lewis Theobald, Jun. Some of these names are scarcely very concealing of Lovecraft's identity. The Lewis Theobald pseudonym, of course, derives from the hapless Shakespearian scholar whom Pope pilloried in the first version (1728) of *The Dunciad*.

In some cases Lovecraft used pseudonyms merely because he was contributing poetry so voluminously to the amateur press—especially to C. W. Smith's *Tryout*—that he perhaps did not wish to create the impression that he was hogging more space than he deserved. In other instances, Lovecraft may have genuinely wished to disguise his identity because of the anomalous content of the poem involved. But it becomes very difficult to characterize some of Lovecraft's pseudonyms, especially those under which a large number of works were published, and he evidently used them merely as the spirit moved him and without much thought of creating any genuine persona for the pseudonyms in question.

Many of Lovecraft's early poems were on political subjects. Political events of the period 1914–17 offered abundant opportunities for Lovecraft's polemical pen, given his early attitudes on race, social class, and militarism. Lovecraft could of course not know that his entry into amateur journalism in April 1914 would occur only four months before the outbreak of the First World War; but once the war did commence, and once he saw that his country was not about to enter it any time soon to stand with his beloved England, Lovecraft's ire was stirred. For prose attacks on world affairs his chosen vehicle was the *Conservative*; his verses on world affairs were scattered far and wide throughout amateurdom.

Lovecraft could not abide Americans not standing with their English brethren to battle the Huns, and it must have infuriated him not merely that the government failed to intervene in the European war but that American public opinion was resolutely against such intervention. Even the sinking of the *Lusitania* on 7 May 1915—resulting in the loss of 128 Americans in its death toll of more than 1200–only began a slow change in people's minds against Germany. The incident led Lovecraft to write a thunderous polemic in verse, 'The Crime of Crimes: Lusitania, 1915'. There is no question of Lovecraft's burning sincerity in this poem; but the antiquated metre and diction he has used here makes it difficult to take the poem seriously, and it gains an unintentional air of frivolity, almost of self-parody. This could be said for much of Lovecraft's political verse.

'The Crime of Crimes' has the distinction of being Lovecraft's first separately published work. It appeared in a Welsh amateur journal, *Interesting Items*, for July 1915, and apparently at about the same time was issued as a four-page pamphlet by the editor of the paper, Arthur Harris of Llandudno, Wales. This item is now one of the rarest of Lovecraft's publications; only three copies are known to exist. I do not know how Lovecraft came in touch with Harris; perhaps he sent him the first issue of the *Conservative*. In any event, Lovecraft stayed sporadically in touch with Harris for the rest of his life.

The *Lusitania* incident led to President Woodrow Wilson's celebrated utterance, 'There is such a thing as a man being too proud to fight', something that infuriated Lovecraft and which he threw back in Wilson's teeth at every opportunity, especially in poems. Lovecraft published an array of anti-pacifist poems ('Pacifist War Song—1917', *Tryout*, March 1917; 'The Peace Advocate', *Tryout*, May 1917) and articles ('The Renaissance of Manhood', *Conservative*, October 1915), along with any number of truly awful poems expressing loyalty to England ('1914', *Interesting Items*, March 1915; 'An American to Mother England', *Poesy*, January 1916; 'The Rose of England', *Scot*, October 1916; 'Britannia Victura', *Inspiration*, April 1917; 'An American to the British Flag', *Little Budget*, December 1917).

Lovecraft's immediate reaction to the war, however, was a curious one. He did not care what the actual causes of the war were, or who was to blame; his prime concern was in stopping what he saw was a suicidal racial civil war between the two sides of 'Anglo-Saxondom'. It is here that Lovecraft's racism comes fully to the forefront: 'In the unnatural racial alignment of the various warring powers we behold a defiance of anthropological principles that cannot but bode ill for the future of the world.' This is from 'The Crime of the Century', one of the salvoes in Lovecraft's first issue (April 1915) of the *Conservative*. What makes the war so appalling for Lovecraft is that England and Germany (as well as Belgium, Holland, Austria, Scandinavia, and Switzerland) are all part of the Teutonic race, and therefore should on no account be battling each other. Political enemies though they may be, England and Germany are racially one:

> The Teuton is the summit of evolution. That we may consider intelligently his place in history we must cast aside the popular nomenclature which would confuse the names 'Teuton' and 'German', and view him not nationally but racially, identifying his fundamental stock with the tall, pale, blue-eyed, yellow-haired, long-headed 'Xanthochroi' as described by Huxley, amongst whom the class of languages we call 'Teutonic' arose, and who today constitute the majority of the Teutonic-speaking population of our globe.

We have already seen Lovecraft's prejudice against blacks manifest so early as the age of fourteen; whence did these ideas of Teutonic superiority arise? The above passage itself suggests one source: Thomas Henry Huxley. Huxley's work is too complex and nuanced to be branded as racist, and he was very circumspect when it came to notions of racial superiority or inferiority; but in 'The Crime of the Century' Lovecraft has made explicit reference to two essays by Huxley, 'On the Methods and Results of Ethnology' (1865) and 'On the Aryan Question' (1890), both included in *Man's Place in Nature and Other Anthropological Essays* (1894). In the former essay Huxley coins the term 'Xanthochroi' (races that are yellow-haired and pale in complexion), applying it to the inhabitants of northern Europe, ultimate descendants of the 'Nordic' barbarians. Along with the Melanochroi (pale-complexioned but dark-haired) who occupy the Mediterranean lands and the Middle East, the Xanthochroi were and are the pinnacle of civilization: 'It is needless to remark upon the civilization of these two great stocks. With them has originated everything that is highest in science, in art, in law, in politics, and in mechanical inventions. In their hands, at the present moment, lies the order of the social world, and to them its progress is committed.'[10]

Although Lovecraft's statements make it evident that he was appealing to evolutionary theories in his vaunting of the Teuton, it had been fashionable for nearly a century to praise Teutons, Anglo-Saxons, Nordics, or Aryans (all these terms being extremely nebulous and frequently interchangeable in their application) as the summit of civilization. English and American historians in particular—beginning with Sir Francis Palgrave's *Rise and Progress of the English Commonwealth* (1832), and continuing on through such distinguished scholars as Edward A. Freeman, J. R. Green, Francis Parkman, William H. Prescott, and John Fiske—became enamoured of the idea that the virtues of the English (hence the American) and German political systems owed their existence to the Teuton or Anglo-Saxon. Lovecraft read many of these writers and had their books in his library. With authorities like these, it is not surprising that he would echo their racial theories, even if in a particularly strident and pompous manner.

L. Sprague de Camp has maintained[11] that Lovecraft was significantly influenced by Houston Stewart Chamberlain's *Foundations of the Nineteenth Century*, published in German in 1899 and translated into English in 1911. But there is not a single reference to Chamberlain in any documents by Lovecraft that I have seen; and even a cursory examination of the specific tenets of Chamberlain's racism shows that Lovecraft's beliefs are very different. Chamberlain, according to one scholar, 'set himself to reconcile Christianity, the religion of humility and forgiveness, with aggressive German nationalism',[12] something Lovecraft never concerned himself about; indeed, Lovecraft's anti-Christianity only gained force as he encountered Nietzsche around 1918. Chamberlain also praised the Teutonic barbarians who overthrow Rome, as being the bearers of 'true Christianity' (i.e., a 'strong' Christianity shorn of its elements of pity and tolerance), a view Lovecraft could never adopt given the belief he maintained to the end of his life that 'To me the Roman Empire will always seem the central incident of human history'.[13] In these and other ways did Lovecraft's racism differ fundamentally from Chamberlain's, so that any influence of the latter seems remote, especially given the total absence of documentary evidence that Lovecraft was even familiar with Chamberlain.

Later in 1915 the issue of blacks was raised again. We have already seen how Lovecraft attacked Charles D. Isaacson's championing of Walt Whitman in his amateur paper *In a Minor Key*. The bulk of Isaacson's paper, however, was a plea for racial tolerance, especially for blacks. He is particularly harsh on D. W. Griffith's film *The Birth of a Nation*, asserting that it presented a false view of the relations between blacks and whites after the Civil War and that it incited racial hatred.

Lovecraft, in 'In a Major Key' (*Conservative*, July 1915), makes the astounding claim that 'Mr. Isaacson's views on racial prejudice … are too subjective to be impartial'. In regard to *The Birth of a*

Nation, Lovecraft states that he has not yet seen the film (he would do so later[14]), but says that he has read both the novel (*The Clansman*, 1905) by Thomas Dixon, Jr, and the dramatic adaptation of the novel on which the film was based. He then launches into a predictable paean to the Ku Klux Klan, 'that noble but much maligned band of Southerners who saved half of our country from destruction at the close of the Civil War'. It is certainly odd that Lovecraft's remarks were made at exactly the time when the Klan was being revived in the South by William J. Simmons, although it was not a force to be reckoned with until the 1920s. It can be pointed out here that Lovecraft is strangely silent on the thousands of lynchings of blacks throughout the early decades of the century; but he never mentions the KKK again until very late in life, and then he repudiates it.

As, however, with the pestiferous astrologer J. F. Hartmann, Lovecraft underestimated his opponent. The responses by both Isaacson and James Ferdinand Morton in the second issue of *In a Minor Key* (undated, but published in late 1915) are devastating, particularly Morton's. James Ferdinand Morton (1870–1941) was a remarkable individual. He had gained a simultaneous B.A. and M.A. from Harvard in 1892, and became a vigorous advocate of black equality, free speech, the single tax, and secularism. He wrote many pamphlets on these subjects, most of them published either by himself or by The Truth Seeker Co. He had been President of the NAPA in 1896–97, and would later become President of the Thomas Paine Natural History Association and Vice President of the Esperanto Association of North America. He would end his career (1925–41) as Curator of the Paterson (New Jersey) Museum.

In '"Conservatism" Gone Mad' Morton begins by stating presciently that 'I presume that Mr. H. P. Lovecraft ... is a rather young man, who will at some future day smile at the amusing dogmatism with which he now assumes to lay down the law.' There then follows a broadside attacking Lovecraft's racism, and a concluding prediction:

> From the sample afforded in the paper under discussion it is evident that Mr. Lovecraft needs to serve a long and humble apprenticeship before he will become qualified to sit in the master's seat and to thunder forth *ex cathedra* judgments. The one thing in his favor is his evident sincerity. Let him once come to realize the value of appreciating the many points of view shared by persons as sincere as he, and better informed

in certain particulars, and he will become less narrow and intolerant. His vigor of style, when wedded to clearer conceptions based on a wider comprehension, will make him a writer of power.[15]

It is passages like this that led Lovecraft ultimately to make peace with Morton, who would then become one of his closest friends.

But that was several years in the future. At the moment Lovecraft had in mind no thought but a towering rebuttal. But the interesting thing is that no genuine rebuttal ever appeared. Lovecraft did write a magnificent satirical poem, 'The Isaacsonio-Mortoniad', around September 1915; but he did not allow it to be published, and there is no evidence that he even showed it to anyone. It is a splendid verse satire, as scintillating as some of the 'Ad Criticos' pieces.

Lovecraft did more than merely write about the war. On 16 May 1917, he himself applied for enlistment with the Rhode Island National Guard. What has not been observed by commentators is that this entire episode with the R.I.N.G. occurred *before* President Wilson's signing of the draft bill (18 May 1917), and well before the institution of the draft itself. Lovecraft must have felt that, with the declaration of war in April, it was now appropriate for him to attempt to enter the hostilities himself as a matter of patriotic duty.

It is difficult to conceive of Lovecraft making this decision. He had been saying repeatedly since at least 1915 that he was an 'invalid' who could scarcely muster enough strength to get out of the house. But consider his most detailed account of his attempt at enlistment in the R.I.N.G.:

> Some time ago, impressed by my entire uselessness in the world, I resolved to attempt enlistment despite my almost invalid condition. I argued that if I chose a regiment soon to depart for France; my sheer nervous force, which is not inconsiderable, might sustain me till a bullet or piece of shrapnel could more conclusively & effectively dispose of me. Accordingly I presented myself at the recruiting station of the R.I. National Guard & applied for entry into whichever unit should first proceed to the front. On account of my lack of technical or special training, I was told that I could not enter the Field Artillery, which leaves first; but was given a blank of application for the Coast Artillery, which

will go after a short preliminary period of defence service at one of the forts of Narragansett Bay. The questions asked me were childishly inadequate, & so far as physical require-ments are concerned, would have admitted a chronic invalid. The only diseases brought into discussion were specific ail-ments from which I had never suffered, & of some of which I had scarcely ever heard. The medical examination related only to major organic troubles, of which I have none, & I soon found myself (as I thought) a duly enrolled private in the 9th Co. R.I.N.G.![16]

This tells us a number of important things. First, Lovecraft, if he had actually become a member of the R.I.N.G., would probably not have been sent overseas into actual combat, but instead would have been merely stationed near home (a later letter declares that the 9th Coast Artillery was stationed at Fort Standish in Boston Harbour[17]) in an auxiliary capacity. Second, Lovecraft took an actual physical examination which, however cursory, revealed no major physical ailments.

If Lovecraft passed the examination, how was it that he was not serving in the R.I.N.G.? Let him tell the story:

As you may have deduced, I embarked upon this desperate venture without informing my mother; & as you may also have deduced, the sensation created at home was far from slight. In fact, my mother was almost prostrated with the news, since she knew that only by rare chance could a weakling like myself survive the rigorous routine of camp life. Her activities soon brought my military career to a close for the present. It required but a few words from our family physician regarding my nervous condition to annul the enlistment, though the army surgeon declared that such an annulment was highly unusual & almost against the regula-tions of the service … my final status is that of a man 'Rejected for physical disability.'[18]

This account too is full of interest. One wonders what exactly Susie and Lovecraft's physician told the R.I.N.G. officials. Some have speculated that the latter might have revealed the fact of Winfield Lovecraft's paretic condition. The connection between paresis and syphilis had been established in 1911, and it is likely that both Susie and the physician now had a pretty good idea of the true cause of Winfield's death. But the physical examination had presumably indicated that Lovecraft himself was not afflicted with paresis or syphilis, so it is not clear what effect the information about Winfield would have had. I think it is safer to concur with Lovecraft's own testimony and assume that the physician's account of Lovecraft's 'nervous condition' caused the annulment.

Psychologically, Lovecraft confessed to a feeling of depression and disappointment: 'I am feeling desolate and lonely indeed as a civilian. Practically all my personal acquaintances are now in some branch of the service, mostly Plattsburg or R.I.N.G. ... it is disheartening to be the one non-combatant among a profusion of proud recruits.'[19] Here was one more indication, for Lovecraft, of his being left behind in life: having failed to finish high school and enter college, he had seen his boyhood friends go on to gain good jobs in journalism, trade, and law enforcement. Now he saw them go off to war while he remained behind to write for the amateur press.

Lovecraft did in fact register for the draft on 5 June; indeed, he was legally obliged to do so. He gave his occupation as 'Writer'. 'I am told that it is possible I may be used even though I fail to pass the physical test for active military service.'[20] Clearly Lovecraft was not so used. His draft record, if it survives, has not come to light.

Another sociopolitical interest that emerged in the earliest part of Lovecraft's amateur journalism phase was temperance. This had, indeed, been an enthusiasm of remarkably early development: so early as 1896 he had read a work by John B. Gough, *Sunlight and Shadow* (1880), on the subject. The fact that this volume was in the Phillips family library is by no means a surprise: recall that the town of Delavan, Illinois, was founded by Lovecraft's maternal ancestors as a temperance town. We have seen that Whipple Phillips spent at least a year there as a young man in the 1850s.

Lovecraft himself did not get a chance to say anything in public on the subject until about 1915. About this time he discovered in the amateur world an ardent colleague in the fight against the demon rum—Andrew Francis Lockhart of Milbank, South Dakota. An article entitled 'More *Chain Lightning*' (*United Official Quarterly*, October 1915) is a paean to Lockhart's efforts in the cause of temperance.

In spite of the fact that prohibition was very unpopular in Rhode Island, it is not at all surprising that Lovecraft would have become converted to temperance, for the movement had strong class- and race-conscious overtones; as one historian notes, it was led by 'old stock, Protestant middle-class Americans'[21] who were repelled by what they considered the excessive drinking habits of immigrants, particularly Germans and Italians.

One has to wonder why Lovecraft became so obsessed with temperance. He himself was fond of declaring that 'I have never tasted intoxicating liquor, and never intend to'.[22] When he remarks that 'I am nauseated by even the distant stink of any alcoholic liquor',[23] one is reminded of his extreme aversion to seafood, and cannot help wondering whether some event in infancy or boyhood triggered this severe physiological and psychological response. We know nothing of the drinking habits of Lovecraft's immediate family; even for his father, whatever other sins he may have committed, we have no evidence of any inclination toward imbibing. It would, therefore, be irresponsible and unjust to make any conjectures on the subject. What must be said is that the cause of temperance is the only aspect of social reform for which Lovecraft showed any enthusiasm in his earlier years—an enthusiasm seemingly out of keeping with the 'cosmic' philosophy he had already evolved, which led him outwardly to maintain a perfect indifference to the fate of the 'flyspeck-inhabiting lice'[24] on this globe.

Lovecraft himself claimed that among the great benefits he derived from amateurdom was the association of sympathetic and like-minded (or contrary-minded) individuals. For one who had been a virtual recluse during the 1908–13 period, amateur journalism allowed Lovecraft a gradual exposure to human society—initially in an indirect manner (via correspondence or discussions in amateur papers), then by direct contact. It would take several years for him to become comfortable as even a limited member of human society, but the transformation did indeed take place; and some of his early amateur associates remained for the rest of his life his closest friends.

Perhaps the three closest colleagues in Lovecraft's early amateur period were Maurice W. Moe, Edward H. Cole, and Rheinhart Kleiner. Moe (1882–1940) was a high school teacher at Appleton High School in Appleton, Wisconsin (later at the West Division High School in Milwaukee) and one of the giants of the amateur world at the time, even though he held relatively few offices. His religious orthodoxy was a constant source of friction with Lovecraft, and it may have helped to develop and refine Lovecraft's own hostility to religion. None of the withering polemics on religion to which Lovecraft treated Moe in his letters seems to have had any effect on their recipient.

Edward H. Cole (1892–1966) was also a well-respected amateur, but he was a staunch supporter of the NAPA and inflexibly hostile to the UAPA. He was Official Editor of the NAPA for 1911–12 and President for 1912–13. His journal, the *Olympian*, is one of the jewels of amateur literature in both contents and typography, even though it lapsed after 1917 and would not resume for two decades. Cole was one of the first amateurs, aside from the members of the Providence Amateur Press Club, whom Lovecraft met. He resided in various Boston suburbs, and attended a meeting of the club in North Providence in late November 1914. Cole became a close correspondent of Lovecraft, who in later years would always look him up when he went to Boston. In spite of his prejudice against the UAPA, Cole in 1917 married Helene E. Hoffman (who had been President of the UAPA in the 1913–14 term, the period when Lovecraft joined) and allowed himself to appear on the UAPA membership list. Lovecraft's early letters to Cole are very stiff and formal, but eventually he unwinds and becomes less self-conscious.

Rheinhart Kleiner (1892–1949) of Brooklyn came in touch with Lovecraft when he received the first issue of the *Conservative* in late March 1915. An immediate and voluble correspondence sprang up, and Kleiner of course sent Lovecraft copies of his own sporadic amateur paper, the *Piper*. The two first met on 1 July 1916, when Kleiner and some others were passing through Providence on the way to the NAPA convention in Boston. Thereafter—especially when Lovecraft himself lived in Brooklyn in 1924–26—he and Kleiner would form a strong bond of friendship.

In the summer of 1916 Moe suggested to Lovecraft that a rotating correspondence cycle be formed amongst UAPA members. Lovecraft, already a voluminous correspondent, readily assented to the plan and suggested Kleiner as a third member. Moe suggested a fourth—Ira A. Cole, an amateur in Bazine, Kansas, and editor of the *Plainsman*. The correspondence cycle started up, under the name (invented by Moe) Kleicomolo, derived from the first syllables of the last names of each member. Each member would write a letter addressed to the other three. The idea at the outset was to rescue letter-writing as an art form from oblivion; whether or not the group succeeded, it certainly gave an impetus to

Lovecraft's own letter-writing and to the development of his philosophical thought.

In the meantime changes of some significance were occurring in Lovecraft's family life. He had been living alone with his mother at 598 Angell Street since 1904: with his grandfather Whipple Phillips dead, his younger aunt Annie married and living in Cambridge, Massachusetts, and his elder aunt Lillian married and living in Providence but some distance away, the atmosphere of 598 might well have been becoming somewhat claustrophobic. I have already noted Clara Hess describing the 'strange and shutup air' of the house at about this time.

Then, on 26 April 1915, after thirteen years of marriage to Lillian, Lovecraft's uncle Franklin Chase Clark died at the age of sixty-seven. It is difficult to know how close Lovecraft was to Clark beyond his teenage years. We can certainly not gauge Lovecraft's emotions about Dr Clark from his 'Elegy on Franklin Chase Clark, M.D.', which appeared in the *Providence Evening News* three days after his death, for a more wooden, lifeless, and mechanical poem would be difficult to find.

About a year and a half later, on the very last day of 1916, Lovecraft's cousin Phillips Gamwell died of tuberculosis at the age of eighteen. Phillips, the only one of Annie E. Phillips Gamwell's and Edward F. Gamwell's children to survive beyond infancy, was the only male member of Lovecraft's family of his own generation. Lovecraft's various references to him make it clear that he was very fond of Phillips, even though he could have seen him only when he visited Cambridge or when Phillips came down to Providence. Lovecraft observes that about this time Phillips, then twelve years old, had 'blossomed out as a piquant letter-writer eager to discuss the various literary and scientific topics broached during our occasional personal coversations',[25] and Lovecraft attributes his fondness for letter-writing to four or five years' correspondence with Phillips.

Annie had taken her son to Roswell, Colorado, in October 1916 for his health, but his tuberculosis had obviously advanced too far and he died there on 31 December 1916. Lovecraft's 'Elegy on Phillips Gamwell, Esq.', published in the *Providence Evening News* for 5 January 1917, is as uninspired as his tribute to Dr Clark. After Phillips's death, Annie returned to Providence, apparently living with her brother Edwin until his death on 14 November 1918 (and it is remarkable that Lovecraft says nothing about his death in any letters of the period or later), then probably in various rented quarters until early 1919, when she moved in with Lovecraft at 598 Angell Street.

Lovecraft, so far as I can tell, was not actually doing much during this period aside from writing; but he had discovered one entertaining form of relaxation—moviegoing. Lovecraft's enthusiasm for the drama had waned by around 1910, the very time that film was emerging as a popular, if not an aesthetically distinguished, form of entertainment. By 1910 there were already five thousand nickleodeons throughout the country, even if these were regarded largely as entertainment for the working classes. Lovecraft reports that the first cinema shows in Providence were in March 1906; and, even though he 'knew too much of literature & drama not to recognise the utter & unrelieved hokum of the moving picture', he attended them anyway—'in the same spirit that I had read Nick Carter, Old King Brady, & Frank Reade in nickel-novel form'.[26] One develops the idea that watching films may have occupied some, perhaps much, of the 'blank' years of 1908–13, as a letter of 1915 suggests: 'As you surmise, I am a devotee of the motion picture, since I can attend shows at any time, whereas my ill health seldom permits me to make definite engagements or purchase real theatre tickets in advance. Some modern films are really worth seeing, though when I first knew moving pictures their only value was to destroy time.'[27]

When Rheinhart Kleiner wrote 'To Mary of the Movies' in the *Piper* for September 1915, Lovecraft immediately responded with 'To Charlie of the Comics' (*Providence Amateur*, February 1916). It is no surprise that the two poets chose to pay tribute to Mary Pickford and Charlie Chaplin, as they were the first true 'stars' of the film industry. Lovecraft's undistinguished poem is notable only for its relative modernity of subject and style and its use of octosyllabic quatrains. Lovecraft clearly had a fondness for Chaplin, remarking: 'Chaplin is infinitely amusing—too good for the rather vulgar films he used to appear in—and I hope he will in future be an exponent of more refined comedy.'[28]

For three years Lovecraft had written reams of essays, poems, and reviews of amateur papers. Would he ever resume the fiction writing that had showed such promise up to 1908? In 1915 Lovecraft wrote to G. W. Macauley: 'I wish that I could write fiction, but it seems almost an impossibility.'[29] Macauley claims that he 'violently disagreed'—not because he had actually seen any of Lovecraft's fiction but because, having sent a story to Lovecraft for comment, he had received such an acute and elaborate analysis that he became convinced that Lovecraft had the short-story writing faculty within him. Criticism of fiction and fiction-writing are, of course, two different things, but in Lovecraft's case one cannot help feeling that the frequency with which he remarks on the failings of stories published in the amateur press points to a growing urge to prove that he can do better. Fiction was, of course, always the weakest point in the amateur press, not only because it is generally harder to master than prose nonfiction but because the space limitations in amateur papers did not allow the publication of much beyond sketches or vignettes.

Lovecraft finally allowed 'The Alchemist' to be printed in the *United Amateur* for November 1916. It was to be expected that he would himself attack it in the 'Department of Public Criticism' (*United Amateur*, May 1917), saying that 'we must needs beg all the charitable indulgence the Association can extend to an humble though ambitious tyro'. The single word 'ambitious' may suggest Lovecraft's desire to write more fiction if this one specimen, however much he may deprecate it himself, receives favourable notice. It appears to have done just that, but even so it would still be more than half a year before Lovecraft would break his self-imposed nine-year ban on fiction-writing. That he finally did so, writing 'The Tomb' and 'Dagon' in quick succession in the summer of 1917, can be attributed in large part to the encouragement of a new associate, W. Paul Cook of Athol, Massachusetts, who would be a significant presence throughout the rest of Lovecraft's life.

CHAPTER SEVEN
Feverish and Incessant Scribbling (1917–19)

W. Paul Cook (1881–1948) had long been a giant in the amateur world. Cook was unmistakably a New Englander: he had been born in Vermont; he was a direct descendant of the colonial governor Benning Wentworth of New Hampshire; and he resided for much of his adult life in Athol, Massachusetts. For years he was the head of the printing department of the *Athol Transcript*, and his access to printing equipment and his devotion to the amateur cause permitted him to be a remarkable philanthropist in printing amateur journals virtually at cost. He began printing *The Conservative* in 1917. During his term as President of the UAPA Lovecraft appointed Cook Official Printer, a position he held for three consecutive years (1917–20) and again for three more years in 1922–25. Curiously, at the same time he served as Official Editor of the NAPA (1918–19) and its President (1919–20).

Cook was one of the few amateurs who had a strong taste in weird fiction; Lovecraft would later admit that Cook's 'library was the most remarkable collection of fantastic & other material that I have ever seen assembled in one place',[1] and he would frequently borrow many rare books to which he himself did not have access. It is scarcely to be doubted that Cook, during his visit with Lovecraft in September 1917 (for which see further below), discussed this topic of mutual interest. Whether at this time he convinced Lovecraft to let him print his other juvenile tale, 'The Beast in the Cave', is not clear; at any rate, that story appeared in Cook's *Vagrant* (a NAPA paper) for June 1918.

Lovecraft makes it very clear that Cook's encouragement was instrumental in his resumption of weird writing; and this encouragement was both private and public. One instance of the latter is Cook's effusive article entitled 'Howard P. Lovecraft's Fiction', prefacing his printing of 'Dagon' in the *Vagrant* for November 1919, a perspicacious piece of work even though it conjectures that Lovecraft may have been influenced by Maupassant, whom he had probably not read by this time.

Poe, of course, is the dominant influence on Lovecraft's early tales, and looms large over the bulk of Lovecraft's fiction up to at least 1923. And yet, even 'The Tomb' and 'The Outsider' (1921), Lovecraft's most obviously Poe-esque tales, are far from being mere pastiches; but it is evident that Lovecraft found in Poe a model both in style and in overall short-story construction.

In particular, the idiom Lovecraft evolved in his early tales—dense, a little overheated, laced with archaic and recondite terms, almost wholly lacking in 'realistic' character portrayal, and almost entirely given over to exposition and narration, with a near-complete absence of dialogue—is clearly derived from Poe. So much did Lovecraft customarily acknowledge the Poe influence that he would sometimes exaggerate it, as in his famous lament of 1929: 'There are my "Poe" pieces & my "Dunsany" pieces—but alas—where are any "Lovecraft" pieces?'[2]

The most obvious stylistic feature common to both Poe and Lovecraft is the use of adjectives. In Lovecraft's case this has been derisively termed 'adjectivitis', as if there is some canonical number of adjectives per square inch that is permissible and the slightest excess is cause for frenzied condemnation. But this sort of criticism is merely a holdover from an outmoded and superficial realism that vaunted the barebones style of a Hemingway or a Sherwood Anderson as the sole acceptable model for English prose. Lovecraft was predominantly influenced by the 'Asianic' style of Johnson and Gibbon as opposed to the 'Attic' style of Swift and Addison; and few nowadays—especially now that such writers as Thomas Pynchon and Gore Vidal have restored richness of texture to modern English fiction—will condemn Lovecraft without a hearing for the use of such a style.

Nevertheless, I think a case could be made that Lovecraft spent the better part of his fictional career in attempting to escape—or, at best, to master or refine—the stylistic influence of Poe, as is suggested by his frequent remarks in the last decade of his life on the need for simplicity of expression and his exemplification of this principle in the evolution of his later 'scientific' manner.

The tales of Lovecraft's early period do not require much analysis; on the whole, they are relatively conventional, showing only hints of the dynamic conceptions that would infuse his later work. Some of the tales are more interesting for their genesis than for their actual content. 'The Tomb', written in the summer of 1917, tells the story of Jervas Dudley, a 'dreamer and a visionary' who appears to be possessed by the spirit of his eighteenth-century ancestor. It was inspired by Lovecraft's stroll in Swan Point Cemetery in June, in the company of his aunt Lillian. They had come upon a tombstone dating to 1711, causing Lovecraft to ponder: 'Here was a link with my favourite aera of periwigs ... Why could I not talk with him, and enter more intimately into the life of my chosen age? What had left his body, that it could no longer converse with me?'[3]

'Polaris', written in the summer of 1918, strikingly anticipates Lovecraft's later 'Dunsanian' tales, but was written a full year before he ever read Lord Dunsany. The story was inspired by a dream occurring in late spring of that year, when Lovecraft saw himself hovering as a disembodied intelligence over 'a strange city—a city of many palaces and gilded domes, lying in a hollow betwixt ranges of grey, horrible hills'.[4]

Most curious of all, 'Beyond the Wall of Sleep' (1919), depicting the psychic possession of a backwoods denizen of the Catskill Mountains region of New York state by some cosmic entity, was inspired by a newspaper article in the *New York Tribune* about the State Constabulary's encounter with just such denizens in that region.[5] This article appeared on 27 April 1919, and actually mentions a backwoods family named Slater or Slahter, the exact character name used by Lovecraft in his story.

'Dagon', the second tale of Lovecraft's maturity, is of interest chiefly for its contemporaneousness of setting (we are clearly in the midst of the First World War) and for its suggestion of an entire alien civilization that had once dwelt literally on the underside of the world. It is a theme that Lovecraft would develop exhaustively in his later work.

In this period Lovecraft also learned to express weird conceptions in verse. Whereas up to 1917 his poetry had been wholly Georgian in character, Lovecraft now began to see that poetry could do more than merely recapture the atmosphere of the eighteenth century. The dominant influence on his early weird verse is, of course, Poe; for although Lovecraft owned and read the 'Graveyard Poets' of the later eighteenth century—James Hervey's *Meditations and Contemplations* (1746–47), Edward Young's *Night-Thoughts* (1742–45), among others—they do not appear to have influenced him appreciably. Probably the most notable piece of work is is a 302-line poem written some time in 1916, 'The Poe-et's Nightmare', the central section of which expresses some tremendous cosmic conceptions in Miltonic blank verse. Another long weird poem—the 312-line 'Psychopompos', begun in the fall of 1917 but not completed until May or June of 1918—is interesting in adopting a kind of ballad narrative form akin to that employed by Sir Walter Scott. Many other poems unfortunately tend, however, toward stock images or contrived shudders. Even Lovecraft's most famous early weird poem, 'Nemesis' (written in the 'sinister small hours of the black morning after Hallowe'en' of 1917[6]), is open to the charge of vagueness and empty horrific imagery.

Meanwhile political events were not failing to attract Lovecraft's attention. Even if he could not himself serve in the Great War, he could at least closely follow the course of that conflict—especially the United States' belated entry into it. Lovecraft predictably wrote a number of poems commemorating the United States' joining of her 'mother' England to battle Germany or more generally urging on the British soldiers. A number of these poems were reprinted in the *National Enquirer*. None of them amounts to anything.

In terms of the actual progress of the war, Lovecraft remarks in late 1917: 'As to the general situation, it seems very discouraging just now. It may take a second war to adjust things properly.'[7] This comment—seemingly but unwittingly prophetic—was made at the lowest point of the war for the Allies: the Germans were making considerable headway and seemed on the brink of winning the war before the new American forces could be mobilized. It is therefore possible that Lovecraft was actually conceiving the possibility of a victory for the Germans, so that the 'second war' would be one required to restore national borders to the pre-1914 state. Curiously enough, I cannot find any remark by Lovecraft on the actual end of the war; but this may only be because many letters of the 1918–19 period have probably been lost or destroyed.

Lovecraft's ponderous essay, 'The League' (*Conservative*, July 1919)—a cynical meditation on the uselessness of the League of Nations, or any other international body, to prevent war—shows that he was paying considerable attention to the peace conference at Versailles. Lovecraft no doubt gained tremendous satisfaction that the United States in early 1920 failed to ratify American entry into the League, the brainchild of the hated President Wilson. He predictably accepted the anti-Communist paranoia of the 'Red Scare' of the postwar period in the essay 'Bolshevism' (*Conservative*, July 1919), speaking of the 'noxious example of the almost sub-human Russian rabble'. More distinctly allied to his racism is the essay 'Americanism' (*United Amateur*, July 1919). For Lovecraft, Americanism is nothing more than 'expanded Anglo-Saxondom'; accordingly, the notion of a 'melting-pot' is rejected summarily:

> Most dangerous and fallacious of the several misconceptions of Americanism is that of the so-called 'melting-pot' of races and traditions. It is true that this country has received a vast influx of non-English immigrants who come hither to enjoy without hardship the liberties which our British ancestors carved out in toil and bloodshed. It is also true that such of them as belong to the Teutonic and Celtic races are capable of assimilation to our English types and of becoming valuable acquisitions to the population. But from this it does not follow that a mixture of really alien blood or ideas has accomplished or can accomplish anything but harm ... Immigration cannot, perhaps, be cut off altogether, but it should be understood that aliens who choose America as their residence must accept the prevailing language and culture as their own; and neither try to modify our institutions, nor to keep alive their own in our midst.

This statement, offensive as it may be to many, was not in any way unusual amongst Yankees of Lovecraft's class. Let us bypass the flagrant untruth that immigrants have somehow come merely to enjoy the 'liberties' carved out by those sturdy Saxons: again Lovecraft's complete ignorance of the hardships willingly endured by immigrants to establish themselves in the United States has betrayed him into clownish error. The critical term here is 'assimilation'—the idea that foreign culture-streams should shed their own cultural heritage and adopt that of the prevailing (Anglo-Saxon) civilization. In Lovecraft's time it was *expected* that immigrants would 'assimilate'; as one modern historian has noted: 'The predominant expectation [in the early twentieth century] has been that the newcomer, no matter what his place of origin, would conform to Anglo-Saxon patterns of behavior.'[8] Lovecraft, although on the far right in his views on the First World War and on the League of Nations, was a centrist in the matter of immigrant assimilation.

I have no doubt that Lovecraft approved of the three important immigration restriction laws of the period: those of 1917 (which introduced a literacy test), of 1921 (which limited immigration from Europe, Australia, the Near East, and Africa to 3 per cent of each foreign nation's population then residing in the United States), and, most significantly, of 1924 (reducing the quota to 2 per cent, but taking as its basis the census of 1890, which had the added effect of radically reducing immigration from eastern and southern Europe, since immigrants from those countries were an insignificant number in 1890). Lovecraft does not mention any of these immigration laws, but his general silence on the matter of foreign incursions in the 1920s (except during his New York period) suggests that he felt this matter had been, at least for the time being, satisfactorily dealt with. Politics during the relatively tranquil and Republican-governed 1920s becomes for Lovecraft less a matter of immediate crises than an opportunity for theoretical speculation. It was during this time that he evolved his notions of aristocracy and 'civilization', ideas that would undergo significant modification with the onset of the Depression but retain their fundamental outlines, leading to his piquant evolution of 'fascistic socialism'.

The late 1910s saw Lovecraft emerge as a towering figure in the tiny world of amateur journalism. Having been elected President for the 1917–18 term, Lovecraft seemed in a good position to carry out his programme for a UAPA that would both promote pure literature and serve as a tool for education. Under the capable official editorship of Verna McGeoch (pronounced Ma-GOO), who held the office for two consecutive terms (1917–19), the *United Amateur* really did flower into a substantial literary organ.

One idea Lovecraft put forward to encourage amateur activity was the issuing of co-operative papers—papers in which a number of individuals would pool their resources, both financial and literary. He attempted to teach by example by participating in such a journal, *The United Co-operative*, which published three issues: December 1918, June 1919, and April 1921. Lovecraft had contributions in each issue. Winifred Jackson—with whom Lovecraft had earlier collaborated on two mediocre short stories, 'The Green Meadow' and 'The Crawling Chaos'—was also one of the co-operative editors.

When Lovecraft's term as President expired in the summer of

1918, he was appointed to his old job of Chairman of the Department of Public Criticism by the new president, Rheinhart Kleiner. For the 1919–20 term Lovecraft held no office. In the summer of 1920, however, he was elected Official Editor, serving for four of the next five years. He was now in still greater control of the editorial content of the *United Amateur*, and he made the most of it, opening its pages to literary matter by many of his colleagues old and new. Moreover, he wrote editorials for nearly every issue and was also in charge of writing 'News Notes' recounting comings and goings of various amateurs, including himself.

The rumblings of discontent from some members became more emphatic around this time. By November 1920 he was having to respond to accusations of 'excessive centralisation of authority' ('Editorial', *United Amateur*, November 1920). It is true that for the period 1917-22 a relatively small number of people held office in the UAPA; but it seems as if a certain apathy had set in amongst UAPA members whereby they were content to have these individuals continue holding office year in and year out. Individual papers were declining, and Lovecraft's own *Conservative*, because of his other official involvements, appeared only annually in 1918 and 1919, and then ceased altogether until 1923.

But there is also evidence that Lovecraft himself, if not his colleagues, was beginning to conduct himself in a sort of fascistic way. Perhaps irritated at the slowness of the progress in literary development on the part of most members, he increasingly called for improvement by main force. In a lecture entitled 'Amateur Journalism: Its Possible Needs and Betterment' (delivered at an amateur convention in Boston on 5 September 1920), he proposes establishing 'some centralised authority capable of exerting a kindly, reliable, and more or less invisible guidance in matters aesthetic and artistic'. Lovecraft anticipates the objections of 'any idealistic and ultra-conscientious person' who might object to the plan's 'possible oligarchical tendencies' by pointing to the fact that all great periods in literature—Periclean Athens, Augustan Rome, eighteenth-century England—were led by 'dominant coteries'. It is evident that Lovecraft has simply reached the limit of his patience with sporting pages, bad poetry, and unhelpful official criticism. It is needless to say that the plan was never adopted.

Lovecraft must, however, have been taken aback when the October 1921 *Woodbee* contained an attack upon him by Leo Fritter, a long-time UAPA member whom Lovecraft himself had supported for president in 1915. Fritter had cited a 'wide-spreading dissatis-faction' with Lovecraft's editorial policy in the *United Amateur* and went on to accuse Lovecraft of trying to force the members into a mould he had arbitrarily cast according to his own ideas. Lovecraft attempted to counter that he himself had received 'numerous and enthusiastic assurances of an opposite nature' ('Editorial', *United Amateur*, September 1921). When Lovecraft concluded that 'The question is one which should ultimately be decided at the polls', he spoke better than he knew, as we shall see presently.

This period, however, saw Lovecraft evolving socially from an extreme misfit to one who, while by no means gregarious, could take his place in the society of congenial individuals. This trans-formation, as successive waves of friends—most of them amateurs —came to visit him or as he actually ventured forth on brief excursions, is heart-warming to see.

Two visits by amateurs occurring in 1917 are instructive by their very contrast. In mid-September 1917 W. Paul Cook, who had only recently become acquainted with Lovecraft, paid him a call in Providence. Cook tells the story piquantly:

> The first time I met Howard I came very near not meeting him ... I was bound from New York to Boston, and broke my trip in Providence purposely to see Lovecraft. I was traveling by train, which enabled me to announce in advance the time of my arrival and with a variation of only a few minutes. Arriving at the address on Angell street which later was to be the best known street address in Amateur journalism, I was met at the door by Howard's mother and aunt. Howard had been up all night studying and writing, had just now gone to bed, and must under no circumstances be disturbed. If I would go to the Crown hotel, register, get a room and wait, they would telephone when, and if, Howard woke up. This was one of the occasions in my life when I have blessed the gods for giving me a sense of humor, however perverted. It was essential that I be in Boston early that evening, which allowed me about three hours in Providence, but there was a train leaving in half an hour which I could catch if I kept moving. I had a life-like picture of myself hanging around Providence until His Majesty was ready to receive me! In later years Mrs. Clark and I laughed more than once in recalling the incident. I was part way to

the sidewalk and the door was almost latched when Howard appeared in dressing gown and slippers. Wasn't that W. Paul Cook and didn't they understand that he was to see me immediately on my arrival? I was almost forcibly ushered by the guardians of the gate and into Howard's study.[9]

Cook's account of the three hours spent with Lovecraft—they mostly talked amateur journalism, naturally enough—is unremarkable save in one detail I shall consider later. Lovecraft's account of the meeting is recorded in a letter to Rheinhart Kleiner:

> Just a week ago I enjoyed the honour of a personal call from Mr. W. Paul Cook … I was rather surprised at his appearance, for he is rather more rustic & carelessly groomed than I had expected of a man of his celebrity to be. In fact, his antique derby hat, unpressed garments, frayed cravat, yellowish collar, ill-brushed hair, & none too immaculate hands made me think of my old friend Sam Johnson … But Cook's conversation makes up for whatever outward deficiencies he may possess.[10]

Before examining these accounts, let us now turn to Rheinhart Kleiner's meeting with Lovecraft, which also occurred some time in 1917—presumably after Cook's visit. Kleiner tells the story as follows: 'I was greeted at the door of 598 Angell Street by his mother, who was a woman just a little below medium height, with graying hair, and eyes which seemed to be the chief point of resemblance between herself and her son. She was very cordial and even vivacious, and in another moment had ushered me into Lovecraft's room.'[11]

Why the very different responses by his mother to Cook and Kleiner? I believe that the overriding factor is social snobbery. Cook's unkempt appearance could not have sat well with either Susie or Lillian, and they were manifestly going to make it as difficult as possible for Cook to pass through their door. Lovecraft confesses in a candid moment that 'Of amateurdom in general her [Susie's] opinion was not high, for she had a certain aesthetic hypersensitiveness which made its crudenesses very obvious and very annoying to her'.[12] Elsewhere he goes on to admit that Lillian also did not care for amateurdom—'an institution whose extreme democracy and occasional heterogeneity have at times made it necessary for me to apologise for it'.[13] If these were the reasons why Lillian did not like amateurdom, then it is very clear that social considerations weighed heavily in her mind: 'democracy and occasional heterogeneity' can scarcely stand for anything but the fact that people of all classes and educational backgrounds were involved in the amateur movement. Kleiner, a polished and debonair Brooklynite, was cordially received because his social standing was, in Susie's eyes, at least equal to Lovecraft's.

These accounts are among the most illuminating as to Lovecraft's life—and his relations with his mother—in this period. Both Cook and Kleiner are united on the extreme solicitude exercised by Susie and Lillian over Lovecraft. Cook notes: 'Every few minutes Howard's mother or his aunt, or both, peeped into the room to see if he had fainted or shown signs of strain.' Kleiner tells a more remarkable story: 'I noticed that at every hour or so his mother appeared in the doorway with a glass of milk, and Lovecraft forthwith drank it.' It is this constant babying of Lovecraft by Susie and Lillian that no doubt helped to foster in Lovecraft's own mind a sense of his 'invalidism'.

Kleiner suggested that they go out for a stroll, and Lovecraft took him to see the colonial antiquities of Providence—a tour he invariably gave to all his out-of-town guests, for he never tired of showing off the wondrous remains of the eighteenth century in his native city. But Lovecraft's unfamiliarity with normal social conduct is made evident when Kleiner states:

> On our way back to his home, and while we were still downtown, I suggested stopping in at a cafeteria for a cup of coffee. He agreed, but took milk himself, and watched me dispose of coffee and cake, or possibly pie, with some curiosity. It occurred to me later that this visit to a public eating-house—a most unpretentious one—might have been a distinct departure from his own usual habits.

This is very likely to be the case: not only because of the family's dwindling finances, but because of Lovecraft's continuing hermitry in spite of his ever-growing correspondence, a trip to a restaurant was at this time not likely to have been a common occurrence.

That correspondence, however, did lead at this time to Lovecraft's contact with two individuals, each remarkable in their own way, who would become lifelong friends—Samuel Loveman and Alfred Galpin. Loveman (1887–1976)—a friend of three of the most distinctive writers in American literature (Ambrose Bierce, Hart Crane, and H. P. Lovecraft) and also well acquainted with

George Sterling and Clark Ashton Smith—appears to be merely a sort of hanger-on to the great. But he was himself an accomplished poet—a greater poet than any in the Lovecraft circle except, perhaps, Clark Ashton Smith, and vastly superior to Lovecraft himself. His infrequently issued amateur journal, *The Saturnian*, contained his own exquisite, neo-Grecian, *fin-de-siècle* poems as well as translations from Baudelaire and Heine; and he scattered his poetry in other amateur or little magazines with insouciance. His greatest work is a long poem, *The Hermaphrodite* (written perhaps in the late teens and published in 1926 by W. Paul Cook), a gorgeous evocation of the spirit of classical Greece.

Lovecraft came in direct contact with Loveman in 1917. Loveman was at this time stationed at an army base, Camp Gordon, in Georgia, where he was in Company H of the 4th Infantry, Replacement Regiment. According to the UAPA membership lists, he remained there until the middle of 1919, when he returned to his native Cleveland. Loveman had, however, been out of organized amateurdom for some years, and he attests that Lovecraft's first letter was essentially a query as to whether Loveman was in fact still in the land of the living.[14] Loveman, finding the antique diction of the letter both charming and faintly ridiculous, duly relieved Lovecraft's doubts on this score. For several years their association was largely conducted on paper, but in 1922 they met in Cleveland and then, in 1924–26, they became close friends in New York.

Alfred Galpin (1901–83) is an entirely different case. This brilliant individual—as gifted in pure intellect as Loveman was in aesthetic sensitivity—would eventually become a philosopher, composer, and teacher of French, although perhaps his rapid alterations in intellectual aspirations prevented him from distinguishing himself in any one of them. Galpin first came to Lovecraft's attention in late 1917, when he was appointed to the new position of 4th Vice-President, in charge of recruiting high-school students into amateurdom. This appointment was very likely suggested by Maurice W. Moe, since Galpin was at that time already emerging as a star pupil in the Appleton (Wis.) High School and specifically in Moe's Appleton High School Press Club. By January 1918, the date of the first surviving letter by Lovecraft to Galpin, the two were already cordial correspondents.

Galpin's most profound effect upon Lovecraft may have been philosophical, for as early as August 1918 Lovecraft is announcing that Galpin's 'system of philosophy ... comes nearest to my own beliefs of any system I have ever known', and in 1921:

> he is intellectually *exactly like me* save in degree. In degree he is immensely my superior—he is what I should like to be but have not brains enough to be. Our minds are cast in precisely the same mould, save that his is finer. He alone can grasp the direction of my thoughts and amplify them. And so we go down the dark ways of knowledge; the poor plodding old man, and ahead of him the alert little link-boy holding the light and pointing out the path.[15]

This obviously is meant half in jest, although Lovecraft clearly believes there is more than a grain of truth to it; and perhaps Galpin did indeed help to give shape to Lovecraft's still nebulous philosophical conceptions, helping this 'old man' of thirty-one to hone his mechanistic materialism. But it is not that that I wish to study here; rather, Galpin had a more immediate effect upon Lovecraft's literary work, and it involved the production of some delightfully playful poetry.

Lovecraft of course wrote some more or less conventional tributes to Galpin, especially on his birthday. Galpin appears to have had amorous inclinations toward various girls in his high school, and Lovecraft has great fun with the whole subject, especially in such poems as 'Damon and Delia, a Pastoral' (*Tryout*, August 1918), 'To Delia, Avoiding Damon' (*Tryout*, September 1918), 'Damon—a Monody' (*United Amateur*, May 1919), and perhaps 'Hylas and Myrrha' (*Tryout*, May 1919) and 'Myrrha and Strephon' (*Tryout*, July 1919), if these latter two are in fact about Galpin. Damon in these poems is clearly Galpin; the name is derived from the shepherd who is featured in the eighth eclogue of Virgil. Many of these poems are very amusing, and some of the best of Lovecraft's parodic love poetry is found in letters to Galpin.

Lovecraft's final word on Galpin's schoolboy crushes occurs in the delightful two-act play in pentameter blank verse entitled *Alfredo: A Tragedy*, the manuscript of which declares it to be 'By Beaumont and Fletcher' and which is dated 14 September 1918. This date makes it clear that two of the chief characters—Rinarto, King of Castile and Aragon, and Alfredo, the Prince Regent—are meant to be Kleiner and Galpin, since Kleiner was president of the UAPA and Galpin was 1st vice-president during the 1918–19 term. Other obviously recognizable characters are Mauricio (= Maurice

W. Moe), a cardinal, and Teobaldo (= Lovecraft), the prime minister.

I don't know that we need read a great deal into all these mock-love poems about Galpin: certainly Lovecraft's beloved Georgians had made a specialty of it, and *The Rape of the Lock* is only the best-known example. But by consistently deflating the emotion of love in these and other poems, Lovecraft may be shielding himself from falling under its influence. The probability that he would so fall was, at the moment, comparatively small, but he was not taking any chances. During his involvement with the Providence Amateur Press Club in 1914–16 a few of the members decided to play a rather malicious joke on him by having one of the female members call him up and ask him to take her out on a date. Lovecraft stated soberly, 'I'll have to ask my mother', and of course nothing came of the matter.[16] In a letter to Galpin Lovecraft notes in passing that 'so far as I know, no feminine freak ever took the trouble to note or recognise my colossal and transcendent intellect'.[17] Whether this was exactly true or not is something I shall take up later.

Although amateur journalism was still the focal point of Lovecraft's world, he was slowly—probably from his mother's urging—making tentative forays at professional employment. His scorn of commercial writing prevented him from submitting his work to paying magazines, and the small number of his poems that were reprinted in the *National Magazine* all saw prior publication in amateur journals, and moreover were presumably not sent in by Lovecraft but were selected by the editors of the magazine itself from an examination of amateur papers. But if Lovecraft was not at the moment inclined to make money by writing, in what way could he earn an income? Whipple Phillips's inheritance, some of it already squandered by bad investments, was slowly but inexorably diminishing; even Lovecraft probably saw that he could not indulge himself as a gentleman-author forever.

The first sign we have that Lovecraft was actually attempting to earn an income occurs in a letter to John T. Dunn in October 1916. In explaining why he is unable to participate as thoroughly in amateur affairs as he would like, Lovecraft states: 'Many of my present duties are outside the association, in connexion with the Symphony Literary Service, which is now handling a goodly amount of verse.'[18] This was a revisory or ghostwriting service featuring Lovecraft, Anne Tillery Renshaw (who edited the amateur journal *The Symphony*), and Mrs J. G. Smith, a colleague of Renshaw's (although not in the UAPA), both of whom lived at this time in Coffeeville, Mississippi. It does not appear that this service, as such, was in business for very long.

This is the first indication that Lovecraft had commenced what would become his only true remunerative occupation: revising and ghostwriting. He never managed to turn this occupation into anything like a regular source of income, as he generally took on jobs only from colleagues and very sporadically placed advertisements for his services. In many senses it was exactly the wrong job for him in terms of his creative work: first, it was too similar in nature to his fiction-writing, so that it frequently left him too physically and mentally drained to attempt work of his own; and second, the very low rates he charged, and the unusual amount of effort he would put into some jobs, netted him far less money than a comparable amount of work in some other profession would have done.

What of Lovecraft and his family at this time? We have seen that aunt Lillian, upon the death of her husband Franklin Chase Clark in 1915, lived in various rented quarters in the city. W. Paul Cook's account of his visit in 1917 makes it clear that she spent considerable time with her sister and nephew. Aunt Annie, upon her separation from Edward F. Gamwell (whenever that might have been) and the death of her son Phillips at the end of 1916, returned from Cambridge and probably lived with her brother Edwin in Providence. The death of Edwin E. Phillips on 14 November 1918 passes entirely unnoticed in the surviving correspondence by Lovecraft that I have seen. Letters from this period are admittedly few, but the silence is none the less significant.

Meanwhile Lovecraft himself, as he had been doing since 1904, continued to live alone with his mother at 598 Angell Street. The nature of their relations for much of the period 1904–19 is a mystery. All in all, they could not have been very wholesome. Lovecraft was still doing almost no travelling outside the city, and the lack of a regular office job must have kept him at home nearly all day, week after week. And yet, Clara Hess, their neighbour of twenty-five years, remarks disturbingly: 'In looking back, I cannot ever remember to have seen Mrs. Lovecraft and her son together. I never heard one speak to the other. It probably just happened that way, but it does seem rather strange.'[19]

Then, in May 1917, came Lovecraft's attempt at enlistment in the R.I.N.G. and, later, in the regular army. We have seen how

Susie put a stop to the first of these efforts by pulling strings. Lovecraft's comment that 'If I had realised to the full how much she would suffer through my enlistment, I should have been less eager to attempt it'[20] reveals a staggering failure of communication and empathy between mother and son. Susie must have been aware of Lovecraft's militarism and his eagerness to see the United States enter the war on England's side; but she must genuinely have been caught off guard at this attempt at enlistment—which, let us recall, came before President Wilson's announcement of the resumption of the draft.

Kenneth W. Faig, Jr, is surely correct in noting that 'Susie's sharp decline ... seems to have begun at about the time of her brother's death'[21] in November 1918. Edwin was the closest surviving male member of Susie's generation. From now on, Susie, Lillian, and Annie were all wholly reliant on Whipple Phillips's and (in the case of Lillian) Franklin C. Clark's estates for their income. (Since Annie never formally divorced her husband, Edward F. Gamwell, it is not clear whether she received any financial support from him; I think it unlikely.) Lovecraft was the only viable wage-earner in the family, and he was clearly not doing much to support himself, let alone his mother and aunts.

The result, for Susie, was perhaps inevitable. In the winter of 1918–19 she finally cracked under the strain of financial worries. On 18 January 1919 Lovecraft writes to Kleiner: 'My mother, feeling no better here, has gone on a visit to my elder aunt for purposes of complete rest; leaving my younger aunt as autocrat of this dwelling.'[22] On 13 March, Susie, 'showing no signs of recovery',[23] was admitted to Butler Hospital, where her husband had died more than twenty years before and where she herself would remain until her death two years later.

Lovecraft notes in his January letter to Kleiner that 'such infirmity & absence on her part is so *unprecedented*', but one wonders whether this was really the case. Once again Clara Hess provides some very disturbing testimony:

> I remember that Mrs. Lovecraft spoke to me about weird and fantastic creatures that rushed out from behind buildings and from corners at dark, and that she shivered and looked about apprehensively as she told her story.
>
> The last time I saw Mrs. Lovecraft we were both going 'down street' on the Butler Avenue car. She was excited and

apparently did not know where she was. She attracted the attention of everyone. I was greatly embarrassed, as I was the object of all her attention.[24]

I believe that these incidents occurred just before Susie's breakdown. Again, if Lovecraft was oblivious of Susie's gradual decline, he must have had very little close or meaningful contact with his mother.

And yet, Lovecraft himself was profoundly shaken by Susie's nervous collapse. In the January letter to Kleiner he writes:

you above all others can imagine the effect of maternal illness & absence. I cannot eat, nor can I stay up long at a time. Penwriting or typewriting nearly drives me insane. My nervous system seems to find its vent in feverish & incessant scribbling with a pencil … She writes optimistic letters each day, & I try to make my replies equally optimistic; though I do not find it possible to 'cheer up', eat, & go out, as she encourages me to do.

It is obvious that Lovecraft felt very close to his mother, however much he may have failed to understand her or she to understand him. I have no warrant for saying that his response to her illness is pathological; rather, I see it as part of a pattern whereby any serious alteration in his familial environment leads to extreme nervous disturbance. The death of his grandmother in 1896 led to dreams of 'night-gaunts'; the death of his father in 1898 brought on some sort of 'near-breakdown'; the death of Whipple Phillips and the loss of his birthplace in 1904 caused Lovecraft seriously to consider suicide. Even less tragic events resulted in severe traumas: school attendance in 1898–99 and violin lessons produced another 'near-breakdown'; yet another breakdown caused or was caused by his inability to complete high school, and led to a several-year period of vegetation and hermitry.

The state of Lovecraft's own health during this entire period is somewhat of a mystery, since we have only his own testimony on the matter. He obviously had no physical ailments: his R.I.N.G. examination, however cursory, was clear on that score. To Arthur Harris, Lovecraft makes the remarkable assertion in 1915: 'I can remain out of bed but three or four hours each day, and those three or four hours are generally burdened with an array of amateur work far beyond my capabilities.'[25] His letters to John Dunn and Alfred Galpin of the period 1915–18 are full of references to his pseudo-invalidism. Clearly, Lovecraft's ailments were largely psychological—perhaps fostered, as I have noted before, by his mother's and his aunts' oversolicitousness; whenever he became engrossed in some intellectual subject, his 'ill health' would be sloughed off and he would pursue studies as vigorously as anyone. It is perhaps not too early to bring in the testimony of a relatively impartial witness, George Julian Houtain, who met Lovecraft in Boston in 1920:

> Lovecraft honestly believes he is not strong—that he has an inherited nervousness and fatigue wished upon him. One would never suspect in his massive form and well constructed body that there could be any ailment. To look at him one would think seriously before 'squaring off.' …
>
> Many of us are Lovecrafts, in the peculiar sense, that we have lots of things wished upon us—and are ignorant how to throw them off. We react always to the suggestion—shall I call it curse?—placed upon us. It was never intended in the great scheme of things that such a magnificent physique should succumb to any mental dictation that commanded it to be subject to nervous ills and fatigue—nor that that wonderful mentality should weakly and childishly listen to that—WHICH ISN'T.[26]

Lovecraft responded to this in a letter to Frank Belknap Long:

> If Houtain knew how constant are my struggles against the devastating headaches, dizzy spells, and spells of poor concentrating power which hedge me in on all sides, and how feverishly I try to utilise every available moment for work, he would be less confident in classifying my ills as imaginary. I do not arbitrarily pronounce myself an invalid *because* of a nervous heredity. The condition itself is only too apparent—the hereditary part is only one explanatory factor.[27]

Lovecraft's account must be given its due, but in the event it appears that Houtain was more on the mark, and eventually Lovecraft realized it:

> Lovecraft did not express surprise at my pronouncements. In fact he was receptive to them. I came to the conclusion that he was willing to overcome this and would but he isn't allowed to do so, because others in his immediate household won't permit him to forget this hereditary nervousness. As it

is Lovecraft is a mental and physical giant, not because of, but in spite of these conditions. I venture the prediction that were he to lose all thoughts of this handed down idea, get out in the world, and rub elbows with the maddening crowd, that he would stand out as a National figure in Belles-Lettres; that his name would top the list in the annals of the literature of the day and I will go so far as to say it would become a house-hold name throughout the breadth and length of this land.

Even now that final pronouncement is a bit of an exaggeration, but it is more accurate than Houtain—or Lovecraft—could ever have imagined. How Lovecraft finally emerged—intellectually, creatively, and personally—from the claustrophobic influence of 598 Angell Street to become the writer, thinker, and human being we know will be the subject of the subsequent chapters of this book.

CHAPTER EIGHT

Cynical Materialist (1919–21)

The immediate effects of Susie's absence from the household at 598 Angell Street were mixed: at times Lovecraft seemed incapable of doing anything because of 'nerve strain'; at other times he found himself possessed of unwonted energy: 'I wrote an entire March critical report [i.e., the 'Department of Public Criticism' for March 1919] one evening recently, & I am this morning able to write letters after having been up all night'.[1] In a sense, this turn of events—especially in light of Lovecraft's repeated assurances, which he himself no doubt received from Susie's doctors, that she was in no physical danger—may have been a relief, for it definitively moved Susie out of the picture as far as Lovecraft's daily life was concerned.

What exactly was the matter with Susie is now difficult to say, since her Butler Hospital records were among those destroyed in a fire several decades ago. Winfield Townley Scott, however, consulted them when they were still in existence, and he paraphrases them as follows:

> She suffered periods of mental and physical exhaustion. She wept frequently under emotional strains. In common lingo, she was a woman who had gone to pieces. When interviewed, she stressed her economic worries, and she spoke … of all she had done for 'a poet of the highest order'; that is, of course, her son. The psychiatrist's record takes note of an Oedipus complex, a 'psycho-sexual contact' with the son, but observes that the effects of such a complex are usually more important on the son than on the mother, and does not pursue the point.[2]

The most seemingly spectacular item is the curious mention of a 'psycho-sexual contact'; but it is surely inconceivable that any actual abuse could have occurred between two individuals who so obviously shared the rigid Victorian sexual mores of the time. There seems every reason to regard Susie's collapse as primarily brought on by financial worries: there was, let us recall, only $7500 for the two of them from Whipple's estate, and in addition there was a tiny sum in mortgage payments (usually $37.08 twice a year, in February and August) from a quarry in Providence, the Providence Crushed Stone and Sand Co., managed by a tenant, Mariano de Magistris.

It was perhaps inevitable that Susie's absence from 598 produced at least the possibility of a certain liberation on Lovecraft's part, if only in terms of his physical activities. By now a giant in the world of amateur journalism, he was increasingly in demand at various local and national amateur conventions. It was some time before Lovecraft actually ventured forth; but, when he did so, it betokened the definitive end of his period of 'eccentric reclusiveness'. Kleiner visited him in Providence in 1918. In October 1919 (as I shall relate later) he accompanied several amateurs to Boston to hear his new literary idol, Lord Dunsany. On the evening of 21 June 1920, Edward F. Daas came to Providence for a two-day visit. That summer and fall Lovecraft himself made three separate trips to Boston for amateur gatherings.

The first meeting took place at 20 Webster Street in the suburb of Allston. This house—occupied jointly by Winifred Jackson, Laurie A. Sawyer, and Edith Miniter—was at the time a central meeting-place for the Hub Club. Lovecraft arrived on Monday 4 July, in the company of Rheinhart Kleiner, who had come to Providence the day before. On this occasion Lovecraft spent the night under a roof other than his own for the first time since 1901. His sleeping-place was the home of Alice Hamlet at 109 Greenbriar Street in Dorchester. But, lest we look askance at Lovecraft's spending the night alone in a young lady's home, let us be reassured: a convention report in the *Epgephi* for September 1920 discreetly informs us that 'he said he'd just got to have a "quiet room to himself"' and that he and Hamlet were properly chaperoned by Michael Oscar White and a Mrs Thompson.[3] The Dorchester party returned to 20 Webster Street the next day to resume festivities, and Lovecraft caught a train home in the early evening.

Miniter (1869–1934) was perhaps the most noted literary figure at this gathering. In 1916 she had published a realistic novel, *Our Natupski Neighbors*, to good reviews, and her short stories had been widely published in professional magazines. But, in spite of her professional success, she was devoted to the amateur cause. Her loyalty, however, extended to the NAPA and not the UAPA. Among her amateur journals was at least one issue of *The Muffin Man* (April 1921), which contained her exquisite parody of Lovecraft, 'Falco Ossifracus: By Mr. Goodguile.' It is, perhaps, the first such work of its kind.

Miniter invited Lovecraft to attend the Hub Club picnic on 7 August. This gathering consisted largely of old-time amateurs who had been active well before the turn of the century. At one point, as the group was wandering through the Middlesex Fells Reservation, Miniter fashioned a chaplet of bays for Lovecraft and insisted that he wear them at a banquet that evening in honour of his triple laureateship.

Lovecraft's third Boston trip began on 5 September. He arrived at noon at 20 Webster Street and unexpectedly encountered James F. Morton: 'Never have I met so thoroughly erudite a conversationalist before, and I was quite surprised by the geniality and friendliness which overlay his unusual attainments. I could but regret the limited opportunities which I have of meeting him, for Morton is one who commands my most unreserved liking.'[4] Clearly, the rancour surrounding Isaacson's *In a Minor Key* had died away. Lovecraft would later have plenty of opportunities to meet Morton during his two-year stay in New York. In the afternoon Lovecraft delivered his lecture, 'Amateur Journalism: Its Possible Needs and Betterment'.

Some months earlier, at the very beginning of 1920, Lovecraft came in touch with an individual who would play a very large role in his life: Frank Belknap Long, Jr (1901–94). At this time Long, a lifelong New Yorker, was not quite nineteen, and would enter New York University that fall to study journalism, transferring two years later to Columbia. His family was quite well-to-do—his father was a prominent New York dentist—and resided in comfortable quarters on the Upper West Side of Manhattan, at 823 West End Avenue. Long had developed an interest in the weird, and he exercised his talents both in prose and in poetry. He joined the UAPA around the end of 1919.

It is not difficult to see why Lovecraft took to Long, and why he saw in him a sort of pendant to his other young disciple, Alfred Galpin. Long may not have had Galpin's incandescent brilliance as a philosopher, but he was an aesthete, fictionist, and poet; and it was exactly at this time that Lovecraft's own creative focus was shifting from arid antiquarian poetry and essays to weird fiction. Long's early Poe-esque work (including the striking tale 'The Eye

Above the Mantel', *United Amateur*, March 1921), by no means markedly inferior to Lovecraft's, no doubt helped convince the latter that the new direction in which he was heading was a potentially fruitful one.

Toward the end of 1919 Lovecraft and Kleiner began a desultory discussion of women, love, and sex. Kleiner, apparently, had always been susceptible to the temptations of the fair, and Lovecraft looked upon his varied involvements with a mixture of mild surprise, amusement, and perhaps a certain lofty contempt. At one point he remarks:

> Of course, I am unfamiliar with amatory phenomena save through cursory reading. I always assumed that one waited till he encountered some nymph who seemed radically different to him from the rest of her sex, and without whom he felt he could no longer exist. Then, I fancied, he commenced to lay siege to her heart in businesslike fashion, not desisting till either he won her for life, or was blighted by rejection.[5]

But is it really the case that Lovecraft was 'unfamiliar with amatory phenomena'? There is perhaps some small reason for doubt on the matter; and it centres upon an individual who has been mentioned sporadically during the last chapter—Winifred Virginia Jackson (1876–1959).

According to research done by George T. Wetzel and R. Alain Everts, Jackson had married Horace Jordan, a black man, around 1915; at that time she resided at 57 Morton Street in Newton Centre, Massachusetts, a suburb of Boston. Wetzel and Everts believe that she divorced in early 1919,[6] although she continued to be listed in the UAPA membership list under her married name until September 1921. By January 1920 she was living, along with two other female amateurs, at 20 Webster Street in Allston.

Jackson and Lovecraft certainly do seem to have done a considerable amount of amateur work together. Along with several others, they edited and published three issues of *The United Co-operative* (1918–21), and she was associate editor of *The Silver Clarion* at a time when Lovecraft was giving a certain amount of attention to that journal. Jackson was Second Vice-President of the UAPA for three consecutive years (1917–20), when Lovecraft was President (1917–18) and Chairman of the Department of Public

Criticism (1918–19). Then, of course, there are the two stories co-written by Jackson and Lovecraft.

None of this would suggest that Lovecraft and Jackson were anything but occasionally close working colleagues were it not for some remarks made by Willametta Keffer, an amateur of a somewhat later period, to George T. Wetzel in the 1950s. According to Wetzel, Keffer told him that (and here Wetzel is paraphrasing a letter by Keffer) 'everybody in Amateur Journalism thought Lovecraft would marry Winifred Jordan'; Keffer herself stated to Wetzel, 'A long time member of NAPA who knew and met both HPL and Winifred Virginia told me of the "romance"'.

It is difficult to know what to make of this. Lovecraft must have met Jackson in person no later than the summer of 1920, since she was then residing at 20 Webster Street in Allston, where Lovecraft stopped on at least two occasions; but, strangely enough, he does not mention her in any of his various accounts of his trips there. He did write an effusive article, 'Winifred Virginia Jackson: A "Different" Poetess', in the *United Amateur* for March 1921; and he spent Christmas Day of 1920 writing a quaint poem upon receiving a photograph of her—presumably her Christmas gift to him, 'On Receiving a Portraiture of Mrs. Berkeley, ye Poetess'.

Jackson really was a very attractive woman, and the fact that she was fourteen years older than Lovecraft need not preclude a romance between the two. But one other fact must now be adduced: although by this time divorced, Jackson (according to Wetzel and Everts) was carrying on an affair with the noted black poet and critic William Stanley Braithwaite (1878–1962), and she would remain involved with him for many years. Did Lovecraft know this? I find it impossible to believe, given his extraordinarily strict views on the need to maintain an absolute 'colour line' prohibiting any sort of sexual union between blacks and whites; if he had known, he would have dropped Jackson immediately even as a colleague. He might not even have known that Horace Jordan was black. Lovecraft of course did know of Braithwaite, who by this time was already the most prominent black critic in the country; he would correspond with him briefly in 1930. As literary editor of the influential *Boston Transcript* and as editor of the annual *Anthology of Magazine Verse* (1913–29), Braithwaite occupied a formidable position in American poetry at this time.

There is one further bit of evidence that seems to clinch the matter of a romance between Lovecraft and Jackson. Lovecraft's wife Sonia Davis told R. Alain Everts in 1967 that 'I stole HPL away from Winifred Jackson'.[7] How this happened will be the subject of a later chapter; but this romance, if it could really be called that, appears to have been very languidly pursued on both sides. There is no evidence that Jackson ever came to Providence to visit Lovecraft, as Sonia frequently did even though she lived much farther away (Brooklyn), and after Sonia 'stole' him we hear little of Winifred either from Lovecraft or in the amateur press generally.

Meanwhile Lovecraft was not done travelling. Two more trips to Boston were made in the early months of 1921, both again for amateur conventions. On 22 February the Boston Conference of Amateur Journalists was held at Quincy House. In the afternoon session Lovecraft delivered a paper, written the previous day, on a prescribed subject, 'What Amateurdom and I Have Done for Each Other'. Later Lovecraft engaged in various discussion—mostly with W. Paul Cook and George Julian Houtain—but declined an invitation to sing, even though he had apparently done so at the September 1920 gathering. So Lovecraft's days as a plaintive tenor were not wholly over!

A month later Lovecraft returned to Boston for a St Patrick's Day gathering of amateurs on 10 March. This took place at 20 Webster Street. Members were seated in a circle in the parlour, and literary contributions were recited in sequence. Lovecraft on this occasion read the story 'The Moon-Bog', written expressly for the occasion; it received abundant applause, but did not win the prize.

Lovecraft was planning yet another trip in early June, this time to New Hampshire to visit Myrta Alice Little in Hampstead, near Westville (just over the Massachusetts border, a few miles north of Haverhill). But Lovecraft's one surviving letter to Little, written on 17 May 1921, in which he outlined the plans for the trip, was written only a week before the most traumatic event of his entire life up to this point: the death of his mother on 24 May.

In 'A Confession of Unfaith' Lovecraft suggests that the immediate postwar period led to the solidification of his philosophical thought:

> The Peace Conference, Friedrich Nietzsche, Samuel Butler (the modern), H. L. Mencken, and other influences have perfected my cynicism; a quality which grows more intense as the advent of middle life removes the blind prejudice whereby youth clings to the vapid 'all's right with the world' hallucination from sheer force of desire to have it so.

These 'influences' are certainly a heterogeneous lot, and they seem primarily influential in Lovecraft's ethical, political, and social philosophy. What he does not state here are what appear to be the two central influences on his metaphysical thought of the time— Ernst Haeckel's *The Riddle of the Universe* (1899; English translation 1900) and Hugh Elliot's *Modern Science and Materialism* (1919).

When Lovecraft stated his philosophy as 'mechanistic materialism', he was intent on denying certain key tenets of idealistic or religious philosophy; specifically, that any event can occur in the universe beyond the bounds of natural law (although all natural laws may not currently be known, or may never be known); that any 'immaterial' substance (such as the 'soul') can exist; and that the universe as a whole is progressing toward any particular goal. The denial of God, the soul, and an afterlife is implicit in all these formulations.

Mechanistic materialism as a philosophy, of course, goes back to the Presocratics, specifically Leucippus and Democritus, the co-founders of atomism and very strong proponents of determinism. Among modern thinkers materialism made considerable headway in the seventeenth (Hobbes), eighteenth (Helvétius, La Mettrie, d'Holbach), and nineteenth centuries, in part through the redis-covery of the ancient materialists and much more importantly through increasing advances in science. Indeed, Lovecraft's chief philosophical influences are all from the nineteenth century— Darwin, Huxley, Haeckel, and others who by their pioneering work in biology, chemistry, and physics systematically brought more and more phenomena under the realm of the known and the natural.

One of the greatest weapons Lovecraft found in his battle against religious metaphysics was anthropology. The anthropological thought of the later nineteenth century had, in Lovecraft's mind, so convincingly accounted for the natural *origin* of religious belief that no further explanation was required for its tenacious hold on human beings. This conception is discussed at length in the essay 'Idealism and Materialism—A Reflection', which was published in an issue of the *National Amateur* dated July 1919. The notion that primitive human beings were, to put it crudely, merely bad philosophers who misapprehended the true nature of phenomena was evolved by a number of important anthropologists of the later nineteenth century. I would like to believe that Lovecraft read Edward Burnett Tylor's *Primitive Culture* (1871), a landmark work in its field that is still of value, but can find no evidence that he ever did so. We are on more certain ground if we contend that Lovecraft's anthropology of religion comes from John Fiske's *Myths and Myth-Makers* (1872) and Sir James George Frazer's *The Golden Bough* (1890f.), which he clearly did read (although Frazer perhaps not this early). Fiske's book was in his library. Like Haeckel, John Fiske (1842–1901) has suffered somewhat of a decline in esteem, but in his day he was highly noted as an anthropologist, philosopher, and (in his later years) historian.

I want at last to address certain curious statements made in 'A Confession of Unfaith', wherein Lovecraft attests to his 'cynical materialism' and his 'pessimistic cosmic views', for they will provide a transition to a study of Lovecraft's early ethics. Why cynical? why pessimistic? What is there in materialism or cosmicism that could lead to such an ethical stance? Well, as a matter of pure logic, nothing: materialism and cosmicism, as metaphysical principles, have no direct ethical corollaries, and it therefore becomes our task to ascertain how and why Lovecraft felt that they did. Let us consider some statements of the 1919–20 period:

> There is a real restfulness in the scientific conviction that nothing matters very much; that the only legitimate aim of humanity is to minimise acute suffering for the majority, and to derive whatever satisfaction is derivable from the exercise of the mind in the pursuit of truth.[8]

> The secret of true contentment ... lies in the achievement of a *cosmical* point of view.[9]

Once again it must be emphasized that neither of these ethical precepts is a direct corollary of cosmicism; they are, rather, varying *psychological* responses to Lovecraft's awareness of the cosmic insignificance of humanity in a boundless universe.

A passage in a letter of 1920 is one of his most poignant early ethical remarks, and here he explicitly ties Epicureanism, Schopenhauerianism, and cosmicism into a neat (if not logically defensible) whole:

> About the time I joined the United I was none too fond of existence. I was 23 years of age, and realised that my infirmities would withhold me from success in the world at large. Feeling like a cipher, I felt I might as well be erased. But later I realised that even success is empty. Failure though I be, I shall reach a level with the greatest—and the

smallest—in the damp earth or on the final pyre. And I saw that in the interim trivialities are not to be despised. Success is a relative thing—and the victory of a boy at marbles is equal to the victory of an Octavius at Actium when measured by the scale of cosmic infinity. So I turned to observe other mediocre and handicapped persons about me, and found pleasure in increasing the happiness of those who could be helped by such encouraging words or critical services as I am capable of furnishing. That I have been able to cheer here and there an aged man, an infirm old lady, a dull youth, or a person deprived by circumstances of education, affords to me a sense of being not altogether useless, which almost forms a substitute for the real success I shall never know. What matter if none hear of my labours, or if those labours touch only the afflicted and mediocre? Surely it is well that the happiness of the unfortunate be made as great as possible; and he who is kind, helpful, and patient with his fellow-sufferers, adds as truly to the world's combined fund of tranquillity as he who, with greater endowments, promotes the birth of empires, or advances the knowledge of civilisation and mankind.[10]

This quotation above may help us to understand why Lovecraft initially derived pessimism from cosmicism. His various comments to the contrary notwithstanding, I suspect he did suffer a sort of disillusion when he contemplated the myriad worlds of infinite space; the first reaction may well have been one of exhilaration, but perhaps not much later there came to him the sensation of the utter futility of all human effort in light of the vastness of the cosmos and the inconsequentiality of mankind in it. At a still later stage Lovecraft turned this pessimism to his advantage, and it became a bulwark against the tragedies of his own existence—his failure to graduate from high school and enter college; his failure to secure a job; his dissatisfaction with the progress of his writing—since these things could be regarded as cosmically unimportant, however large they loomed in his own circumstances. Lovecraft largely abandoned Schopenhauerian pessimism over the next decade or so, evolving instead his notion of 'indifferentism'; but this should be treated at a later stage.

Philosophy was only one of Lovecraft's many concerns in this period. Perhaps more significantly for his future career, he simultaneously began—or attempted to begin—separating himself from amateur activity and turning determinedly to fiction-writing. We can at last study the influence of Lord Dunsany on his fiction, as well as the many other tales of supernatural horror that laid the groundwork for his later, more substantial fiction.

Edward John Moreton Drax Plunkett (1878–1957) became the eighteenth Lord Dunsany (pronounced Dun-SAY-ny) upon the death of his father in 1899. He could trace his lineage to the twelfth century, but few members of this Anglo-Norman line had shown much aptitude for literature. Dunsany himself did not do so in his early years, spent alternately in various homes in England and in Dunsany Castle in County Meath. He had gone to Eton and Sandhurst, had served in the Boer War, and appeared on his way to occupying an undistinguished place amongst the Anglo-Irish aristocracy as sportsman, hunter, and socialite. He married Beatrice Villiers, daughter of the Earl of Jersey, in 1904.

In 1904 Dunsany sat down and wrote *The Gods of Pegāna*. Having no literary reputation, he was forced to pay for its publication with Elkin Mathews of London. Never again, however, would Dunsany have to resort to vanity publishing.

The Gods of Pegāna, with its rhythmic prose and cosmic subject matter, both self-consciously derived from the King James Bible, introduced something unique to literature. Here was an entire theogony whose principal motivation was not the expression of religious fervour (Dunsany was in all likelihood an atheist) but an instantiation of Oscar Wilde's imperishable dictum: 'The artist is the creator of beautiful things.'[11] While there are a number of provocative philosophical undercurrents in *The Gods of Pegāna*, as in Dunsany's work as a whole, its main function is merely the evocation of beauty—beauty of language, beauty of conception, beauty of image. Readers and critics alike responded to this rarefied creation of exotic loveliness, with its seamless mixture of naivety and sophistication, archaism and modernity, sly humour and brooding horror, chilling remoteness and quiet pathos.

By the time Lovecraft discovered him, Dunsany had published much of the fiction and drama that would gain him fame, even adulation, on both sides of the Atlantic: *Time and the Gods* (1906); *The Sword of Welleran* (1908); *A Dreamer's Tales* (1910); *The Book of Wonder* (1912); *Five Plays* (1914); *Fifty-one Tales* (1915); *The Last Book of Wonder* (1916); *Plays of Gods and Men* (1917). *Tales of Three Hemispheres* would appear at the very end of 1919, marking the definite end of this phase of his work. By this time, however, Dunsany had achieved idolatrous fame in America. In 1916 he had five plays simultaneously produced in New York, as each of the *Five Plays* appeared in a different 'little' theatre off Broadway. His work was appearing in the most sophisticated and highbrow magazines—*Vanity Fair, The Smart Set, Harper's*, and (a little later) the *Atlantic Monthly*. By 1919 Dunsany would probably have been considered one of the ten greatest living writers in the English-speaking world.

An examination of Dunsany's early tales and plays reveals many thematic and philosophical similarities with Lovecraft: cosmicism (largely restricted to *The Gods of Pegāna*); the exaltation of Nature; hostility to industrialism; the power of dream to transform the mundane world into a realm of gorgeously exotic beauty; the awesome role of Time in human and divine affairs; and, of course, the evocative use of language. It is scarcely to be wondered at that Lovecraft felt for a time that Dunsany had said all he wished to say in a given literary and philosophical direction.

Lovecraft could hardly have been unaware of Dunsany's reputation. He admits to knowing of him well before he read him in 1919, but he had passed him off as a writer of whimsical, benign fantasy of the J. M. Barrie sort. The first work he read was not Dunsany's own first volume, *The Gods of Pegāna*, but *A Dreamer's Tales*, which may well be his best single short story collection in its diversity of contents and its several powerful tales of horror. Lovecraft admits: 'The book had been recommended to me by one whose judgment I did not highly esteem.'[12] This person was Alice M. Hamlet, an amateur journalist residing in Dorchester, Massachusetts, and probably a member of Winifred Virginia Jackson's informal coterie of writers.

Lovecraft would repeatedly say, even late in life, that Dunsany 'has certainly influenced me more than any other living writer'.[13] The first paragraph of *A Dreamer's Tales* 'arrested me as with an electrick shock, & I had not read two pages before I became a Dunsany devotee for life'.[14]

Hamlet had given Lovecraft *A Dreamer's Tales* in anticipation of Dunsany's lecture at the Copley Plaza in Boston on 20 October 1919, part of his extensive American tour. Lovecraft attended the lecture in the company of Miss Hamlet and her aunt. The group secured seats in the very front row, 'not ten feet' from Dunsany; it was the closest Lovecraft would ever come to meeting one of his literary idols, since he was too diffident to meet or correspond with Machen, Blackwood, or M. R. James.

Dunsany must at this time have agreed to act as Laureate Judge of Poetry of the UAPA for the 1919–20 term. In this function he probably read some of Lovecraft's poetry published during that period, but in his letter to UAPA President Mary Faye Durr announcing his decision he makes no reference to any work by Lovecraft. Hamlet, however, presented Dunsany a copy of the *Tryout* for November 1919, which contained one of two poems written on Dunsany by Lovecraft. 'To Edward John Moreton Drax Plunkett, 18th Baron Dunsany' must have been written very shortly after Lovecraft's attendance of the lecture; it is a dreadful, wooden poem that starkly reveals the drawbacks of using the Georgian style for subjects manifestly unsuited to it. Dunsany, however, remarked charitably in a letter published in the *Tryout* that the tribute was 'magnificent' and that 'I am most grateful to the author of that poem for his warm and generous enthusiasm, crystallised in verse'.[15] A few months later Lovecraft wrote a much better tribute in three simple stanzas of quatrains, 'On Reading Lord Dunsany's *Book of Wonder*' (*Silver Clarion*, March 1920). Dunsany apparently never read this poem.

It is easy to see why a figure like Dunsany would have had an immediate appeal for Lovecraft: his yearning for the unmechanized past, his purely aesthetic creation of a gorgeously evocative ersatz mythology, and his 'crystalline singing prose' (as Lovecraft would memorably characterize it in 'Supernatural Horror in Literature') made Lovecraft think that he had found a spiritual twin in the Irish fantaisiste. As late as 1923 he was still maintaining that 'Dunsany *is myself* ... His cosmic realm is the realm in which I live; his distant, emotionless vistas of the beauty of moonlight on quaint and ancient roofs are the vistas I know and cherish.'[16] And one must also conjecture that Dunsany's position as an independently wealthy nobleman who wrote what he chose and paid no heed to popular expectations exercised a powerful fascination for Lovecraft: here was an 'amateur' writer who had achieved tremendous popular and critical success; here was a case where the aristocracy of blood and the aristocracy of intellect were conjoined.

The string of Dunsanian pastiches that Lovecraft produced in 1919–21 are scarcely worth studying in detail. Their actual debt to Dunsany—except in several surface features and, of course, in overall style and otherworldly content—has perhaps been exaggerated, and many of them do reveal concerns central to Lovecraft's own temperament; but on the whole they are not among his finest tales, even of his early period. 'The White Ship', written in October 1919 and superficially based on Dunsany's 'Idle Days on the Yann' (in *A Dreamer's Tales*), is an interesting allegory on the loss of hope. Somewhat similar, and considerably more poignant, is 'The Quest of Iranon', perhaps the best of Lovecraft's Dunsanian tales. 'The Cats of Ulthar' (written on 15 June 1920) is one of his most celebrated tales, and remained one of his own favourites in its portrayal of how the cats of the mythical city of Ulthar avenged the death of a kitten at the hands of a cruel couple in that town. 'Celephaïs' (written in November 1920) is somewhat embarrassingly derivative of Dunsany's 'The Coronation of Mr. Thomas Shap' (in *The Book of Wonder*), in which a man takes to imagining himself a king of a mythical region of the imagination, to the degree that his work in the real world suffers and he is put in a madhouse. In 'Celephaïs' much the same thing happens: an unsuccessful writer dreams of the realm of Celephaïs, a realm that he had in fact imagined as a boy; later he occupies the realm permanently, while his body is found washed up by the tide.

Several stories written during this time that have not been considered 'Dunsanian' in fact owe something to Dunsany. 'The Terrible Old Man' (written on 28 January 1920) is set in the real world (the Massachusetts town of Kingsport, invented for this tale), and deals with the comeuppance of three potential robbers of a seemingly decrepit individual of excessively lengthy years. It recalls many of the tales in *The Book of Wonder*, which similarly deal with owlish gravity of attempted robberies which usually end badly for the perpetrators.

'The Street' was written in late 1919, and may have been inspired by some of the war parables in Dunsany's *Tales of War* (1919). The basic plot involves the transformation of some unspecified street (but clearly one in New England) from one occupied by 'men of strength and honour' to one inhabited by foreigners. The entire history of the United States is encapsulated in obvious allusions. Finally the Street itself rebels against its occupation by a band of foreign terrorists by blowing itself up.

Lovecraft supplies the genesis of the story in a letter—a strike of the Boston police for much of September and October 1919, during which time the state militia had to be called on to patrol the streets.[17] No doubt it was a very disturbing event, but at this time unionisation and strikes were almost the only option available to the working class for better wages and better working conditions.

'The Street' is nothing more than a prose version of such early poems as 'New England Fallen' and 'On a New-England Village Seen by Moonlight': there is the same naive glorification of the past, the same attribution of all evils to 'strangers' (who seem to have ousted those hardy Anglo-Saxons with surprising ease), and, remarkably, even a gliding over of the devastating economic and social effects of the industrial revolution. It is among his poorest works.

What, then, did Lovecraft learn from Dunsany? The answer may not be immediately evident, since it took several years for the Dunsany influence to be assimilated, and some of the most interesting and important aspects of the influence are manifested in tales that bear no superficial resemblance to Dunsany. Perhaps Lovecraft's most perceptive account of Dunsany's influence on him occurs in a letter of March 1920: 'The flight of imagination, and the delineation of pastoral or natural beauty, can be accomplished as well in prose as in verse—often better. It is this lesson which the inimitable Dunsany hath taught me.'[18] This comment was made in a discussion of Lovecraft's verse writing; and it is no accident that his verse output declined dramatically after 1920. There had been a dichotomy between Lovecraft's fictional and poetic output ever since he had resumed the writing of stories: how could tales of supernatural horror have any relation to the empty but super-ficially 'pretty' Georgianism of his verse? With the decline of verse writing, that dichotomy disappears—or, at least, narrows—as the quest for pure beauty now finds expression in tales.

More to the point, Lovecraft learned from Dunsany how to enunciate his philosophical, aesthetic, and moral conceptions by means of fiction, beyond the simple cosmicism of 'Dagon' or 'Beyond the Wall of Sleep'. The relation of dream and reality—dimly probed in 'Polaris'—is treated exhaustively and poignantly in 'Celephaïs'; the loss of hope is etched pensively in 'The White Ship' and 'The Quest of Iranon'. Lovecraft found *Time and the Gods* 'richly philo-sophical',[19] and the whole of Dunsany's early—and later—work offers simple, affecting parables on fundamental human issues. Lovecraft would in later years express his philosophy in increas-ingly complex ways as his fiction itself gained in breadth, scope, and richness.

In spite of his own assertions to the contrary, Lovecraft's 'Dun-sanian' fantasies are far more than mechanical pastiches of a revered master: they reveal considerable originality of conception while being only superficially derived from Dunsany. Interestingly, Dunsany himself came to this conclusion: when Lovecraft's work was posthumously published in book form, Dunsany came upon it and confessed that he had 'an odd interest in Lovecraft's work because in the few tales of his I have read I found that he was writing in my style, entirely originally & without in any way borrowing from me, & yet with my style & largely my material'.[20] Lovecraft would have been grateful for the acknowledgment.

During this period Lovecraft of course did not cease to write tales of supernatural horror, and a number of these display his increasing grasp of short story technique; some of them are also rather good in their own right. One of the most well-known, at least in terms of its genesis, is 'The Statement of Randolph Carter', written in late December 1919 and, apparently, a virtual literal transcript of a dream in which Lovecraft and Samuel Loveman explore some centuried graveyard, during which Loveman descends the steps of an ancient tomb, never to return. It is an effective, if predictable, story, and first appeared in W. Paul Cook's *Vagrant* for May 1920.

'The Temple' (probably written in the fall of 1920) requires little discussion, being a confused tale of a German U-boat commander who descends to the bottom of the ocean and comes upon a city built by some ancient civilization. The story is poorly conceived, having an excess of supernatural phenomena that are never adequately explained. Considerably better is 'Facts concerning the Late Arthur Jermyn and His Family' (also written in late 1920), a compact story of miscegenation: Sir Arthur Jermyn learns to his horror that his ancestor, Sir Wade Jermyn, had, during his explorations of the Congo, married a 'white ape', leading to the physical and psychological aberrations of the Jermyn line. Curiously enough, Lovecraft admits that the story was actually inspired in part by Sherwood Anderson's *Winesburg, Ohio* (1919).[21] Evidently Lovecraft found Anderson's exposure of the family secrets of a small American town a bit tame, so he devised a much darker 'skeleton' in the Jermyn closet.

'From Beyond' (written on 16 November 1920) is almost a caricature of the 'mad scientist' tale, but is of interest in that it was clearly derived from some passages in Elliot's *Modern Science and Materialism*, particularly those referring to the notion that most material objects consist largely of empty space. In the story,

Crawford Tillinghast devises a machine that breaks down the barriers that prevents us from seeing all the loathsome entities that pass by and *through* us at every moment.

One of the finest tales—or, perhaps, vignettes—of Lovecraft's early period is the prose poem 'Nyarlathotep', written in late 1920. This brief story is nothing more than an allegory on the decline of civilization. The mysterious Nyarlathotep is a kind of itinerant showman whose displays of bizarre phenomena involving light and electricity fascinate the public, but he appears to be a harbinger for the downfall of all human culture. Will Murray has made the plausible conjecture that the figure of Nyarlathotep in this tale may have been based on the eccentric scientist (and part charlatan) Nikola Tesla.[22]

Another strong tale is 'The Picture in the House', written on 12 December 1920. This simple tale of what a young man travelling through backwoods New England discovers in an apparently abandoned house makes mention of Lovecraft's second, and most famous, fictional town, Arkham. Beyond that, the story is the first of Lovecraft's tales not merely to utilize an authentic New England setting but to draw upon what Lovecraft himself clearly felt to be the weird heritage of New England history, specifically the history of Massachusetts. To Lovecraft, the seventeenth century, with its Puritan theocracy, represented a kind of American 'dark ages' precisely analogous to the medieval period, and its culminating event—the Salem witchcraft trials of 1692—only confirmed Lovecraft's impression of it as an epoch of ignorance, darkness, and potential terror. 'The Picture in the House' only broaches some of these issues, but later works would elaborate upon them considerably.

'The Nameless City', written in January 1921, is, conversely, one of Lovecraft's poorest tales, but one for which he himself retained an inexplicable fondness. This wild, implausible, histrionic tale of an explorer who tunnels beneath the sands of the Arabian desert and discovers a city formerly inhabited by alien creatures (preserved like mummies in upright coffins) has little to recommend it. It is, however, the first time that Abdul Alhazred is mentioned in Lovecraft's fiction. 'The Moon-Bog', written for that St Patrick's meeting in March 1921, is similarly a conventional tale of supernatural revenge.

Of 'The Outsider'—which many believe to be Lovecraft's signature tale—it is difficult to speak in small compass. To be sure, its depiction of a strange individual who burrows out of what appears to be a subterranean castle and, entering a brightly lit mansion, discovers that he himself is the horrible, decaying monster that has frightened off a band of merry-makers is a poignant exemplar of 'the soul-shattering consequences of self-knowledge';[23] but its excessive reliance on Poe-esque diction makes one wonder whether it is much more than an exercise in pastiche. Lovecraft himself came to such a judgment:

> Others ... agree with you in liking 'The Outsider', but I can't say that I share this opinion. To my mind this tale—written a decade ago—is too glibly *mechanical* in its climactic effect, & almost comic in the bombastic pomposity of its language. As I re-read it, I can hardly understand how I could have let myself be tangled up in such baroque & windy rhetoric as recently as ten years ago. It represents my literal though unconscious imitation of Poe at its very height.[24]

Many have conjectured on the influences behind the tale, specifically the culminating image of the entity seeing himself in a mirror. The most plausible suggestion, I believe, is that Lovecraft is borrowing from the scene in Mary Shelley's *Frankenstein* when the monster first sees himself in a pool of water.

It is, however, now time to examine the question of the story's autobiographical character. The opening sentence reads: 'Unhappy is he to whom the memories of childhood bring only fear and sadness.' One of the Outsider's final remarks—'I know always that I am an outsider; a stranger in this century and among those who are still men'—has been taken, perhaps not unjustly, as proto-typical of Lovecraft's entire life, the life of an 'eccentric recluse' who wished himself intellectually, aesthetically, and spiritually in the rational haven of the eighteenth century. I think we have already learnt enough about Lovecraft to know that such an interpretation greatly overstates the case: without denying his emphatic and sincere fondness, and even to some degree nostalgia, for the eighteenth century, he was also very much a part of his time, and was an 'outsider' only in the sense that most writers and intellectuals find a gulf between themselves and the commonality of citizens. Lovecraft's childhood was by no means unhappy, and he frequently looked back upon it as idyllic, carefree, and full of pleasurable intellectual stimulation and the close friendship of at least a small band of peers.

Is, then, 'The Outsider' a symbol for Lovecraft's own self-image, particularly the image of one who always thought himself ugly and whose mother told at least one individual about her son's 'hideous' face? I find this interpretation rather superficial, and it would have the effect of rendering the story maudlin and self-pitying. I think it is more profitable not to read too much autobiographical significance in 'The Outsider': its large number of apparent literary influences seem to make it more an experiment in pastiche than some deeply felt expression of psychological wounds.

It is difficult to characterise the non-Dunsanian stories of this period. Lovecraft was still experimenting in different tones, styles, moods, and themes in an effort to find out what might work the best. Perhaps the fact that so many of these tales were inspired by dreams is the most important thing about them. Lovecraft's letters of 1920 are full of accounts of incredibly bizarre dreams, some of which served as the nuclei for tales written years later. It would be a facile and inexpert psychoanalysis to maintain that Lovecraft's worries over Susie's health were the principal cause of these disturbances in his subconscious; as a matter of fact, it appears that Susie's health had, after a fashion, stabilized and that there was no suspicion of any impending collapse until only a few days before her death. Suffice it to say that the dozen or more stories Lovecraft wrote in 1920—more than he wrote in any other year of his life— point to a definitive shift in his aesthetic horizons. Lovecraft still did not know it yet, but he had come upon his life-work.

CHAPTER NINE
The High Tide of My Life
(1921–22)

Sarah Susan Phillips Lovecraft died on 24 May 1921, at Butler Hospital. Her death, however, was not a result of her nervous breakdown but rather of a gall bladder operation from which she did not recover. Winfield Townley Scott, who had access to Susie's now destroyed medical records, tells the story laconically: 'She underwent a gall-bladder operation which was thought to be successful. Five days later her nurse noted that the patient expressed a wish to die because "I will only live to suffer." She died the next day.'[1]

Lovecraft's reaction was pretty much what one might expect: 'The death of my mother on May 24 gave me an extreme nervous shock, and I find concentration and continuous endeavour quite impossible ... I cannot sleep much, or labour with any particular spirit or success.'[2] Later on in this letter, written nine days after the event, Lovecraft adds disturbingly:

> For my part, I do not think I shall wait for a natural death; since there is no longer any particular reason why I should exist. During my mother's life-time I was aware that voluntary euthanasia on my part would cause her distress, but it is now possible for me to regulate the term of my existence with the assurance that my end would cause no one more than a passing annoyance.

Evidently his aunts did not figure much in this equation. But it was a passing phase, as we shall shortly see.

What, in the end, are we to make of Lovecraft's relations with his mother? Susie Lovecraft has not fared well at the hands of Lovecraft's biographers, and her flaws are readily discernible: she was overly possessive, clearly neurotic, failed (as Lovecraft himself and the rest of his family did) to foresee the need for training her son in some sort of remunerative occupation, and psychologically damaged

Lovecraft at least to the point of declaring him physically hideous and perhaps in other ways that are now irrecoverable.

But the verdict on Susie should not be entirely negative. Kenneth W. Faig, Jr, correctly remarks: 'Lovecraft's finely honed aesthetic sensibilities and seasoned artistic judgment undoubtedly owed something to the early influence of his mother ... The wonderful home which Susie and her young son shared with her parents and sisters at 454 Angell Street during the 1890s must have been truly a delight.'[3] Her indulging Lovecraft in many of his early whims—the *Arabian Nights*, chemistry, astronomy—may seem excessive, but it allowed him fully to develop these intellectual and aesthetic interests, and so to lay the groundwork for both the intellect and the creativity he displayed in later years.

The critical issue is whether Lovecraft knew and acknowledged— at least to himself—the ways in which his mother affected him, both positively and adversely. In letters both early and late he speaks of her with nothing but praise and respect. In many letters of the 1930s, when recalling his early years, he makes statements such as: 'My health improved vastly and rapidly, though without any ascertainable cause, about 1920–21';[4] which gives—or appears to give—not the slightest hint that Susie's death might actually have been a liberating factor of some kind. But was Lovecraft really so lacking in self-awareness on this issue? I have already cited Sonia's noting that Lovecraft once admitted to her that Susie's influence upon him had been 'devastating'. Another very interesting piece of evidence comes not from a letter or an essay, or from a memoir by a friend, but from a story.

'The Thing on the Doorstep' (1933) tells the tale of Edward Derby, who was an only child and 'had organic weaknesses which startled his doting parents and caused them to keep him closely chained to their side. He was never allowed out without his nurse, and seldom had a chance to play unconstrainedly with other children.' A little later the narrator remarks: 'Edward's mother died when he was thirty-four, and for months he was incapacitated by some odd psychological malady. His father took him to Europe, however, and he managed to pull out of his trouble without visible effects. Afterward he seemed to feel a sort of grotesque exhilaration, as if of partial escape from some unseen bondage.' That last sentence is all the evidence we need: it makes it abundantly clear that Lovecraft knew (by 1933, at any rate) that Susie's death had in a sense made the rest of his own life possible. It is telling that, in his litany of 'near-breakdowns' beginning in 1898, he lists no break-down of 1921.

In the short term Lovecraft did the most sensible thing he could have done: continue the normal course of his existence. He may not, like Derby, have travelled to Europe, but there was always New Hampshire. He went ahead with his visit to Myrta Alice Little on 8–9 June, also seeing 'Tryout' Smith in Haverhill. He repeated the trip in August. Later that month he went with his old school chum Harold Munroe to their old clubhouse in Rehoboth (which Lovecraft was delighted to find nearly intact), and still later he took in another amateur meeting in Boston.

Meanwhile events in the amateur world were heating up. Love-craft had easily been elected Official Editor for the 1920–21 and 1921–22 terms, and his 'literary' faction was in both political and editorial control of the association: Alfred Galpin was President in 1920–21 (serving, anomalously, also as Chairman of the Department of Public Criticism), and Ida C. Haughton of Columbus, Ohio, was President in 1921–22; other associates of Lovecraft such as Paul J. Campbell, Frank Belknap Long, and Alice Hamlet all held official positions.

But the picture was by no means rosy. Lovecraft had consider-able disagreements with President Haughton, and years later he claimed that she 'ran the very gamut of abuse & positive insult—culminating even in an aspersion on my stewardship of the United funds!'[5] In response, Lovecraft wrote 'Medusa: A Portrait' in late 1921. This is the most vicious and unrestrained of his poetic satires, and in it he mercilessly flays Haughton for her large bulk and her supposed foulness of temper. The poem was published in the *Tryout* for December 1921.

There was trouble on other fronts also. In the *Woodbee* for January 1922 Fritter continued his attacks on Lovecraft and his literary coterie. Although Lovecraft responded tartly in his 'Editorial' in the January 1922 *United Amateur*, in this case he was not to prevail. In the UAPA election in July 1922, the 'literature' side lost out to its opponents. Lovecraft himself lost to Fritter for Official Editor by a vote of 44 to 29. It was, no doubt, a staggering blow, and may have gone a long way in showing Lovecraft that this phase of his amateur career was coming to an end.

But Lovecraft had the last laugh. The new official board did manage to produce six issues of the *United Amateur*, but at the convention in late July 1923 Lovecraft's literary party was almost entirely voted back into office; incredibly, Sonia H. Greene was elected President even though she had not knowingly placed herself on the ballot. This whole turn of events appeared to rile Fritter and his colleagues, and they acted in an obstructionist manner toward the new official board; the Secretary-Treasurer, Alma B. Sanger, withheld funds and failed to answer letters, so that no *United Amateur* could be printed until May 1924. No convention was held in 1924, and evidently the official board for that year was re-elected by a mail vote; but that administration produced only one more issue (July 1925)—an issue remarkable for its complete dominance by members of Lovecraft's literary circle (Frank Belknap Long, Samuel Loveman, Clark Ashton Smith, and of course Lovecraft himself). This ended Lovecraft's official involvement with the UAPA. Although he strove valiantly to establish the next official board (Edgar J. Davis as President, Victor E. Bacon as Official Editor), it never really took off and, after one or two skimpy issues of the *United Amateur*, it died some time in 1926.

Lovecraft was by no means aloof from the affairs of the NAPA. It is somewhat ironic that the only two national conventions he ever attended, in 1921 and 1930, were those of the NAPA, not the UAPA. The NAPA convention of 1921 was held on 2–4 July in Boston. At the banquet on 4 July Lovecraft himself gave a speech; it survives under the title 'Within the Gates: By "One Sent by Providence"'. Next to some of his humorous short stories, it is the wittiest of Lovecraft's prose performances. The speech is full of genial barbs directed at Houtain, Edith Miniter, and other ama-teurs, and concludes by apologizing for the 'long and sonorous intellectual silence' of the speech (it is less than a thousand words).

One of the individuals who must have been in the audience was Sonia Haft Greene (1883–1972). Sonia had been introduced to amateur journalism by James F. Morton, whom she had known since 1917. She was one of a contingent of NAPA members from the New York area (among them Morton, Rheinhart Kleiner, and others) to go to the convention, and Kleiner later testified that he introduced her to Lovecraft at the event.[6] Very shortly thereafter Sonia became an ardent supporter of the amateur cause, and not only joined the UAPA but contributed the unheard-of sum of $50.00 to the Official Organ Fund.

It is a pity that we know so relatively little about the woman whom Lovecraft would marry less than three years later. She was born Sonia Haft Shafirkin on 16 March 1883, in Ichnya (near Kiev) in the Ukraine. Her father, Simyon Shafirkin, apparently died when she was a child. Her mother, Racille Haft, left Sonia with her brother in Liverpool—where Sonia received her first schooling—and herself came to America, where she married Solomon H—— (full name unknown) in 1892. Sonia joined her mother later that year. She married Samuel Seckendorff in 1899—she was not quite sixteen, her husband twenty-six. A son, born in 1900, died after three months, and a daughter, Florence, was born on 19 March 1902. Seckendorff, a Russian, later adopted the name Greene from a friend in Boston, John Greene. The marriage was apparently very turbulent, and Samuel Greene died in 1916, apparently by his own hand.

Sonia had taken some extension courses at Columbia University, and had secured an executive position (with a salary of $10,000 a year) at Ferle Heller's, a clothing store. (The store had two outlets, one at 36 West 57th Street and the other at 9 East 46th Street; Sonia, whose specialty was hats, worked at the former shop.) She resided at 259 Parkside Avenue in the then fashionable Flatbush section of Brooklyn.

Kleiner describes her physically as 'a very attractive woman of Junoesque proportions'; Galpin, while using exactly the same classical adjective, paints a more piquant portrait:

> When she dropped in on my reserved and bookish student life at Madison [in 1921 or 1922], I felt like an English sparrow transfixed by a cobra. Junoesque and commanding, with superb dark eyes and hair, she was too regal to be a Dostoievski character and seemed rather a heroine from some of the most martial pages of *War and Peace*. Proclaiming the glory of the free and enlightened human personality, she declared herself a person unique in depth and intensity of passion and urged me to Write, to Do, to Create.[7]

Sonia was taken with Lovecraft from the start. She bluntly confesses that, when first meeting Lovecraft, 'I admired his personality but frankly, at first, not his person'[8]—a clear reference to Lovecraft's very plain looks (tall, gaunt frame, lantern jaw, possible problems with facial hair and skin) and perhaps also his stiff, formal conduct and (particularly annoying to one in the fashion industry) the archaic cut of his clothes.

But a correspondence promptly ensued. Lovecraft heard from Sonia as early as mid- to late July of 1921, by which time she had already read some of Lovecraft's stories that had appeared in the amateur press. Lovecraft professed to be taken with her, at least as an intellect.

It was Sonia who took things into her own hands. She visited Lovecraft in Providence on 4–5 September, staying at the Crown Hotel. Lovecraft, as had already become customary with his out-of-town visitors, showed her the antiquarian treasures of Providence, took her back to 598 and introduced her to aunt Lillian. The next day Sonia invited Lovecraft and his aunt to come to the Crown for a noon meal.

In the meantime Sonia contributed to the amateur cause in other than monetary ways. In October 1921 the first of two issues of her *Rainbow* appeared; both would be forums for the poetic, fictional, essayistic, and polemical outpourings of Lovecraft and his inner circle of amateur colleagues. Lovecraft contributed a piece entitled 'Nietzscheism and Realism', which he declares was a series of extracts made from two letters to Sonia.[9] This compendium of philosophical *bon mots* comprises, sadly enough, almost the sole remnant (aside from a handful of postcards and one other item to be discussed later) of what must have been an extensive and exceptionally fascinating correspondence—one which we would, from a biographical perspective, wish to have perhaps more than any other of Lovecraft's. But Sonia is clear on its fate: 'I had a trunkful of his letters which he had written me throughout the years but before leaving New York for California [around 1935] I took them to a field and set a match to them.'[10] No doubt Sonia, after all she had been through, was within her rights to do this, but all students of Lovecraft must groan when reading this terse utterance.

Being a professional amateur was perfectly suited to Lovecraft's aristocratic temperament, but, as time went on and the family inheritance increasingly dwindled, some thought had to be paid to making money. Lovecraft was surely aware of the principal reason for his mother's nervous collapse—her worries about the financial future of herself and her son. Perhaps it was this that finally led him to make some effort at earning an income; for it is at this time that David Van Bush appears on the scene.

Bush had joined the UAPA in 1916. Lovecraft first mentions him, to my knowledge, in the summer of 1918. From 1915 into the late

1920s Bush wrote an appalling number of poetry volumes and pop psychology manuals, most of them self-published. It is a dreary possibility that Lovecraft revised the bulk of these books, both prose and verse.

The fact is that Bush did become quite popular as a writer and lecturer on popular psychology. Lovecraft did not begin working in earnest for Bush until around 1920, and it is no accident that Bush's titles begin appearing at a rapid rate thereafter. Lovecraft regarded Bush with a mixture of annoyance and lofty condescension. He met Bush in the summer of 1922, when the latter was lecturing in Cambridge, Massachusetts, and paints a vivid portrait of him:

> David V. Bush is a short, plump fellow of about forty-five, with a bland face, bald head, and very fair taste in attire. He is actually an immensely good sort—kindly, affable, winning, and smiling. Probably he has to be in order to induce people to let him live after they have read his verse. His keynote is a hearty good-fellowship, and I almost think he is rather sincere about it. His 'success-in-life' stuff is no joke so far as finance is concerned; for with his present 'psychological' mountebank outfit, his Theobaldised books of doggerel, and his newly-founded magazine, *Mind Power Plus*, he actually shovels in the coin at a very gratifying rate. Otherwise he'd never have a suite at the Copley-Plaza.[11]

The letter goes on at some length, touching on Bush's rural up-bringing, his wife, his odd jobs (trick cyclist in a circus, 'ham' actor, clergyman), and his 'new gospel of dynamic pychology' ('which has all the virtues of "New Thought" plus a saving vagueness which prevents its absurdity from being exposed before the credulous public amongst whom his missionary labours lie').

Lovecraft could not afford to scorn David Van Bush: he was a regular customer, and he paid promptly and well. In 1917 Lovecraft was charging a rate of $1.00 for sixty lines of verse; by 1920 Bush had agreed to pay $1.00 for forty-eight lines; and by September 1922 Bush was paying him $1.00 for every eight lines of verse revised. This is a pretty remarkable rate, given that the best Lovecraft could do with his own professionally published poetry was to get 25 cents per line for verse in *Weird Tales*. Lovecraft goes on to note: 'I told him that only at this high price could I guarantee my own personal service—he doesn't like Morton's work so well, and asked me to do as much as possible myself.'[12] What this clearly means is that Lovecraft and Morton have teamed up to do revisory work. How formal was such an arrangement? It is difficult to tell, but consider the following ad that appeared in the amateur journal *L'Alouette* (edited by Charles A. A. Parker) in September 1924:

> THE CRAFTON SERVICE BUREAU offers the expert assistance of a group of highly trained and experienced specialists in the revision and typing of manuscripts of all kinds, prose or verse, at reasonable rates.
>
> THE BUREAU is also equipped with unusual facilities for all forms of research, having international affiliations of great importance. Its agents are in a position to prepare special articles on any topic at reasonable notice. It has a corps of able translators, and can offer the best of service in this department, covering all of the important classical and modern languages, including the international language Esperanto. It is also ready to prepare and supervise courses of home study or reading in any field, and to furnish expert confidential advice with reference to personal problems.
>
> APPLICATIONS and INQUIRIES may be addressed to either of the heads of THE BUREAU:
>
> Howard P. Lovecraft,
> 598 ANGELL STREET,   PROVIDENCE, R.I.
> James F. Morton, Jr.,
> 211 WEST 138TH STREET,   NEW YORK, N.Y.

Lovecraft (or Morton) has certainly caught the spirit of advertising! I have no idea how much business this wildly exaggerated ad— suggesting that Lovecraft and Morton were 'heads' of a non-existent bureau of editors, revisors, translators, and solvers of 'personal problems'—brought in; Bush seemed to remain Lovecraft's chief revision client until well into the 1920s. It is likely that many of the 'services' noted above were provided by Morton. Even those 'personal problems' were probably under Morton's jurisdiction, since among his published works was at least one collaborative treatise on sex morality. It is, in any case, difficult to imagine Lovecraft at this stage dealing with anyone's personal problems but his own.

In the midst of all this activity, both amateur and professional, Lovecraft finally embarked upon a career of professional fiction publication; inevitably, the opportunity was afforded him by amateur connections. Around September of 1921 George Julian Houtain (who had married the amateur writer E. Dorothy MacLoughlin) conceived the idea of launching a peppy and slightly off-colour humour magazine named *Home Brew*. As contributors he called upon his various amateur colleagues, and managed to secure pieces from James F. Morton, Rheinhart Kleiner, and others for early issues. For some strange reason he wished Lovecraft to write a serial horror story, even though such a thing would seemingly clash with the general humorous tone of the magazine. He offered Lovecraft the princely sum of $5.00 per two-thousand-word instalment (a quarter of a cent per word). 'You can't make them too morbid', Lovecraft reports Houtain telling him.[13] The first issue of the magazine duly appeared in February 1922, featuring the first instalment of 'Herbert West—Reanimator', which Houtain ran under the title 'Grewsome Tales' ('grewsome' was a legitimate spelling variant of 'gruesome' at this time).

Lovecraft takes a certain masochistic pleasure in complaining at being reduced to the level of a Grub Street hack. Over and over for the next several months he emits whines like the following:

> Now this is manifestly inartistic. To write to order, to drag one figure through a series of artificial episodes, involves the violation of all that spontaneity and singleness of impression which should characterise short story work. It reduces the unhappy author from art to the commonplace level of mechanical and unimaginative hack-work. Nevertheless, when one needs the money one is not scrupulous—so I have accepted the job![14]

One gets the impression that Lovecraft actually got a kick out of this literary slumming.

In spite of the fact that the six episodes of 'Herbert West—Reanimator' were clearly written over a long period—October 1921 to mid-June 1922—the tale does maintain unity of a sort, and Lovecraft seems to have conceived it as a single entity from the beginning: in the final episode all the imperfectly resurrected corpses raised by Herbert West come back to dispatch him hideously. In other ways the story builds up a certain cumulative power and suspense, and it is by no means Lovecraft's poorest fictional work. The structural weaknesses necessitated by the serial format are obvious and unavoidable: the need to recapitulate the plot of the foregoing episodes at the beginning of each new one, and the need for a horrific climax at the end of each episode.

No one would deem 'Herbert West—Reanimator' a masterpiece of subtlety, but it is rather engaging in its lurid way. It is also my belief that the story, while not *starting out* as a parody, *became* one as time went on. In other words, Lovecraft initially attempted to write a more or less serious, if quite 'grewsome', supernatural tale but, as he perceived the increasing absurdity of the enterprise, abandoned the attempt and turned the story into what it in fact was all along, a self-parody.

The question of influence might be worth studying briefly. It has casually been taken for granted that the obvious influence upon the story is *Frankenstein*; but I wonder whether this is the case. The method of West's reanimation of the dead (whole bodies that have died only recently) is very different from that of Victor Frankenstein (the assembling of a huge composite body from disparate parts of bodies), and only the most general influence can perhaps be detected. The core of the story is so elementary a weird conception that no literary source need be postulated.

It has frequently been believed—based upon Lovecraft's remark in June 1922 that 'the pay was a myth after the second cheque'[15]— that Lovecraft was never fully paid for the serial; but a letter to Samuel Loveman in November 1922 reports that Houtain has 'paid up his past debts' and even advanced Lovecraft $10 for the first two segments of 'The Lurking Fear'.[16]

Lovecraft managed to write two other stories while working desultorily on 'Herbert West—Reanimator', and they are very different propositions altogether. 'The Music of Erich Zann' appears to have been written in late 1921, probably December. The first of its many appearances was in the *National Amateur* for March 1922. The story—recounting the tale of Erich Zann, a mute viol-player who dwells in a lofty garret in Paris and apparently plays his bizarre music in order to ward off some nameless entity lurking just outside his window—justifiably remained one of Lovecraft's own favourite stories, for it reveals a restraint in its supernatural manifestations (bordering, for one of the few times in his entire work, on obscurity), a pathos in its depiction of its protagonist, and a general polish in its language that Lovecraft rarely achieved in later years.

The other story of this period is 'Hypnos', probably written in March 1922 and first published in the *National Amateur* for May

1923. It is a curious but quite substantial tale that has not received the attention it deserves, perhaps because Lovecraft himself in later years came to dislike it. 'Hypnos' tells of a sculptor who encounters another man at a railway station, becomes fascinated with him, and apparently undertakes weird dream-travels through space and time in his company. After a particularly horrifying experience, the two men strive to stay awake as much as possible, in an attempt to ward off the strange dreams. Later the friend disappears, and all that is left is an exquisite bust of him in marble, with the Greek word HYPNOS (sleep) inscribed at the base.

It would seem that the interpretation of this story rests on whether the narrator's friend actually existed or not; but this point may not affect the analysis appreciably. What we have here, ultimately, is, as with 'The Other Gods', a case of hybris, but on a much subtler level. At one point the narrator states: 'I will hint— only hint—that he had designs which involved the rulership of the visible universe and more; designs whereby the earth and the stars would move at his command, and the destinies of all living things be his.' This sounds somewhat extravagant, but in the context of the story it is powerful and effective, even though not much evidence is offered as to how the person could have effected this rulership of the universe. In the end, 'Hypnos' is a subtilization of a theme already broached in several earlier tales, notably 'Beyond the Wall of Sleep'—the notion that certain 'dreams' provide access to other realms of entity beyond that of the five senses or waking world.

Shortly after writing 'Hypnos' Lovecraft began a series of peregrinations that would not end until October. First on the agenda was Lovecraft's first trip out of New England—his New York jaunt of 6– 12 April. The trip was, of course, arranged by Sonia. She had visited Cleveland on business some time in late 1921 or early 1922, and there met both Samuel Loveman and Alfred Galpin, who had temporarily settled there after finishing his work at Lawrence College. Developing the idea of convening a group of Lovecraft's best friends in New York, Sonia persuaded Loveman to come to the metropolis to look for work. Loveman arrived on 1 April but had little success in job-hunting. As a way of keeping him in the city— and, coincidentally, of uprooting Lovecraft from his hermitry— Sonia telephoned Lovecraft and urged him to come down to meet his longtime correspondent. Loveman, Morton, and Kleiner added their encouragement, and Lovecraft's new protégé Frank Long was also likely to be on hand. These massed invitations did the trick, and Lovecraft caught the 10.06 train from Providence on the 6th.

Five hours later he saw the 'Cyclopean outlines of New-York'[17] for the first time. There followed an endless round of discussion with his friends, along with museum visiting, sightseeing (they ascended to the top of the Woolworth Building, then the tallest structure in the city), bookstore-hunting, and all the other things that most tourists of a bookish sort do when they hit the big city. Sonia magnanimously turned over her own apartment at 259 Parkside Avenue in Brooklyn to Loveman and Lovecraft, herself sleeping in a neighbour's apartment. She reports in her memoir at being 'amazed at myself' for her 'boldness'[18] in inviting two men to be guests in her flat.

Certainly the high point for Lovecraft was meeting two of his closest friends, Loveman and Long. Of course, he met often with Sonia, and even once met her 'flapper offspring' Florence—a 'pert, spoiled, and ultra-independent infant rather more hard-boiled of visage than her benignant mater'.[19] Sonia cooked several meals for the gang at her place, which even the ascetic Lovecraft admitted to enjoying. One of the most provocative passages in her memoir relates to an event toward the end of Lovecraft's stay:

> Soon S. L. returned to Cleveland and H. P. remained. My neighbor who so kindly made room for me had a beautiful Persian cat which she brought to my apartment. As soon as H. P. saw that cat he made 'love' to it. He seemed to have a language that the feline brother understood, for it curled right up in his lap and purred contentedly.
>
> Half in earnest, half in jest I remarked, 'What a lot of perfectly good affection to waste on a mere cat, when some woman might highly appreciate it!' His retort was, 'How can any woman love a face like mine?' My counter-retort was, 'A mother can and some who are not mothers would not have to try very hard.' We all laughed while Felis was enjoying some more stroking.[20]

At this point one hardly need belabour Lovecraft's inferiority complex about his appearance. But Sonia's intentions were already becoming clear, although perhaps she herself was not yet wholly aware of them.

In late May he visited Myrta Alice Little again in New Hampshire.

In early or mid-June was the Cambridge trip to hear David Van Bush lecture. Later that month Sonia, striking while the iron was hot, found a way to spend time in New England and do much visiting with Lovecraft, taking him to Magnolia, Massachusetts, a fashionable watering-place north of Boston. Sonia persuaded Lovecraft to spend several days with her in Magnolia and Gloucester in late June and early July. One evening, while they were strolling along the esplanade on the cliffs of Magnolia, the view of the moon reflecting its light upon the ocean so struck Sonia that she evolved the plot of a horror tale. Encouraged by Lovecraft, she presently wrote it, and Lovecraft revised it. The result was 'The Horror at Martin's Beach', a wild and improbable story about a sea monster that appeared in *Weird Tales* for November 1923 (under Sonia's name only) as 'The Invisible Monster'.

Another story that may have been written at this time is a short macabre tale called 'Four O'Clock'. In a letter to Winfield Townley Scott, Sonia declares that Lovecraft only suggested changes in the prose of the tale;[21] hence I concluded that it does not belong in the Lovecraft corpus and did not include it in the revised version of *The Horror in the Museum and Other Revisions* (1989). Judging, however, from her later memoir, Sonia does not seem to have been a very skilled, polished, or even coherent writer, so that Lovecraft probably did contribute something to this story, which is even slighter than its predecessor.

Sonia adds a startling note about what happened the day after 'The Horror at Martin's Beach' was conceived:

> His continued enthusiasm the next day was so genuine and sincere that in appreciation I surprised and shocked him right then and there by kissing him. He was so flustered that he blushed, then he turned pale. When I chaffed him about it he said he had not been kissed since he was a very small child and that he was never kissed by any woman, not even by his mother or aunts, since he grew to manhood, and that he would probably never be kissed again. (But I fooled him.)[22]

This really is pretty remarkable. First, if Lovecraft's statement here is true, it certainly makes his 'romance' with Winifred Jackson an exceptionally platonic one. Second, the matter of his not being kissed even by his aunts or mother since he was a young man makes us wonder about the degree of reserve in this old New

England family. Lovecraft's affection for his aunts—and theirs for him—is unquestioned; but such an unusual lack of physical intimacy is anomalous even for the time and for their social milieu. No wonder Lovecraft was so slow to respond to a woman who so openly expressed affection for him. His emotions had clearly been stunted in this direction.

This week-long trip with Sonia was, as far as I can tell, the first time Lovecraft had spent any considerable amount of time alone in the company of a woman to whom he was not related. Sonia was keen on pursuing matters and managed to get up to Rhode Island again on Sunday 16 July, when she and Lovecraft went to Newport.

Ten days later, on Wednesday 26 July, we find Lovecraft writing again from Sonia's apartment in Brooklyn: somehow she had managed to persuade him to undertake a trip to Cleveland to see Galpin and Loveman. He spent only three days in a stopover in New York, for on Saturday 29 July, at 6.30 p.m., he boarded the Lake Shore Limited at Grand Central Station for the long train ride to Cleveland. The ride took sixteen hours, and Lovecraft arrived in Cleveland at 10.30 a.m. on the 30th.

Lovecraft stayed until 15 August, mostly at Galpin's residence at 9231 Birchdale Avenue (the building is now no longer standing). Their habits were roughly in accord with Lovecraft's own behaviour-patterns at home: 'We rise at noon, eat twice a day, and retire after midnight.' An interesting note on the state of Lovecraft's physical and psychological health is recorded in a later letter to Lillian:

> As for the kind of time I am having—it is simply great! I have just the incentive I need to keep me active & free from melancholy, & I look so well that I doubt if any Providence person would know me by sight! I have no headaches or depressed spells—in short, I am for the time being really alive & in good health & spirits. The companionship of youth & artistic taste is what keeps one going![23]

Freedom from his mother's (and, to a lesser degree, his aunts') stifling control, travel to different parts of the country, and the company of congenial friends who regarded him with fondness, respect, and admiration will do wonders for a cloistered recluse who never travelled a hundred miles away from home up to the age of thirty-one.

Naturally, they met Samuel Loveman (staying at the Lonore Apartments around the corner) frequently, and it was through

Loveman that Lovecraft met several other distinguished littérateurs —George Kirk (1898–1962), the bookseller who had just published Loveman's edition of Ambrose Bierce's *Twenty-one Letters* (1922), and, most notably, the young Hart Crane (1899–1932) and his circle of literary and artistic friends. Lovecraft reports attending a meeting of 'all the members of Loveman's literary circle':

> It gave me a novel sensation to be 'lionised' so much beyond my deserts by men as able as the painter Summers [*sic*], Loveman, Galpin, &c. I met some new figures—Crane the poet, Lazar [*sic*], an ambitious young literary student now in the army, & a delightful young fellow named Carroll Lawrence, who writes weird stories & wants to see all of mine.[24]

I shall have more to say about both Kirk and Crane later, since Lovecraft would meet them again during his New York period; for now we can note this brief meeting with William Sommer, the watercolourist and draughtsman; William Lescaze, later to become an internationally known architect; Edward Lazare (whom Lovecraft would meet again in New York, and who in later years would become a long-time editor of *American Book-Prices Current*); and others of Crane's circle. Crane had just begun to publish his poetry in magazines, although his first volume, *White Buildings*, would not appear until 1926. Lovecraft must, however, have read Crane's 'Pastorale' (in the *Dial* for October 1921), for he wrote a parody of it entitled 'Plaster-All'. While an amusing take-off of what Lovecraft believed to be the formless free verse of the modernists, the poem is really a sort of impressionistic—dare one say imagistic?—account of his Cleveland trip.

Another person with whom Lovecraft came into contact at this time, although only by correspondence, was Clark Ashton Smith. Loveman and Smith were long-time correspondents, and the former showed Lovecraft Smith's paintings and sketches, while Galpin and Kirk, respectively, presented Lovecraft with copies of Smith's early collections of poetry, *The Star-Treader and Other Poems* (1912) and *Odes and Sonnets* (1918). So taken was Lovecraft with both the pictorial and literary material that he forthwith wrote Smith a fan letter toward the end of his Cleveland stay. This almost effusively flattering letter initiated a fifteen-year correspondence that would end only with Lovecraft's death.

Clark Ashton Smith (1893–1961) has suffered an anomalous fate precisely because his work is so distinctive and unclassifiable.

His early collections of poetry are in a *fin-de-siècle* vein somewhat in the manner of Swinburne or George Sterling (Smith's early mentor), but very distinctively Smith's own. Indeed, upon the publication of that first volume, at the age of nineteen, Smith—a native of California who was born in Long Valley and lived most of his life in Auburn—was hailed by local reviewers as a new Keats or Shelley. These accolades were perhaps not far from the truth. To my mind, Smith's early poems are quite superior to the 'cosmic' poetry of George Sterling, although he has clearly learnt much from Sterling's *The Testimony of the Suns* (1903) and *A Wine of Wizardry* (1907). The problem for Smith—or, rather, for his recognition as a significant poet—is that the tradition of weird or fantastic poetry is not very deep or substantial; moreover, modern enthusiasts (and critics) of weird literature seem uncomfortable with poetry, so that the tremendous body of Smith's verse has been ignored by exactly those readers who might be expected to champion it and keep it alive. And although Smith wrote some free verse, much of his work is written both in formal metres and in a very elevated, metaphor-laden diction in utter contrast to the flat, conversational, and (in my judgment) entirely prosaic work of the 'poets' who, following the dreary example of William Carlos Williams and Ezra Pound, are currently fashionable. Is it any wonder that Smith's poetry, after its initial praise on the West Coast, fell on deaf ears and remains one of the lost jewels of twentieth-century literature?

Smith did not help his cause by churning out reams of fantasy and science fiction tales in the late 1920s and early 1930s, some (perhaps much) of it written under Lovecraft's encouragement. This body of work hangs on after a fashion as a very acquired taste, but to me it is much inferior to his verse; I shall have more to say of it later. If Smith did any good work in prose, it is in the prose-poems, some of which Lovecraft read and admired in the volume *Ebony and Crystal* (1918). This work is toweringly impressive, and it could be maintained quite plausibly that Smith is the best prose-poet in English; but this form is too recondite to inspire much of a following or much critical attention.

As for Smith's art work, I find it quite amateurish and crude, and have no idea why Lovecraft so rhapsodized over it. Smith was a self-taught artist, and it shows; this work is, to be sure, reminiscent of primitive art, and occasionally some startlingly weird effects are produced, but much of it—in pen and ink, crayon, watercolour, and oil—is imaginatively powerful but technically very backward. His small sculptures and figurines are somewhat more interesting. Lovecraft, however, never ceased to admire Smith as another Blake who could both write great work and illustrate it.

For the time being, however, it was the benefits and delights of travel that were in the forefront of Lovecraft's mind. Leaving for New York on 15 August, he spent at least two months as Sonia's guest in Brooklyn, making an unheard-of total of nearly three solid months away from 598 Angell Street. This long trip was made possible by the unstinting generosity of Lovecraft's friends: just as Loveman, Galpin, and Kirk insisted on picking up many of his expenses (especially meals) in Cleveland, so did Long (or, more precisely, his parents) frequently have Lovecraft over for lunch or dinner, and no doubt Sonia made or paid for many meals as well. I do not believe there was any condescension in this: Lovecraft's friends surely knew of his lean purse, but their hospitality was a product of both their own kindness and genuine fondness for Lovecraft and their desire to have him stay as long as possible. We shall find this becoming a repeated pattern in all Lovecraft's peregrinations for the rest of his life.

How did the aunts take this extended departure of their only nephew? As early as 9 August, in Cleveland, Lovecraft writes to Lillian, rather touchingly: 'I am sorry you miss me—though much flattered that you should do so!' In September Sonia and Lovecraft attempted to persuade one or both of the aunts to come and join them in New York; the staid Lillian declined, but Annie—who in her younger days was very much the socialite—accepted.

On the evening of 16 September Lovecraft and Kleiner explored the exquisite Dutch Reformed Church (1796) on Flatbush Avenue in Brooklyn, quite near to Sonia's apartment. This magnificent structure contains a sinister old churchyard at its rear, full of crumbling slabs in Dutch. What did Lovecraft do?

> From one of the crumbling gravestones—dated 1747—I chipped a small piece to carry away. It lies before me as I write—& ought to suggest some sort of a horror-story. I must some night place it beneath my pillow as I sleep … who can say what *thing* might not come out of the centuried earth to exact vengeance for his desecrated tomb?[25]

True enough, the incident led directly to the writing of 'The Hound', probably in October after he returned home. This story involves the escapades of the narrator and his friend St John (based very loosely on Kleiner, whom Lovecraft referred to in correspondence as Randolph St John, as if he were a relative of Henry St John, Viscount Bolingbroke) in that 'hideous extremity of human outrage, the abhorred practice of grave-robbing'.

'The Hound' has been roundly abused for being wildly overwritten; but it has somehow managed to escape most critics' attention that the story is clearly a self-parody. This becomes increasingly evident from obvious literary allusions as well as from such grotesque utterances as 'Bizarre manifestations were now too frequent to count'. And yet, the story is undeniably successful as an experiment in sheer flamboyance and excess, so long as one keeps in mind that Lovecraft was clearly aiming for such an effect and was doing so at least partially with tongue in cheek.

Lovecraft finally returned home in mid-October. Houtain was already asking him for another serial, this time to run in four parts. Lovecraft dawdled on the task through mid-November, but—perhaps because Houtain finally paid up for 'Herbert West—Reanimator' and advanced him half the payment for the new story—finally got down to work and wrote 'The Lurking Fear' later in the month. Since this story was written in a far more condensed period of time than 'Herbert West—Reanimator', it presents a somewhat greater impression of unity than its predecessor, in spite of the need to provide a shocking conclusion at the end of each segment.

No one is likely to regard 'The Lurking Fear' as one of Lovecraft's masterworks, even among his early tales; and yet, it is not as contemptible a tale as many critics have deemed it, and once again it contains many foreshadowings of techniques and devices used to better advantage in later works. The tale moves briskly in its account of the narrator's search for the unknown entity that had wreaked havoc amongst the squatters of the Catskills near the Martense mansion. In the end we learn that there is not a single entity, but a legion of mutants who are nothing less than the result of centuries of interbreeding among members of the ancient and formerly aristocratic Martense family.

'The Lurking Fear' appeared in *Home Brew* from January to April 1923. Presumably at Lovecraft's request, Clark Ashton Smith was commissioned to illustrate the serial, supplying two illustrations per instalment. The last issue announces that the magazine will change its name to *High Life*; after this change of name the magazine folded in 1924. No doubt Lovecraft was glad to be rid of the 'vile rag'.[26]

Although it was late in the year and Lovecraft's sensitivity to cold would not allow him to venture abroad very much, his travels for 1922 were not quite over. In mid-December he visited Boston to participate in a Hub Club meeting with Edith Miniter and others. Afterward he decided to do some solitary antiquarian exploration of some of the towns on the North Shore, specifically Salem. Salem was certainly a delight—it was Lovecraft's first true experience of the seventeenth century, and he canvassed the Witch House (1642), the House of the Seven Gables, and other celebrated sites— but while there he learnt from natives that there was another town a little farther up the coast called Marblehead that was even quainter. Taking a bus there, Lovecraft was 'borne into the most marvellous region I had ever dream'd of, and furnished with the most powerful single aesthetick impression I have receiv'd in years'.[27]

Marblehead was—and, on the whole, today remains—one of the most charming little backwaters in Massachusetts, full of well-restored colonial houses, crooked and narrow streets, and a spectral hilltop burying-ground from which one can derive a magnificent panoramic view of the city and the nearby harbour. In the old part of town the antiquity is strangely *complete*, and very little of the modern intrudes there. It was this that so captivated Lovecraft. More than seven years later Lovecraft was still attesting to the poignancy of his initial witnessing of the place:

> God! Shall I ever forget my first stupefying glimpse of MARBLEHEAD'S huddled and archaick roofs under the snow in the delirious sunset glory of four p.m., Dec. 17, 1922!!! I did not know until an hour before that I should ever behold such a place as Marblehead, and I did not know *until that moment itself* the full extent of the wonder I was to behold. I account that instant—about 4:05 to 4:10 p.m., Dec. 17, 1922—the most powerful single emotional climax experienced during my nearly forty years of existence. In a flash all the past of New England—all the past of Old England—all the past of Anglo-Saxondom and the Western World—swept over me and identified me with the stupendous totality of all things in such a way as it never did before and never will again. That was the high tide of my life.[28]

What exactly was it about Marblehead that so struck him? Lovecraft clarifies it himself: with his tremendous imaginative faculty—and with the visible tokens of the present almost totally banished for at least a short interval—Lovecraft felt himself united with his entire cultural and racial past. As he said in another context: 'The past is *real*—it is *all there is.*'[29]

It would take Lovecraft nearly a year—and several more trips to Marblehead—to internalize his impressions and transmute them into fiction; but when he did so, in 'The Festival' (1923), he would be well on his way to revivifying New England in some of the most topographically and historically rooted weird fiction ever written. He had begun haltingly to head in this direction, with 'The Picture in the House'; but New England was still relatively undiscovered territory to him, and it would take many more excursions for him to imbibe the essence of the area—not merely its antiquities and its history, but its people and their intimate and centuried relations with the soil—and render it fit for fictional use. And it would also take those two years away from New England to make him realize how much he really was moulded of its flesh, so that he could express both the terror and the beauty of this ancient land.

CHAPTER TEN

For My Own Amusement
(1923–24)

At just the time when Lovecraft's activity in the UAPA seemed on the wane, his involvement with the NAPA took on a sudden and wholly unforeseen turn: it was nothing less than his appointment, on 30 November, as interim President to replace William J. Dowdell, who was forced to resign. It is not clear what led to Dowdell's decision: Lovecraft later commented that Dowdell 'ran off with a chorus girl in 1922'.[1]

Lovecraft made the first of five official reports (four 'President's Messages' and a 'President's Annual Report') for the issue of the *National Amateur* dated November 1922–January 1923. The report, written on 11 January 1923, is an eloquent plea for the resumption of activity in light of the confusion involving the official board and the general apathy apparently overtaking all amateurdom; Lovecraft himself promised to issue another number or two of his *Conservative*, and came through on the promise. Most incredible of all, given his chronic poverty, Lovecraft himself contributed $10 (the equivalent of a week's rent in his New York period) to the official organ fund. Approaching the completion of his ninth year of amateur activity, Lovecraft found himself still drawn to the cause.

As early as February, Edward H. Cole was urging Lovecraft to run for President for the 1923–24 term. Lovecraft blanched at the idea, for he profoundly disliked the tedious administrative burdens that went with the office; in any event, his re-election as Official Editor of the UAPA in July 1923 compelled him to turn his attention back to his original amateur organization. It would be a decade before he would resume ties with the NAPA.

One notable event was Lovecraft's first appearance in hardcover, in a volume entitled *The Poetical Works of Jonathan E. Hoag*. Hoag was the ancient poet (born 1831) in Troy, New York, for whom Lovecraft had been writing annual birthday odes since 1918. Now he wished to see a bound book of his verse, and enlisted Lovecraft to gather, revise, and publish his work. Lovecraft in turn called upon Loveman and Morton to aid him. Hoag was clearly footing the bill for the entire enterprise—a point worth emphasizing, since it has long been believed that Lovecraft himself helped to subsidize the book, a highly unlikely prospect given the leanness of his purse. The finished book emerged late in the spring; incredibly, Lovecraft waived 'all monetary remuneration for my share of the editing'[2] in exchange for twenty copies of the book!

Meanwhile there was much more travel in the offing. Lovecraft visited the Salem–Marblehead area at least three times early in 1923—in early February, in March, and again in April. On the third trip he went to Danvers—the town, once called Salem-Village, founded in 1636 by some members of the original settlement of 1626, and where the 1692 witch trials had taken place—and thoroughly explored the Samuel Fowler house (1809), occupied by two hideous old crones who were descendants of the original owner. He then proceeded out into the countryside, seeking the farmhouse built by Townsend Bishop in 1636—the place where Rebekah Nurse lived in 1692 when she was accused of witchcraft by the slave woman Tituba and, at the age of seventy, hanged on Gallows Hill. He found both the farmhouse and Rebekah Nurse's grave some distance away. Unlike the Fowler place, the farmhouse was of a cramped seventeenth-century design with low rooms and massive wooden beams.

The next day (14 April) Lovecraft set out for Merrimac, where his young amateur friend Edgar J. Davis (age fifteen) lived. The two of them visited graveyards in nearby Amesbury (where the poet Whittier had lived), and the next day they headed for Newburyport. This coastal town has now been made into a yuppie resort, but in 1923 it was a quiet little backwater that preserved its antiquities in almost as complete a state as Marblehead. So little life did the town have that Lovecraft and Davis rode the trolley car all the way through it without realizing that they had passed through the centre of town, which was their destination. Returning on foot to the central square, Lovecraft and Davis revelled in the atmosphere of the past of a once-thriving colonial seaport.

Sonia paid Lovecraft a call in Providence on 15–17 July. This is the first we hear of the two meeting since Lovecraft's visit to New York the preceding September, but Sonia makes clear that in the two years preceding their marriage in March 1924 they engaged in 'almost daily correspondence—H. P. writing me about everything he did and everywhere he went, introducing names of friends and his evaluation of them, sometimes filling 30, 40 and even 50 pages of finely written script'.[3] What a shame that Sonia felt the need to burn all those letters! The visit in July was a joint business-pleasure trip on her part: on Monday the 16th Lovecraft showed Sonia the customary antiquities of Providence; then, on Tuesday the 17th, the two of them went to the coastal town of Narragansett Pier, in the southern part of the state overlooking the ocean, passing through Apponaug, East Greenwich, and Kingston along the way. On the return trip Sonia continued on to Boston while Lovecraft went home.

On 10 August occurred no less momentous an event than Lovecraft's first personal visit with his longtime friend Maurice W. Moe, who was making a tour of the East. Lovecraft met him at the Providence YMCA that morning, showing him all the local sites before boarding a bus to Boston, where they would meet Cole, Albert A. Sandusky, and Moe's wife and two children, Robert (age eleven) and Donald (age nine). The next day Lovecraft performed his customary tour-guide act, as Cole relates in a memoir:

> I recall vividly the Saturday afternoon ... when Lovecraft, Maurice Moe, Albert Sandusky, and I went to Old Marblehead to visit the numerous Colonial houses and other places of interest with which Howard was thoroughly familiar. He was so insistent that our friend from the West should not miss a single relic or point of view over lovely town and harbor that he walked us relentlessly for miles, impelled solely by his inexhaustible enthusiasm until our bodies rebelled and, against his protests, we dragged ourselves to the train. Lovecraft was still buoyant.[4]

So much for the sickly recluse of a decade before!

Although he was scarcely aware of it at the time, the summer of 1923 brought a radical change in Lovecraft's literary career—perhaps as radical as his discovery of amateur journalism nine years previously. Whether the change was all for the good is a matter we shall have to consider at a later stage. In March of 1923 the first issue of *Weird Tales* appeared, and a month or two later Lovecraft was urged—initially by Everett McNeil (an author of boys' books whom Lovecraft had met in New York) and Morton, but probably by Clark Ashton Smith and others as well—to submit to it.

Weird Tales was the brainchild of Jacob Clark Henneberger, who with J. M. Lansinger founded Rural Publications, Inc., in 1922 to publish a variety of popular magazines. Henneberger had already achieved great success with the magazine *College Humor*, and he now envisioned founding a line of varied periodicals in the detective and horror field. Henneberger had received assurances from such established writers as Hamlin Garland and Ben Hecht that they would be willing to contribute stories of the 'unconventional' which they could not land in the 'slicks' or other magazines, but they failed to come through when the magazine was actually launched.[5] As later events will show, Henneberger founded *Weird Tales* not out of some altruistic goal of fostering artistic weird literature but largely in order to make money by featuring big-name writers; and when this did not happen, he quickly freed himself of his creation. *Weird Tales* never made any significant amount of money, and on several occasions—especially during the Depression—it came close to folding; but somehow it managed to hang on for thirty-one years and 279 issues, an unprecedented run for a pulp magazine.

Henneberger selected Edwin Baird (1886–1957) as editor, with assistance from Farnsworth Wright and Otis Adelbert Kline. Baird did not appear to have any great sensitivity to the weird. The first several issues—which varied in dimensions from 6 by 9 inches to an ungainly 'bedsheet' size, all with very crude and amateurish covers—are a decidedly mixed bag: the March 1923 issue featured a striking novelette, 'Ooze' by Anthony M. Rud, which Lovecraft enjoyed, but otherwise contained a rag-tag farrago of amateurish and outlandish stories largely written by beginning writers. Few established writers, even from the pulp field, appeared in the early issues: Harold Ward, Vincent Starrett, Don Mark Lemon, and Francis Stevens are the only recognizable names. Throughout its run *Weird Tales* was much more congenial to new writers than other pulps, a policy that had both advantages and drawbacks.

Lovecraft no doubt read those early issues of *Weird Tales*, finding some of the tales quite powerful. Indeed, even if Morton and others had not advised him to submit to *Weird Tales*, he might eventually have done so on his own; for he was clearly making efforts—naive and clumsy as they may have been—to break into professional print on a higher grade than *Home Brew*. As early as 1919, at the urging of one of his aunts, he submitted 'The Tomb' to the *Black Cat*;[6] at some later date he submitted 'Dagon' to *Black Mask*. Both stories were rejected. This was perhaps not the wisest choice in either instance. Although Lovecraft had read some of the early issues of *Black Cat* around the turn of the century, the magazine was not primarily devoted to weird fiction and published, proportionately, much less of it than the Munseys. As for *Black Mask*, it was founded in 1920 as an all-purpose fiction magazine; but by the mid–1920s the earliest stories by Carroll John Daly and Dashiell Hammett were appearing in it, and under the editorship of Joseph T. Shaw, who took over in November 1926, *Black Mask* would become the nurturing ground for the hard-boiled school of detective fiction. The occasional ghost story did appear, but such an excursion into archaic, Poe-esque horror as 'The Tomb' was not likely to find a home there.

What is more, when Lovecraft did submit to *Weird Tales*, he sent five tales simultaneously—'Dagon', 'Arthur Jermyn', 'The Cats of Ulthar', 'The Hound', and 'The Statement of Randolph Carter'—along with a cover letter that took pains to point out the rejection of 'Dagon' by *Black Cat*. Baird replied to Lovecraft in a personal letter, saying that he would consider accepting these tales if they were typed double-spaced. (Lovecraft, used to the relatively informal policies of the amateur journals and probably wanting to save paper, had typed them single spaced.) For one whose loathing of the typewriter would in later years reach phobic proportions, the prospect of having to undergo such a labour for what he believed to be a not entirely certain assurance of acceptance was formidable; but he finally typed 'Dagon', which was accepted, as were the other four.

It is one of the many anomalies of Lovecraft's involvement with *Weird Tales* that his first published work in the magazine was not a story but a letter. With a certain impishness, Baird printed the bulk of Lovecraft's cover letter accompanying his five tales; this letter appeared in the September 1923 issue, by which time his tales had been accepted. Here are some extracts:

> My Dear Sir: Having a habit of writing weird, macabre, and fantastic stories for my own amusement, I have lately been simultaneously hounded by nearly a dozen well-meaning friends into deciding to submit a few of these Gothic horrors to your newly-founded periodical ...

> I have no idea that these things will be found suitable, for I pay no attention to the demands of commercial writing. My object is such pleasure as I can obtain from the creation of certain bizarre pictures, situations, or atmospheric effects; and the only reader I hold in mind is myself ...
>
> I like *Weird Tales* very much, though I have seen only the April number. Most of the stories, of course, are more or less commercial—or should I say conventional?—in technique, but they all have an enjoyable angle ...

No wonder Baird added at the end of this letter: 'Despite the foregoing, or because of it, we are using some of Mr. Lovecraft's unusual stories.' One would like to think that the letter was in some senses a self-parody, but it does not appear to be. Highbrow and condescending as it may appear, it quite accurately reflects the aesthetic theory Lovecraft had by this time evolved.

Lovecraft quickly became a fixture with *Weird Tales*, appearing in five of the six issues from October 1923 to April 1924 (there was no issue for December 1923). He might even be thought to have appeared in all six, if the publication of Sonia Greene's 'The Horror at Martin's Beach' (retitled, to Lovecraft's chagrin, 'The Invisible Monster') in the November 1923 issue can count as one of his appearances.

Lovecraft no doubt found the money he received from the magazine a small but welcome relief from poverty. *Weird Tales* paid upon publication, not (as the better grade of pulps and all the 'slicks' did) on acceptance; and, judging from the evidence of his early payments, he appears initially to have received much better than the standard 1 cent a word. For 'Dagon', a story of scarcely 2500 words, he received $55, a rate of more than 2 cents a word. Later this rate would decline, but Lovecraft would still receive *Weird Tales*' 'highest' rate of $1\frac{1}{2}$ cents a word.

Another event of the summer of 1923 that significantly affected Lovecraft's weird fiction was the discovery of the great Welsh writer Arthur Machen (1863–1947; pronounced MACK-en). As with his discoveries of Ambrose Bierce and Lord Dunsany in 1919, it is a wonder that he had not read him earlier, for Machen's greatest celebrity had been in the 1890s and by 1923 he was already regarded as having done his best work long before. Machen had attained not merely fame but actual notoriety with such works as *The Great God Pan and The Inmost Light* (1894), *The Three Impostors*

(1895), *The House of Souls* (1906), and *The Hill of Dreams* (1907), which many believed to be the outpourings of a diseased mind. In fact, Machen himself subscribed to the same Victorian sexual pruderies he so seemingly flouted; and the covert intimations of aberrant sex in such tales as 'The Great God Pan' and 'The White People' were as horrifying to him as they were to his audience. Temperamentally Machen was not at all similar to Lovecraft: an unwavering Anglo-Catholic, violently hostile to science and materialism, seeking always for some mystical sense of 'ecstasy' that might liberate him from what he fancied to be the prosiness of contemporary life, Machen would have found Lovecraft's mechanistic materialism and atheism repugnant in the extreme. They may have shared a general hostility to the modern age, but they were coming at it from very different directions. And yet, because Machen so sincerely feels the sense of sin and transgression in those things that 'religion brands with outlawry and horror',[7] he manages to convey his sentiments to the reader in such a way that his work remains powerful and effective. Lovecraft himself came to regard 'The White People' as second to Algernon Blackwood's 'The Willows' as the greatest weird tale of all time; he may well be right.

Although Lovecraft dutifully read as much of Machen as he could, it was the horror tales that remained closest to his heart. In particular, a whole series of works—including 'The White People', 'The Shining Pyramid', 'Novel of the Black Seal' (a segment of the episodic novel *The Three Impostors*), and others—make use of the old legends of the 'Little People', a supposedly pre-Aryan race of dwarfish devils who still live covertly in the secret places of the earth and occasionally steal human infants, leaving one of their own behind. Lovecraft would transform this topos into something even more sinister in some of his later tales.

Lovecraft seems to have owed the discovery of Machen to Frank Long. I cannot detect any Machen influence on Lovecraft's tales prior to 1926, but the Welshman's work clearly filtered into Lovecraft's imagination and eventually emerged in a quite transformed but still perceptible manner in some of his best-known stories.

Lovecraft had, indeed, not written any stories since 'The Lurking Fear' in November 1922; but then, in a matter of two or three months, he wrote three in quick succession—'The Rats in the Walls', 'The Unnamable', and 'The Festival'. All three are of considerable interest, and the first is without question the greatest tale of Lovecraft's early period.

The plot of 'The Rats in the Walls' (probably written in late August or early September) is deceptively simple. A Virginian of British ancestry, a man named Delapore, decides to spend his latter years in refurbishing and occupying his ancestral estate in southern England, Exham Priory, whose foundations go disturbingly far back in time, to a period even before the Roman conquest of the first century A.D. Delapore hears of some strange legends attached to the house—including the tale of a huge army of rats that devoured everything in its path in the Middle Ages—but dispenses them as pure myth. A variety of weird manifestations (many of them sounding like rats scurrying in the walls of the castle) then begin to appear following Delapore's occupation of the place on 16 July 1923, culminating in an exploration (with a number of learned scientists) of the cellar of the castle. There the explorers come upon an immense expanse of bones, and it becomes evident that Delapore's own ancestors were the leaders of a cannibalistic witch-cult that had its origins in primitive times. Delapore goes mad, descends the evolutionary scale (heralded by the increasing archaism of the oaths he utters at the end), and is found bent over the half-eaten form of his friend, Capt. Norrys.

It is difficult to convey the richness and cumulative horror of this story in any analysis; next to *The Case of Charles Dexter Ward*, it is Lovecraft's greatest triumph in the old-time 'Gothic' vein—although even here the stock Gothic features (the ancient castle with a secret chamber; the ghostly legendry that proves to be founded on fact) have been modernized and refined so as to be wholly convincing. And the fundamental premise of the story—that a human being can suddenly reverse the course of evolution—could only have been written by one who had accepted the Darwinian theory.

Certain surface features of the tale—and perhaps one essential kernel of the plot—were taken from other works. As Steven J. Mariconda has pointed out,[8] Lovecraft's account of the 'epic of the rats' appears to be derived from a chapter in S. Baring-Gould's *Curious Myths of the Middle Ages* (1869). Some portions of Delapore's concluding cries were lifted directly from Fiona Macleod's 'The Sin-Eater', which Lovecraft read in Joseph Lewis French's anthology, *Best Psychic Stories* (1920).

More significantly, the very idea of atavism or reversion to type seems to have been derived from a story by Irvin S. Cobb, 'The Unbroken Chain', published in *Cosmopolitan* for September 1923 (the issue, as is still customary with many magazines, was probably on the stands at least a month before its cover date). Lovecraft admits that Long gave him the magazine in 1923.[9] This tale deals with a Frenchman who has a small proportion of negroid blood from a slave brought to America in 1819. When he is run down by a train, he cries out in an African language—'*Niama tumba!*'—the words that his black ancestor shouted when he was attacked by a rhinoceros in Africa.

'The Rats in the Walls' was first submitted, not to *Weird Tales*, but to the *Argosy All-Story Weekly*, a Munsey magazine whose managing editor, Robert H. Davis, rejected it as being (in Lovecraft's words) 'too horrible for the tender sensibilities of a delicately nurtured publick'.[10] Lovecraft then sent the story to Baird, who accepted it and ran it in the March 1924 issue.

'The Unnamable' and 'The Festival', Lovecraft's two other original stories of 1923, return to New England in their different ways. The former is slight, but could be thought of as a sort of veiled justification for the type of weird tale Lovecraft was evolving; much of it reads like a treatise on aesthetics. At the beginning there is a lengthy discussion on the weird between Randolph Carter and Joel Manton (clearly based upon Maurice W. Moe). Manton does not believe that there can be anything in life or literature that could be 'unnamable'; but he finds out differently when such an entity attacks them as they are sitting in a New England churchyard.

Aside from its interesting aesthetic reflections, 'The Unnamable' fosters that sense of the lurking horror of New England history and topography which we have already seen in 'The Picture in the House', and which would become a dominant trope in Lovecraft's later work. The tale is set in Arkham, but the actual inspiration for the setting—a 'dilapidated seventeenth-century tomb' and, nearby, a 'giant willow in the centre of the cemetery, whose trunk has nearly engulfed an ancient, illegible slab'—is the Charter Street Burying Ground in Salem, where just such a tree-engulfed slab can be found.

'The Festival' (written probably in October) can be considered a virtual three-thousand-word prose-poem for the sustained modulation of its prose. The first-person narrator comes back to Kingsport and is led into an underground chamber beneath a church and encounters spectacular winged horrors that fly off into the unknown, bearing the inhabitants of the town on their backs. This is the first story in which the mythical town of Kingsport (first cited in 'The Terrible Old Man') is definitively identified with Marblehead.

Much of the topography cited in the story corresponds exactly with that of Marblehead, although some of the actual sites mentioned have only recently been identified by Donovan K. Loucks. For example, the church that is the focal point of the tale is probably not St Michael's Episcopal Church, as has long been thought. If Lovecraft had a specific church in in mind, he may have been referring either to the First Meeting House (built in 1648 on Old Burial Hill) or the Second Congregational Church (built in 1715 at 28 Mugford Street), or a fusion of the two.

There is, in addition to the topography of Marblehead, a literary (or scientific) influence to the story. In 1933 Lovecraft stated in reference to the tale: 'In intimating an alien race I had in mind the survival of some clan of pre-Aryan sorcerers who preserved primitive rites like those of the witch-cult—I had just been reading Miss Murray's *The Witch-Cult in Western Europe*.'[11] This landmark work of anthropology by Margaret A. Murray, published in 1921, made the claim (now regarded by modern scholars as highly unlikely) that the witch-cult in both Europe and America had its origin in a pre-Aryan race that was driven underground but continued to lurk in the hidden corners of the earth. Lovecraft—having just read a very similar fictional exposition of the idea in Machen's stories of the 'Little People'—was much taken with this conception, and would allude to it in many subsequent references to the Salem witches in his tales; as late as 1930 he was presenting the theory seriously.

Meanwhile Lovecraft had actually met a writer of weird fiction in his own hometown—Clifford Martin Eddy, Jr (1896–1971), who with his wife Muriel became fairly close to Lovecraft in the year or two preceding his marriage. The Eddys were at that time residents of East Providence, across the Seekonk River, and, after an initial round of correspondence and a few telephone calls, Lovecraft walked three miles to visit them at their home in August 1923.

But how did Lovecraft come into contact with the Eddys at all? There is some doubt on the matter. Muriel Eddy wrote two significant memoirs of Lovecraft, one published in 1945, the other in 1961. The first memoir seems on the whole quite reliable; the second, written in a gushing and histrionic manner, makes many statements not found in the first, including the claim that Lovecraft's mother and Eddy's mother (Mrs Grace Eddy) had become friends by meeting at a women's suffrage meeting and that at this time (probably in in 1918, although Muriel Eddy supplies no date) the two of them discovered their their sons were both enthusiasts of the weird.[12] This is a remarkable assertion, and I am frankly sceptical of it. There is no other indication that Susie Lovecraft was interested in women's suffrage. Lovecraft does not, to my knowledge, mention the Eddys in correspondence prior to October 1923, at which time he refers to Eddy as 'the new Providence amateur'.[13] He certainly gives no indication that he had once been in touch with the Eddys and was only now re-establishing contact. My feeling, then, is that the whole story about Susie Lovecraft and Grace Eddy—and about the Eddys' early association with Lovecraft—is a fabrication, made by Muriel so as to augment the sense of her and her husband's importance in Lovecraft's life.

In any event, C. M. Eddy was already a professionally published author by this time. He was working on stories to submit to *Weird Tales*, whose editor, Edwin Baird, he knew. Two of these—'Ashes' and 'The Ghost-Eater'—had already been rejected, but Lovecraft 'corrected'[14] them and Baird thereupon accepted them. 'Ashes' (*Weird Tales*, March 1924) is perhaps the single worst tale among Lovecraft's 'revisions', and no one would suspect his hand in it if he had not admitted it himself. This maudlin and conventional story about a mad scientist who has discovered a chemical compound that will reduce any substance to fine white ashes contains a nauseously fatuous romance element that must have made Lovecraft queasy. 'The Ghost-Eater' (*Weird Tales*, April 1924) is a little better, although it is nothing but a stereotypical werewolf story. Here again I cannot detect much actual Lovecraft prose, unless he was deliberately altering his style to make it harmonize with Eddy's more choppy, less prose-poetic idiom.

In late October Eddy was working on another story, entitled 'The Loved Dead'. Lovecraft clearly had a greater hand in this story than in the two previous ones; indeed, the published version (*Weird Tales*, May–June–July 1924) reads as if Lovecraft wrote the entire thing. The tale is, of course, about a necrophile who works for one undertaking establishment after another so as to secure the intimacy with corpses he desires. 'The Loved Dead' seems to be a parody, both of itself and of this sort of lurid, sensationalist fiction. But, as we shall see, when it was published not everyone found it quite so amusing. Lovecraft revised one final story for Eddy, 'Deaf, Dumb, and Blind' (*Weird Tales*, April 1925), around February 1924, just prior to his move to New York.

In 1929 Lovecraft made the following evaluation of the progression of his aesthetic thought:

> I can look back ... at two distinct periods of opinion whose foundations I have successively come to distrust—a period before 1919 or so, when the weight of classic authority unduly influenced me, and another period from 1919 to about 1925, when I placed too high a value on the elements of revolt, florid colour, and emotional extravagance or intensity.[15]

Simply put, these two phases (which would then be followed by a third and final phase combining the best features of both the previous two, and which might best be called 'cosmic regionalism') are Classicism and Decadence. The classical phase I have treated already: Lovecraft's early absorption of the Augustan poets and essayists and the Graeco-Roman classics (either in the original or in translations deriving from the Augustan age), and his curious sense of psychic union with the eighteenth century, fostered a classicism that simultaneously condemned his poetry to antiquarian irrelevance and made him violently opposed to the radical aesthetic movements emerging in the early part of the century.

How, then, does an individual who professed himself, for the first thirty years of his life, more comfortable in the periwig and small-clothes of the eighteenth century suddenly adopt an attitude of 'revolt, florid colour, and emotional extravagance or intensity'? How does someone who, in 1919, maintained that 'The literary genius of Greece and Rome ... may fairly be said to have completed the art and science of expression' come to write, in 1923: 'What is art but a matter of impressions, of pictures, emotions, and symmetrical sensations? It must have poignancy and beauty, but nothing else counts. It may or may not have coherence'?[16] The shift may seem radical, but there are many points of contact between the older and the newer view; and in many ways the change of perspective occurring in Lovecraft's mind was a mirror of the change occurring in Anglo-American aesthetics in general. Much as he might have found the idea surprising or even repellent, Lovecraft was becoming contemporary; he was starting to live, intellectually, in the twentieth, not the eighteenth, century.

I do not wish to underestimate the extent and significance of the shift in Lovecraft's aesthetic; clearly he himself thought that something revolutionary was occurring. No longer was he concerned with antiquated notions of 'metrical regularity' or the 'allowable rhyme'; broader, deeper questions were now involved. Specifically, Lovecraft was attempting to come to terms with certain findings in the sciences that might have grave effects upon artistic creation, in particular the work of Sigmund Freud. Consider a revealing statement in 'The Defence Reopens!' (January 1921):

> Certainly, they [Freud's doctrines] reduce man's boasted nobility to a hollowness woeful to contemplate ... we are forced to admit that the Freudians have in most respects excelled their predecessors, and that while many of Freud's most important details may be erroneous ... he has nevertheless opened up a new path in psychology, devising a system whose doctrines more nearly approximate the real workings of the mind than any heretofore entertained.

Although Lovecraft rejects Freud's central notion of the libido as the principal motivating factor in human psychology—something he would have found difficult to comprehend, since his own libido seems to have been so sluggish—he nevertheless accepts the view that many of our beliefs and mental processes are the result not of disinterested rationalism, but of aggression (Nietzsche's will to power), ego-assertion, and in some cases pure irrationalism. Under the placid-seeming façade of civilized bourgeois life teem powerful emotional forces that social restraints are ill-equipped to control. The effect on art will necessarily be telling. Lovecraft expounds his view in 'Lord Dunsany and His Work' (1922):

> Modern science has, in the end, proved an enemy to art and pleasure; for by revealing to us the whole sordid and prosaic basis of our thoughts, motives, and acts, it has stripped the world of glamour, wonder, and all those illusions of heroism, nobility, and sacrifice which used to sound so impressive when romantically treated. Indeed, it is not too much to say that psychological discovery, and chemical, physical, and physiological research, have largely destroyed the element of emotion among informed and sophisticated people by resolving it into its component parts—intellectual idea and animal impulse. The so-called 'soul' with all its hectic and mawkish attributes of sentimentality, veneration, earnestness, devotion, and the like, has perished on analysis

This is an intensely interesting utterance. In spite of Lovecraft's claim of intellectual independence from his time, it is clear that he had absorbed enough of the Victorian belief in 'heroism, nobility, and sacrifice' to be shaken by the revelation, via Freud and Nietzsche, of their 'sordid and prosaic basis'. For the moment he adopted a sort of aesthetic Decadence that might allow these illusions to be preserved after a fashion precisely by recognizing their artificiality. We cannot regain that blissful ignorance of our triviality in the cosmic scheme of things and of the hollowness of our lofty ideals which allowed prior ages to create the illusion of significance in human affairs. The solution—for now—is to 'worship afresh the music and colour of divine language, and take an Epicurean delight in those combinations of ideas and fancies which we know to be artificial'. If there is any literary source for any of these views, it is Oscar Wilde. It is not likely that Wilde actually generated Lovecraft's views; rather, Lovecraft found Wilde a highly articulate spokesman for the sort of views he was nebulously coming to adopt.

There are two general caveats that should be borne in mind when studying Lovecraft's Decadent stance: first, he clearly wished to believe that his position did not commit him entirely, or at all, to the avant-garde; and second, he had no wish to follow the Decadents in the repudiation of Victorianism on the level of personal conduct. As to the first point, let me quote in full that statement from 'In the Editor's Study' of July 1923 which I cited earlier:

> What is art but a matter of impressions, of pictures, emotions, and symmetrical sensations? It must have poignancy and beauty, but nothing else counts. It may or may not have coherence. If concerned with large externals or simple fancies, or produced in a simple age, it is likely to be of a clear and continuous pattern; but if concerned with individual reactions to life in a complex and analytical age, as most modern art is, it tends to break up into detached transcripts of hidden sensation and offer a loosely joined fabric which demands from the spectator a discriminating duplication of the artist's mood.

This statement—particularly the remark about 'life in a complex and analytical age'—is remarkably similar to T. S. Eliot's celebrated definition and justification of modernism, as expressed in 'The Metaphysical Poets' (1921), especially the point that 'poets in our civilization, as it exists at present, must be *difficult*'.[17] But Lovecraft pulls back at the last; perhaps aware that his amateur audience would be dumbfounded by the perception of the antiquated fossil Lovecraft becoming avant-garde, he hastily adds that he is 'no convert to Dadaism', concluding:

> Nothing, on the contrary, seems more certain ... than that the bulk of radical prose and verse represents merely the extravagant extreme of a tendency whose truly artistic application is vastly more limited. Traces of this tendency, whereby pictorial methods are used, and words and images employed without conventional connexions to excite sensations, may be found throughout literature; especially in Keats, William Blake, and the French symbolists. This broader conception of art does not outrage any eternal tradition, but honours all creations of the past or present which can shew genuine ecstatic fire and a glamour not tawdrily founded on utterly commonplace emotions.

Lovecraft is slowly carving out a place for himself between Victorian conventionality and modernist radicalism: in this way he can continue to fulminate against such things as free verse, stream-of-consciousness, or the chaoticism of Eliot and Joyce as illegitimate extensions of his Decadent principles.

The second point in this entire issue—Decadence as a mode of conduct—is clarified in Lovecraft's discussion with Frank Long in 1923–24 about the merits of Puritanism. This discussion occasionally becomes a little frivolous, and Lovecraft seems at times to be uttering hyperbole in a deliberate attempt to tease Long. After condemning 'Bohemians' for their 'wild lives',[18] he goes on to say:

> An intellectual Puritan is a fool—almost as much of a fool as is an anti-Puritan—but a Puritan in the conduct of life is the only kind of man one may honestly respect. I have no respect or reverence whatever for any person who does not live abstemiously and purely—I can like him and tolerate him, and admit him to be a social equal as I do Clark Ashton Smith and Mortonius and Kleiner and others like that, but in my heart I feel him to be my inferior—nearer the abysmal amoeba and the Neanderthal man—and at times cannot veil a sort of condescension and sardonic contempt for him, no matter how much my aesthetick and intellectual superior he may be.[19]

Of course, the various code words in this utterance ('abstemiously', 'purely') are a thin veil for restraint in sexual behaviour; the mentions of Smith and Kleiner-—both of whom were openly fond of female companionship and boasted of their conquests of various women, single or married—are also telling. Lovecraft had, therefore, sloughed off (or, in reality, never really adopted) the *aesthetics* of Victorianism but could not—or did not wish to—relinquish the sexual Puritanism he had no doubt gained at his mother's knee.

And yet, Lovecraft was by no means in the modernist camp. Several intensely interesting documents of this period bear this out with much emphasis. It is certainly odd that the two great landmarks of modernism—Joyce's *Ulysses* and Eliot's *The Waste Land*—appeared in the same year, 1922; but their fortuitously joint appearance compelled Lovecraft to address them in some fashion or other. He read *The Waste Land* in its first American appearance, in the *Dial* for November 1922 (it had appeared in England in Eliot's magazine, the *Criterion*, for October). Shortly thereafter, he wrote one or both of his responses to the poem. The first is an editorial in the March 1923 *Conservative* headed 'Rudis Indigestaque Moles' (taken from Ovid's *Metamorphoses*: 'A rough and unfinished mass'). Lovecraft asserts: 'The old heroics, pieties, and sentimentalities are dead amongst the sophisticated; and even some of our appreciations of natural beauty are threatened.' *The Waste Land* is one result of this state of confusion and turbulence:

> We here behold a practically meaningless collection of phrases, learned allusions, quotations, slang, and scraps in general; offered to the public (whether or not as a hoax) as something justified by our modern mind with its recent comprehension of its own chaotic triviality and disorganisation. And we behold th[e] public, or a considerable part of it, receiving this hilarious melange as something vital and typical; as 'a poem of profound significance,' to quote its sponsors.

This is one of the most notorious pieces of evidence of Lovecraft's supposed insensitivy to modernism and of his innate aesthetic conservatism; but it is difficult to see what other reaction he could have made at this stage of his development. It should also be pointed out that many other reviewers—not merely stodgy Victorians like J. C. Squire but level-headed modernists like Conrad

Aiken—also found the poem incomprehensible or at least ambiguous and incoherent, although some did not think it a bad poem on that account. As for Lovecraft, he may by this time have given up his literal adherence to eighteenth-century forms—or, at least, his requirement that all other poets do so—but the outward form of *The Waste Land* with its free verse and its seemingly random progression so offended him that he saw in the poem an actual instance of the aesthetic fragmentation of modern civilization that other reviewers felt it to be expressing.

I think too much has been made of the supposed similarities in philosophy and temperament of Eliot and Lovecraft: to be sure, they may both have been classicists (of a sort) and believed in continuity of culture; but Lovecraft rightly scorned Eliot's later royalism as a mere ostrich-act and heaped even more abuse on Eliot's belief in religion as a necessary foundation or bulwark of civilization.

But Lovecraft's other response to *The Waste Land*—the exquisite parody 'Waste Paper: A Poem of Profound Insignificance'—merits greater attention; for this is his best satirical poem. One wishes, therefore, that there was even the least bit of evidence as to when this poem was written and when it appeared in 'the newspaper', as Lovecraft casually notes a decade later.[20] This is the only occasion, so far as is known, that Lovecraft even mentions his poem; searches have been made in several of the Providence papers of the period with no results.

What Lovecraft very simply seeks to do in this work is to carry to a *reductio ad absurdum* his own claim in the *Conservative* editorial that *The Waste Land* is a 'practically meaningless collection of phrases, learned allusions, quotations, slang, and scraps in general'. In many parts of this quite lengthy poem (135 lines) he has quite faithfully parodied the insularity of modern poetry—its ability to be understood only by a small coterie of readers who are aware of intimate facts about the poet. The ending can only be quoted:

> Henry Fielding wrote *Tom Jones*.
> And cursed be he that moves my bones.
> Good night, good night, the stars are bright
> I saw the Leonard-Tendler fight
> Farewell, farewell, O go to hell.
> Nobody home
> In the shantih.

That delightful final pun 'confirms the jerrybuilt quality of modern life and art', as Barton L. St Armand and John H. Stanley remark; and as for the poem as a whole, its 'scraps of twentieth-century conversations, news bulletins, public announcements, newspaper headlines, and advertising jingles reflect the mundane tawdriness of the present as contrasted to the epic grandeur of the past'.[21]

Meanwhile Lovecraft had simultaneously been hammering out a theory of the weird tale that would, with some modifications, serve him his entire life. This theory is, like his aesthetics in general, an intimate outgrowth of his entire philosophical thought, especially his metaphysics and ethics. The central document here is the *In Defence of Dagon* essays—a series of three articles he wrote to an Anglo-American correspondence group, the Transatlantic Circulator, in defence of his philosophical and aesthetic views. He begins by dividing fiction, somewhat unorthodoxly, into three divisions—romantic, realistic, and imaginative. The first 'is for those who value action and emotion for their own sake; who are interested in striking events which conform to a preconceived artificial pattern'. The second 'is for those who are intellectual and analytical rather than poetical or emotional ... It has the virtue of being close to life, but has the disadvantage of sinking into the commonplace and the unpleasant at times.' Lovecraft does not provide an explicit definition of imaginative fiction, but implies that it draws upon the best features of both the other two: like romanticism, imaginative fiction bases its appeal on emotions (the emotions of fear, wonder, and terror); from realism it derives the important principle of truth—not truth to fact, as in realism, but truth to human feeling. As a result, Lovecraft comes up with the somewhat startling deduction that 'The imaginative writer devotes himself to art in its most essential sense.'

The attack on what Lovecraft called 'romanticism' is one he never relinquished. The term must not be understood here in any historical sense—Lovecraft had great respect and fondness for such Romantic poets as Shelley, Keats, and Coleridge—but purely theoretically, as embodying an approach not only to literature but to life generally:

> The one form of literary appeal which I consider *absolutely unsound, charlatanic, and valueless*—frivolous, insincere, irrelevant, and meaningless—is that mode of handling human events and values and motivations known as *romanticism*.

Dumas, Scott, Stevenson—my gawd! Here is sheer puerility—
the concoction of false glamours and enthusiasms and
events out of an addled and distorted background which has
no relation to anything in the genuine thoughts, feelings,
and experiences of evolved and adult mankind.[22]

This remark, although made in 1930, makes clear that his enemy
here is his whipping-boy of 1923, Victorianism. It was this
approach—the instilling of 'glamour' or significance into certain
phases of human activity (notably love)—that Lovecraft believed to
be most invalidated by the findings of modern science. And yet, his
vehemence on this issue may stem from another cause as well: the
possibility that his very different brand of weird fiction might
conceivably be confused with (or be considered an aspect of)
romanticism. Lovecraft knew that the weird tale had emerged in
the course of the romantic movement of the late eighteenth and
early nineteenth centuries, so that, in the eyes of many, weird
fiction itself was a phase of Romanticism and might be thought to
have 'no relation to anything in the genuine thoughts, feelings, and
experiences of evolved and adult mankind'.

Accordingly, Lovecraft always strove to ally weird fiction with
realism, which he knew to be the dominant mode of contemporary
expression. This realism extended not merely to technique ('a tale
should be plausible—even a bizarre tale *except for the single element
where supernaturalism is involved*', he says in a letter of 1921[23]), but
in terms of philosophical orientation. Of course, it cannot be
realistic in terms of *events*, so it must be realistic in terms of *human
emotions*. Lovecraft again contrasts romanticism (an 'overcoloured
representation of *what purports to be real life*') with fantasy: 'But
fantasy is something altogether different. Here we have an art
based on the imaginative life of the human mind, *frankly recognised
as such*; and in its way as natural and scientific—as truly related to
natural (even if uncommon and delicate) psychological processes
as the starkest of photographic realism.'[24]

When asked by A. H. Brown, a Canadian member of the
Transatlantic Circulator, why he didn't write more about 'ordinary
people', since this might increase the audience for his work,
Lovecraft replied with towering scorn:

I could not write about 'ordinary people' because I am not in
the least interested in them. Without interest there can be
no art. Man's relations to man do not captivate my fancy. It

is man's relation to the cosmos—to the unknown—which alone arouses in me the spark of creative imagination. The humanocentric pose is impossible to me, for I cannot acquire the primitive myopia which magnifies the earth and ignores the background.

This is Lovecraft's first *explicit* expression of the view he would later call 'cosmicism'. Cosmicism is at once a metaphysical position (an awareness of the vastness of the universe in both space and time), an ethical position (an awareness of the insignificance of human beings within the realm of the universe), and an aesthetic position (a literary expression of this insignificance, to be effected by the minimizing of human character and the display of the titanic gulfs of space and time). The strange thing about it is that it was so late in being articulated, and also that it was so feebly exhibited in his weird fiction up to this time—indeed, really up to 1926.

One interesting development in Lovecraft's pure metaphysics occurred in May of 1923:

I have no opinions—I believe in nothing … My cynicism and scepticism are increasing, and from an entirely new cause— the Einstein theory. The latest eclipse observations seem to place this system among the facts which cannot be dismissed, and assumedly it removes the last hold which reality or the universe can have on the independent mind. All is chance, accident, and ephemeral illusion—a fly may be greater than Arcturus, and Durfee Hill may surpass Mount Everest—assuming them to be removed from the present planet and differently environed in the continuum of space-time. There are no values in all infinity—the least idea that there are is the supreme mockery of all. All the cosmos is a jest, and fit to be treated only as a jest, and one thing is as true as another.[25]

The history of the acceptance of the theory of relativity would make an interesting study in itself. The theory was propounded by Einstein in 1905 but was the source of much scepticism on the part of philosophers and scientists; some merely ignored it, perhaps hoping it would go away. Lovecraft's mentor Hugh Elliot dismisses Einstein in a nervous footnote in *Modern Science and Materialism*. The theory indeed remained largely deductive until the results of observations of a total solar eclipse on 21 September 1922 were finally reported in the *New York Times* on 12 April 1923, leading many scientists to accept relativity and inspiring Lovecraft's comment.

It is hardly worth remarking that Lovecraft's wild conclusions from Einstein, both metaphysical and ethical, are entirely unfounded; but his reaction is perhaps not atypical of that of many intellectuals—especially those who could not in fact understand the precise details and ramifications of relativity—at the time. We will see that Lovecraft fairly quickly snapped out of his naive views about Einstein and, by no later than 1929, actually welcomed him as another means to bolster a modified materialism that still outlawed teleology, theism, spirituality, and other tenets he rightly believed to be outmoded in light of nineteenth-century science. In so doing he evolved a metaphysical and ethical system not at all dissimilar to that of his two later philosophical mentors, Bertrand Russell and George Santayana.

Some words about Lovecraft's political views might be in order. American entry into the world war had relieved him of the burden of fulminating against the 'craven pacifism' of Woodrow Wilson. I find little mention in Lovecraft's letters of the aftermath of the war, especially in regard to the harsh penalties imposed upon Germany by the Allies: Lovecraft later came to believe the terms of the Versailles treaty unjust, although he thought them more of a tactical error than a matter of abstract ethics.

In the relative political tranquillity of a Republican-dominated decade, Lovecraft reflected more abstractly on the issues of government. 'Nietzscheism and Realism' contains a lot of cocksure aphorisms on the subject, largely derived from Nietzsche but with a sort of Schopenhauerian foundation. For example: 'I believe in an aristocracy, because I deem it the only agency for the creation of those refinements which make life endurable for the human animal of high organization.' Lovecraft naturally assumed that he was one of those animals of high organisation, and it was entirely logical for him, when speaking abstractly of the ideal government, to look for one that would suit his own requirements. What he seems to imagine is a society like that of Periclean Athens, Augustan Rome, or Augustan England, where the aristocracy both symbolized refinement and culture (if they did not always practise it) and provided enough patronage of artists to produce those 'ornaments of life' that result in a rich and thriving civilization. It is, certainly—at least in the abstract—an appealing system, but Lovecraft surely did not fancy that it could have much relevance to present-day concerns.

When he does address such concerns, it is in tones of magisterial condemnation. Democracy earns his wholesale scorn. Consider a letter of February 1923: 'democracy ... is a false idol—a mere catchword and illusion of inferior classes, visionaries, and dying civilisations'.[26] This is manifestly Nietzschean: 'I have ... character-ised modern democracy ... as the *decaying form* of the state.'[27] I do not know that Lovecraft ever espoused democracy, but certainly his reading of Nietzsche just after the war seems to have given him the intellectual backbone to support his view.

The letter in which the above comment is imbedded occurs in a discussion of Mussolini and fascism. No one should be surprised that Lovecraft supported Mussolini's takeover of Italy (completed in late October 1922) and that he was attracted by the fascist ideology—or, at any rate, what he took it to be. I doubt that Lovecraft had any real understanding of the internal political forces that led to Mussolini's rise. Fascism was, at its base, opposed both to conventional liberalism and to socialism; its popularity grew rapidly after the end of the war when the socialists, winning a majority in 1919, could accomplish little to restore Italian society. Mussolini's takeover of the government was indeed supported, as Lovecraft would later remark, by a majority of the Italian populace; but each group wished different benefits from it, and, when after several years these benefits were not forthcoming, there was so much discontent that very repressive measures had to be adopted.

For the time being, however, Lovecraft could revel in the fact that here was a 'strong' ruler who scorned liberalism and could 'get the sort of authoritative social and political control which alone produces things which make life worth living'.[28] It cannot, cer-tainly, be said that fascism produced any sort of artistic renaissance; but that was not of much concern to Lovecraft at the moment.

The end of 1923 saw still more small travels—to the new private museum of George L. Shepley on Benefit Street, and (in the com-pany of C. M. Eddy and James F. Morton) to the exquisite First Baptist Church (1775) on North Main Street. Here Lovecraft ascended to the organ loft and attempted to play 'Yes, We Have No Bananas' but was foiled 'since the machine is not a self-starter'.[29]

Weird Tales, meanwhile, was throwing a lot of work in Lovecraft's direction, in particular a rush ghostwriting job for Harry Houdini. But in the midst of all this literary activity we find an anomalous change of personal circumstances. On 9 March 1924, Lovecraft writes a letter to his aunt Lillian from 259 Parkside Avenue, Brooklyn, New York. Was this another visit of longer or shorter duration, as the two New York trips of 1922 had been? Not exactly.

On 3 March, at St Paul's Chapel at Broadway and Vesey Streets in lower Manhattan, H. P. Lovecraft had married Sonia Haft Greene.

CHAPTER ELEVEN
Ball and Chain (1924)

New York in 1924 was an extraordinary place. Far and away the largest city in the country, its five boroughs totalled (in 1926) 5,924,138 in population, of which Manhattan had 1,752,018 and Brooklyn (then and now the largest of the boroughs both in size and in population) had 2,308,631. A remarkable 1,700,000 were of Jewish origin, while the nearly 250,000 blacks were already concentrating in Harlem (extending from 125th to 151st Streets on the west side and 96th Street northward on the east side of Manhattan) because of the severe prejudice that prevented their occupying many other areas of the city. The subway system, begun in 1904, was allowing easy access to many regions of the metropolis, and was supplemented by the extensive above-ground or elevated lines, now nearly all eliminated. Lovecraft, on some of his more remote jaunts around the area in search of antiquarian oases, nevertheless found it necessary to take the more expensive trolleys rather than the 5-cent subways or elevateds. The Hudson Tubes (now called the PATH trains) were constructed in 1908–10 to link Manhattan with the commuter terminals in Hoboken and Jersey City, New Jersey; ferry service was also common between the two states. The remoter areas of the region—Long Island to the east, or Westchester County to the north of the Bronx—were less easy of access, although the N.Y.N.H.&H. (New York, New Haven, and Hartford) railway lines brought in commuters from Connecticut. The mayor of the city was John F. Hylan; but he was ousted in 1925, and James J. Walker was elected in 1926. The governor was the Democrat Alfred E. Smith (1923–28).

It is difficult to convey in capsule form any impression of the vast metropolis, which then as now was as diverse as any place on the globe. The city's character can change in a single block, and the whole region defies neat generalization. When we speak of Harlem or Hell's Kitchen or Greenwich Village, we are in danger of letting stereotypes take the place of realities. Lovecraft discovered the city gradually over two years of peregrinations, but his heart was in those surprisingly numerous pockets of antiquity (many of them now sadly obliterated) that still remained even in the heart of Manhattan. Some of the outer boroughs also preserved such pockets, and Lovecraft sought them out with the zeal of desperation. The Flatbush section of Brooklyn where he and Sonia settled was then on the outskirts of the borough, and was then (as it is not now) the residence of choice for the well-to-do in the area. It was not Providence, but neither was it a wholly inferior substitute.

There is no question that, at least for the first few months, the euphoria of his marriage and of his residence in the nation's centre of publishing, finance, art, and general culture helped to ward off any doubts about the precipitancy of his departure from Providence. With a new wife, many friends, and even reasonably good job prospects Lovecraft had reason to believe that a promising new phase of his life was beginning.

Lovecraft's marriage seems to have produced, among his friends and associates, reactions ranging from surprise to shock to alarm. Rheinhart Kleiner writes:

> I do remember very well that it was while riding in a taxi with Mr. and Mrs. Houtain … that the news of the Lovecraft–Greene marriage was imparted to me. At once, I had a feeling of faintness at the pit of my stomach and became very pale. Houtain laughed uproariously at the effect of his announcement, but agreed that he felt as I did.[1]

The silence that Lovecraft maintained about his marriage plans up to—and, indeed, beyond—the last minute is attested by one of the most remarkable letters ever written by Lovecraft: the letter to his aunt Lillian announcing his marriage—*six days after the fact*. It is manifestly obvious that he simply boarded the 11.09 train on Sunday morning, 2 March, married Sonia the next day, began settling in at 259 Parkside, and finally decided to spill the news to his elder aunt. Indeed, Lovecraft sent Lillian several postcards on 4 and 5 March from both New York and Philadelphia (where the couple honeymooned), but without any indication of the true state of affairs.

Some parts of the laborious preamble to the actual announcement in this letter are astounding:

> [A] more active life, to one of my temperament, demands
> many things which I could dispense with when drifting
> sleepily and inertly along, shunning a world which
> exhausted and disgusted me, and having no goal but a phial
> of cyanide when my money should give out. I had formerly
> meant to follow the latter course, and was fully prepared to
> seek oblivion whenever cash should fail or sheer ennui grow
> too much for me; when suddenly, nearly three years ago,
> our benevolent angel S. H. G. stepped into my circle of
> consciousness and began to combat that idea with the
> opposite one of effort and the enjoyment of life through the
> rewards which effort will bring.

Well, perhaps marriage and a move to the big city is better than
suicide from poverty or boredom. But what about the critical issue
of the pair's affection for each other?

> meanwhile—egotistical as it sounds to relate it—it began to
> be apparent that I was not alone in finding psychological
> solitude more or less of a handicap. A detailed intellectual
> and aesthetic acquaintance since 1921, and a three-months
> visit in 1922 wherein congeniality was tested and found
> perfect in an infinity of ways, furnished abundant proof not
> only that S. H. G. is the most inspiriting and encouraging
> influence which could possibly be brought to bear on me,
> but that she herself had begun to find me more congenial
> than anyone else, and had come to depend to a great extent
> on my correspondence and conversation for mental
> contentment and artistic and philosophical enjoyment.[2]

This is, certainly, one of the most glaring examples of Lovecraft's
inability to speak of 'love' or anything remotely connected to it. His
natural reserve in talking of such matters to his aunt should
certainly be taken into account; but we will also have to deal later
with Sonia's own admission that Lovecraft never said the word
'love' to *her*.

What were Sonia's feelings on the whole matter? In speaking of
the year or two prior to their marriage, she writes: 'I well knew that
he was not in a position to marry, yet his letters indicated his desire
to leave his home town and settle in New York.'[3] The first part of
the statement presumably refers merely to financial capability; as
for the second, although of course we do not have access to
Lovecraft's letters to Sonia, I have to believe that this is somewhat

of an exaggeration. Sonia goes on to say that she requested Love-craft to inform his aunts of the marriage plans before the ceremony, but that he preferred to surprise them. 'In the matter of securing the marriage license, buying the ring and other details incumbent upon a marriage, he seemed to be so jovial. He said one would think that he was being married for the nth time, he went about it in such a methodical way.'[4]

What Sonia does not say is that she had written to Lillian a full month before the marriage, and in a manner that should clearly have signalled to Lillian that something was afoot. In a letter dated 9 February 1924, Sonia writes:

> I have nothing in life to attract me to Life and if I can help the good and beautiful soul of Howard Lovecraft find itself financially as it has found itself spiritually, morally and mentally, my efforts shall not have been in vain ...
>
> Therefore little Lady, fear nothing. I am just as desirous of his success for his own sake as you are, and I am just as anxious, perhaps more so, that you should live to enjoy the fruits of his labor and the honors that will be heaped upon his beautiful and blessed name, as you may be.[5]

That 'fear nothing' must have been in response to some letter by Lillian, perhaps asking Sonia bluntly what her 'intentions' toward her nephew actually were.

Lovecraft's joviality during the ceremony is borne out by several amusing letters to his closest friends. To James Morton he writes, after another long and teasing preamble about the seeming strangeness of his residence at 259 Parkside:

> Yes, my boy, you got it the first time. Eager to put Colonial architecture to all of its possible uses, I hit the ties hither last week; and on Monday, March the Third, seized by the hair of the head the President of the United—S. H. G.—and dragged her to Saint Paul's Chapel, ... where after consider-able assorted genuflection, and with the aid of the honest curate, Father George Benson Cox, and of two less betitled ecclesiastical hangers-on, I succeeded in affixing to her series of patronymics the not unpretentious one of Lovecraft. Damned quaint of me, is it not? You never can tell what a guy like me is gonna do next![6]

It is as if Lovecraft is regarding the whole thing as a lark; and, indeed, we will see increasing evidence that he was quite taken with the charm and novelty of being married but was simply not aware of the amount of effort it takes to make a marriage actually work. Lovecraft was, in all honesty, not emotionally mature enough for such an undertaking.

It is worth pausing to ponder the sources for Lovecraft's attraction for Sonia. It seems facile to say that he was looking for a mother replacement; and yet the emergence of Sonia into his life a mere six weeks after his mother's death is certainly a coincidence worth noting. Granted that the affection may initially have been more on Sonia's side than his—she came to Providence far more frequently than he came to New York—Lovecraft may nevertheless have felt the need to confide his thoughts and feelings to someone in a way that he does not seem to have done with his aunts.

Sonia was, of course, nothing like Susie Lovecraft: she was dynamic, emotionally open, contemporary, cosmopolitan, and perhaps a little domineering (this is the exact term Frank Belknap Long once used in describing Sonia to me), whereas Susie, although perhaps domineering in her own way, was subdued, emotionally reserved, even stunted, and a typical product of American Victorianism. But let us recall that at this moment Lovecraft was still in the full flower of his Decadent phase: his scorn of Victorianism and his toying with the intellectual and aesthetic avant-garde may have found a welcome echo in a woman who was very much an inhabitant of the twentieth century.

Sonia has made one further admission that is of some interest. In a manuscript (clearly written after the dissolution of the marriage, as it is signed Sonia H. Davis) entitled 'The Psychic Phenominon [sic] of Love' she has incorporated a part of one of Lovecraft's letters to her. In a note on the manuscript she has written: 'It was Lovecraft's part of this letter that I believe made me fall in love with him; but he did not carry out his own dictum; time and place, and reversion of some of his thoughts and expressions did not bode for happiness.'[7] The letter was published as 'Lovecraft on Love'. It is a very strange document. Going on for about 1200 words in the most abstract and pedantic manner, Lovecraft thoroughly downplays the erotic aspect of love as a product of the fire of extreme youth, saying instead that

> By forty or perhaps fifty a wholesome replacement process begins to operate, and love attains calm, cool depths based on tender association beside which the erotic infatuation of

> youth takes on a certain shade of cheapness and degrada-
> tion. Mature tranquillised love produces an idyllic fidelity
> which is a testimonial to its sincerity, purity, and intensity.[8]

And so on. There is actually not much substance in this letter, and some parts of it should have made Sonia a little nervous, as when he says that 'True love thrives equally well in presence or in absence' or that each party 'must not be too antipodal in their values, motive-forces, perspectives, and modes of expression and fulfilment' for compatibility.

But the months preceding and following the marriage were sufficiently hectic that neither had much time for reflection. In the first place, Lovecraft had to finish the ghostwriting job for *Weird Tales*. The magazine was not doing well on the newsstands, and in an effort to bolster sales owner J. C. Henneberger enlisted the services of the escape artist Harry Houdini (born Ehrich Weiss, 1874–1926), then at the height of his popularity, to write a column and other items. Henneberger also enlisted Lovecraft to write up a strange tale that Houdini was attempting to pass off as an actual occurrence that purportedly took place in Egypt. Lovecraft quickly discovered that the account was entirely fictitious, so he persuaded Henneberger to let him have as much imaginative leeway as he could in writing up the story, which as it stands seems to be entirely Lovecraft's in its prose and largely in its conception. By 25 February he had not yet begun to write it, even though it was due on 1 March. Somehow he managed to finish it just shortly before he boarded the train to New York on 2 March; but in his rush he left the typescript behind somewhere in Union Station in Providence. Although he took out an advertisement that appeared the next day in the lost and found column of the *Providence Journal* (in which the story is titled 'Under the Pyramids'), the typescript was never recovered. It appeared as 'Imprisoned with the Pharaohs' in the first anniversary issue (May–June–July 1924) of *Weird Tales*.

Lovecraft's concern at the moment, however, was to get a newly typed version to Henneberger as quickly as possible. Fortunately, he had brought along the autograph manuscript, so the morning of the 3rd found him at the office of 'The Reading Lamp' (on which more later) frantically retyping the long story; but he was only half done when it was time to go to St Paul's Chapel for the service. They completed the typing job one or two evenings later in Philadelphia. The story was sent to *Weird Tales* immediately, and Lovecraft received payment of $100—the largest sum he had hitherto earned as a fiction-writer—on 21 March. It was the only occasion on which he was paid by *Weird Tales* in advance of publication.

'Under the Pyramids' is quite an able piece of work, and it remains a much undervalued tale, even if some of the earlier parts read like a travelogue or encyclopedia. Some of the imagery of the story probably derives from Théophile Gautier's superb non-supernatural tale of Egyptian horror, 'One of Cleopatra's Nights'. Lovecraft owned Lafcadio Hearn's translation of *One of Cleopatra's Nights and Other Fantastic Romances* (1882).

One bizarre postscript to this entire affair concerns C. M. Eddy's 'The Loved Dead', which appeared in the same issue of *Weird Tales*. Lovecraft had, of course, revised this tale. When the issue appeared, it was promptly banned on the grounds that 'The Loved Dead' was about necrophilia (true enough, indeed) and apparently considered obscene. It is not entirely clear what actually happened, but it seems that the magazine was banned only in the state of Indiana.[9] To what degree the notoriety of the banning affected sales of *Weird Tales* is also in doubt: it can certainly not be said that this banning somehow 'saved' the magazine by causing a run on the issue, especially since it would be four months before the next issue appeared. We may discover, however, that less fortunate conse-quences occurred—at least, as far as Lovecraft was concerned—in later years.

Meanwhile, Lovecraft was becoming very much involved with *Weird Tales*—perhaps more than he would have liked. In mid-March he reports that Henneberger 'is making a radical change in the policy of *Weird Tales*, and that he has in mind a brand new magazine to cover the field of Poe–Machen shudders. This maga-zine, he says, will be "right in my line", and he wants to know if I would consider moving to CHICAGO to edit it!'[10] There is a certain ambiguity in this utterance, but I believe the sense is not that Henneberger would start a 'brand new magazine' but that *Weird Tales* itself would be made over into a 'new' magazine featuring Poe–Machen shudders. Lovecraft had earlier noted that Baird had been ousted as editor and that Farnsworth Wright had been placed in his stead;[11] this was only a stop-gap measure, and Lovecraft was indeed Henneberger's first choice for editor of *Weird Tales*.

Lovecraft has frequently been criticized for failing to take up this opportunity just at the time when, as a new husband, he needed a steady income; the thinking is that he should have overcome his purely aesthetic distaste of the modern architecture of Chicago and accepted the offer. But the matter is more complicated than this scenario suggests. First, although Sonia was in favour of the move, it would have meant either Sonia's search for uncertain job prospects in Chicago or the couple's having to live a thousand miles away from each other merely for the sake of employment. Second, Lovecraft knew that Henneberger was deeply in debt: Henneberger had lost $51,000 on his two magazines, *Weird Tales* and *Detective Tales*, and there was no guarantee that either enterprise would continue in operation much longer. If Lovecraft had therefore left for Chicago, he might after a few months have been stranded there with no job and with little prospect of getting one. Lovecraft was, in my view, wise to decline the offer. In any case, even in the most ideal financial circumstances, he might not have made the best editor of a magazine such as *Weird Tales*. His fastidious taste would have rejected much that was actually published in its pages: there was simply not enough artistically polished weird fiction to fill what was really nothing more than a cheap pulp magazine paying a penny a word.

What actually happened to *Weird Tales* in this crisis was that Henneberger sold off his share of *Detective Tales* to the co-founder of Rural Publications, J. M. Lansinger (who retained Baird as editor of that magazine), appointed Farnsworth Wright as permanent editor of *Weird Tales* (he would retain that position until 1940), and then—as the only way to make up the $40,000 debt he had accrued—came to an agreement with B. Cornelius, the printer of the magazine, as follows: 'Cornelius became chief stockholder with an agreement that if the $40,000 owed him was ever repaid by profits from the magazine, Henneberger would be returned the stock.'[12] A new company, the Popular Fiction Publishing Co., was formed to issue the magazine, with the stockholders being Cornelius, Farnsworth Wright, and William Sprenger (*Weird Tales'* business manager); after a several-month hiatus *Weird Tales* resumed publication with the November 1924 issue. Although Henneberger retained a minor interest in the new company, *Weird Tales* never made sufficient profits for him to buy it back; in any case, he seems to have lost interest in the venture after a few years and finally drifted entirely out of the picture.

Farnsworth Wright (1888–1940) deserves some mention, as Lovecraft would eventually develop a very curious relationship with him. He had been the magazine's first reader from the very beginning, and had several undistinguished stories in early issues. He had served in the First World War and afterwards was music critic for the *Chicago Herald and Examiner*, continuing in this latter activity for a time even after he took over the editorship of *Weird Tales*. By early 1921 he had contracted Parkinson's disease, and the illness worsened throughout the rest of his life, so that by the end of the decade he could not sign his name.

It is difficult to gauge Wright's success as editor of *Weird Tales*, especially since very different yardsticks can be used to measure 'success' in something of this kind. It is, certainly, something in his favour that he managed to keep the magazine going even during the worst years of the Depression; but there can similarly be no denying that he published an appalling amount of trite, hackneyed, and simply bad fiction that would never have appeared elsewhere and should never have been published in the first place. Lovecraft felt that Wright was erratic, capricious, and even a little hypocritical, at least as regards his handling of Lovecraft's own work; and, in spite of those who have come to Wright's defence on this score, this view seems plausible. Lovecraft may have had excessively high expectations of his success with Wright, so that rejections came with added bitterness. In some senses his irritation stemmed from what he eventually realized was a naive view that aesthetically meritorious work should be rewarded commensurately. It would be years before he learned that writing for the pulps was simply a business, and that Wright looked upon the matter in that light. If most of *Weird Tales'* readership wanted cheap, formula-ridden hackwork, Wright would make sure to give it to them.

In the short term, however, Lovecraft and Sonia had a household to set in order. The first thing to do was to persuade aunt Lillian (and perhaps Annie as well) to come to New York to live with them. This seems to have been an entirely sincere desire on the part of both Lovecraft and Sonia. Lillian was, however, at this time almost sixty-six years old and probably in declining health; it is clear that she herself had no desire to move—especially after her nephew failed to take her into his confidence regarding the most dramatic change in his personal circumstances.

One occupant the couple would not have to worry about was Sonia's daughter. Florence Carol Greene appears to have had a falling out with her mother a few years previously: she had fallen in love with her half-uncle Sydney (only five years her elder), and Sonia, enraged, had adamantly refused to allow her to marry him. (Such a marriage would, in any event, have been prohibited by the tenets of Orthodox Judaism.) This dispute led to a schism which, unfortunately, lasted the duration of both women's lives. Florence left Sonia's apartment some time after she came of age (19 March 1923), although continuing to remain in New York. There are reports that she herself did not care for Lovecraft and did not approve of her mother's marrying him. Florence's later life is both distinguished and tragic: she married a newspaperman named John Weld in 1927 but divorced him in 1932; she herself went to Europe and became a reporter, attaining celebrity as the first reporter to cover the romance of the Prince of Wales (the future Edward VIII) and Mrs Wallis Simpson. Returning to America, she worked for newspapers in New York, later moving to Florida and becoming a film publicist. She died on 31 March 1979. But in all that time she refused to speak to her mother. And aside from a passing reference in her memoir, Sonia never speaks of her. Lovecraft too alludes to her only twice in all the correspondence I have seen.

In the meantime, however, Lovecraft had to think of work. Sonia had been making $10,000 per year at Ferle Heller's—a princely sum considering that the 'minimum health and decency' wages for a family of four in the 1920s was $2000—but had already lost this position, evidently, by February 1924. Nevertheless, she had savings in five figures,[13] so perhaps there was no immediate need to replenish the coffers.

A likely prospect seemed in the offing in something called 'The Reading Lamp'. So far as I can tell, this was a magazine (although no file of it exists in any library in the world) as well as a literary agency that would generate commissioned articles or books on behalf of its clients; it was run by one Gertrude E. Tucker. Edwin Baird had recommended Lovecraft to Tucker in January 1924; Sonia, learning of this, took it upon herself to see Tucker and bring a sheaf of Lovecraft's manuscripts to her. On 10 March Lovecraft interviewed at the Reading Lamp office, with the following result:

> Miss T. thinks a book of my antiquarian & other essays would be quite practicable, & urges me to prepare at least three as samples at once. Also, she thinks she can get me a contract with a chain of magazines to write minor matter to order. And more—as soon as my MSS. arrive, she wants to

see all of them, with a view to a weird book ... What Miss T. wants in the way of essays is quaint stuff with a flavour of the supernatural.[14]

All this sounds promising, and at one point Lovecraft even reports the possibility that The Reading Lamp might be able to secure him a regular position at a publishing house, although this clearly did not happen. Later in the month he reports working on several chapters of a book on American superstitions; the idea evidently was that he would do three chapters and Tucker would then try to get a contract from a book publisher for the project. But since on 1 August he reports the 'non-materialisation of sundry literary prospects',[15] the obvious inference is that the Reading Lamp business came to nothing.

But Lovecraft always had Bush to rely on. He met him on 25 May, and reports doing 'Bush work' in July. Bush published at least eight books in 1924 and 1925 (all of them psychology manuals—he had evidently given up poetry), and no doubt Lovecraft derived at least a modest income from revising them. Cheques from *Weird Tales* were no doubt trickling in also—for 'The Hound' (February), 'The Rats in the Walls' (March), 'Arthur Jermyn' (April), and 'Hypnos' (May–June–July) along with 'Under the Pyramids', although I have no information on how much any of these stories aside from the Houdini job actually brought in.

The couple, indeed, felt so relatively prosperous that in May they placed a down payment on two pieces of property in Bryn Mawr Park, a development in Yonkers. In her autobiography Sonia declares that a home for Lovecraft, herself, and his two aunts was planned for the larger property and that the other would be used for speculation. Yonkers is the city immediately north of the Bronx in lower Westchester County, and within easy commuting distance of Manhattan by trolley or train. Since the turn of the century it had become a fashionable bedroom community for New Yorkers; but it was still an idyllic small town with plenty of greenery and a sort of New England feel to it, and might have been the ideal place for Lovecraft to have settled so long as he needed to remain in the New York area for purposes of employment. However, by late July Lovecraft wrote to the real estate company that he could no longer afford to pay the monthly fees for the lots. What exactly had happened to the couple's finances?

Sonia had apparently attempted to start her own hat shop. This strikes me as an extremely risky undertaking. In days when all men and women wore hats in public, the millinery business was an extraordinarily competitive one: the 1924–25 city directory for Manhattan and the Bronx lists at least 1200 milliners. My only thought is that Sonia, as a married woman, did not wish to do the extensive amount of travelling that her position at Ferle Heller's evidently required her to do, and wished to open a shop of her own so as to remain in the city as much as possible. But if this was the case, the ironic circumstance is that Sonia remained out of work for much of the rest of the year and was then forced to take a series of jobs in the Midwest, separating her far more from her husband than her Ferle Heller's position would have been likely to do. She says nothing about this whole matter at all in her memoir; but Lovecraft, writing to Lillian on 1 August, makes clear reference to 'the somewhat disastrous collapse of S. H.'s *independent* [my emphasis] millinery venture', with the result that there is now 'something of a shortage in the exchequer'.[16]

The upshot of all this was that Lovecraft was forced to look much more vigorously for a job—any job—than before. Now, and only now, begins the futile and rather pathetic hunting through the classified ads every Sunday in the *New York Times* for any position that might conceivably be available; but Lovecraft came face to face with a realization as true then as now: 'Positions of every kind seem virtually unattainable to persons without experience …'[17] What Lovecraft says is the job that 'came nearest to materialisation' was a salesman's position with the Creditors' National Clearing House, located at 810 Broad Street in Newark, New Jersey. This was a bill collecting agency, and Lovecraft would be responsible not for actually collecting bills but for selling the agency's services amongst wholesalers and retailers in New York City. He appears to have been hired on a trial basis in late July, but it was painfully evident that Lovecraft simply did not have the brazenness or suavity to be a successful salesman, and he quickly resigned.

This whole episode—as well as a later one in which Lovecraft tried to secure a job in the lamp-testing department of an electrical laboratory—shows how difficult it was for Lovecraft to secure the job that most suited him, namely something in the writing or publishing business. There is no reason why, with his experience, he should not have been able to secure some such position; but he was unable to do so. Several of his friends have commented on a notorious letter of application that he sent out around this time, the first paragraph of which reads as follows:

> If an unprovoked application for employment seems some-
> what unusual in these days of system, agencies, & advertising,
> I trust that the circumstances surrounding this one may help
> to mitigate what would otherwise be obtrusive forwardness.
> The case is one wherein certain definitely marketable
> aptitudes must be put forward in an unconventional manner
> if they are to override the current fetish which demands
> commercial experience & causes prospective employers to
> dismiss unheard the application of any situation-seeker
> unable to boast of specific professional service in a given
> line.[18]

And so on for six more paragraphs, commenting pointedly that he
has, in the last two months, answered over a hundred advertisements without a single response.

To be sure, this may not have been the ideal letter, but standards
of business writing were different seventy years ago. Nevertheless,
Kleiner remarks of this letter, and others like it: 'I think I am
justified in saying that they were the sort of letters a temporarily
straitened English gentleman might have written in an effort to
make a profitable connection in the business world of the day
before yesterday.'[19]

Then, in the classified section of the *New York Times* for Sunday
10 August, appeared the following advertisement in the 'Situations
Wanted—Male' category:

> WRITER AND REVISER, free-lance, desires regular and per-
> manent salaried connection with any responsible enterprise
> requiring literary services; exceptionally thorough experience
> in preparing correct and fluent text on subjects assigned, and
> in meeting the most difficult, intricate and extensive prob-
> lems of rewriting and constructive revision, prose or verse;
> would also consider situation dealing with such proof-
> reading as demands rapid and discriminating perception,
> orthographical accuracy, stylistic fastidiousness and a keenly
> developed sense of the niceties of English usage; good typist;
> age 34, married; has for seven years handled all the prose
> and verse of a leading American public speaker and editor. Y
> 2292 Times Annex.

This advertisement—taking many phrases from his application
letter—is rather more open to criticism than the letter itself, for it is
far longer than any other one in this section and really does go on

at needless length when a more compact notice would have conveyed many of the same points far more cheaply. The expense was, indeed, quite considerable: the rate for ads in the 'Situations Wanted' section was 40 cents per word, and this ad—99 words—cost a full $39.60. This would be the equivalent of a month's rent in the one-room apartment Lovecraft would occupy in 1925–26. I am amazed that Sonia let Lovecraft take out an ad of this length, for surely she paid for it.

Then, in September, an old friend reappeared on the scene—J. C. Henneberger. Lovecraft states that Henneberger had hired him for a 'new magazine' at the rate of $40 per week. What kind of magazine was it? *College Humor*, founded in 1922, was going strong and was not likely to need a new editor; but there was another magazine called the *Magazine of Fun* that Henneberger started about this time, and, incredible as it seems, the editorship of this magazine or something like it is what Henneberger appears to have been offering. Lovecraft speaks of Henneberger telephoning him and 'want[ing] me to turn out some samples of my adapting of jokes for his proposed magazine'.[20] It was on the basis of these samples that Henneberger 'hired' Lovecraft in mid-September.

Of course, nothing came of the plans. The promised pay for Lovecraft's editorial work metamorphosed into a $60 credit at the Scribner Book Shop; and although Lovecraft tried to get this credit converted to cash, he was unable to do so and finally, on 9 October, he took Long to the bookstore to purchase a sheaf of books, mostly weird. Frank Long treats the whole episode engagingly in his memoir,[21] but seems under the impression that the credit was a payment for stories in *Weird Tales*, when in fact it was for this editorial job that never materialized.

Lovecraft accordingly returned to answering the want ads, although by this time the strain was becoming severe for someone who had no particular business sense and may perhaps have felt the whole activity somewhat beneath his dignity. He writes to Lillian in late September: 'That day [Sunday] was one of gloom and nerves—more advertisement answering, which has become such a psychological strain that I almost fall unconscious over it!'[22] Anyone who has been out of work for any length of time has felt this way.

Meanwhile Lovecraft's friends were trying to lend a hand. Houdini was impressed with 'Under the Pyramids', and in late September put Lovecraft in touch with one Brett Page, the head of a newspaper syndicate; but Page had no actual position to offer. In mid-November Samuel Loveman attempted to set up Lovecraft with the head of the cataloguing department of a bookshop on 59th Street, but this too proved fruitless.

Sonia was not, to be sure, unemployed during this entire period; no doubt she was also answering want ads, and she had been employed in either a milliner's or a department store for a few weeks in September. But she felt that this position was insecure and was looking around for something better. But then things took a turn very much for the worse. On the evening of 20 October Sonia was stricken with 'sudden gastric spasms ... whilst resting in bed after a day of general ill-feeling'.[23] Lovecraft took her in a taxicab to Brooklyn Hospital, only a few blocks away. She would spend the next eleven days there, finally being released on the 31st.

There can hardly be any question but that Sonia's illness was in large part nervous or psychological in origin. She must have been acutely worried over the many disasters, financial and otherwise, that had overtaken the couple, and no doubt sensed Lovecraft's increasing discouragement at his failed job-hunting efforts and perhaps his belief that his entire life had taken a wrong turn. Lovecraft never makes any such statement in his letters of the period, but I have trouble believing that something of the sort was not going through his mind.

Lovecraft was unusually solicitous to Sonia in the hospital: he visited her every day (this representing his first time he had actually set foot in a hospital), bringing her books, stationery, and— what must have been a great sacrifice in the name of married bliss—relearned the game of chess so that he could play it with Sonia. She beat him every time. In turn he began learning to be more independent in the running of a household: he made coffee, a twenty-minute egg, and even spaghetti from Sonia's written instructions, and showed obvious pride in keeping the place well cleaned and dusted for her return. These remarks on cooking suggest that he had never made a meal for himself up to this time.

One of Sonia's doctors, Dr Westbrook, actually recommended an operation for the removal of her gall bladder; but Lovecraft—quite consciously remembering that his mother had died of just such an operation—strongly urged Sonia to get a second opinion, and another doctor advised against surgery; either this doctor or Dr Kingman, a nerve specialist, then recommended six weeks' rest in the country before Sonia resumed work. Accordingly, she checked into a private rest home in New Jersey on 9 November, planning to stay for six days. This was actually a farm run by a Mrs R. A. Craig and her two sons near Somerville, New Jersey, in the central part of the state. Lovecraft himself stayed overnight at the farm, then left the next morning to spend the rest of the week in Philadelphia examining colonial antiquities. Returning on the 15th, he was surprised to find that Sonia had come home the day before, one day early; evidently she had not found the place entirely to her liking. She felt, however, good enough after only six days to resume job-hunting efforts.

Almost immediately after Sonia's return, a dramatic decision was made: Sonia would leave for a job in the Midwest while Lovecraft would relocate to a smaller apartment in the city. The couple planned to move out of 259 Parkside as early as the end of November, but as it happened the dispersal did not occur until the end of December. Lovecraft's first choice for a place to settle was Elizabeth, New Jersey, which he had visited earlier in the year and found a delightful haven of colonial antiquity. If this could not be managed, then Lovecraft would opt for Brooklyn Heights, where Loveman and Hart Crane lived.

Lillian came to New York around 1 December to help in the transition. The month of December is a blank, since Lillian stayed the entire month and into early January, so naturally Lovecraft wrote no letters to her; no letters to others have come to light either. The one thing that remains unclear is exactly when or how Sonia secured her job in the Midwest. Neither she nor Lovecraft has anything of consequence to say on the subject.

It should be pointed out that this separation was not—at least outwardly—anything other than an economic move; there is no real indication that any dispute or emotional crisis had occurred. Are we permitted to wonder whether Lovecraft was secretly pleased at this turn of events? Did he prefer a marriage by correspondence rather than one in person? It is time to backtrack and see what we can learn about the actual personal relations between Sonia and Lovecraft.

Sonia's dry remark that, after typing the Houdini manuscript, they were 'too tired and exhausted for honey-mooning or anything else' is surely a tactful way of referring to the fact that she and Lovecraft did not have sex on their first night together. The matter of Lovecraft's sexual conduct must inevitably be addressed, although the information we have on the subject is very sparse. We learn from R. Alain Everts, who interviewed Sonia on the matter, that: first, he was a virgin at the time he married; second, prior to his marriage he had read several books on sex; and third, he *never* initiated sexual relations, but would respond when Sonia did so.[24]

None of these, except the second, is a surprise. One wonders what books Lovecraft might have read (one hopes it was not David Van Bush's *Practical Psychology and Sex Life* (1922)!—quite possibly he may have read some of James F. Morton's writings on the subject). His Victorian upbringing—especially from a mother whose husband died under distasteful circumstances—clearly made him very inhibited as far as sex is concerned; but there is also every reason to believe that Lovecraft was simply one of those individuals who have a low sex drive, and for whom the subject is of relatively little interest. It is mere armchair psychoanalysis to say that he somehow sublimated his sex urges into writing or other activities.

Sonia herself has only two comments on the matter. 'As a married man he was an adequately excellent lover, but refused to show his feelings in the presence of others. He shunned promiscuous association with women before his marriage.'[25] I do not know what an 'adequately excellent' lover is. The other remark is a trifle more embarrassing: 'H. P. was inarticulate in expressions of love except to his mother and to his aunts, to whom he expressed himself quite vigorously; to all other[s] it was expressed by deep appreciation only. One way of expression of H. P.'s sentiment was to wrap his "pinkey" finger around mine and say "Umph!"'[26] Move over, Casanova! The note about 'appreciation' leads to one of the most celebrated passages in her memoir: 'I believe he loved me as much as it was possible for a temperament like his to love. He'd never mention the word *love*. He would say instead "My dear, you don't know how much I appreciate you." I tried to understand him and was grateful for any crumbs from his lips that fell my way.'[27] Again, none of this is entirely surprising given what we know about Lovecraft's upbringing.

If Sonia could not make Lovecraft perform sexually quite as much as she would like, she could change him in other ways. First there was his diet. Although he had put on considerable weight in the 1922–23 period, Sonia nevertheless remarks:

> When we were married he was tall and gaunt and 'hungry-looking'. I happen to like the apparently ascetic type but H. P. was too much even for my taste, so I used to cook a

well-balanced meal every evening, make a substantial breakfast (he loved cheese soufflé—rather an untimely dish for breakfast) and I'd leave a few (almost Dagwoodian) sandwiches for him, a piece of cake and some fruit for his lunch (he loved sweets), and I'd tell him to be sure to make some tea or coffee for himself.[28]

Elsewhere she says: 'Living a normal life and eating the food I provided made him take on much extra weight, which was quite becoming to him.'[29] She may have thought so, but Lovecraft didn't: he would later refer to himself as a 'porpoise',[30] and indeed he ballooned to nearly 200 pounds, which is certainly overweight for someone of his general build.

Another thing Sonia didn't like about Lovecraft, aside from his lean and hungry look, was his attire.

I remember so well when I took him to a smart haberdashery how he protested at the newness of the coat and hat I persuaded him to accept and wear. He looked at himself in the mirror and protested, 'But my dear, this is entirely too stylish for "Grandpa Theobald"; it doesn't look like me. I look like some fashionable fop!' To which I replied, 'Not all men who dress fashionably are necessarily fops.'[31]

To someone in the fashion business, the conservative clothing customarily worn by Lovecraft must have been irritating indeed. Sonia adds with some tartness, 'I really think he was glad that this coat and the new suit purchased that day were later stolen.'

This simple incident may go far in suggesting what went wrong with the marriage. Although in later years Lovecraft charitably claimed that the marriage's failure was '98% financial',[32] in reality both Sonia and Lovecraft had deceived themselves into thinking that they shared a 'congeniality' (as Lovecraft stated in his marriage-announcement letter to Lillian) that went beyond intellectual and aesthetic matters and covered actual modes of behaviour and basic values. Granting that financial considerations were indeed of considerable—even paramount—importance, these differences in values would have emerged in time and doomed the marriage sooner or later. In some senses it was better—at least for Lovecraft—that it occurred sooner than later.

But in those first few months the euphoria of being married, the excitement of the big city (and of fairly promising job prospects), the fortuitous arrival of Annie Gamwell at the end of March, and of course his many friends in the area kept Lovecraft in a buoyant mood. Amateur work was still taking up some time: Sonia, as President, and Lovecraft, as Official Editor of the UAPA, managed to issue a *United Amateur* for May 1924, although it must have been a month or so late, as Sonia's 'President's Message' is dated 1 May.

Social activity with amateurs still remained on the agenda. Sonia took Lovecraft frequently to the monthly meetings of the Blue Pencil Club (a NAPA group) in Brooklyn; Lovecraft did not much care for this group but would go to please his wife, and in 1925–26, when he was alone, he would skip meetings except when Sonia happened to be in town and made him go. There was some group called The Writers' Club whose meetings Lovecraft attended in March, although this does not seem to have been an amateur organization. When asked by Morton if he would attend a meeting in May, he writes: 'It all depends on the ball-and-chain.' However we are to take the 'ball-and-chain' remark (one hopes it is meant in genial flippancy), Lovecraft adds rather touchingly: 'She generally has to hit the hay early, and I have to get home in proportionate time, since she can't get to sleep till I do.'[33] The couple did share a double bed, and no doubt Sonia had already become accustomed to having her husband beside her and felt uncomfortable when he was not there.

Lovecraft found the support of his friends indispensable for maintaining emotional equilibrium during this entire period, when the many changes in his social and professional life and, later, the successive disappointments and hardships threatened to disrupt his own mental stability. The most heart-warming portions of his letters to his aunts of 1924 are not those involving Sonia (she is mentioned with remarkable infrequency) but those dealing with his surpisingly numerous outings with friends old and new. This was, of course, the heyday of the Kalem Club, although that term was not coined until early the next year.

Some of these men (and they were all men) we have met already—Kleiner (then a bookkeeper at the Fairbanks Scales Co. and living somewhere in Brooklyn), Morton (living in Harlem; I am not sure of his occupation at this time), and Long (living at 823 West End Avenue in the upper West Side of Manhattan with his parents and studying journalism at New York University). Now others joined 'the gang'.

There was Arthur Leeds (1882–1952?), a kind of rolling stone who had been with a travelling circus as a boy and now, at the age of roughly forty, eked out a bare living as a columnist for *Writer's Digest* and occasional pulp writer for *Adventure* and other magazines; he had two stories in *Weird Tales*. He was perhaps the most indigent of this entire group of largely indigent aesthetes. At this time he was living at a hotel in West 49th Street in Hell's Kitchen.

There was Everett McNeil (1862–1929), who like Morton earned an entry in *Who's Who in America*, on the strength of sixteen novels for boys published between 1903 and 1929, mostly for E. P. Dutton. The majority of these were historical novels in which McNeil would sugarcoat the history with stirring tales of action on the part of explorers or adventurers battling Indians or colonizing the American frontier. The most popular was perhaps *In Texas with Davy Crockett* (1908), which was reprinted as late as 1937. George Kirk describes him in a letter to his fiancée as 'an oldster—lovely purely white hair, writes books for boys and does not need to write down to them, he is quite equal mentally'.[34] Kirk did not mean that last remark at all derogatorily. Lovecraft—who had already met McNeil on one of his New York trips of 1922—felt the same way and cherished McNeil's naive simplicity, even though gradually McNeil fell out of favour with the rest of the gang for being tiresome and intellectually unstimulating. He was living, as in 1922, in Hell's Kitchen, not far from Leeds.

There was George Kirk himself (1898–1962), who had of course met Lovecraft in Cleveland in 1922 and arrived in New York in August (just before Samuel Loveman, who came in early September) to pursue his bookseller's trade, settling at 50 West 106th Street in Manhattan. His one venture into publishing was *Twenty-one Letters of Ambrose Bierce* (1922), Loveman's edition of Bierce's letters to him. He had become engaged to Lucile Dvorak in late 1923 but did not wish to marry until he had established himself as a bookseller in New York; this took nearly three years, and in the interim he wrote letters to Lucile that rival Lovecraft's letters to his aunts in their detailed vignettes of 'the gang'. They are the only other contemporaneous documents of the sort that we have, and they are of considerable help in filling in gaps in Lovecraft's own letters and in rounding out the general picture of the group.

The Kalem Club existed in a very rudimentary—and nameless—form prior to Lovecraft's arrival in the city; Kleiner, McNeil, and perhaps Morton appear to have met occasionally at each other's homes. But clearly the group—whose chief bond was their correspondence and association with Lovecraft—fully solidified as a club only with Lovecraft's arrival.

Frank Long provides a piquant glimpse at Lovecraft's conduct at these meetings:

> Almost invariably ... Howard did most of the talking, at least for the first ten or fifteen minutes. He would sink into an easy chair—he never seemed to feel at ease in a straight-backed chair on such occasions and I took care to keep an extremely comfortable one unoccupied until his arrival—and words would flow from him in a continuous stream.
>
> He never seemed to experience the slightest necessity to pause between words. There was no groping about for just the right term, no matter how recondite his conversation became. When the need for some metaphysical hair-splitting arose, it was easy to visualize scissors honed to a surgical sharpness snipping away in the recesses of his mind ...
>
> In general the conversation was lively and quite variegated. It was a brilliant enough assemblage, and the discussions ranged from current happenings of a political or sociological nature, to some recent book or play, or to five or six centuries of English and French literature, art, philosophy, and natural science.[35]

This may be as good a place as any to explore the question of Lovecraft's voice, since several of Lovecraft's New York colleagues have given us their impressions of it. There seems general consensus that his voice was somewhat high-pitched. Sonia has the most detailed discussion:

> His voice was clear and resonant when he read or lectured but became thin and high-pitched in general conversation, and somewhat falsetto in its ring, but when reciting favorite poems he managed to keep his voice on an even keel of deep resonance. Also his singing voice, while not strong, was very sweet. He would sing none of the modern songs, only the more favored ones of about a half century ago or more.[36]

Wilfred Blanch Talman offers a less flattering account:

> His voice had that flat and slightly nasal quality that is sometimes stereotyped as a New England characteristic. When he laughed aloud, a harsh cackle emerged that reversed the impression of his smile and to the uninitiated might be con-

sidered a ham actor's version of a hermit's laughter. Companions avoided any attempt to achieve more than a smile in conversation with him, so unbecoming was the result.[37]

The Kalem Club began meeting weekly on Thursday nights, but later shifted to Wednesdays. It was after one such meeting that Lovecraft began the diligent if unsystematic discovery of the antiquities of the metropolitan area. On Thursday 21 August, there was a gang meeting at Kirk's place at 106th Street. The meeting broke up at 1.30 a.m. and the group started walking down Broadway, leaving successively at various subway or elevated stations on their respective ways home. Finally only Kirk and Lovecraft remained, and they continued walking all the way down Eighth Avenue through Chelsea into Greenwich Village, exploring all the colonial remnants (still existing) along Grove Court, Patchin and Milligan Places, Minetta Lane, and elsewhere. It was now almost dawn, but they continued walking, down the (now largely destroyed) 'colonial expanse' of Varick and Charlton Streets to City Hall. They must have covered at least seven or eight miles on this entire trip. Finally they broke up around 8 a.m., Lovecraft returning home by 9. (So much for his coming home early so that he and Sonia could retire together. On a slightly earlier all-night excursion with Kleiner and Leeds, he returned home at 5 a.m., and, 'having successfully dodged the traditional fusilade of conjugal flatirons and rolling-pins, I was with Hypnos, Lord of Slumbers'.[38] One assumes Lovecraft is being whimsical and not literal here.)

On 19 September Lovecraft went to Loveman's apartment at 78 Columbia Heights and met Crane. He reports that 'Crane is writing a long poem on Brooklyn Bridge in a modern medium':[39] this would, of course, be Crane's masterpiece, *The Bridge* (1930), on which he had begun work as early as February 1923. Crane was rather less charitable to Lovecraft in his various letters than Lovecraft was to Crane. Writing on 14 September to his mother and grandmother, Crane notes Loveman's arrival in the city but says that he has not spent much time with him because he has been occupied with his many friends:

> Miss Sonia Green [*sic*] and her piping-voiced husband, Howard Lovecraft, (the man who visited Sam in Cleveland one summer when Galpin was also there) kept Sam traipsing around the slums and wharf streets until four this morning looking for Colonial specimens of architecture, and

until Sam tells me he groaned with fatigue and begged for the subway![40]

The former 'invalid' Lovecraft had already become famous for outwalking all his friends!

Kleiner, in a memoir, supplies a partial answer to a question that has perhaps occurred to nearly everyone reading of Lovecraft's long walks all around Manhattan at night, whether alone or with others: how is it that he escaped being the victim of a crime? Kleiner writes:

> In Greenwich Village, for whose eccentric habitants he had little use, he was fond of poking about in back alleys where his companions preferred not to go. In prohibition years, with murderous affrays among bootleggers and rum-runners likely to break out anywhere, this was a particularly dangerous business. Every other house in this neighborhood was open to suspicion as a speakeasy. I recall that at least once, while stumbling around old barrels and crates in some dark corner of this area, Lovecraft found a doorway suddenly illuminated and an excited foreigner, wearing the apron that was an almost infallible sign of a speakeasy bartender, enquiring hotly what he wanted. Loveman and Kirk went in after Lovecraft and got him safely out. None of us, surely, was under any illusion as to what might very well happen in such an obscure corner of the city.[41]

Lovecraft was certainly fearless—perhaps a little foolhardy—on these jaunts. He was, of course, at this time a fairly imposing physical specimen at nearly six feet and 200 pounds; but physical size means nothing when one is faced with a knife or gun, and many criminals are also not put off by a prospective victim's apparent lack of prosperity. Lovecraft was, in effect, simply lucky in not coming to harm on these peregrinations.

On the evening of 26 September there was a Blue Pencil Club meeting, and the prescribed topic for literary contributions was 'The Old Home Town'. It was a theme close to Lovecraft's heart, and he produced the thirteen-stanza poem 'Providence' for the occasion—virtually the first creative writing he had done since writing 'Under the Pyramids' in February. It was published in the *Brooklynite* for November 1924 and, some time in November, in the *Providence Evening Bulletin*, for which he received $5.00.

Early October saw his first visit to Elizabeth, New Jersey (which

Lovecraft persistently calls by its eighteenth-century name of Eliza-bethtown). He was alerted to the existence of colonial antiquities there by an editorial in the *New York Times*, and he was entirely captivated. His visit proved to be the catalyst for his first story in eight months, 'The Shunned House'. He had come upon 'a terrible old house—a hellish place where night-black deeds must have been done in the early seventeen-hundreds'[42] (no longer standing) and it made him think of a house in Providence at 135 Benefit Street, where Lillian had resided in 1919–20 as a companion for Mrs C. H. Babbit. This house had been built around 1763, and is a magnificent structure—with basement, two storeys, and attic—built on the rising hill, with shuttered doors in the basement leading directly out into the sidewalk. It has been considerably restored since Lovecraft's day, but at that time it must have been a spectral place. Lovecraft spent the whole of 16–19 of October writing a draft of the story, making considerable 'eliminations & rearrangements' and doing more revision the next day after having read it to Frank Long. (It was in the evening of this day that Sonia was stricken with her gastric attack and had to be taken to the hospital.)

'The Shunned House' deals with a house that has exercised a fascination upon the first-person narrator since boyhood. After conducting exhaustive historical research on the place, he comes to suspect that some nameless object or entity is causing the frequent deaths in the place by somehow sucking the vitality out of the house's occupants. With his uncle, Elihu Whipple, the narrator spends a night in the house, during which the uncle dies hideously. The next day the narrator brings six carboys of sulphuric acid to the house, digs up the earth where a doubled-up anthropomorphic shape lies, and pours the acid down the hole—realizing only then that the shape was merely the 'titan *elbow*' of some huge and hideous monster.

What is remarkable about 'The Shunned House' is the exquisite linkage of real and imagined history throughout the tale. Much of the history of the house is real, as are other details. But on the other hand, there are sly insertions of fictitious events and connections into the historical record. The most interesting elaboration upon history in the story is the figure of Etienne Roulet, a kind of vampire from the seventeenth century who is discovered to have caused the haunting of the house. This figure is mythical, but his purported descendant, Jacques Roulet of Caude, is very real. Lovecraft's brief mention of him is taken almost verbatim from the account in John Fiske's *Myths and Myth-Makers* (1872), which we have already seen was a significant source of Lovecraft's early views on the anthropology of religion.

The most interesting part of the story—in terms of Lovecraft's future development as a writer—is a passage in which the narrator attempts to come to grips with the exact nature of the malevolent entity. He comes to believe that the peculiar entity 'was surely not a physical or biochemical impossibility in the light of a newer science which includes the theories of relativity and intra-atomic action'. This remarkable passage suddenly transforms 'The Shunned House' into a sort of proto-science-fiction story, in that it enunciates the crucial principle of a scientific rationale for a seemingly supernatural occurrence or event. A year and a half after he had expressed bafflement and perturbation at the Einstein theory, Lovecraft is making convenient use of it in fiction. The reference to 'intra-atomic action' is some sort of bow to the quantum theory, although I have not found any discussions of it at this time in letters. Whether this scientific account is at all convincing or plausible is not quite to the point; it is the gesture that is important. That the entity is killed not by driving a stake through its heart but by sulphuric acid is telling.

Lovecraft read the story to the gang on 16 November and was heartened at their enthusiastic response. Loveman was particularly keen, and wanted Lovecraft to type it by the 19th so that he could show it to a reader at Alfred A. Knopf. This did not happen, as Lovecraft did not finish typing the story until the 22nd, but Loveman continued throughout the next year to try to promote the story. We shall discover, indeed, that its experiences in print were not very happy.

Lovecraft moved to a one-room apartment (with two alcoves) at 169 Clinton Street in Brooklyn Heights on 31 December, the same day that Sonia caught a train to Cincinnati. The couple had cohabited for only ten continuous months; the occasions on which Sonia returned to New York from the Midwest over the next year and a quarter amounted to a net total of about thirteen weeks. It is too early to pass judgment on Lovecraft as a husband; we must first examine what the next fifteen months would bring. He may or may not have been secretly pleased at Sonia's departure; but if he thought that 1924 was a year he would rather forget, he had no idea what 1925 would be like.

CHAPTER TWELVE
Moriturus Te Saluto (1925–26)

Lovecraft found the first-floor apartment at 169 Clinton Street pleasing, since the two alcoves—one for dressing and the other for washing—allowed him to preserve a study-like effect in the room proper. There were no cooking facilities in the apartment. The only thing he found disappointing, at least initially, was the seediness of the general area; but he knew that beggars could not be choosers. At $40 a month the place was a pretty good deal, especially since Sonia—during her infrequent visits there—could be accommodated well enough, as the sofa could be unfolded into a double bed. When Sonia was not there, Lovecraft would frequently lie on the couch without opening it, or sometimes doze in the morris chair.

Let us first examine the precise degree to which, in the year 1925, Lovecraft was alone. Sonia's job at Mabley & Carew's, the Cincinnati department store, evidently allowed her to make monthly trips of a few days to New York. But as early as late February Sonia had either lost or had resigned from this position. She also spent a short time on two separate occasions in a private hospital in Cincinnati. Accordingly, Sonia returned to Brooklyn for an extended period in February and March, deciding belatedly to take the six weeks' rest recommended by her doctors. She spent most of the period from late March to early June in the home of a woman physician in Saratoga Springs, in upstate New York.

Sonia spent another extended period in June and July in Brooklyn. In mid-July she secured some sort of position with a hat shop or department store in Cleveland, leaving on the 24th. By mid-October, however, she had again either lost or given up this position (which was on a commission basis). By mid-November at the latest, and probably somewhat earlier, Sonia had secured a new position, this time with Halle's, then (and, up to about a decade ago, when it went out of business) the leading department store in Cleveland. This position appears to have lasted well into 1926.

The upshot of all this is that Sonia was at 169 Clinton Street for a total of only 89 days in 1925, on nine different occasions as follows:

11–16 January; 3–6 February; 23 February–19 March; 8–11 April ; 2–5 May; 9 June–24 July; 15–20 August; 16–17 September; 16–18 October. She had wanted to come during the Christmas holidays, but work at Halle's was too heavy to permit it. In the three and a half months that Lovecraft spent in Brooklyn in 1926, Sonia was there for a period of about three weeks, from roughly 15 January to 5 February. In other words, for the fifteen and a half months of Lovecraft's stay at 169 Clinton Street in 1925–26, Sonia was present for a net total of just over three months at widely scattered intervals; the six weeks in June and July constituted the longest single visit.

If Sonia's record of employment during this period was chequered, Lovecraft's was completely hopeless. There are, in the 160,000 words of correspondence to Lillian for 1925–26, only three references to looking through the Sunday *Times* want ads for work; none of these came to anything. It is evident that, with Sonia out of the way, Lovecraft simply stopped looking very hard for work. I am not sure there is anything to criticize in this: many individuals who suffer prolonged unemployment become discouraged, and, in spite of the clumsiness and inexperience with which Lovecraft attempted to find work in 1924, he did make the attempt with determination and zeal.

Lovecraft's job attempts in 1925 were largely a product of various tips he received from his friends. The one that seemed most promising was freelance work on a trade journal in which Arthur Leeds was involved with another man named Yesley. This does not exactly sound like work for which Lovecraft would be suited, but all it really took is facility at writing, which he certainly had. Difficult as it may be to imagine Lovecraft writing advertising copy, we have the evidence in front of us in the form of five such pieces found among his effects (evidently unpublished). R. H. Barlow bestowed upon them the generic title of 'Commercial Blurbs'. Sadly, the venture did not pan out, and through no fault of Lovecraft's. In February Morton secured his position with the Paterson Museum; it would last the rest of his life. By mid-July Lovecraft was talking about the possibility that Morton might hire him as an assistant, and this rather dim prospect continued to be bruited about sporadically all the way up to Lovecraft's departure from New York in April 1926.

There was, of course, money trickling in from *Weird Tales*. Lovecraft had five stories published in the magazine in 1925. We know the amounts received for three of these: $35 for 'The Festival' (January), $25 for 'The Unnamable' (July), and $50 for 'The Temple' (September); we do not know the amounts for the other two ('The Statement of Randolph Carter' (February) and 'The Music of Erich Zann' (May)), but they each probably averaged in the $30 range. These five sales make a rough total of $170 for the year—barely equivalent to four months' rent.

Where was the other money—for food, laundry, modest travel, clothing, household items, and of course the other eight months' rent—coming from? Clearly Sonia was largely supporting him, and his aunts were contributing as best they could. Sonia, however, speaks very bitterly on this subject in a letter to Samuel Loveman: 'When we lived at 259 Parkside, his aunts sent him five dollars ($5) a week. They expected me to support him. When he moved to Clinton St., they sent him $15 a week. His rent was $40 a month. Food, carfare, and laundry and writing materials cost more than $5 a week. It was this "more" that I supplied.'[1] And yet, Sonia has perhaps exaggerated a little. Lovecraft frequently acknowledges receipt of (mostly unspecified) sums from Lillian, and Annie was paying for his daily subscription to the *Providence Evening Bulletin*. In other words, there is every reason to believe that the aunts were contributing as best they could, although no doubt Sonia was still bearing the lion's share of Lovecraft's expenses.

The absence of remunerative work, of course, simply left Lovecraft that much more time to hang around with his friends. The year 1925 is the real pinnacle of the Kalem Club. Lovecraft and Kirk continued to be close; although Kirk was nominally employed as the owner of a bookstore, he could essentially set his own hours, and so made very congenial company for Lovecraft the night owl.

There is scarcely a day in the entire year when Lovecraft did not meet with one or the other of his friends—either as they came over to his place or as they met at various cafeterias in Manhattan or Brooklyn or at the formal Wednesday meetings. So busy was he with these social obligations—as well as apparently voluminous correspondence relating to the UAPA—that he wrote almost nothing during the first seven months of the year save a handful of poems, and many of these were written to order for meetings of the Blue Pencil Club.

Kirk writes to his fiancée on 6 February about the actual naming of the club: 'Because all of the last names of the permanent members of our club begin with K, L or M, we plan to call it the KALEM

KLYBB. Half a dozen friends are to be here tonight. Mostly they're bores. All but me and HPL …'[2] I wonder whether the exact form of the name had anything to do with an old film company of 1905 called Kalem, formed on exactly the same principle by George Kleine, Samuel Long, and Frank Marion. It is possible that one or more of the members subconsciously recollected this name in forming the name of their club. Lovecraft, however, never refers to the group as the Kalems in the correspondence of this period, citing it merely as 'the gang' or 'The Boys'.

Lovecraft at first did make the attempt to spend time with Sonia on her infrequent visits into town: he notes that he skipped a meeting of the Boys on 4 February because she was not feeling well. But as time went on—and especially during Sonia's long stay in June and July—he became less conscientious. Even during her stay in February–March Lovecraft would stay out so late that he would come home well after Sonia was asleep and wake up late in the morning (or even early in the afternoon) to find that she had already gone out.

The one thing Lovecraft could do during Sonia's absence is control his eating habits. He told Moe that after passing 193 pounds he refused to mount a pair of scales; but in January his reducing plan began in earnest. The upshot is that in a few months Lovecraft went from close to 200 pounds to 146; from a 16 collar to 14½. All his suits had to be retailored, and each week he bought smaller and smaller collars. What was the reaction by his friends, family, and wife to this radical reduction?

> As you may imagine, my wife protested fearfully at what seemed an alarming decline. I received long scolding letters from my aunts, and was lectured severely by Mrs. Long every time I went up to see Little Belknap. But I knew what I was doing, and kept on like grim death … I now publickly avow my personal mastery of my diet, and do not permit my wife to feed me in excess of it.[3]

Lovecraft's letters to his aunts elaborate considerably upon this account. He writes in April:

> Diet & walking are the stuff—which reminds me that tonight I've begun my home dining programme, having spent *30 cents* for a lot of food which ought to last about *3* meals:

```
1 loaf bread ........................................................ 0.06
1 medium can beans ......................................... 0.14
¼ lb cheese ...................................................... 0.10
Total ................................................................ 0.30⁴
```

Lovecraft seems to have written the above in an effort to prove his skill at economizing during lean times, and he no doubt expected to be praised for his frugality; but his next letter suggests that the response was very different:

> As to my dietary programme—bosh! I *am* eating enough! Just you take a medium-sized loaf of bread, cut it in four equal parts, & add to each of these ¼ can (medium) Heinz beans & a goodly chunk of cheese. If the result isn't a full-sized, healthy day's quota of fodder for an Old Gentleman, I'll resign from the League of Nations' dietary committee!! It only costs 8 cents—but don't let that prejudice you! It's good sound food, & many vigorous Chinamen live on vastly less. Of course, from time to time I'll vary the 'meat course' by getting something instead of beans—canned spaghetti, beef stew, corned beef, &c. &c. &c.—& once in a while I'll add a dessert of cookies or some such thing. Fruit, also, is conceivable.⁵

This is surely one of the most remarkable passages in all Lovecraft's correspondence. It suggests many things at once—the crippling poverty under which he was at this time living (and, although under somewhat less straitened circumstances, he would continue to live for the rest of his life, even back in Providence); the fact that he had largely abandoned restaurant meals in the interest of economy; and the rather schoolboyish tone of the entire passage, as if he were a teenager attempting to justify his behaviour to his parents.

There is a still more depressing note in all this. In October Lovecraft was forced to buy an oil heater for the winter, since the heat provided by his landlandy, Mrs Burns—especially in the wake of a nationwide coal strike organized by the United Mine Workers and lasting from September 1925 to February 1926—was insufficient. The heater came with a stove-top attachment, so that Lovecraft could now indulge in the luxury of 'the preparation of *hot dinners*. No more cold beans & spaghetti for me ...'⁶ Does this mean that, for the first nine and a half months of the year, Lovecraft was eating cold meals, mostly out of cans? In spite of an earlier remark about heating beans on a 'sterno' (a tin of a waxlike flammable substance), this seems to be a dismal probability—else why would he boast about the prospect of hot dinners?

The room at 169 Clinton Street really was rather dismal—in a run-down neighbourhood, with a dubious clientele, and infested with mice. For this last problem Lovecraft purchased 5-cent mouse-traps, as recommended by Kirk, 'since I can throw them away without removing the corpus delicti, a thing I should hate to do with a costlier bit of mechanism'.[7] (Later he found even cheaper traps at two for 5 cents.) Lovecraft has been ridiculed for this squeamishness, but I think unjustly. Not many of us would wish to handle the corpses of mice.

The final insult came on the morning of Sunday 24 May. While Lovecraft was sleeping on the couch after an all-night writing session, his dressing alcove was broken into from the connecting apartment and he was robbed of nearly all his suits, along with sundry other abstractions. The thieves removed three of his suits (dating from 1914, 1921, and 1923), one overcoat (the fashionable 1924 coat that Sonia had purchased for him), a wicker suitcase of Sonia's (although the contents were later found in the thieves' apartment), and an expensive $100 radio set that Loveman had been storing in the alcove. All that Lovecraft was left with, in terms of suits, was a thin 1918 blue suit hanging on a chair in the main room, which the thieves did not enter. Lovecraft did not discover the robbery until 1.30 a.m. on Tuesday the 26th, since he had had no previous occasion to enter the alcove.

The property was of course never recovered, although a police detective came over and promised to do his best. And yet, after an initial outburst of anger and frustration, Lovecraft managed to respond to the whole situation with surprising good humour, for only two days later he wrote a long letter to Lillian on the matter and in the process made light of the situation:

> Alas for the robes of my infancy, perennial in their bloom, &
> now cut off—or snatched off—in the finest flowering of their
> first few decades! They knew the slender youth of old, &
> expanded to accomodate [sic] the portly citizen of middle
> life—aye, & condensed again to shroud the wizened shanks
> of old age! And now they are gone—gone—& the grey, bent
> wearer still lives to bemoan his nudity; gathering around his
> lean sides as best he may the strands of his long white beard
> to serve him in the office of a garment![8]

What now transpired was a five-month hunt for the cheapest but most tasteful suits Lovecraft could endure to wear; in the process Lovecraft gained a considerable knowledge of discount clothing stores and even the rudiments of haggling. He could not feel comfortable without four suits—two light and two dark, one each for summer and winter. He really did not think it possible—based on conversations with Long, Leeds, and others—to get a good suit for under $35, but in early July, when Sonia was in town, he found a good suit for $25 at Monroe Clothes, a chain store. This was a summer suit, and Lovecraft began wearing it immediately. In October he decided to buy a heavy suit for winter, since the weather was turning colder. This, he knew, would be a considerably more difficult proposition, for really good winter suits can rarely be secured at bargain prices. To his dismay he found, on his weary peregrinations, that 'In this age of well-heated houses men have stopped wearing the heavy clothing they used to wear ... so that the unhappy victim of a menage in which the name *Burns* applies to the family instead of the fuel is very literally left out in the cold!'[9]

Finally he seemed to come across just what he wanted, at the Borough Clothiers in Fulton Street in Brooklyn. Lovecraft was very shrewd in dealing with the salesman: he said that he really wanted only a provisional suit until he could get a better one, therefore implying that he might buy another suit from the place later (not mentioning that it might be more than a year before he did so); the salesman, accordingly, consulted with a superior and showed him a more expensive suit but priced it at only $25. Lovecraft bought it, and took to calling it 'the triumph'.

But he quickly came to the conclusion that he would need to buy a cheap winter suit in order not to wear out the good one, so in late October he undertook yet another long quest for a suit under $15 for everyday wear. The first place Lovecraft went was the row of stores on 14th Street between Sixth and Seventh Avenues in Manhattan, then (as now) the haven of discount clothing in the city. What he found, after trying 'a dozen coats of varying degrees of impossibility', was a coat that was 'a limp rag; crushed, dusty, twisted, & out-of-press, but I saw that cut, fabric, & fit were just right'. It was part of a $9.95 sale; but the problem was that there was no exactly matching set of trousers. Accompanying it were one trouser that was too long and two that were too short. The salesman was trying to get Lovecraft to accept the short trousers, but Lovecraft wanted the long one; after considerable haggling

Lovecraft persuaded the salesman to sell him the coat, the long
trousers, and one of the short trousers, all for $11.95. This was all
pretty clever on Lovecraft's part, and a tailor repaired the coat and
trousers the next day. This entire adventure, too, is narrated by
Lovecraft in a long and piquant letter to Lillian; in the course of
which he indulges in a long tirade on the subject:

> in general I think I have developed an eye for the difference
> between the clothing a gentleman wears & that which a
> gentleman doesn't. What has sharpened this sense is the
> constant sight of these accursed filthy rabbles that infest the
> N.Y. streets, & whose clothing presents such systematic
> differences from the normal clothing of real people along
> Angell St. & in Butler Ave. or Elmgrove Ave. cars that he
> comes to feel a tremendous homesickness & to pounce
> avidly on any gentleman whose clothes are proper & tasteful
> & suggestive of Blackstone Boulevard rather than Borough
> Hall or Hell's Kitchen … Confound it, I'll be either in good
> Providence taste or in a bally bathrobe!! Certain lapel
> cuts, textures, & fits tell the story. It amuses me to see how
> some of these flashy young 'boobs' & foreigners spend
> fortunes on various kinds of expensive clothes which they
> regard as evidences of meritorious taste, but which in reality
> are their absolute social & aesthetic damnation—being little
> short of placards shrieking in bold letters: *'I am an ignorant
> peasant'*, *'I am a mongrel gutter-rat'*, or *'I am a tasteless & unsoph-
> isticated yokel.'*

To which he adds, with complete ingenuousness, 'And yet perhaps
these creatures are not, after all, seeking to conform to the absolute
artistic standard of gentlefolk.'[10] This remarkable passage testifies to
Lovecraft's inability to dissociate himself from the codes of attire
and general social behaviour inculcated in him in youth. But now
Lovecraft had his four suits, and he need think no more about the
matter.

Not having a job at least meant that Lovecraft could go out with the
boys at almost any time and also indulge in modest travels. His
diary and letters are full of accounts of trips to Van Cortlandt Park,
Fort Greene Park, Yonkers, and elsewhere; there were the usual
walks through the colonial parts of Greenwich Village, and any
number of walks across the Brooklyn Bridge.

On the night of 11 April Lovecraft and Kirk, wishing to take advantage of a special $5 excursion fare to Washington, D.C., boarded the night train at Pennsylvania Station at midnight and arrived at dawn in the capital. They would have only a single morning and afternoon in the city, so they intended to make the most of it. Thanks to the presence of two colleagues who could act as tour guides, Anne Tillery Renshaw (who had a car) and Edward L. Sechrist, the group saw an astonishing number of sites in a few hours: the Library of Congress, the Capitol, the White House, the Washington Monument, the Lincoln Memorial, Georgetown (the colonial town founded in 1751), Christ Church (an exquisite late Georgian structure in Alexandria), Mount Vernon (Washington's home), Arlington (the manor of the Custis family), and the enormous Memorial Amphitheatre completed in 1920, which Lovecraft considered 'one of the most prodigious and spectacular architectural triumphs of the Western World'.[11] They caught the 4.35 train back to New York just in time.

During Sonia's long stay Lovecraft did some travelling with her. The two of them went to Scott Park in Elizabeth on 13 June. On the 28th they went to the Bryn Mawr Park section of Yonkers, where they had attempted to purchase property the previous year. With Long, Lovecraft again visited the Cloisters in Fort Tryon Park, in the far northwest tip of Manhattan.

On 2 July Sonia and Lovecraft took a trip to Coney Island, where he had cotton candy for the first time. On this occasion Sonia had a silhouette of herself made by a black man named Perry; Lovecraft had had his own silhouette done on 26 March. This silhouette has become very well known in recent years, and its very faithful (perhaps even a little flattering) rendition has caused Lovecraft's profile to become an icon; the silhouette of Sonia, on the other hand, is so little known that few have had any idea of its very existence.

Now that Sonia was out of the way and his amateur work apparently finished (he managed to get out the July 1925 *United Amateur* only a few weeks late, and also helped set up the next editorial board through a mail election), Lovecraft felt that the time had come to buckle down to some real creative work. On 1 and 2 August he wrote 'The Horror at Red Hook', which he describes in a letter to Long (who was away on vacation) as follows: 'it deals with hideous cult-practices behind the gangs of noisy young loafers whose essential mystery has impressed me so much. The tale is rather long and rambling, and I don't think it is very good; but it represents at least an attempt to extract horror from an atmosphere to which you deny any qualities save vulgar commonplaceness.'[12] Lovecraft is sadly correct in his analysis of the merits of the story, for it is one of the poorest of his longer efforts.

Red Hook is a small peninsula of Brooklyn facing Governor's Island, about two miles southwest of Borough Hall. Lovecraft could easily walk to the area from 169 Clinton Street, and seems to have done so on several occasions. It was then and still remains one of the most dismal slums in the entire metropolitan area. In the story Lovecraft describes it not inaccurately, although with a certain jaundiced tartness; but of course it is not merely the physical decay that is of interest to him:

> The population is a hopeless tangle and enigma; Syrian, Spanish, Italian, and negro elements impinging upon one another, and fragments of Scandinavian and American belts lying not far distant. It is a babel of sound and filth, and sends out strange cries to answer the lapping of oily waves at its grimy piers and the monstrous organ litanies of the harbour whistles.

Here, in essence, is the heart of the story; for 'The Horror at Red Hook' is nothing but a shriek of rage and loathing at the 'foreigners' who have taken New York away from the white people to whom it presumably belongs.

Sonia in her memoir claims to supply the inspiration for the tale: 'It was on an evening while he, and I think Morton, Sam Loveman and Rheinhart Kleiner were dining in a restaurant somewhere in Columbia Heights that a few rough, rowdyish men entered. He was so annoyed by their churlish behavior that out of this circumstance he wove "The Horror at Red Hook".'[13] Lovecraft may have mentioned this event in a letter to her; but I am not entirely convinced that it was any one incident that gave birth to the story, but rather the cumulative depression of New York after a year and a half of poverty and futility.

The plot of 'The Horror at Red Hook' is simple, and is presented as an elementary good-versus-evil conflict between Thomas Malone, an Irish police detective working out of the Borough Hall station, and Robert Suydam, a wealthy man of ancient Dutch ancestry who becomes the focus of horror in the tale. What strikes us about this tale, aside from the hackneyed supernatural manifestations, is the sheer poorness of its writing. The perfervid rhetoric that in other tales provides such harmless enjoyment here comes off sounding forced and bombastic. Lovecraft cannot help ending the story on a note of dour ponderousness ('The soul of the beast is omnipresent and triumphant') and with a transparent indication that the horrors that were seemingly suppressed by the police will recur at some later date. It is a fittingly stereotyped ending for a story that does nothing but deal in stereotypes—both of race and of weird fictional imagery.

The figure of Malone is of some interest in relation to the possible genesis—or, at any rate, the particular form—of the story. Some time before writing 'The Horror at Red Hook' Lovecraft had submitted 'The Shunned House' to *Detective Tales*, the magazine that had been founded together with *Weird Tales* and of which Edwin Baird was the editor. In spite of the fact that *Detective Tales* did occasionally print tales of horror and the supernatural, Baird rejected the story. By late July Lovecraft is speaking of writing a 'novel or novelette of Salem horrors which I may be able to cast in a sufficiently "detectivish" mould to sell to Edwin Baird for *Detective Tales*',[14] but he does not appear to have begun such a work. What this all suggests, however, is that Lovecraft is attempting to develop, however impractically, an alternative market to *Weird Tales*—and is calling upon the man who, as editor of *Weird Tales*, accepted all his stories to aid him in the attempt. Sure enough, in early August Lovecraft speaks of planning to send 'The Horror at Red Hook' to *Detective Tales*; whether he actually did so is unclear, but, if he did, the tale was obviously rejected. Lovecraft would later remark that the story was consciously written with *Weird Tales* in mind,[15] and sure enough it appeared in the January 1927 issue.

'The Horror at Red Hook' presents as good an opportunity as any for discussing the development (if it can be called that) of Love-craft's racial attitudes during this period. There is no question that his racism flared to greater heights at this time—at least on paper (as embodied in letters to his aunts)—than at any subsequent period in his life. There is no need to dwell upon the seeming paradox of Lovecraft's marrying a Jewess when he exhibited marked anti-Semitic traits, for Sonia in his mind fulfilled his requirement that aliens assimilate themselves into the American population, as did other Jews such as Samuel Loveman. Never-theless, Sonia speaks at length about Lovecraft's attitudes on this subject. One of her most celebrated comments is as follows:

> Although he once said he loved New York and that hence-
> forth it would be his 'adopted state', I soon learned that he
> hated it and all its 'alien hordes'. When I protested that I too
> was one of them, he'd tell me I 'no longer belonged to these
> mongrels'. *'You are now Mrs. H. P. Lovecraft of 598 Angell St.,
> Providence, Rhode Island!'*[16]

Let it pass that Lovecraft and Sonia never resided at 598 Angell
Street. A later remark is still more telling: 'Soon after we were
married he told me that whenever we have company he would
appreciate it if there were "Aryans" in the majority.'[17] This must
refer to the year 1924, as they would not have done much entertaining in 1925. Sonia's final remark on the matter is still more
damning. Sonia claims that part of her desire to have Lovecraft and
Loveman meet in 1922 was to 'cure' Lovecraft of his bias against
Jews by actually meeting one face to face. She continues:

> Unfortunately, one often judges a whole people by the
> character of the first ones he meets. But H. P. assured me
> that he was quite 'cured'; that since I was so well assimilated
> into the American way of life and the American scene he felt
> sure our marriage would be a success. But unfortunately
> (and here I must speak of something I never intended to
> have publicly known), whenever he would meet crowds of
> people—in the subway, or, at the noon hour, on the side-
> walks in Broadway, or crowds, wherever he happened to
> find them, and these were usually the workers of minority
> races—he would become livid with anger and rage.[18]

Again, there is nothing here that need surprise us. And yet, in spite
of what his previous biographer, L. Sprague de Camp, has suggested,
comments on aliens are relatively rare in the correspondence to his
aunts during this period. A long letter in early January goes on at
length about the fundamental inassimilability of Jews in American
life, maintaining that 'vast harm is done by those idealists who
encourage belief in a coalescence which never can be'. When he
goes on to note that 'On our side there is a shuddering physical
repugnance to most Semitic types',[19] he is unwittingly reaching the
heart of the issue, at least as far as he himself is concerned: in spite
of Lovecraft's talk about cultural inassimiliability, what he really
finds offensive about foreigners (or, more broadly, non-'Aryans',

since many of the ethnics in New York were already first- or second-generation immigrants) is the fact that they look funny to him.

Of course, Lovecraft's hostility was exacerbated by his increasingly shaky psychological state as he found himself dragging out a life in an unfamiliar, unfriendly city where he did not seem to belong and where he had few[prospects for work or permanent comfort. Foreigners made convenient scapegoats, and New York City, then and now the most cosmopolitan and culturally heterogeneous city in the country, stood in stark contrast to the homogeneity and conservatism he had known in the first thirty-four years of his life in New England. The city that had seemed such a fount of Dunsanian glamour and wonder had become a dirty, noisy, overcrowded place that dealt repeated blows to his self-esteem by denying him a job in spite of his abilities and by forcing him to hole up in a seedy, mice-infested, crime-ridden dump where all he could do was write racist stories like 'The Horror at Red Hook' as a safety-valve for his anger and despair.

Lovecraft was, however, not finished with creative work. Eight days after writing the story, on 10 August, he began a long, lone evening ramble that led through Greenwich Village to the Battery, then to the ferry to Elizabeth, which he reached at 7 a.m. He purchased a 10-cent composition book at a shop, went to Scott Park, and wrote the story 'He'. It is interesting that in this instance Lovecraft had to leave New York in order to write about it. 'He', while much superior to 'The Horror at Red Hook', is as heart-wrenching a cry of despair as its predecessor—quite avowedly so. Its opening is celebrated:

> I saw him on a sleepless night when I was walking desperately to save my soul and my vision. My coming to New York had been a mistake; for whereas I had looked for poignant wonder and inspiration in the teeming labyrinths of ancient streets that twist endlessly from forgotten courts and squares and waterfronts to courts and squares and waterfronts equally forgotten, and in the Cyclopean modern towers and pinnacles that rise blackly Babylonian under waning moons, I had found instead only a sense of horror and oppression which threatened to master, paralyse, and annihilate me.

In this story Lovecraft presents a kind of sociology of New York: the immigrants who have clustered there really have no 'kinship' with it because the city was founded by the Dutch and the English, and these immigrants are of a different cultural heritage altogether. This sophism allows Lovecraft to conclude that 'this city of stone and stridor is not a sentient perpetuation of Old New York as London is of Old London and Paris of Old Paris, but that it is in fact quite dead, its sprawling body imperfectly embalmed and infested with queer animate things which have nothing to do with it as it was in life'. The immigrants are now considered to be on the level of maggots.

The narrator, like Lovecraft, seeks out Greenwich Village in particular; and it is here, at two in the morning one August night, that he meets 'the man', who leads him to an ancient manor-house and shows him spectacularly apocalyptic visions of past and future New York through a window. Can the specific locale of the story be identified? At the end of the tale the narrator finds himself 'at the entrance of a little black court off Perry Street'; and this is all we need to realize that this segment of the tale was inspired by a similar expedition to Perry Street that Lovecraft took on 29 August 1924, inspired by an article in the *New York Evening Post* for that day, in a regular column entitled 'Little Sketches About Town'. The exact site is 93 Perry Street, where an archway leads to a lane between three buildings. What is more, according to an historical monograph on Perry Street, this general area was heavily settled by Indians (they had named it Sapohanican), and, moreover, a sump-tuous mansion was built in the block bounded by Perry, Charles, Bleecker, and West Fourth Streets sometime between 1726 and 1744, being the residence of a succession of wealthy citizens until it was razed in 1865.[20] Lovecraft almost certainly knew the history of the area, and he has deftly incorporated it into his tale.

Farnsworth Wright accepted 'He' in early October, and it appear-ed in *Weird Tales* for September 1926. Strangely enough, Lovecraft had not yet submitted 'The Shunned House' to Wright, but when he did so (probably in early September) Wright eventually turned it down on the grounds that it began too gradually. Lovecraft does not make any notable comment on this rejection, even though it was the first rejection he had ever had from *Weird Tales*.

The writing of 'He', however, did not put an entire end to Lovecraft's fictional efforts. The Kalem meeting on Wednesday, 12 August, broke up at 4 a.m.; Lovecraft immediately went home and mapped out 'a new story plot—perhaps a short novel' which he titled 'The Call of Cthulhu'.[21] Although he confidently reports that 'the writing itself will now be a relatively simple matter', it would be more than a year before he would write this seminal story. It is a little sad to note how Lovecraft attempts to justify his state of chronic unemployment by suggesting to Lillian that a lengthy story of this sort 'ought to bring in a very decent sized cheque'; he had earlier noted that the projected Salem novelette or novel, 'if accepted, would bring in a goodly sum of cash'.[22] It is as if he is desperately seeking to convince Lillian that he is not a drain on her (and Sonia's) finances in spite of his lack of a regular position and his continual cafeteria-lounging with the boys.

Some time in August Lovecraft received a plot idea from C. W. Smith, editor of the *Tryout*. The resulting tale, 'In the Vault', written on 18 September, is poorer than 'He' but not quite as horrendously bad as 'The Horror at Red Hook'; it is merely mediocre. This elementary supernatural revenge tale, recounting what happens to George Birch, a careless and thick-skinned undertaker, who finds himself trapped in the receiving-tomb of the cemetery he runs, is a curiously conventional tale for Lovecraft to have written at this stage of his career. He attempts to write in a more homespun, colloquial vein, but the result is not successful. August Derleth developed an unfortunate fondness for this tale, so that it still stands embalmed among volumes of Lovecraft's 'best' stories.

The tale's immediate fortunes were not very happy, either. Lovecraft dedicated the story to C. W. Smith, and it appeared in Smith's *Tryout* for November 1925. Of course Lovecraft also sought professional publication; and although it would seem that 'In the Vault', in its limited scope and conventionally macabre orientation, would be ready-made for *Weird Tales*, Wright rejected it in November. The reason for the rejection, according to Lovecraft, is interesting: 'its extreme gruesomeness would not pass the Indiana censorship'.[23] The reference, of course, is to the banning of Eddy's 'The Loved Dead'. Here then is the first—but not the last—instance where the apparent uproar over 'The Loved Dead' had a negative impact upon Lovecraft.

There was, however, better news from Wright. Lovecraft had evidently sent him 'The Outsider' merely for his examination, as it was already promised to W. Paul Cook—apparently for the *Recluse*, which Cook had conceived around September. Wright liked the story so much that he pleaded with Lovecraft to let him print it. Lovecraft managed to persuade Cook to release the story, and Wright accepted it some time around the end of the year; its appearance in *Weird Tales* for April 1926 would be a landmark.

The rest of the year was spent variously in activity with the Kalems, in receiving out-of-town guests, and in solitary travels of an increasingly wider scope in search of antiquarian oases. Lovecraft took pleasure in acting as host to the Kalems on occasion, and his letters display how much he enjoyed treating his friends to coffee, cake, and other humble delectables on his best blue china. On 29 July he bought for 49 cents an aluminum pail with which to fetch hot coffee from the deli at the corner of State and Court Streets.

Some new colleagues emerged on Lovecraft's horizon about this time. One, Wilfred Blanch Talman (1904–1986), was an amateur of Dutch ancestry who was attending Brown University. The two met in late August, and Lovecraft took to him immediately. Talman went on to become a reporter for the *New York Times* and later an editor of the *Texaco Star*, a paper issued by the oil company. He made random ventures into professional fiction, and would later have one of his stories subjected to (possibly unwanted) revision by Lovecraft. Talman was perhaps the first addition to the core membership of the Kalem Club, although he did not begin regular attendance until after Lovecraft had left New York.

A still more congenial colleague was Vrest Teachout Orton (1897–1986). Orton was a friend of W. Paul Cook, and at this time worked in the advertising department of the *American Mercury*. Later he would achieve distinction as an editor at the *Saturday Review of Literature* and, still later, as the founder of the Vermont Country Store. Orton became perhaps the second honorary member of the Kalems, although his attendance at meetings was also irregular until after Lovecraft's departure from New York. Orton did a little literary work of his own—he compiled a bibliography of Theodore Dreiser, *Dreiserana* (1929), founded the *Colophon*, a bibliophiles' magazine, and later founded the Stephen Daye Press in Vermont, for which Lovecraft would do some freelance work— but he had little interest in the weird. Nevertheless, their mutual New England background and their loathing of New York gave the two men much to talk about.

Aside from activities with friends, Lovecraft engaged in much solitary travel in the latter half of 1925. One of his most extensive trips of the season was a three-day trip to Jamaica, Mineola, Hempstead, Garden City, and Freeport on Long Island. Jamaica was then a separate community but is now a part of Queens; the other towns are in Nassau County, east of Queens. On 27 September Lovecraft went to Jamaica, which 'utterly astonisht' him: 'There, all about me, lay a veritable New-England village; with wooden colonial houses, Georgian churches, & deliciously sleepy & shady streets where giant elms & maples stood in dense & luxurious rows.'[24] Things are, I fear, very different now. Thereafter he went north to Flushing, also once separate and also now part of Queens. This was a Dutch settlement, and it too retained gratifying touches of colonialism. One structure—the Bowne house (1661) at Bowne Street and 37th Avenue—particularly delighted him.

The 29th, however, was his great Long Island journey. Reaching Garden City, he saw the extensive college-like brick buildings of Doubleday, Page & Co., now (after many years as Doubleday, Doran) simply Doubleday; the publisher has moved its editorial offices to Manhattan but still retains a considerable presence in its city of origin. Continuing southward on foot, he came to Hempstead, which captivated him utterly. Once again it was the churches that delighted him—St George's Episcopal, Methodist, Christ's First Presbyterian, and others. He spent considerable time in Hempstead, then continued south on foot to Freeport, which he found pleasant but undistinguished from an antiquarian point of view. All this walking must have covered close to ten miles.

The importance of these expeditions to Lovecraft's psyche can scarcely be overestimated. The shimmering skyscrapers of Manhattan had proved, upon closer examination, to be an oppressive horror; as he had noted when refusing the offer to edit *Weird Tales* in Chicago, 'it is colonial atmosphere which supplies my very breath of life'.[25] Lovecraft had, indeed, developed an uncanny nose for antiquity, whether it be in Manhattan, Brooklyn, or in the further reaches of the metropolitan area.

After September Lovecraft lapsed again into literary quiescence. Then, in mid-November, he announces that 'W. Paul Cook wants an article from me on the element of terror & weirdness in literature'[26] for his new magazine, the *Recluse*. He goes on to say that 'I shall take my time about preparing it', which was true enough: it would be close to a year and a half before he put the finishing touches on what would become 'Supernatural Horror in Literature'.

Lovecraft began the actual writing of the article in late December; by early January he had already written the first four chapters and was reading Emily Brontë's *Wuthering Heights* preparatory to writing about it at the end of Chapter V; by March he had written Chapter VII, on Poe; and by the middle of April he had gotten 'half through Arthur Machen' (Chapter X).[27] It is not entirely clear from his initial mention that Cook actually wished an historical monograph—an essay 'on the element of terror & weirdness' could just as well have been theoretical or thematic—but Lovecraft clearly interpreted it this way.

Lovecraft had, of course, read much of the significant weird literature up to his time, but he was still making discoveries. Two of the writers whom he would rank very highly were encountered only at about this time. He had first read Algernon Blackwood (1869–1951) as early as 1920, at the recommendation of James F. Morton, but did not care for him at all at this time. Then, in late September 1924, he read *The Listener and Other Stories* (1907), containing 'The Willows', 'perhaps the most devastating piece of supernaturally hideous suggestion which I have beheld in a decade'.[28] In later years Lovecraft would unhesitatingly (and, I think, correctly) deem 'The Willows' the single greatest weird story ever written, followed by Machen's 'The White People'.

As with Machen and Dunsany, Blackwood is an author Lovecraft should have discovered earlier than he did. His first book, *The Empty House and Other Stories* (1906), is admittedly slight, although with a few notable items. *John Silence—Physician Extraordinary* (1908) became a bestseller, allowing Blackwood to spend the years 1908–14 in Switzerland, where he did most of his best work. *Incredible Adventures* (1914)—the very volume toward which Lovecraft was so lukewarm in 1920—is one of the great weird collections of all time.

Blackwood was frankly a mystic. In his autobiography, *Episodes Before Thirty* (1923), he admits to relieving the heavy and conventional religiosity of his household by an absorption of Buddhist philosophy, and he ultimately developed a remarkably vital and intensely felt pantheism that emerges most clearly in his novel *The Centaur* (1911), the central work in his corpus and the equivalent of a spiritual autobiography. In a sense Blackwood sought the same sort of return to the natural world as Dunsany. But because he was, unlike Dunsany, a mystic, he would see in the return to Nature a shedding of the moral and spiritual blinders which in his view modern urban civilization places upon us; hence his ultimate goal is an expansion of consciousness that opens up to our perception the boundless universe with its throbbing presences. Several of his novels deal explicitly with reincarnation, in such a way as to suggest that Blackwood himself clearly believed in it. Philosophically, therefore, Blackwood and Lovecraft were poles apart; but the latter never let that bother him, and there is much in Blackwood to relish even if one does not subscribe to his world view.

Montague Rhodes James (1862–1936) is a much different proposition. Weird writing represents a quite small proportion of his writing, and was indeed merely a diversion from his work as educator, authority on medieval manuscripts, and Biblical scholar. His edition of the Apocryphal New Testament (1924) long remained standard. James took to telling ghost stories while at Cambridge, and his first tales were recited at a meeting of the Chitchat Society in 1893. He later became Provost of Eton and began telling his tales to his young charges at Christmas. They were eventually collected in four volumes: *Ghost-Stories of an Antiquary* (1904); *More Ghost Stories of an Antiquary* (1911); *A Thin Ghost and Others* (1919); and *A Warning to the Curious* (1925). This relatively slim body of work is none the less a landmark in weird literature. If nothing else, it represents the ultimate refinement of the conventional ghost story. James was a master at short story construction; he also was one of the few who could write in a chatty, whimsical, and bantering style without destroying the potency of his horrors. Like Lovecraft and Machen, James has attracted a somewhat fanatical cadre of devotees. But in all honesty, much of James's work is thin and insubstantial: he had no vision of the world to put across, as Machen, Dunsany, Blackwood, and Lovecraft did, and many of his tales seem like academic exercises in shudder-mongering. Lovecraft seems first to have read James in mid-December 1925. Although his enthusiasm for him was high at the time, it would later cool off. In 'Supernatural Horror in Literature' he would rank James as a 'modern master', but by 1932 he declared that 'he isn't really in the Machen, Blackwood, & Dunsany class. He is the earthiest member of the "big four"'.[29]

There was not much criticism of weird fiction up to this time upon which Lovecraft could draw for his treatise. He read Edith Birkhead's *The Tale of Terror* (1921), a landmark study of Gothic fiction, in late November; it is quite clear that he borrowed heavily from this treatise in his chapters (II–V) on the Gothics, both in the structure of his analysis and in some points of evaluation. Eino Railo's *The Haunted Castle* (1927) came out just about the time of Lovecraft's own essay; it is a very penetrating historical and thematic study that Lovecraft later read with appreciation. Conversely, the only exhaustive study of *modern* weird fiction was Dorothy Scarborough's *The Supernatural in Modern English Fiction* (1917), which Lovecraft would not read until 1932; but, when he did so, he rightly criticized it as being overly schematic in its thematic analyses and hampered by an amusing squeamishness in the face of the explicit horrors of Stoker, Machen, and others.

Lovecraft's essay, accordingly, gains its greatest originality as an historical study in its final six chapters. His lengthy chapter on Poe is, I think, one of the most perceptive short analyses ever written, in spite of a certain flamboyancy in its diction. Lovecraft could not summon up much enthusiasm for the later Victorians in England, but his lengthy discussions of Hawthorne and Bierce in Chapter VIII are illuminating. And his greatest achievement, perhaps, was to designate Machen, Dunsany, Blackwood, and M. R. James as the four 'modern masters' of the weird tale; a judgment that has been justified by subsequent scholarship. Indeed, the only 'master' lacking from this list is Lovecraft himself.

Lovecraft admitted that the writing of this essay produced two good effects; first: 'It's good preparation for composing a new series of weird tales of my own';[30] and second: 'This course of reading & writing I am going through for the Cook article is excellent mental discipline, & a fine gesture of demarcation betwixt my aimless, lost existence of the past year or two & the resumed Providence-like hermitage amidst which I hope to grind out some tales worth writing.'[31] The second effect is one more in a succession of resolutions to cease his all-day and all-night gallivanting with the gang and get down to real work; how successful this was, it is difficult to say, in the absence of a diary for 1926. As for the first effect, it came to fruition in late February, when 'Cool Air' was apparently written.

'Cool Air' is the last and perhaps the best of Lovecraft's New York stories. It is a compact exposition of pure physical loathsomeness, dealing with what happens when a Dr Muñoz, who requires constant coolness in his New York apartment, finds his air conditioning unit malfunctioning, and the narrator is unable to find anyone to fix it. The result is that Muñoz, who is actually dead but is trying to keep himself alive by artificial preservation, ends as a 'kind of dark, slimy trail [that] led from the open bathroom to the hall door' and that 'ended unutterably'.

The apartment house that serves as the setting of the tale is based on the brownstone occupied by George Kirk both as a residence and as the site of his Chelsea Book Shop at 317 West 14th Street in Manhattan for two months during the late summer of 1925. In regard to literary influences, Lovecraft later admitted that the chief inspiration was not Poe's 'Facts in the Case of M. Valdemar' but Machen's 'Novel of the White Powder' (an episode from *The Three Impostors*),[32] where a hapless student unwittingly takes a drug that reduces him to a loathsome mass of liquescence. And yet, one can hardly deny that M. Valdemar, the man who, after his presumed death, is kept alive after a fashion for months by hypnosis and who at the end collapses 'in a nearly liquid mass of loathsome—of detestable putridity', was somewhere in the back of Lovecraft's mind in the writing of 'Cool Air'. This story, much more than 'The Horror at Red Hook', is Lovecraft's most successful evocation of the horror to be found in the teeming clangour of America's only true megalopolis.

Farnsworth Wright incredibly and inexplicably rejected 'Cool Air', even though it is just the sort of safe, macabre tale he would have liked. Perhaps, as with 'In the Vault', he was afraid of its grisly conclusion. In any event, Lovecraft was forced to sell the story for $18 to the short-lived *Tales of Magic and Mystery*, where it appeared in the March 1928 issue.

Meanwhile Lovecraft finally secured some employment, even if it was of a temporary and, frankly, ignominious sort. In September Loveman had secured work at the prestigious Dauber & Pine bookshop at Fifth Avenue and 12th Street, and he convinced his superiors to hire Lovecraft as an envelope-addresser for three weeks, probably beginning on 7 March. Lovecraft had helped Kirk out at this task on several occasions in 1925, doing the work for free because of Kirk's many kindnesses to him. The pay at the Dauber & Pine job would be $17.50 per week. Lovecraft speaks of the enterprise as a lark ('Moriturus te saluto! Before the final plunge into the abyss I am squaring all my indebtedness to mankind'[33]), but he probably found the work highly tedious, as he never relished repetitive, mechanical tasks of this sort.

Lovecraft himself does not say anything to Lillian about liking or disliking the job. Perhaps he did not wish to seem unwilling to earn a living; but perhaps, by 27 March, he had other things on his mind. His letter to Lillian of that date begins:

> Well!!! All your epistles arrived & received a grateful welcome, but the third one was the climax that relegates everything

else to the distance!! Whoop! Bang! I had to go on a cele-
bration forthwith, ... & have now returned to gloat & reply.
A E P G's letter came, too—riotous symposium!! ...

And now about your invitation. Hooray!! Long live the
State of Rhode-Island & Providence-Plantations!!![34]

In other words, Lovecraft had at last been invited to return to
Providence.

CHAPTER THIRTEEN
Paradise Regain'd (1926)

The saga of Lovecraft's efforts to return to Providence can be said to commence around April 1925, when he writes to Lillian that 'I couldn't bear to see Providence again till I can be there for ever'.[1] Lillian had clearly suggested that Lovecraft pay a visit, perhaps to relieve the tedium and even depression that his lack of work, his dismal Clinton Street room, and the rocky state of his marriage had engendered.

When Lovecraft stated in November 1925 that 'My mental life is really at home'[2] in Providence, he was not exaggerating. For the entirety of his New York stay, he subscribed to the *Providence Evening Bulletin*, reading the *Providence Sunday Journal* (the *Bulletin* published no Sunday edition) along with the *New York Times* on Sunday. He mentally attempted to stay in touch with Providence in other ways, specifically by reading as many books on Providence history as he could.

But reading books was clearly not enough. One of the most remarkable passages in Lovecraft's letters to his aunts is on the subject of personal possessions, and it is an accurate gauge of his temper during the worst of his New York period. Lillian had made the comment (perhaps as a consequence of Lovecraft's long-winded account of purchasing his best suit) that 'possessions are a burden'; Lovecraft, in August 1925, flung this remark back in her face:

> It so happens that I am unable to take pleasure or interest in anything but a mental re-creation of other & better days— for in sooth, I see no possibility of ever encountering a really congenial milieu or living among civilised people with old Yankee historic memories again—so in order to avoid the madness which leads to violence & suicide I must cling to the few shreds of old days & old ways which are left to me. Therefore no one need expect me to discard the ponderous furniture & paintings & clocks & books which help to keep 454 always in my dreams. When they go, I shall go, for they are all that make it possible for me to open my eyes in the

morning or look forward to another day of consciousness without screaming in sheer desperation & pounding the walls & floor in a frenzied clamour to be waked up out of the nightmare of 'reality' & my own room in Providence. Yes— such sensitivenesses of temperament are very inconvenient when one has no money—but it's easier to criticise than to cure them. When a poor fool possessing them allows himself to get exiled & sidetracked through temporarily false perspective & ignorance of the world, the only thing to do is to let him cling to his pathetic scraps as long as he can hold them. They are life for him.[3]

A treatise could be written on this poignant passage. How Lillian reacted to her only nephew speaking with apparent seriousness— or, at least, with extreme bitterness—about suicide and screaming and pounding the walls, it is not possible to say.

There is a very curious sidelight to this entire matter. Winfield Townley Scott claims that, according to Samuel Loveman, Lovecraft during the latter part of his New York period 'carried a phial of poison with him' (Loveman's words) so as to be able to put an end to his existence if things became too unbearable.[4] In all honesty, I find this notion preposterous. I flatly believe that Loveman has invented this story. Loveman turned against Lovecraft's memory later in life, largely on the belief that Lovecraft's anti-Semitism (about which he learned from Sonia as early as 1948) made him a hypocrite. It is also possible that Loveman simply misunderstood something that Lovecraft had said—perhaps something meant as a sardonic joke. There is certainly no independent confirmation of this anecdote, and no mention of it by any other friend or correspondent; and one suspects that Lovecraft would have confided in Long more than in Loveman on a matter of such delicacy. I think it is quite out of character for Lovecraft to have come so close to suicide even during this difficult period; indeed, the general tenor of his letters to his aunts, even taking into consideration such passages as I have quoted above, is by no means uniformly depressed or lugubrious.

The subject of Lovecraft's return was broached again in December. At this time he says that 'S H fully endorses my design of an ultimate return to New England, & herself intends to seek industrial openings in the Boston district after a time', then proceeds to sing Sonia's praises in a very touching way in spite of its almost bathetic tone:

S H's attitude on all such matters is so kindly & magnanimous that any design of permanent isolation on my part would seem little short of barbaric, & wholly contrary to the principles of taste which impel one to recognise & revere a devotion of the most unselfish quality & uncommon intensity. I have never beheld a more admirable attitude of disinterested & solicitous regard; in which each financial shortcoming of mine is accepted & condoned as soon as it is proved inevitable, & in which acquiescence is extended even to my statements ... that the one *essential* ingredient of my life is a certain amount of quiet & freedom for creative literary composition ... A devotion which can accept this combination of incompetence & aesthetic selfishness without a murmur, contrary tho' it must be to all expectations originally entertained; is assuredly a phenomenon so rare, & so akin to the historic quality of saintliness, that no one with the least sense of artistic proportion could possibly meet it with other than the keenest reciprocal esteem, respect, admiration, & affection.[5]

What I believe has inspired this long-winded passage is a suggestion by Lillian that Lovecraft simply come home and forget about Sonia, leading Lovecraft to counter that he cannot countenance 'any design of permanent isolation' from her given her boundlessly patient and understanding attitude.

But after December, the issue of Lovecraft's return was evidently dropped, perhaps because all parties concerned were waiting to see about the possibility of his securing employment at Morton's museum in Paterson. Three more months passed with no prospect of work for Lovecraft except a temporary job as envelope-addresser; and so, on 27 March, he finally received the invitation to come home.

What, or who, was behind the invitation? Was it merely Lillian's decision? Did Annie add her vote? Were there others involved? There is conflicting evidence on the point. Frank Long told Winfield Townley Scott that he had written to Annie 'urging that arrangements be set in motion to restore [Lovecraft] to Providence';[6] but in his 1975 memoir Long noted that his mother wrote a letter to the aunts.[7] So who wrote the letter, Long or his mother? The latter theory is not at all improbable: during Lillian's month or so in New York during December 1924 and January 1925, she and Lovecraft visited the Longs frequently; and it seems that a bond was established between these two elderly women whose son and nephew, respectively, were such close friends. Still, Long's earlier mentions that he wrote the letter may perhaps be more reliable; or perhaps both Long and his mother did so.

After making the preliminary invitation, Lillian had evidently suggested Boston or Cambridge as a more likely place for Lovecraft to find literary work. Lovecraft grudgingly admitted the apparent good sense of this idea, but then, in words both poignant and a little sad, made a plea for residing in Providence:

> To all intents & purposes I am more naturally isolated from mankind than Nathaniel Hawthorne himself, who dwelt alone in the midst of crowds, & whom Salem knew only after he died. Therefore, it may be taken as axiomatic that the people of a place matter absolutely nothing to me except as components of the general landscape & scenery ... My life lies not among *people* but among *scenes*—my local affections are not personal, but topographical & architectural ... I am always an outsider—to all scenes & all people—but outsiders have their sentimental preferences in visual environment. I will be dogmatic only to the extent of saying that it is *New England* I *must* have—in some form or other. Providence is part of me—I *am* Providence ... Providence is my home, & there I shall end my days if I can do so with any semblance of peace, dignity, or appropriateness ... Providence would always be at the back of my head as a goal to be worked toward—an ultimate Paradise to be regain'd at last.[8]

Lillian shortly afterward decided that her nephew should come back to Providence. She found a place for the two of them at 10 Barnes Street, north of the Brown University campus, and asked Lovecraft whether she should take it. He responded with another near-hysterical letter: 'Whoopee!! Bang!! 'Rah!! For God's sake jump at that room without a second's delay!! I can't believe it—too good to be true! ... Somebody wake me up before the dream becomes so poignant I can't bear to be waked up!!!'[9]

I have quoted these letters at such length—and several of them go on for pages in this vein—to display how close to the end of his tether Lovecraft must have been. He had tried for two years to put the best face on things—had tried to convince Lillian, and perhaps himself, that his coming to New York was *not* a mistake—but when the prospect of going home was held out, he leaped at it with an alacrity that betrays his desperation.

The big question, of course, was where Sonia fitted in—or, perhaps, whether she fitted in. Although Sonia would return from the Midwest to help Lovecraft pack and accompany him home to get him ensconced in his new quarters, there was certainly no thought at this juncture of her actually living in Providence or working there. And yet, such a course was clearly considered at some point—at least by Sonia, and perhaps by Lovecraft as well. In her memoir she remarks: 'He wanted more than anything else to go back to Providence but he also wanted *me* to come along, and this I could not do because there was no situation open there for me; that is, one fitting my ability and my need.' Perhaps the most dramatic passage in her entire memoir relates to this critical period:

> When he no longer could tolerate Brooklyn, I, myself, suggested that he return to Providence. Said he, 'If we could but both return to live in Providence, the blessed city where I was born and reared, I am sure, there I could be happy.' I agreed, 'I'd love nothing better than to live in Providence if I could do my work there but Providence has no particular niche that I could fill.' He returned to Providence himself. I came much later.
>
> H. P. lived in a large studio room at that time, where the kitchen was shared with two other occupants. His aunt, Mrs. Clark, had a room in the same house while Mrs. Gamwell, the younger aunt, lived elsewhere. Then we had a conference with the aunts. I suggested that I would take a large house, secure a good maid, pay all the expenses and have the two aunts live with us at no expense to them, or at least they would live better at no greater expense. H. P. and I actually negotiated the rental of such a house with the option to buy it if we found we liked it. H. P. was to use one side of it as his study and library, and I would use the other side as a business venture of my own. At this time the aunts gently but firmly informed me that neither they nor Howard could afford to have Howard's wife work for a living in Providence. That was that. I now knew where we all stood. Pride preferred to suffer in silence; both theirs and mine.[10]

This account is full of difficulties. First, it is clear that Sonia was not the one who 'suggested that he return to Providence', else Lovecraft would not have told Lillian repeatedly that she was merely 'endorsing' the move. Second, it is cannot be ascertained exactly when this 'conference' in Providence took place. It may have occurred in early summer; then again, Sonia's mention that she came to Providence 'much later' may mean that she came only years later—perhaps as late as 1928, for it was only then that actual divorce proceedings—undertaken at her insistence—were instituted.

The critical issue is the 'pride' cited by Sonia. We here see the clash of cultures and generations at its clearest: on the one side the dynamic, perhaps domineering businesswoman striving to salvage her marriage by taking things into her own hands, and on the other side the Victorian shabby-genteel matrons who could not 'afford' the social catastrophe of seeing their only nephew's wife set up a shop and support them in the very town where the name of Phillips still represented something akin to an aristocracy. The exact wording of Sonia's comment is of note: it carries the implication that the aunts might have countenanced her opening a shop somewhere other than Providence.

Are the aunts to be criticized for their attitude? Certainly, many of those today who believe that the acquisition of money is the highest moral good that human beings can attain will find it absurd, incomprehensible, and offensively class-conscious; but the 1920s in New England was a time when standards of propriety meant more than an income, and the aunts were simply adhering to the codes of behaviour by which they had led their entire lives. If anyone is to be criticized, it is Lovecraft: whether he agreed with his aunts on the issue or not (and, in spite of his Victorian upbringing, my feeling is that at this time he did not), he should have worked a little harder to express his own views and to act as an intermediary so that some compromise could have been worked out. Instead, he seems to have stood idly by and let his aunts make all the decisions for him. In all honesty, it is highly likely that he really wished the marriage to end at this point—or, at the very least, that he was perfectly content to see it continue only by correspondence, as indeed it did for the next several years. All he wanted was to come home; Sonia could shift for herself.

How are we to judge Lovecraft's two-year venture into matrimony? There is, certainly, enough blame to spread to all parties: to the aunts for being cool to the entire matter and for possibly failing to provide adequate support—either financial or emotional—to the struggling couple; to Sonia for feeling that she could mould Lovecraft to suit her wishes; and, of course, to Lovecraft himself for being generally thoughtless, spineless, emotionally remote, and financially incompetent. There is nothing but circumstantial evidence for this first point; but let us consider the last two more carefully.

Sonia's memoir makes it clear that she found in Lovecraft a sort of raw material which she wished to shape to her own desires. The fact that a great many women enter into marriage with such conceptions is no great mitigating factor. In essence, she wanted to remake his entire personality—ostensibly to benefit him, but really to make him more satisfactory to herself. She bluntly declared that she initially wished Lovecraft and Loveman to meet in order to 'cure' Lovecraft of his race prejudice; it would certainly have been a good thing if she had succeeded, but clearly that was beyond her powers.

It seems hardly profitable at this juncture to blame Lovecraft for his many failings as a husband—nothing can be accomplished now by such a schoolmasterly attitude—but much in his behaviour is inexcusable. The most inexcusable, of course, is the decision to marry at all, a decision he made with very little awareness of the difficulties involved (beyond any of the financial concerns that emerged unexpectedly at a later date) and without any sense of how unsuited he was to be a husband. Here was a man with an unusually low sex drive, with a deep-seated love of his native region, with severe prejudice against racial minorities, suddenly deciding to marry a woman who, although several years older than he, clearly wished both a physical and an intellectual union, and deciding also to uproot himself from his place of birth to move into a bustling, cosmopolitan, racially heterogeneous megalopolis without a job and, it appears, entirely content to be supported by his wife until such time as he got one.

Once actually married, Lovecraft displayed singularly little consideration for his wife. He found it much more engaging to spend most of his evenings, and even nights, with the boys. He did make a concerted effort to find work in 1924, but virtually gave up the attempt in 1925–26. Once he came to the realization that married life did not suit him, he became content—when Sonia was forced to move to the Midwest in 1925—to conduct a marriage at long distance by correspondence.

Three years after the debacle Lovecraft pondered the whole matter, and to his words not much need be added. He plainly admitted that a fundamental difference in character caused the breakup:

> I haven't a doubt but that matrimony can become a very helpful and pleasing permanent arrangement when both parties happen to harbour the potentialities of parallel mental and imaginative lives—similar or at least mutually comprehensible reactions to the same salient points in environment, reading, historic and philosophic reflection, and so on; and corresponding needs and aspirations in geographic, social, and intellectual milieu … With a wife of the same temperament as my mother and aunts, I would probably have been able to reconstruct a type of domestic life not unlike that of Angell St. days, even though I would have had a different status in the household hierarchy. But years brought out basic and essential diversities in reactions to the various landmarks of the time-stream, and antipodal ambitions and conceptions of value in planning a fixed joint milieu. It was the clash of the abstract-traditional-individual-retrospective-Apollonian aesthetic with the concrete-emotional-present-dwelling-social-ethical-Dionysian aesthetic; and amidst this, the originally fancied congeniality, based on a shared disillusion, philosophic bent, and sensitiveness to beauty, waged a losing struggle.[11]

Abstract as this sounds, it reveals a clear grasp of the fundamentals of the matter: he and Sonia were simply not temperamentally suited to each other.

What is more remarkable is that in later years Lovecraft would in many instances actually conceal the fact that he ever was married. When giving the essentials of his life to new correspondents, he would mention the New York episode but not Sonia or his marriage; and only if some correspondent bluntly and nosily asked him point-blank whether or not he was ever married would he admit that he was. It is as if his marriage, and his entire New York stay, had never happened.

Meanwhile there was the actual move from Brooklyn to Providence to undertake. Lovecraft's letters to his aunts for the first half of April are full of mundane details on the matter—what moving company to hire, how to pack up his books and other belongings, when he will arrive, and the like. I have previously mentioned that Sonia was planning to come back to assist in the move; indeed, she notes rather tartly that 'it was out of my funds that [the move] was paid for, including his fare'.[12]

Lovecraft boarded a train in the morning of Saturday 17 April, and arrived early in the afternoon. He tells the story inimitably in a letter to Long:

> Well—the train sped on, & I experienced silent convulsions of joy in returning step by step to a waking & tridimensional life. New Haven—New London—& then quaint *Mystic*, with its colonial hillside & landlocked cove. Then at last a still subtler magick fill'd the air—nobler roofs & steeples, with the train rushing airily above them on its lofty viaduct—*Westerly*—in His Majesty's Province of RHODE-ISLAND & PROVIDENCE-PLANTATIONS! GOD SAVE THE KING!! Intoxication follow'd—Kingston—East Greenwich with its steep Georgian alleys climbing up from the railway —Apponaug & its ancient roofs—Auburn—just outside the city limits—I fumble with bags & wraps in a desperate effort to appear calm—THEN—a delirious marble dome outside the window—a hissing of air brakes—a slackening of speed— surges of ecstasy & dropping of clouds from my eyes & mind—HOME—UNION STATION—*PROVIDENCE!!!!*[13]

The printed text cannot tell the whole story, for as Lovecraft approaches the triumphant conclusion his handwriting begins to grow larger and larger, until that final word is nearly an inch high. It is symmetrically balanced by four exclamation marks and four underscores. W. Paul Cook made a celebrated remark that the rest of this book will, I trust, instantiate: 'He came back to Providence a human being—and what a human being! He had been tried in the fire and came out pure gold.'[14]

Cook has another imperishable account of Lovecraft's settling in:

> I saw him in Providence on his return from New York and before he had his things all unpacked and his room settled, and he was without question the happiest man I ever saw— he could have posed for an 'After Taking' picture for the medical ads. He *had* taken it and shown that he *could* take it. His touch was caressing as he put his things in place, a real love-light shone in his eyes as he glanced out of the window. He was so happy he hummed—if he had possessed the necessary apparatus he would have purred.[15]

We do not know much of what Lovecraft was doing during the first few months of his return to Providence. In April, May, and

June he reports seeing several parts of the city he had never seen before, at least once in the company of Annie Gamwell. He expresses the wish to do more reading and collecting of Rhode Island matter, and claims that a special corner of the reference room of the Providence Public Library will now be among his principal haunts.

Providence enters into several of the tales he wrote in the year after his return; indeed, this period—from the summer of 1926 to the spring of 1927—represents the most remarkable outburst of fiction-writing in Lovecraft's entire career. Only a month after leaving New York he wrote to Morton: 'It is astonishing how much better the old head works since its restoration to those native scenes amidst which it belongs. As my exile progressed, even reading and writing became relatively slow and formidable processes.'[16] Now things were very different: two short novels, two novelettes, and three short stories, totalling some 150,000 words, were written at this time, along with a handful of poems and essays. All the tales are set, at least in part, in New England.

First on the agenda is 'The Call of Cthulhu', written probably in August or September. This story had, as noted previously, been plotted a full year earlier, on 12–13 August 1925. The plot of this well-known tale does not need elaborate description. The narrator, Francis Wayland Thurston, tells of the peculiar facts he has learned, both from the papers of his recently deceased grand-uncle, George Gammell Angell, and from personal investigation. The upshot of his investigations is the revelation that an awesome cosmic entity, Cthulhu, had come from the stars in the dawn of time and established a stone city, R'lyeh, which then sank into the Pacific Ocean. In early March 1925, the city rose from the waters as the result of an earthquake, and Cthulhu momentarily emerges; but, presumably because the stars are not 'ready', the city sinks again, returning Cthulhu to the bottom of the ocean. But the mere existence of this titanic entity is an unending source of profound unease to Thurston because it shows how tenuous is mankind's vaunted supremacy upon this planet.

It is difficult to convey by this bald summary the rich texture of this substantial work: its implications of cosmic menace, its insidiously gradual climax, its complexity of structure and multitude of narrative voices, and the absolute perfection of its style—sober and clinical at the outset, but reaching at the end heights of prose-poetic horror that attain an almost epic grandeur.

The origin of the tale goes back even beyond the evidently detailed plot-synopsis of 1925. Its kernel is recorded in an entry in his commonplace book (no. 25) that must date to 1920, about a man visiting a museum of antiquities with a statue he has just made. This is a fairly literal encapsulation of a dream Lovecraft had in early 1920, which he describes at length in two letters of the period.

The dominant literary influence on the tale is Guy de Maupassant's 'The Horla'. In 'Supernatural Horror in Literature' Lovecraft writes that it 'relat[es] the advent to France of an invisible being who lives on water and milk, sways the minds of others, and seems to be the vanguard of a horde of extra-terrestrial organisms arrived on earth to subjugate and overwhelm mankind, this tense narrative is perhaps without a peer in its particular department'. Cthulhu is not, of course, invisible, but the rest of the description tallies uncannily with the events of the story. Nevertheless, it must frankly be admitted that Lovecraft himself handles the theme with vastly greater subtlety and richness than Maupassant. There may also be a Machen influence; especially relevant is 'Novel of the Black Seal', where Professor Gregg, like Thurston, pieces together disparate bits of information that by themselves reveal little but, when taken together, suggest an appalling horror awaiting the human race.

Many of the locales in Providence are real, notably the Fleur-de-Lys building at 7 Thomas Street, where the artist Wilcox (who fashioned a sculpture of Cthulhu after dreaming about him) resides. The earthquake cited in the story is also a real event. Steven J. Mariconda, who has written exhaustively on the genesis of the tale, notes: 'In New York, lamps fell from tables and mirrors from walls; walls themselves cracked, and windows shattered; people fled into the street.'[17] Interestingly, the celebrated underwater city of R'lyeh, brought up by this earthquake, was first coined by Lovecraft as L'yeh.[18]

The true importance of 'The Call of Cthulhu', however, lies not in its incorporation of autobiographical details nor even in its intrinsic excellence, but in its being the first significant contribution to what came to be called the 'Cthulhu Mythos'. This tale contains nearly all the elements that would be utilized in subsequent 'Cthulhu Mythos' fiction by Lovecraft and others. There is, to be sure, something going on in many of the tales of Lovecraft's last decade of writing: they are frequently interrelated by a complex series of cross-references to a constantly evolving body of imagined myth, and many of them build upon features—superficial or profound as the case may be—in previous tales. But certain basic points can now be made, although even some of these are not without controversy: first, Lovecraft himself did not coin the term 'Cthulhu Mythos'; second, Lovecraft felt that *all* his tales embodied his basic philosophical principles; third, the mythos, if it can be said to be anything, is not the tales themselves nor even the philosophy behind the tales, but a series of *plot devices* utilized to convey that philosophy. Let us study each of these points further.

First, the term 'Cthulhu Mythos' was invented by August Derleth after Lovecraft's death; of this there is no question. The closest Lovecraft ever came to giving his invented pantheon and related phenomena a name was when he made a casual reference to 'Cthulhuism & Yog-Sothothery',[19] and it is not at all clear what these terms really signify.

Second, Lovecraft utilized his pseudomythology as one (among many) of the ways to convey his fundamental philosophical message, whose chief feature was cosmicism. This point is made clear in a letter written to Farnsworth Wright in July 1927 upon the resubmittal of 'The Call of Cthulhu' to *Weird Tales* (it had been rejected upon initial submission):

> Now all my tales are based on the fundamental premise that common human laws and interests and emotions have no validity or significance in the vast cosmos-at-large. To me there is nothing but puerility in a tale in which the human form—and the local human passions and conditions and standards—are depicted as native to other worlds or other universes. To achieve the essence of real externality, whether of time or space or dimension, one must forget that such things as organic life, good and evil, love and hate, and all such local attributes of a negligible and temporary race called mankind, have any existence at all.[20]

This passage maintains that *all* Lovecraft's tales emphasize cosmicism in some form or another. If, then, we segregate certain of Lovecraft's tales as employing the framework of his 'artificial pantheon and myth-background' (as he writes in 'Some Notes on a Nonentity'), it is purely for convenience, with a full knowledge that Lovecraft's work is not to be grouped arbitrarily, rigidly, or exclusively into discrete categories ('New England tales', 'Dunsanian tales', and 'Cthulhu Mythos tales', as Derleth decreed), since it is transparently clear that these (or any other) categories are not well-defined or mutually exclusive.

Third, it is careless and inaccurate to say that the Lovecraft Mythos is Lovecraft's philosophy: his philosophy is mechanistic materialism and all its ramifications, and, if the Lovecraft Mythos is anything, it is a series of plot devices meant to facilitate the expression of this philosophy. These various plot devices need not concern us here except in their broadest features. They can perhaps be placed in three general groups: first, invented 'gods' and the cults or worshippers that have grown up around them; second, an ever-increasing library of mythical books of occult lore; and third, a fictitious New England topography (Arkham, Dunwich, Innsmouth, etc.). It will readily be noted that the latter two were already present in nebulous form in much earlier tales; but the three features came together only in Lovecraft's later work. Indeed, the third feature does not appreciably foster Lovecraft's cosmic message, and it can be found in tales that are anything but cosmic (e.g., 'The Picture in the House'); but it is a phenomenon that has exercised much fascination and can still be said to be an important component of the Lovecraft Mythos. It is an unfortunate fact, of course, that these surface features have frequently taken precedence with readers, writers, and even critics, rather than the philosophy of which they are symbols or representations.

It is at this point scarcely profitable to examine some of the misinterpretations foisted upon the Lovecraft Mythos by August Derleth; the only value in so doing is to serve as a prelude to examining what the mythos actually meant to Lovecraft. The principal error is that Lovecraft's 'gods' can be differentiated between 'Elder Gods', who represent the forces of good, and the 'Old Ones', who are the forces of evil.

Derleth, a practising Catholic, was unable to endure Lovecraft's bleak atheistic vision, and so he invented out of whole cloth the 'Elder Gods' as a counterweight to the 'evil' Old Ones, who had been 'expelled' from the earth but are eternally preparing to re-emerge and destroy humanity. This invention of 'Elder Gods' allowed him to maintain that the 'Cthulhu Mythos' is substantially akin to Christianity, therefore making it acceptable to people of his conventional temperament. An important piece of 'evidence' that Derleth repeatedly cited to bolster his claims was the following 'quotation', presumably from a letter by Lovecraft:

> All my stories, unconnected as they may be, are based on the fundamental lore or legend that this world was inhabited at one time by another race who, in practising black magic, lost their foothold and were expelled, yet live on outside ever ready to take possession of this earth again.

In spite of its superficial similarity with the 'Now all my tales ...' quotation previously cited (with which Derleth was familiar), this quotation does not sound at all like Lovecraft—at any rate, it is entirely in conflict with the thrust of his philosophy. When Derleth in later years was asked to produce the actual letter from which this quotation was purportedly taken, he could not do so, and for a very good reason: it does not in fact occur in any letter by Lovecraft. It comes from a letter to Derleth written by Harold S. Farnese, the composer who had corresponded briefly with Lovecraft and who severely misconstrued the direction of Lovecraft's work and thought very much as Derleth did.[21] But Derleth seized upon this 'quotation' as a trump card for his erroneous views.

There is now little need to rehash this entire matter. There is no cosmic 'good-versus-evil' struggle in Lovecraft's tales; there are no 'Elder Gods' whose goal is to protect humanity from the 'evil' Old Ones; the Old Ones were not 'expelled' by anyone and are not (aside from Cthulhu) 'trapped' in the earth or elsewhere. Lovecraft's vision is far less cheerful: humanity is *not* at centre stage in the cosmos, and there is no one to help us against the entities who have from time to time descended upon the earth and wreaked havoc; indeed, the 'gods' of the Mythos are not really gods at all, but merely extraterrestrials who occasionally manipulate their human followers for their own advantage.

And it is here that we finally approach the heart of the Lovecraft Mythos. What Lovecraft was really doing was creating (as David E. Schultz has felicitously expressed it[22]) an *anti-mythology*. What is the purpose behind most religions and mythologies? It is to 'justify the ways of God to men'.[23] Human beings have always considered themselves at the centre of the universe; they have peopled the universe with gods of varying natures and capacities as a means of explaining natural phenomena, of accounting for their own existence, and of shielding themselves from the grim prospect of oblivion after death. Every religion and mythology has established some vital connection between gods and human beings, and it is exactly this connection that Lovecraft is seeking to subvert with his pseudomythology.

From the cosmicism of 'The Call of Cthulhu' to the apparent mundaneness of 'Pickman's Model'—written, apprently, in early September—seems a long step backward; and, while this tale cannot be deemed one of Lovecraft's best, it contains some features of interest. The narrator, Thurber, writing in a colloquial style very unusual for Lovecraft, tells of the painter Richard Upton Pickman of Boston, whose spectacularly horrific paintings violently disturb him. Later Thurber learns that the monsters depicted by Pickman in his paintings are taken 'from life'.

No reader can have failed to predict this conclusion, but the tale is more interesting not for its actual plot but for its setting and its aesthetics. The setting—the North End of Boston, then (as now) a largely Italian district—is portrayed quite faithfully, right down to many of the street names; but, less than a year after writing the story, Lovecraft was disappointed to find that much of the area had been razed to make way for new development. Aside from its topographical accuracy, 'Pickman's Model' expresses, in fictionalized form, many of the aesthetic principles on weird fiction that Lovecraft had just outlined in 'Supernatural Horror in Literature'.

'The Call of Cthulhu' was initially rejected by Farnsworth Wright of *Weird Tales*, but it is predictable that Wright would snap up the more conventional 'Pickman's Model', publishing it in the October 1927 issue.

Lovecraft was doing more than writing original fiction; he was no doubt continuing to make a meagre living by revision, and in the process was slowly attracting would-be weird writers who offered him stories for correction. In the summer of 1926 his new friend Wilfred B. Talman came to him with a story entitled 'Two Black Bottles'. Lovecraft found promise in the tale—Talman, let us recall, was only twenty-two at this time, and writing was not his principal creative outlet—but felt that changes were in order. By October the tale was finished, more or less to both writers' satisfaction. The end result is nothing to write home about, but it managed to land with *Weird Tales* and appeared in the August 1927 issue.

A revision job of a very different sort on which Lovecraft worked in October was *The Cancer of Superstition*. This appears to have been a collaborative project on which Lovecraft and C. M. Eddy worked at the instigation of Harry Houdini. Houdini performed in Providence in early October, at which time he asked Lovecraft to do a rush job—an article attacking astrology—for which he paid

$75.00. This article has not come to light; but perhaps it supplied the nucleus for what was apparently to be a full-length polemic against superstitions of all sorts. Houdini had himself written several works of this kind—including *A Magician among the Spirits* (1924), a copy of which he gave to Lovecraft with an inscription—but he now wished something with more scholarly rigour.

But Houdini's sudden death on 31 October put an end to the endeavour, as his wife did not wish to pursue it. This may have been just as well, for the existing material is undistinguished and largely lacks the academic support a work of this kind needs. Lovecraft may have been well versed in anthropology for a layman, but neither he nor Eddy had the scholarly authority to bring this venture to a suitable conclusion.

Shortly after the writing of 'Pickman's Model', something strange occurs—Lovecraft is back in New York. He arrived no later than Monday, 13 September, for he speaks of seeing a film with Sonia that evening. I am not certain of the purpose of this visit—it clearly was only a visit, and I suspect the impetus came from Sonia. Lovecraft, although of course still married to Sonia, seems to have reverted to the guest status he occupied during his 1922 visits: he spent most of his time with the gang, particularly Long, Kirk, and Orton. On Sunday the 19th Lovecraft left for Philadelphia. Sonia had insisted on treating him to this excursion, presumably as recompense for returning to the 'pest-zone'.

With Annie Gamwell, Lovecraft made another excursion in late October, although this one was much closer to home. It was, in fact, nothing less than his first visit to his ancestral region of Foster since 1908. It is heartwarming to read Lovecraft's account of this journey, in which he not only absorbed the intrinsic loveliness of a rural New England he had always cherished but also re-established bonds with family members who still revered the memory of Whipple Phillips.

Echoes of the trip are manifested in his next work of fiction, 'The Silver Key', presumably written in early November. In this tale Randolph Carter—resurrected from 'The Unnamable' (1923)—is now thirty; he has 'lost the key of the gate of dreams' and therefore seeks to reconcile himself to the real world, which he now finds prosy and aesthetically unrewarding. He tries all manner of literary and physical novelties until one day he does find the key—or, at any rate, a key of silver in his attic, which somehow takes him back in time so that he is again a nine-year-old boy. Sitting down to dinner with his aunt and uncle, Carter finds perfect content as a boy who has sloughed off the tedious complications of adult life for the eternal wonder of childhood.

'The Silver Key' is, clearly, an exposition of Lovecraft's own social, ethical, and aesthetic philosophy. It is not even so much a story as a parable or philosophical diatribe. He attacks literary realism, conventional religion, and bohemianism in exactly the same way as he does in his letters. But, as Kenneth W. Faig, Jr, has exhaustively pointed out, 'The Silver Key' is in large part a fictionalized account of Lovecraft's recent Foster visit.[24] Details of topography, character names, and other similarities make this conclusion unshakable. Just as Lovecraft felt the need, after two rootless years in New York, to restore connections with the places that had given him and his family birth, so in his fiction did he need to announce that, henceforth, however far his imagination might stray, it would always return to New England and look upon it as a source of bedrock values and emotional sustenance.

'The Silver Key', with its heavily philosophical burden, is by no means oriented toward a popular audience, and it is no surprise that Farnsworth Wright rejected it for *Weird Tales*. In the summer of 1928, however, Wright asked to see the tale again and this time accepted it for $70.

'The Strange High House in the Mist', written on 9 November, shows that the Dunsany influence had now been thoroughly internalised so as to allow for the expression of Lovecraft's own sentiments through Dunsany's idiom and general atmosphere. Indeed, the only genuine connections to Dunsany's work may perhaps be in some details of the setting and in the manifestly philosophical, even satiric purpose which the fantasy is made to serve. We are now again in Kingsport, a city to which Lovecraft had not returned since 'The Festival' (1923), and Thomas Olney learns of the strange creatures that haunt an ancient house on a high cliff north of the city. After he returns to his family, Olney's soul no longer longs for wonder and mystery; instead, he is content to lead his prosy bourgeois life with his wife and children.

On various occasions Lovecraft admits that he had no specific locale in mind when writing this tale: he states that memories of the 'titan cliffs of Magnolia'[25] in part prompted the setting, but that there is no house on the cliff as in the story. 'The Strange High House in the Mist' contains little in the way of specific topographical description, and we are clearly in a never-never land where—anomalously for Lovecraft—the focus is on human character.

For the strange transformation of Thomas Olney is at the heart of the tale. The Terrible Old Man states: 'somewhere under that grey peaked roof, or amidst inconceivable reaches of that sinister white mist, there lingered still the lost spirit of him who was Thomas Olney'. The body has returned to the normal round of things, but the spirit has remained with the occupant of the strange high house in the mist; Olney realizes that it is in this realm of nebulous wonder that he truly belongs. His body is now an empty shell, without soul and without imagination.

But Lovecraft was by no means done with writing. In a departure from his normal habits, he wrote 'The Silver Key' and 'The Strange High House in the Mist' while simultaneously at work on a much longer work. Writing to August Derleth in early December, he notes: 'I am now on page 72 of my dreamland fantasy.'[26] The result, finished in late January, would be the longest work of fiction he had written up to this time—*The Dream-Quest of Unknown Kadath*.

CHAPTER FOURTEEN
Cosmic Outsideness (1927–28)

The Dream-Quest of Unknown Kadath was finished at 43,000 words on 22 January 1927. Even while writing it, Lovecraft expressed doubts about its merits: 'Actually, it isn't much good; but forms useful practice for later and more authentic attempts in the novel form.'[1] That remark is about as accurate a judgment as can be delivered on the work. More than any other of Lovecraft's major stories, it has elicited antipodally opposite reactions even from devotees: L. Sprague de Camp compared it to George MacDonald's *Lilith* and *Phantastes* and the *Alice* books, while other Lovecraft scholars find it almost unreadable. For my part, I think it is a charming but relatively insubstantial work: Carter's adventures through dreamland do indeed pall after a time, but the novel is saved by its extraordinarily poignant conclusion. Its chief feature may be its autobiographical significance: it is, in fact, Lovecraft's spiritual autobiography for this precise moment in his life.

It is scarcely worth while to pursue the rambling plot of this short novel, which in its continuous, chapterless meandering consciously resembles not only Dunsany (although Dunsany never wrote a long work exactly of this kind) but William Beckford's *Vathek* (1786); several points of plot and imagery also bring Beckford's Arabian fantasy to mind. Lovecraft resurrects Randolph Carter in a quest through dreamland for his 'sunset city', which is described as follows:

> All golden and lovely it blazed in the sunset, with walls, temples, colonnades, and arched bridges of veined marble, silver-basined fountains of prismatic spray in broad squares and perfumed gardens, and wide streets marching between delicate trees and blossom-laden urns and ivory statues in gleaming rows; while on steep northward slopes climbed tiers of red roofs and old peaked gables harbouring little lanes of grassy cobbles.

This certainly sounds—except for some odd details at the end—like some Dunsanian realm of the imagination; but what does Carter discover as he leaves his hometown of Boston to make a laborious excursion through dreamland to the throne of the Great Ones who dwell in an onyx castle on unknown Kadath? Nyarlathotep, the messenger of the gods, tells him in a passage as moving as any in Lovecraft:

> 'For know you, that your gold and marble city of wonder is only the sum of what you have seen and loved in youth. It is the glory of Boston's hillside roofs and western windows aflame with sunset; of the flower-fragrant Common and the great dome on the hill and the tangle of gables and chimneys in the violet valley where the many-bridged Charles flows drowsily. These things you saw, Randolph Carter, when your nurse first wheeled you out in the springtime, and they will be the last things you will ever see with eyes of memory and of love …
>
> 'These, Randolph Carter, are your city; for they are yourself. New-England bore you, and into your soul she poured a liquid loveliness which cannot die. This loveliness, moulded, crystallised, and polished by years of memory and dreaming, is your terraced wonder of elusive sunsets; and to find that marble parapet with curious urns and carven rail, and descend at last those endless balustraded steps to the city of broad squares and prismatic fountains, you need only to turn back to the thoughts and visions of your wistful boyhood.'

We suddenly realize why that 'sunset city' contained such otherwise curious features as gables and cobblestoned lanes. And we also realize why it is that the various fantastic creatures Carter meets along his journey—zoogs, gugs, ghasts, ghouls, moonbeasts—touch no chord in us: they are not meant to. They are all very charming, in that 'Dresden-china' way Lovecraft mistook Dunsany to be; but they amount to nothing because they do not correspond to anything in our memories and dreams. So all that Carter has to do—and what he does in fact do at the end—is merely to wake up in his Boston room, leave dreamland behind, and realize the beauty to be found on his doorstep.

Lovecraft's resurrection of the Dunsanian idiom—not used since 'The Other Gods' (1921)—seems to me meant not so much as an homage as a repudiation of Dunsany, at least of what Lovecraft at this moment took Dunsany to be. Just as, when he wrote 'Lord

Dunsany and His Work' in 1922, he felt that the only escape from modern disillusion would be to 'worship afresh the music and colour of divine language, and take an Epicurean delight in those combinations of ideas and fancies which we know to be artificial', so in 1926—after two years spent away from the New England soil that he now realized was his one true anchor against chaos and meaninglessness—he felt the need to reject these decorative artificialities. By 1930—only seven years after claiming, in pitiable wish-fulfilment, that 'Dunsany *is myself*'—he made a definitive break with his once-revered mentor:

> What I do not think I shall use much in future is the Dunsanian pseudo-poetic vein—not because I don't admire it, but because I don't think it is natural to me. The fact that I used it only sparingly before reading Dunsany, but immediately began to overwork it upon doing so, gives me a strong suspicion of its artificiality so far as I am concerned. That kind of thing takes a better poet than I.[2]

In later years Lovecraft repudiated the novel, refusing several colleagues' desires to prepare a typed copy of the manuscript. The text was not published until it was included in *Beyond the Wall of Sleep* (1943).

It is remarkable that, almost immediately after completing *The Dream-Quest of Unknown Kadath* in late January 1927, Lovecraft plunged into another 'young novel',[3] *The Case of Charles Dexter Ward*. Actually, at the outset he did not regard it as anything more than a novelette, but by the time it was finished on 1 March, it had reached 147 manuscript pages. At approximately 51,000 words, it is the longest work of fiction Lovecraft would ever write. While it does betray a few signs of haste, and while he would no doubt have polished it had he made the effort to prepare it for publication, the fact is that he felt so discouraged as to its quality—as well as its marketability—that he never made such an effort, and the work remained unpublished until four years after his death.

Perhaps, however, it is not so odd that Lovecraft wrote *The Case of Charles Dexter Ward* in a blinding rush nine months after his return to Providence; for this novel—the second of his major tales (after 'The Shunned House') to be set entirely in the city of his birth—had been gestating for at least a year or more. I have mentioned that in August 1925 he was contemplating a novel about Salem; but then, in September, he read Gertrude Selwyn Kimball's *Providence in*

Colonial Times (1912) at the New York Public Library, and this rather dry historical work clearly fired his imagination. He was, however, still talking of the Salem idea just as he was finishing the *Dream-Quest*; perhaps the Kimball book—as well, of course, as his return to Providence—led to a uniting of the Salem idea with a work about his hometown.

The novel concerns the attempts of the seventeenth-century alchemist Joseph Curwen to secure unholy knowledge by resurrecting the 'essential saltes' of the great thinkers of the world. Curwen also leaves his own essential saltes to be discovered by his twentieth-century descendant, Charles Dexter Ward, so that he is resurrected, only to be put down by the Ward family doctor, Marinus Bicknell Willett. The historical flashback—occupying the second of the five chapters—is as evocative a passage as any in Lovecraft's work.

The house that serves the model for Charles Dexter Ward's residence is the so-called Halsey mansion (the Thomas Lloyd Halsey house at 140 Prospect Street). In late August 1925 Lovecraft heard from Lillian that this mansion was haunted.[4] Although now broken up into apartments, it is a superb late Georgian structure (c. 1800) fully deserving of Lovecraft's encomium. Lovecraft was presumably never in the Halsey mansion, but had a clear view of it from 10 Barnes Street; looking northwestward from his aunt's upstairs back window, he could see it distinctly.

One significant literary influence may be noted here: Walter de la Mare's novel *The Return* (1910). Lovecraft had first read de la Mare (1873–1956) in the summer of 1926; of *The Return* he remarks in 'Supernatural Horror in Literature': 'we see the soul of a dead man reach out of its grave of two centuries and fasten itself upon the flesh of the living, so that even the face of the victim becomes that which had long ago returned to dust'. In de la Mare's novel, of course, there is actual psychic possession involved, as there is not in *Charles Dexter Ward*; and, although the focus in *The Return* is on the afflicted man's personal trauma—in particular his relations with his wife and daughter—rather than the unnaturalness of his condition, Lovecraft has manifestly adapted the general scenario in his own work.

The apparent source for the character Charles Dexter Ward is a very interesting one. Of course, there are many autobiographical touches in the portraiture of Ward; but many surface details appear to be taken from a person actually living in the Halsey mansion at this time, William Lippitt Mauran, who was born in 1910. Lovecraft was probably not acquainted with Mauran, but it is highly likely that he observed Mauran on the street and knew of him. Mauran was a sickly child who spent much of his youth as an invalid, being wheeled through the streets in a carriage by a nurse. Moreover, the Mauran family also owned a farmhouse in Pawtuxet, exactly as Curwen is said to have done. Other details of Ward's character also fit Mauran more closely than Lovecraft.[5]

The early parts of the novel in particular are full of autobiographical details. The opening descriptions of Ward as a youth are filled with echoes of Lovecraft's own upbringing, although with provocative changes. For example, a description of 'one of the child's first memories'—'the great westward sea of hazy roofs and domes and steeples and far hills which he saw one winter afternoon from that great railed embankment, all violet and mystic against a fevered, apocalyptic sunset of reds and golds and purples and curious greens'—is situated in Prospect Terrace, whereas in letters Lovecraft identifies this mystic vision as occurring on the railway embankment in Auburndale, Massachusetts, around 1892. Ward's ecstatic return to Providence after several years abroad can scarcely be anything but a transparent echo of Lovecraft's own return to Providence after two years in New York. The simple utterance that concludes this passage—'It was twilight, and Charles Dexter Ward had come home'—is one of the most quietly moving statements in all Lovecraft's work.

It is a pity that Lovecraft made no efforts to prepare *The Case of Charles Dexter Ward* for publication, even when book publishers in the 1930s were specifically asking for a novel from his pen; but we are in no position to question Lovecraft's own judgment that the novel was an inferior piece of work, a 'cumbrous, creaking bit of self-conscious antiquarianism'.[6] It has now been acknowledged as one of his finest works, and it emphasizes the message of *The Dream-Quest of Unknown Kadath* all over again: Lovecraft is who he is because of his birth and upbringing as a New England Yankee. The need to root his work in his native soil became more and more clear to him as time went on, and it led to his gradual transformation of all New England as the locus of both wonder and terror.

The last tale of Lovecraft's great spate of fiction-writing of 1926–27 is 'The Colour out of Space', written in March 1927. It is unquestionably one of his great tales, and it always remained Lovecraft's own favourite. Here again the plot is too well known to require lengthy description, and focuses on the horrifying effects of a meteorite—or, more specifically, the nebulous entity or entities within the meteorite—after it lands upon a New England farmer's field. Crops grow strangely, animals develop anatomical abnormalities, and finally both humans and animals alike crumble into a greyish dust. At the end there is a tremendous eruption of light from a well: the creatures have returned to their cosmic home.

Lovecraft was correct in calling this tale an 'atmospheric study',[7] for he has rarely captured the atmosphere of inexplicable horror better than he has here. First let us consider the setting. The reservoir mentioned in the tale is a very real one: the Quabbin Reservoir, plans for which were announced in 1926, although it was not completed until 1939. And yet Lovecraft declares in a late letter that it was not this reservoir but the Scituate Reservoir in Rhode Island (built in 1926) that caused him to use the reservoir element in the story.[8] He saw this reservoir when he passed through this area in the west-central part of the state on the way to Foster in late October. I cannot, however, believe that Lovecraft was not also thinking of the Quabbin, which is located exactly in the area of central Massachusetts where the tale takes place, and which involved the abandonment and submersion of entire towns in the region.

The key to the story, of course, is the anomalous meteorite. Is it—or are the coloured globules inside it—animate in any sense we can recognize? Does it house a single entity or many entities? What are their physical properties? More significantly, what are their aims, goals, and motives? The fact that we can answer none of these questions very clearly is by no means a failing; indeed, this is exactly the source of terror in the tale. As Lovecraft said of Machen's 'The White People', 'the *lack of anything concrete* is the *great asset* of the story'.[9] In other words, it is precisely our inability to define the nature—either physical or psychological—of the entities in 'The Colour out of Space' (or even know whether they are entities or living creatures as we understand them) that produces the sense of nameless horror.

Perhaps the most controversial aspect of the tale is the mundane matter of its publication history. 'The Colour out of Space' appeared in *Amazing Stories* for September 1927; but the critical question is whether the tale was ever submitted to *Weird Tales*. Although Sam Moskowitz claimed that it was submitted both there and to the

Argosy, no documentary evidence has emerged to support the contention. Consider also Lovecraft's comment to Farnsworth Wright in his letter of 5 July 1927: 'this spring and summer I've been too busy with revisory and kindred activities to write more than one tale—which, oddly enough, was accepted at once by *Amazing Stories*'.[10] The wording of this letter suggests that this is Lovecraft's first mention of the story to Wright. There is equal silence concerning a possible *Argosy* rejection.

But if Lovecraft was hoping that in *Amazing Stories*—the first authentic science fiction magazine in English—he had found an alternative to *Weird Tales*, he was in for a rude awakening. Although his later work contained a fairly significant scientific element, *Amazing* became a closed market to him when Hugo Gernsback paid him only $25.00 for the story—a mere one-fifth of a cent per word—and this only after three dunning letters. Although in later years Lovecraft briefly considered requests from Gernsback or from his associate editor, C. A. Brandt, for further submissions, he never again sent a tale to *Amazing*. He also took to calling Gernsback 'Hugo the Rat'.

Just before writing 'The Colour out of Space', Lovecraft had to hurry up and type 'Supernatural Horror in Literature', since Cook wished it immediately for the *Recluse*. Lovecraft had been making random additions to the essay based upon recent readings—including the subtle and atmospheric tales of Walter de la Mare—but Cook's rush order compelled him to type up the essay without any further enlargements. Even this, however, was not quite the end. Late in March, after Cook had sent Lovecraft the first proofs, Donald Wandrei lent F. Marion Crawford's superb posthumous collection of horror tales, *Wandering Ghosts* (1911), to Lovecraft, while in April Lovecraft borrowed Robert W. Chambers's early collection *The King in Yellow* (1895) from Cook; he was so taken with these works that he added paragraphs on both writers in the page proofs.

The Recluse appeared in August 1927; although initially planned as a quarterly, this was the only issue ever published. Although not strictly a weird publication, it contains fine work by Clark Ashton Smith, Donald Wandrei, H. Warner Munn, Frank Belknap Long, and Samuel Loveman. Cook wished to send *The Recluse* to certain 'celebrities', in particular to all four of Lovecraft's 'modern masters', Machen, Dunsany, Blackwood, and M. R. James. As it happened, the issue did find its way to some of these figures, and their responses to Lovecraft's essay are of interest. James rather unkindly declared in a letter that Lovecraft's style 'is of the most offensive', but goes on to remark: 'But he has taken pains to search about & treat the subject from its beginning to MRJ, to whom he devotes several columns.'[11] Machen's response can be gauged only from Donald Wandrei's comment to Lovecraft: 'I received a letter to-day from Machen, in which he mentioned your article and its hold on him.'[12] Copies were also apparently sent to Blackwood, Dunsany, Rudyard Kipling, Charlotte Perkins Gilman, Mary E. Wilkins Free-man, and several others.

As early as April 1927 Lovecraft already had a vague idea of expanding 'Supernatural Horror in Literature' for a putative second edition, and Cook occasionally mentioned the possibility of issuing such an edition separately as a monograph. Lovecraft set up a section in his commonplace book entitled 'Books to mention in new edition of weird article', listing several works he read in the subsequent months and years; but Cook's physical and financial collapse confounded, or at least delayed, the plans, and the second edition did not materialize until 1933, and in a form very different from what Lovecraft envisioned.

Lovecraft, having by 1927 already published nearly a score of tales in *Weird Tales*, and finding that amateur work was at a virtual end with the demise of the UAPA, now began gathering colleagues specifically devoted to weird fiction. The last decade of his life would see him become a friend, correspondent, and mentor of more than a dozen writers who would follow in his footsteps and become well known in the fields of weird, mystery, and science fiction.

August Derleth (1909–71) wrote to Lovecraft through *Weird Tales*, and the latter replied in August 1926. From that time on, the two men kept up a very steady correspondence—usually once a week—for the next ten and a half years. Derleth had just finished high school in Sauk City, Wisconsin, and in the fall of 1926 would begin attendance at the University of Wisconsin at Madison. As a fiction writer he would reveal astounding range and precocity. Although his first story in *Weird Tales* dates to his eighteenth year, his weird tales—whether written by himself or in collaboration with the young Mark Schorer—would be in many ways the least interesting aspect of his work; they are conventional, relatively unoriginal, and largely undistinguished, and he readily admitted to Lovecraft that they were written merely to supply cash for his more serious work. That serious work—for which Derleth would eventually gain considerable renown, and which today remains the most significant branch of his output—is a series of regional sagas drawing upon his native Wisconsin and written in a poignant, Proustian, reminiscent vein whose simple elegance allows for evocative character portrayal. The first of these works to be published was *Place of Hawks* (1935), although Derleth was working as early as 1929 on a novel he initially titled *The Early Years*, which was finally published in 1941 as *Evening in Spring*. Those who fail to read these two works, along with their many successors in Derleth's long and fertile career, will have no conception why Lovecraft, as early as 1930, wrote with such enthusiasm about his younger colleague and disciple.

Donald Wandrei (1908–87) got in touch with Lovecraft through Clark Ashton Smith in late 1926, shortly after he had entered the University of Minnesota. Smith was the first writer to whom Wandrei was devoted, and in many ways he remained Wandrei's model in both fiction and poetry. Wandrei was initially attracted to poetry, but he was also experimenting with prose fiction. Some of this early work is quite striking, especially 'The Red Brain' (*Weird Tales*, October 1927). It, along with several other works such as the celebrated 'Colossus' (*Astounding Stories*, January 1934), reveals a staggeringly cosmic imagination second only to Lovecraft's in intensity. Like Derleth, who spent nearly the whole of his life in and around Sauk City, Wisconsin, Wandrei lived almost his entire life in his family home in St Paul, Minnesota, save for various periods in New York in the 1920s and 1930s; but unlike the cheerful Derleth, Wandrei had a brooding and misanthropic streak that often intrigued Lovecraft and may perhaps have helped to shape his own later philosophical views.

I wish I knew more about Bernard Austin Dwyer (1897–1943), but as he published relatively little and was more an appreciator than a creator, he remains a nebulous figure. He lived nearly the whole of his life in and around the tiny village of West Shokan, in upstate New York, near the towns of Hurley, New Paltz, and Kingston. Although attracted to weird fiction and the author of a short poem published in *Weird Tales* ('Ol' Black Sarah' in the October 1928 issue), his chief interest was weird art; and in this capacity he naturally became fast friends with Clark Ashton Smith. One gains the impression that Dwyer was a kind of mute, inglorious Milton. He came in touch with Lovecraft through *Weird Tales* in the early part of 1927.

In the summer of 1927 Lovecraft both played host to a succession of visitors to Providence and undertook several journeys of his own—something that would become a habit every spring and summer, as he roamed increasingly widely in quest of antiquarian oases. First on the agenda was his new friend Donald Wandrei, who undertook a trip from St Paul, Minnesota, to Providence entirely by hitchhiking. One would like to think that such an expedition was a little safer then than it would be now, and perhaps it was; Wandrei seemed to have no difficulty getting rides, even though on occasion he had to spend nights under the open sky, sometimes in the rain.

Arriving on 20 June in Chicago, where he confirmed all Lovecraft's impressions of the place, Wandrei went to the *Weird Tales* office and met Farnsworth Wright. Lovecraft himself had spoken to Wright about Wandrei's work early in the year, and perhaps as a result Wandrei's 'The Red Brain'—rejected a year earlier—was accepted in March. Wandrei felt the need to return the favour, so he spoke to Wright about 'The Call of Cthulhu'. Accordingly, Wright asked Lovecraft to resubmit the tale and accepted it for $165.00; it appeared in the February 1928 issue. This did not, of course, prevent Wright from rejecting 'The Strange High House in the Mist' and 'The Silver Key' later in the summer; but in both cases he asked to see them again, and ultimately accepted them for $70.00 and $55.00, respectively.

On 12 July Wandrei arrived in Providence, staying till the 29th. On the 16th Lovecraft and Wandrei set out for Boston; but the excursion was somewhat of a disappointment. Lovecraft was especially keen on showing Wandrei the sinister, decaying North End where 'Pickman's Model' was set, but was mortified to find that 'the actual alley & house of the tale [had been] utterly demolished; a whole crooked line of buildings having been torn down'.[13] This remark is of interest in indicating that Lovecraft had an actual house in mind for Pickman's North End studio.

On Tuesday, 19 July, Frank Long and his parents drove up from New York City, while simultaneously James F. Morton came down from Green Acre, Maine, where he had been visiting. On the 21st the entire crew went to Newport. The Longs left on the 22nd, whereupon Morton dragged Lovecraft and Wandrei to the rock quarry on which Lovecraft still held the mortgage, and for which he was still receiving his pittance of a payment ($37.08) every six months. The owner, Mariano de Magistris, set his men to hunting up specimens, while his son drove them home in his car. 'That's what I call real Latin courtesy!' Lovecraft remarked in a rare show of tolerance for non-Aryans.[14]

On Saturday the 23rd occurred an historic pilgrimage—to Julia A. Maxfield's in Warren, where Lovecraft, Morton, and Wandrei staged an ice-cream-eating contest. Maxfield's advertised twenty-eight flavours of ice cream, and the contestants sampled them all. Wandrei could not quite keep up with the others, but he at least managed to dip his spoon into the remaining flavours so that he could say he had tasted them all.

That afternoon a contingent from Athol, Massachusetts, arrived —W. Paul Cook and his protégé, H. Warner Munn (1903–81). Lovecraft had no doubt heard something of Munn before. Munn's 'The Werewolf of Ponkert' (*Weird Tales*, July 1925) was apparently inspired by a comment in Lovecraft's letter to Edwin Baird published in the March 1924 issue. He contributed extensively to the pulps and over his long career wrote many supernatural and adventure novels; but perhaps his most distinguished works were historical novels written late in his career, notably *Merlin's Ring* (1974) and *The Lost Legion* (1980). Lovecraft took to Munn readily, finding him 'a splendid young chap—blond and burly';[15] he would visit him frequently when passing through Athol.

On the 29th Wandrei finally left, but Lovecraft's own travels were by no means over. In August, after visits to Worcester, Athol, Amherst, and Deerfield, Lovecraft and Cook went to Vermont to visit the amateur poet Arthur Goodenough. A decade before, Goodenough had praised Lovecraft in a poem ('Lovecraft—an Appreciation') containing the grotesque image, 'Laurels from thy very temples sprout'. Lovecraft had thought Goodenough was spoofing him, and only with difficulty was he prevented by Cook from writing some devastating reply; instead, he wrote a poem in return, 'To Arthur Goodenough, Esq.' (*Tryout*, September 1918). Now, when meeting him, Lovecraft was captivated by Good-enough, and especially by the archaic and rustic charm of his dress and demeanour. Lovecraft later wrote a rhapsodic essay on his entire Vermont visit, 'Vermont—A First Impression', which appeared in Walter J. Coates's regional magazine *Driftwind* for March 1928.

On 25 August Lovecraft visited Portland, Maine. He spent two days there and enjoyed the town immensely: although it was not as rich in antiquities as Marblehead or Portsmouth, it was scenically lovely—it occupies a peninsula with hills at the eastern and

western ends, and has many beautiful drives and promenades—
and at least had things like the two Longfellow houses (birthplace
and principal residence), which Lovecraft explored thoroughly.
Travels to Portsmouth, New Hampshire, and Newburyport, Haverhill, Gloucester, and Ipswich in Massachusetts concluded Lovecraft's two-week trek.

Meanwhile various prospects for the book publication of Lovecraft's stories were developing. One possibility began taking shape
late in 1926 when Farnsworth Wright broached the idea of a
collection. This project would keep Lovecraft dangling for several
years before finally collapsing. The reasons for this are perhaps not
far to seek. In 1927 *Weird Tales* (under its official imprint, the
Popular Fiction Publishing Company) issued *The Moon Terror* by
A. G. Birch and others. For whatever reason, the book was a complete
commercial disaster, remaining in print nearly as long as *Weird Tales*
itself was in existence. And, of course, the onset of the Depression
hit the magazine very hard, and for various periods in the 1930s it
appeared only once every two months; at this time the issuance of
a book was the last thing on the publishers' minds. Nevertheless, in
late December 1927 negotiations were still serious enough for
Lovecraft to write a long letter giving his own preferences as to the
contents. Lovecraft concludes with an interesting remark: 'As for a
title—my choice is *The Outsider and Other Stories*. This is because I
consider the touch of cosmic *outsideness*—of dim, shadowy *non-
terrestrial* hints—to be the characteristic feature of my writing.'[16]
     One story Lovecraft did not offer for the collection (probably just
as well, as Wright had already rejected it for the magazine) was
'The Shunned House', which W. Paul Cook wished to publish as a
small book. Cook had initially conceived of including it in *The
Recluse*, but presumably held off because the magazine had already
attained enormous size. Then, around February 1927, he first
broached the idea of printing it as a chapbook, uniform in format
with two other publications, Frank Long's slim collection of poetry
The Man from Genoa and Samuel Loveman's *The Hermaphrodite*, both
issued in 1926. The issuance of *The Recluse* delayed work on the
book project, but in the spring of 1928 things began to move.
Lovecraft read proofs in early June, even though he was then on
another extensive series of travels. By the end of June *The Shunned
House* was printed but not bound. About three hundred copies were
printed.

Unfortunately, things soured at this very moment. Both Cook's finances and his health were in a very shaky state. *The Shunned House*—which Cook was financing, without any contribution by Lovecraft—had to be put on the back burner. In January 1930 Cook's wife died and Cook suffered another and severer nervous breakdown. The depression completed his devastation, and *The Shunned House*'s emergence became increasingly remote. By the summer of 1930 Lovecraft heard that the sheets had been sent to a binder in Boston, but the book still did not come out. The matter hung fire all the way to Lovecraft's death.

Late in 1927 Lovecraft received *You'll Need a Night Light*, a British anthology edited by Christine Campbell Thomson and published by Selwyn & Blount. It contained 'The Horror at Red Hook', marking the first time that a story of Lovecraft's appeared in hardcover. The volume was part of a series of 'Not at Night' books edited by Campbell; the stories for most of the volumes were culled from *Weird Tales*, and several of Lovecraft's tales and revisions would later be reprinted. Although pleased at its appearance, Lovecraft had no illusions as to the anthology's merits. 'As for that "Not at Night"—that's a mere lowbrow hash of absolutely no taste or significance. Aesthetically speaking, it doesn't exist.'[17]

Rather more significant—and indeed, one of the most important items in the critical recognition of Lovecraft prior to his death—was the appearance of 'The Colour out of Space' on the 'Roll of Honor' of the 1928 volume of Edward J. O'Brien's *Best Short Stories*. Lovecraft sent O'Brien a somewhat lengthy autobiographical paragraph for a section at the back of the book; he expected O'Brien merely to select from it, but instead the latter printed it intact, and it occupied eighteen lines of text, longer than any other biography in the volume. On the whole it is an exceptionally accurate and compact account of Lovecraft's life and beliefs.

In the autumn of 1927 Frank Belknap Long took it into his head to write a longish short story entitled 'The Space-Eaters'. This story can be said to have two distinctive qualities: it is the first work to involve Lovecraft as a character (if we exclude whimsies like Edith Miniter's 'Falco Ossifracus', in which the central character, while modelled on Randolph Carter, shares some chracteristics with Lovecraft), and—although this point is somewhat debatable—it is the first 'addition' to Lovecraft's mythos.

To be perfectly honest, 'The Space-Eaters' is a preposterous story.

This wild, histrionic account of some entities who are apparently 'eating their way through space', are attacking people's brains, but are in some mysterious manner prevented from overwhelming the earth, is frankly an embarrassment. In this sense, however, it is sadly prophetic of most of the 'contributions' other writers would make to Lovecraft's conceptions.

Whether it is indeed an addition to or extrapolation from Lovecraft's mythos is a debatable question. The entities in question are never named, and there are no references to any of Lovecraft's 'gods' (only Cthulhu and Yog-Sothoth had even been invented at this time, the latter in the unpublished *Case of Charles Dexter Ward*). What there is, however, is an epigraph (omitted from the first appearance—*Weird Tales*, July 1928—and many subsequent reprintings) from 'John Dee's Necronomicon'—i.e., from a purported English translation of Olaus Wormius's Latin translation of the *Necronomicon*. Lovecraft made frequent citations of this Dee translation in later stories. This phenomenon would recur throughout Lovecraft's lifetime: a writer—usually a colleague—either devised an elaboration upon some myth-element in Lovecraft's stories or created an entirely new element, which Lovecraft then co-opted in some subsequent story of his own. This whole procedure was largely meant in fun—as a way of investing this growing body of myth with a sense of actuality by its citation in different texts, and also as a sort of tip of the hat to each writer's creations.

Lovecraft, meanwhile, was doing relatively little fiction-writing of his own—he had written nothing since 'The Colour out of Space'. What he did do, however, on Hallowe'en was to have a spectacular dream about ancient Rome that might serve as the nucleus of a story. He subsequently wrote a long account of the dream to several colleagues—Frank Belknap Long, Donald Wandrei, Bernard Austin Dwyer, and perhaps others. One would have liked to see Lovecraft himself write up the dream into an actual story, but he never did anything with it. In 1929 Long asked Lovecraft that he be allowed to use the letter verbatim in a short novel he was writing, and Lovecraft acceded. The result was *The Horror from the Hills*, published in two parts in *Weird Tales* (January and February 1931) and later as a book.

Around this time Lovecraft also wrote a history of his mythical book, the *Necronomicon*, although largely for the purpose of keeping references clear in his own mind. This item bears the title 'History of the *Necronomicon*'. On this draft a sentence is added about Dr.

Dee's translation of the volume, leading one to believe that Lovecraft had written the bulk of the text prior to seeing Long's 'The Space-Eaters'. Since he noted that he had 'just received' that story in late September, 'History of the *Necronomicon*' was probably written just before this time.

In late 1927 Lovecraft declared that he had never yet advertised for his revisory services[18] (he had evidently forgotten about the 'Crafton Service Bureau' ad in *L'Alouette* in 1924), so that new revision clients would have come to him only by referral. Two such clients made their appearance about this time—Adolphe de Castro and Zealia Brown Reed Bishop.

De Castro (1859–1959), formerly Gustav Adolphe Danziger, was an odd case. He met Ambrose Bierce in 1886 and become an enthusiastic devotee and colleague. A few years later he translated Richard Voss's short novel *Der Mönch des Berchtesgaden* (1890–91), and had Bierce revise it; it was published serially as *The Monk and the Hangman's Daughter* in the *San Francisco Examiner* in September 1891 and then as a book in 1892. With Bierce and others, Danziger formed the Western Authors Publishing Association, which issued Bierce's poetry collection *Black Beetles in Amber* (1892) and Danziger's own short story collection, *In the Confessional and the Following* (1893). Shortly thereafter, however, Bierce and Danziger had a falling out—mostly over financial wrangling over the profits from the *Monk* and over Danziger's management of the publishing company—and although Danziger occasionally met up with Bierce on random subsequent occasions, the two did no further work together.

Bierce went down to Mexico in late 1913, evidently to observe or to participate in the Mexican Civil War. Danziger (now de Castro) lived in Mexico between 1922 and 1925 editing a weekly newspaper. In 1923 he managed to talk with Pancho Villa; Villa maintained that he threw Bierce out of his camp when Bierce began praising Carranza. Later, according to this account, Bierce's body was found by the side of a road. De Castro wrote an article in the *American Parade* for October 1926 entitled 'Ambrose Bierce as He Really Was', going on at length about his collaboration on the *Monk* and discussing his search for Bierce in Mexico.

It was at this point that de Castro came in touch with Lovecraft. With the publicity he was now receiving, he felt the time was right to capitalize on his association with Bierce. He knew Samuel

Loveman, and the latter recommended that de Castro write to Lovecraft and seek his help on two projects: a book-length memoir of Bierce, and a revision of the story collection, *In the Confessional*. Lovecraft agreed to do one story—titled 'A Sacrifice to Science' in de Castro's book and published as 'The Last Test' in *Weird Tales* for November 1928—for which he received $16.00 (de Castro received $175.00 from *Weird Tales*).

'The Last Test' is one of the poorest of Lovecraft's revisions. It tells the melodramatic story of a doctor, Alfred Clarendon, who is apparently developing an antitoxin for black fever while in charge of the California State Penitentiary at San Quentin but who in reality has fallen under the influence of an evil Atlantean magus, Surama, who has developed a disease that 'isn't of this earth' to overwhelm mankind. All this is narrated in the most stiff and pompous manner conceivable. Lovecraft has radically overhauled the plot while yet preserving the basic framework—the California setting, the characters (though the names of some have been changed), the search for a cure to a new type of fever, and (although this now becomes only a minor part of the climax) Clarendon's attempt to persuade his sister to sacrifice herself. But—aside from replacing the nebulously depicted assistant of Dr Clarendon ('Dr Clinton' in de Castro) named Mort with the much more re-doubtable Surama—he has added much better motivation for the characters and the story as a whole. This, if anything, was Lovecraft's strong point. He has made the tale about half again as long as de Castro's original; and although he remarked of the latter that 'I nearly exploded over the dragging monotony of [the] silly thing',[19] Lovecraft's own version is not without monotony and prolixity of its own.

If it seems unjust that Lovecraft got less than one-tenth of what de Castro was paid, these were the conditions under which Lovecraft operated his revision service: he was at least assured of his fee whether the end result sold or not. (Occasionally, of course, he had difficulty collecting on this fee, but that is a separate matter.) In many cases the revised or ghostwritten tale did not in fact sell. Lovecraft would, in any case, never have wanted to acknowledge such a piece of drivel as 'The Last Test', and it is in some ways unfortunate that his posthumous celebrity has resulted in the unearthing of such items and their republication under his name—the very thing he was trying to avoid.

Even before Lovecraft finished 'The Last Test', de Castro was pleading with him to help him with his memoirs of Bierce. This was a much more difficult proposition, and Lovecraft was properly reluctant to undertake the task without advance payment. De Castro, being hard up for cash, could not assent to this; so Lovecraft turned him over to Frank Long, who was getting into the revision business himself. Long offered to do the revision for no advance pay if he could write a signed preface to the volume. De Castro agreed to this, and Long did what appears to have been a very light revision—he finished the work in two days! This version, however, was rejected by three publishers, so that de Castro came back to Lovecraft on his knees and asked him to take over the project. Lovecraft demanded that de Castro pay him $150.00 in advance, and once again de Castro declined. He appears then to have gone back to Long. The book did in fact come out—with how much more revision by Long, or anyone else, is unclear—as *Portrait of Ambrose Bierce*, published by The Century Company in the spring of 1929 and with a preface by 'Belknap Long'.

In this whole matter de Castro comes off as both wheedling and sly, trying to get Lovecraft and Long to do work for him for little or no pay and for the mythical prospect of vast revenues at a later date. And yet, he was not a complete charlatan. He had published at least one distinguished book of scholarship with a major publisher (*Jewish Forerunners of Christianity* (E. P. Dutton, 1903)). He also seemed to know many languages and had served as a minor functionary in the United States government for a time. If there is a certain ghoulishness in his attempt to cash in on his friendship with Bierce, he was certainly not alone in this.

Another revision client that came into Lovecraft's horizon at this time was Zealia Brown Reed Bishop (1897–1968). Bishop was studying journalism at Columbia and also writing articles and stories to support herself and her young son. I assume that she was divorced at this point. Finding out about Lovecraft's revisory service through Samuel Loveman, she wrote to him in late spring of 1927. In her memoir of Lovecraft, Bishop expresses great admiration for Lovecraft's intellect and literary skill, but also admits rather petulantly that Lovecraft tried to steer her in directions contrary to her natural inclination: 'Being young and romantic, I wanted to follow my own impulse for fresh, youthful stories. Lovecraft was not convinced that [t]his course was best. I was his protégé[e] and he meant to bend my career to his direction.'[20] Bishop goes on to say that at this point she returned to her sister's ranch in Oklahoma, where she heard some tales by Grandma Compton, her sister's mother-in-law, about a pioneer couple in Oklahoma not far away, and wrote a story called 'The Curse of Yig', which Lovecraft praised highly.

And yet, it can hardly be doubted that the story as we have it is almost entirely the work of Lovecraft except for the bare nucleus of the plot. 'The Curse of Yig' is quite an effective piece of work, telling of the horrible fate of a couple, Walker and Audrey Davis, the former of whom has a morbid fear of snakes. Lovecraft writes of his contribution to the story in a letter to Derleth:

> By the way—if you want to see a new story which is practically mine, read 'The Curse of Yig' in the current W.T. Mrs. Reed is a client for whom Long & I have done oceans of work, & this story is about 75% mine. All I had to work on was a synopsis describing a couple of pioneers in a cabin with a nest of rattlesnakes beneath, the killing of the husband by snakes, the bursting of the corpse, & the madness of the wife, who was an eye-witness to the horror. There was no plot or motivation—no prologue or aftermath to the incident—so that one might say the story, as a story, is wholly my own. I invented the snake-god & the curse, the tragic wielding of the axe by the wife, the matter of the snake-victim's identity, & the asylum epilogue. Also, I worked up the geographic & other incidental colour-getting some data from the alleged authoress, who knows Oklahoma, but more from books.[21]

Lovecraft charged Bishop $17.50 for the tale. She managed to sell the story to *Weird Tales*, where it appeared in the November 1929 issue; she received $45.00 for it.

One letter Lovecraft wrote to Bishop in late spring of 1928 is of interest:

> When you perceive the foregoing temporary address, and correlate it with what I have quite frequently expressed as my unvarnished sentiments toward the New York region, you will probably appreciate the extent of the combined burdens and nerve-taxes which have, through malign coincidence, utterly disrupted my programme this spring, and brought me to the verge of what would be a complete breakdown if I did not have a staunch and brilliant colleague—my

young 'adopted grandchild' Frank B. Long—to whom to lean for coöperation and assistance in getting my tasks in shape.[22]

What could be the meaning of this? The address at the head of this letter—395 East 16th Street, Brooklyn, New York—tells part of the story; the other part—which Lovecraft told almost none of his colleagues (those, at any rate, who did not already know the situation)—is that Sonia had called him back to New York.

CHAPTER FIFTEEN
Fanlights and Georgian Steeples
(1928–30)

Lovecraft arrived in New York no later than April 24. Sonia writes in her memoir: 'Late that spring (1928) I invited Howard to come on a visit once more. He gladly accepted but as a visit, only. To me, even that crumb of his nearness was better than nothing.'[1] How 'gladly' Lovecraft accepted this invitation we have already seen in the letter to Zealia Bishop. To his old friend Morton he is a little more expansive: 'The wife had to camp out here for quite a spell on account of business, and thought it only fair that I drop around for a while. Not having any snappy comeback, and wishing to avoid any domestick civil war, I played the pacifist ... and here I am.'[2]

The 'business' referred to is Sonia's attempt to set up a hat shop in Brooklyn—368 East 17th Street, in the very next block from where she was living. Sonia had invested $1000 of her own money to set up the shop, which formally opened on Saturday the 28th. Lovecraft helped Sonia on 'sundry errands' on several occasions, including one stint of addressing envelopes from 11.30 p.m. to 3.30 a.m. one night.

But let us not be deceived; Lovecraft was by no means resuming his marriage any more than was necessary. Sonia writes with considerable tartness: 'But while visiting me, all I saw of Howard was during the few early morning hours when he would return from his jaunts with either Morton, Loveman, Long, Kleiner, or with some or all of them. This lasted through the summer.'[3] Indeed it did; and his gallivanting began almost as soon as he came to town. And yet, although he did do some exploring of the region with friends—a drive along the Hudson River with Long; a visit to James F. Morton's museum in Paterson; a trip to Talman's home in Spring Valley, in Rockland County just above the New Jersey border—Lovecraft and Sonia did manage to go on 13 May to Bryn Mawr Park, the area in Yonkers where they had purchased property in 1924.

On 7 June Lovecraft unexpectedly received an invitation from Vrest Orton that changed his travel plans significantly. He had been planning to visit Bernard Austin Dwyer in West Shokan, then head south for perhaps a week to Philadelphia or Washington, D.C.; but Orton—although living in the pleasant Riverdale section of the Bronx—was disgusted with New York and wished to move out to a farm near Brattleboro, Vermont, which he had just purchased. He insisted that Lovecraft come along, and it took little persuasion for Lovecraft to accede.

Lovecraft's faint taste of Vermont in 1927 had only whetted his appetite; now he would spend a full two weeks in quaint rusticity, and he made the most of it. Orton was, of course, not coming alone, but brought his whole family—wife, infant son, parents, and maternal grandmother, Mrs Teachout, an eighty-year-old woman whose recollections of the past Lovecraft found fascinating. The entire party arrived around 10 June, and Lovecraft stayed till the 24th.

It is charming to read of the simple chores Lovecraft performed ('I have learned how to build a wood fire, & have helped the neighbours' boys round up a straying cow'[4])—no doubt he could momentarily indulge in the fantasy of being a grizzled farmer. Orton's farm, indeed, had few modern amenities—no plumbing except for a lead pipe to lead in the spring water, and no illumination except with oil lamps and candles.

Most of the time, however, Lovecraft struck out on lone trips of exploration. On the 13th he climbed Governor's Mountain (1823 feet above sea level). The next day he called on his old amateur friend Arthur Goodenough and then went across the Connecticut River into New Hampshire to climb Mount Wantastiquet. On the 18th he went to Deerfield and Greenfield in Massachusetts by bus. On the 17th Lovecraft, Orton, and Walter J. Coates went to Arthur Goodenough's home in Brattleboro for a literary conclave with several other local writers—a gathering that was written up in the *Brattleboro Reformer*.[5] Another newspaper item was an article on Lovecraft by Vrest Orton entitled 'A Weird Writer Is In Our Midst', published in the *Brattleboro Reformer* for 16 June. It appeared in a column called 'The Pendrifter', conducted by Charles Crane. On the afternoon of the 21st a neighbour, Charley Lee, took Lovecraft to meet an eccentric farmer named Bert G. Akley, a self-taught painter and photographer of much native skill. Lovecraft was captivated with this 'veritable jack-of-all-trades' who none the less 'retains the primitiveness of the agrestic yeoman'.[6]

On Friday, 29 June, Lovecraft moved on to another leg of his journey as distinctive as his Vermont stay; for Edith Miniter, the old-time amateur, almost demanded that Lovecraft pay her a visit in Wilbraham, Massachusetts, where she was residing with her cousin, Evanore Beebe. He stayed for eight days, and was charmed by the vast array of antiques collected by Beebe, the seven cats and two dogs who had the run of the place, and especially by the spectral local folklore Miniter told him. In 'Mrs. Miniter—Estimates and Recollections' (1934) Lovecraft writes:

> I saw the ruinous, deserted old Randolph Beebe house where the whippoorwills cluster abnormally, and learned that these birds are feared by the rustics as evil psycho-pomps. It is whispered that they linger and flutter around houses where death is approaching, hoping to catch the soul of the departed as it leaves. If the soul eludes them, they disperse in quiet disappointment; but sometimes they set up a chorused clamour of excited, triumphant chattering which makes the watchers turn pale and mutter—with that air of hushed, awestruck portentousness which only a backwoods Yankee can assume—'They got 'im!'

Finally, in mid-July, Lovecraft prepared for his southern jaunt. Catching trains to New York and then to Philadephia, he reached Baltimore on 11 July. Although the bulk of the town was unmistakably Victorian, he found one poignant landmark—Edgar Allan Poe's grave in the Westminster Presbyterian Churchyard. He was planning to go directly from Baltimore to Washington, but the colonial relics of Annapolis proved a fatal temptation; and they were no disappointment. That evening Lovecraft left for Washington, spending the next three days there. At this point yet another temptation proved alluring—an excursion to the Endless Caverns in New Market, Virginia. This was a good four hours by bus from Washington, but the rate was so cheap ($2.50) that Lovecraft could ill resist. Having written about caves from boyhood, he found that the chance actually to visit one was not to be denied. As with his entire trip, this proved highly stimulating to his imagination.

Shortly after returning to Providence Lovecraft wrote a lengthy account of his spring travels, 'Observations on Several Parts of America'. It is the first of several lengthy travelogues—some of the others are 'Travels in the Provinces of America' (1929), 'An Account of Charleston' (1930), and *A Description of the Town of*

Quebeck (1930–31)—and it is among the best. Its flawless capturing of eighteenth-century diction is matched by the deftness with which it weaves travel impressions, history, and personal asides into a smoothly flowing narrative.

Certain practical souls have shed bitter tears at Lovecraft's 'wasting' his time writing these lengthy accounts, which were manifestly produced with no idea of publication and—in the cases of the latter two documents mentioned above—with not even the prospect of meeting any other eye than their author's. Here is one of many occasions in which later commentators have tried to live Lovecraft's life for him. The only 'purpose' of these items is to afford pleasure to Lovecraft and to some of his friends, and that is enough. The 'Observations' and the 'Travels' are single-spaced typescripts, and in effect are open letters, the first written to Maurice W. Moe although surely circulated to other close associates. A volume of Lovecraft's travelogues would be very welcome.

Lovecraft did manage to do some writing aside from letters and his travelogue; in early August he wrote 'The Dunwich Horror'. This is, certainly, one of his most popular tales, but I cannot help finding serious flaws of conception, execution, and style in it. Its plot is well known, and centres upon the efforts of Wilbur Whateley, his mother Lavinia, and his grandfather, Old Whateley, to bring in a horde of monsters from another dimension to overwhelm the earth. One monster in particular has been locked up in their house for years; and, after Wilbur dies in attempting to pilfer the *Necronomicon* from the Miskatonic University Library, the creature breaks out and causes sundry destruction before being dispatched by means of incantations uttered by the Miskatonic University librarian, Henry Armitage, and two of his colleagues. It is then discovered that the monster in question was Wilbur's twin brother.

It should be evident even from this narration that many points of plotting and characterisation in the story are painfully inept. Let us first consider the *moral* implications of the tale. What we have here is an elementary 'good-versus-evil' struggle between Armitage and the Whateleys. That Lovecraft did not mean to portray Armitage parodically (as has been suggested) is proved by a remark made in a letter to August Derleth just after writing the story: '[I] found myself psychologically identifying with one of the characters (an aged scholar who finally combats the menace) toward the end'.[7]

What 'The Dunwich Horror' did was, in effect, to make the rest of the 'Cthulhu Mythos' (i.e., the contributions by other and less skilful hands) possible. Its luridness, melodrama, and naive moral dichotomy were picked up by later writers (it was, not surprisingly, one of Derleth's favourite tales) rather than the subtler work embodied in 'The Call of Cthulhu', 'The Colour out of Space', and others. In a sense, then, Lovecraft bears some responsibility for bringing the 'Cthulhu Mythos' and some of its unfortunate results upon his own head.

In an important sense, indeed, 'The Dunwich Horror' itself turns out to be not much more than a pastiche. The central premise—the sexual union of a 'god' or monster with a human woman—is taken directly from Machen's 'The Great God Pan'. The use of bizarre footsteps to indicate the presence of an otherwise undetectable entity is borrowed from Blackwood's 'The Wendigo'. Some other features relating to the invisible monster are taken from Anthony M. Rud's 'Ooze' (*Weird Tales*, March 1923). The fact that Lovecraft on occasion borrowed from previous works need not be a source of criticism, for he ordinarily made extensive alterations in what he borrowed; but in this case the borrowings go beyond mere surface details of imagery to the very core of the plot.

'The Dunwich Horror' is, of course, not a complete failure. Its portrayal of the decaying backwoods Massachusetts terrain is vivid and memorable, even if a little more hyperbolic than that of 'The Colour out of Space'; and it is, as should now be evident, largely the result of personal experience. Lovecraft later admitted that Dunwich was located in the Wilbraham area, and it is clear that both the topography and some of the folklore (whippoorwills as psychopomps of the dead) are in large part derived from his visit with Edith Miniter. The forest gorge that Lovecraft calls the Bear's Den, however, is taken from a visit to just such an area, near Athol, that Lovecraft took on 28 June in the company of H. Warner Munn.

It is not at all surprising either that 'The Dunwich Horror' was snapped up by *Weird Tales* (Lovecraft received $240.00 for it, the largest single cheque for original fiction he had ever received) or that, when it appeared in the April 1929 issue, its praises were sung by the readership.

In the fall of 1928 Lovecraft heard from an elderly poet named Elizabeth Toldridge (1861–1940), who five years earlier had been involved in some poetry contest of which Lovecraft was a judge. Toldridge was a disabled person who lived a drab life in various hotels in Washington, D.C. She had published—no doubt at her own expense—two slim volumes of poetry earlier in the century, *The Soul of Love* (1910) and *Mother's Love Songs* (1911). Lovecraft wrote to her cordially and promptly, since he felt it gentlemanly to do so; and, because Toldridge herself wrote with unfailing regularity, the correspondence flourished to the end of Lovecraft's life. Toldridge was, indeed, one of the few later correspondents of Lovecraft not involved in weird fiction.

The correspondence naturally focused on the nature of poetry and its philosophical underpinnings. It was just at this time that Lovecraft was beginning a revaluation of poetic style; and the barrage of old-fashioned poetry Toldridge sent to him helped to refine his views. In response to one such poem he wrote:

> It would be an excellent thing if you could gradually work out of the idea that this kind of stilted & artificial language is 'poetical' in any way; for truly, it is *not*. It is a drag & hindrance on *real* poetic feeling & expression, because *real* poetry means spontaneous expression in the simplest & most poignantly vital *living* language. The great object of the poet is to get rid of the cumbrous & the emptily quaint, & buckle down to the *plain, the direct, & the vital*—the pure, precious stuff of actual life & human daily speech.[8]

Lovecraft knew he was not yet ready to practise what he preached; but the mere fact that he had written very little poetry since about 1922 meant both that prose fiction had become his chief aesthetic outlet and that he had come to be profoundly disappointed in his earlier poetic work.

But if Lovecraft could not yet exemplify his new poetic theories, he could at least help to inculcate them in others. Maurice Moe was preparing a volume entitled *Doorways to Poetry*, which Lovecraft in late 1928 announces as provisionally accepted (on the basis of an outline) by Macmillan. As the book developed, he came to have more and more regard for it; by the fall of 1929 he is calling it 'without exception the best & clearest exposition of the inner essence of poetry that I've ever seen'.[9] Lovecraft refused to accept any payment for the evidently extensive revision he performed on the book. It is, as a result, very unfortunate that the manuscript of the volume does not seem to survive; for, as with so many projects by Lovecraft and his friends, *Doorways to Poetry* was never published.

Before Lovecraft could undertake the southern tour he was planning for the spring of 1929, he had one small matter to take care
of—his divorce from Sonia.

Around the end of 1928 Sonia must have begun pressing for a
divorce. Interestingly enough, Lovecraft was opposed to the move:
'during this period of time he tried every method he could devise to
persuade me how much he appreciated me and that divorce would
cause him great unhappiness; and that a gentleman does not
divorce his wife unless he has a cause, and that he has no cause for
doing so'.[10] It is not, certainly, that Lovecraft was contemplating
any return to cohabitation, either in New York or in Providence; it
is simply that the fact of divorce disturbed him, upsetting his
notions of what a gentleman ought to do. He was perfectly willing
to carry on a marriage by correspondence, and actually put forth
the case of someone he knew who was ill and lived apart from his
wife, only writing letters. Sonia did not welcome such a plan: 'My
reply was that neither of us was really sick and that I did not wish to
be a long-distance wife "enjoying" the company of a long-distance
husband by letter-writing only.'

What subsequently happened is not entirely clear. According to
Arthur S. Koki,[11] who consulted various documents in Providence,
on 24 January a subpoena was issued by the Providence Superior
Court for Sonia to appear on 1 March. On 6 February Lovecraft,
Annie Gamwell, and C. M. Eddy went to the office of a lawyer,
Ralph M. Greenlaw, at 76 Westminster Street (the Turk's Head Build-
ing), and presented testimony to the effect that *Sonia* had deserted
Lovecraft. All this was, of course, a charade; but it was necessary
because of the reactionary divorce laws prevailing in the State of
New York, where until 1933 the only grounds for divorce were
adultery or if one of the parties was sentenced to life imprisonment.
The only other option in New York was to have a marriage annul-
led if it had been entered into 'by reason of force, duress, or fraud'
(the last term being interpreted at a judge's discretion) or if one
party was declared legally insane for five years.[12] Obviously these
options did not exist for Lovecraft and Sonia; and so the fiction that
she 'deserted' him was soberly perpetrated, surely with the knowledge of all parties in question.

The overriding question, however, is this: Was the divorce ever
finalized? The answer is clearly no. The final decree was never
signed. How Sonia could have allowed this to happen is anyone's
guess. One can only believe that Lovecraft's refusal to sign was

deliberate—he simply could not bear the thought of divorcing Sonia, not because he really wanted to be married to her, but because a 'gentleman does not divorce his wife without cause'. This purely abstract consideration, based upon social values Lovecraft was already increasingly coming to reject, is highly puzzling. But the matter had at least one unfortunate sequel. It is certain that Sonia's marriage in 1936 to Dr Nathaniel Davis of Los Angeles was legally bigamous—a fact that disturbed her considerably when she was told of it late in life. It was a fittingly botched ending to the whole affair.

Lovecraft's spring travels commenced on 4 April. On that day Vrest Orton drove him up to a home in Yonkers which he was occupying with his wife, child, and grandmother. The place, built around 1830 and set in an idyllic rural area, charmed Lovecraft. He spent his time visiting the gang in New York, going to various literary gatherings arranged by Orton, and generally enjoying his freedom from responsibility and work.

On 1 May Lovecraft's travels began in earnest. He went right down to Washington, stayed overnight at a cheap hotel (he got a room for $1.00), then caught the 6.45 a.m. bus the next morning to Richmond, Virginia. He stayed in Virginia for only four days but took in an astonishing number of sites—Richmond, Williamsburg, Jamestown, Yorktown, Fredericksburg, and Falmouth. All were delightful. Richmond, although it had no one colonial section, nevertheless revealed substantial traces of antiquity to the diligent searcher; of course, it had suffered terrible damage during the Civil War, but was rapidly rebuilt shortly thereafter, and Lovecraft—sympathetic as he always was to the Confederate cause—found the frequent monuments to the Confederate heroes heartwarming. And, of course, he saw a number of sites relating to Poe, including the Poe Shrine (now the Edgar Allan Poe Museum), which had opened only recently. On 3 May Lovecraft saw Williamsburg (then only in the early stages of its restoration as a colonial village), Jamestown, and Yorktown all in a single day.

On 6 May Lovecraft was back in Washington, where he looked up both old and new friends (Edward Lloyd Sechrist and Elizabeth Toldridge) and explored several museums. Returning to New York on the 9th, Lovecraft found that the Longs were planning a fishing trip upstate, so that they could conveniently take him right to the doorstep of Bernard Austin Dwyer, who was at this time occupying a house at 177 Green Street in Kingston. They left the next morning, reaching Kingston in the early afternoon. For the next several evenings Lovecraft and Dwyer sat up discussing literature and philosophy till far into the night. On the 14th Lovecraft visited the neighbouring towns of Hurley and New Paltz, both of them full of Dutch colonial remains.

After a brief stay with Cook in Athol, Lovecraft returned home around the 18th. It had been a great trip, with ten states plus the District of Columbia traversed; and it had given Lovecraft his first fleeting taste of the South, although in later years he would see far more of it. As with his previous year's travels, he wrote up his 1929 jaunt in a tremendous eighteen-thousand-word travelogue entitled 'Travels in the Provinces of America', which, however, was not published until 1995.

On 13 August the Longs drove through Providence on their way to Cape Cod and picked up Lovecraft to accompany them. New Bedford was explored that day, as well as other towns in the vicinity—Chatham, Orleans, Hyannis, Sandwich. But the best part of the journey for Lovecraft was on the 17th, when he took his first ride in an aeroplane. It was only $3.00, and would fly passengers all over Buzzard's Bay. It proved no disappointment: 'The landscape effect was that of a bird's eye view map—& the scene was such as to lend itself to this inspection with maximum advantage ... This aeroplane ride (which attained a pretty good height at its maximum) adds a finishing touch to the perfection of the present outing.'[13] For someone with so cosmic an imagination as Lovecraft, it is scarcely to be wondered that a ride in an aeroplane would be a powerful imaginative stimulus; and only poverty prevented his ever repeating the experience.

One more trip occurred on 29 August. Lovecraft and Annie Gamwell took yet another sojourn to the ancestral Foster region, renewing their acquaintances of three years earlier and extending their explorations still further. This time they investigated the area called Howard Hill, where Asaph Phillips had built his homestead in 1790. They met several people who recalled Whipple Phillips and Robie Place, saw old Phillips gravestones, and consulted genealogical records that helped Lovecraft fill in details of his ancestry. Later they returned to Moosup Valley, the site of their 1926 trip.

In the fall of 1929 Lovecraft and Derleth engaged in a debate over the best weird stories ever written. This may have been part of the honours thesis Derleth was writing ('The Weird Tale in English

Since 1890', completed in 1930 and published in W. Paul Cook's late amateur journal, the *Ghost*, for May 1945), but, whatever the case, the discussion ended up having an unexpectedly wider audience. Bertrand K. Hart, literary editor of the *Providence Journal*, who ran a column called 'The Sideshow', published a list of the best weird tales that Lovecraft found so tame that he sent in the lists prepared by Derleth and Frank Long, as well as his own.

Lovecraft was tickled by his appearance in the paper. He did not ordinarily like to obtrude himself as a persistent bombarder of letters to the editorial page, feeling it callow and self-promotional; but around this time another matter far more pressing to him than an academic discussion of weird fiction forced him once again into a vigorous letter-writing campaign. In spring it had been announced that the old warehouses along South Water Street would be torn down to make way for what was announced as a new hall of records (adjacent to the very fine neo-Georgian court house, built in 1928–33, at the corner of College and North Main Streets). Appalled at the threatened destruction, he wrote a long letter on 20 March 1929 (published in the *Sunday Journal* for 24 March) appealing almost frantically to the city government not to destroy the buildings. But Lovecraft must have known that the fate of the warehouses was sealed. As a final ploy he resurrected his rusty poetic skills and wrote a poignant twelve-stanza poem, 'The East India Brick Row', on 12 December. It appeared in the *Providence Journal* on 8 January 1930.

'The East India Brick Row' was written in the midst of an unexpected burst of poetry at the end of 1929. At the very beginning of the year, or perhaps in late 1928, Lovecraft had written the powerful weird poem 'The Wood' (*Tryout*, January 1929)—a poem that finally begins to exemplify those principles of poetry as a living language that Lovecraft had now embraced and was inculcating to Elizabeth Toldridge and others.

'The Outpost', written on 26 November, inaugurated the poetic outburst. It is not a great success, and was rejected by Farnsworth Wright as being too long (it is in thirteen quatrains). It speaks of the 'great King who fears to dream' in a palace in Zimbabwe. The poem seems clearly inspired by various anecdotes told to Lovecraft by Edward Lloyd Sechrist, who had actually been to the ruins of Zimbabwe in Africa.

At this point B. K. Hart re-enters the scene. The discussion of weird fiction had about died down when Hart stumbled upon a copy of T. Everett Harrés' *Beware After Dark!* containing 'The Call of Cthulhu'. While enjoying the tale, he was startled to note that Wilcox's residence at 7 Thomas Street was one he himself had once occupied. Hart, in a column published in the *Journal* for 30 November, pretended to take umbrage and made a dire threat: he would send over a monster to Lovecraft's house at 3 a.m. What else could Lovecraft do but, that night at 3 a.m., write 'The Messenger'?

> The thing, he said, would come that night at three
> From the old churchyard on the hill below;
> But crouching by an oak fire's wholesome glow,
> I tried to tell myself it could not be.
> Surely, I mused, it was a pleasantry
> Devised by one who did not truly know
> The Elder Sign, bequeathed from long ago,
> That sets the fumbling forms of darkness free.
>
> He had not meant it—no—but still I lit
> Another lamp as starry Leo climbed
> Out of the Seekonk, and a steeple chimed
> Three—and the firelight faded, bit by bit.
> Then at the door that cautious rattling came—
> And the mad truth devoured me like a flame!

Winfield Townley Scott—he who had referred to the bulk of Lovecraft's verse as 'eighteenth-century rubbish'—calls this 'perhaps as wholly satisfactory as any poem he ever wrote'.[14] B. K. Hart must have been pleased with the piece, for he printed it in his column for 3 December 1929.

'The East India Brick Row' followed in early December, after which Lovecraft wrote what *I* might regard as his single most successful poem, 'The Ancient Track'. 'There was no hand to hold me back / That night I found the ancient track', begins—and ends—this brooding, pensive lyric, written in Poe-esque iambic trimeter. This poem readily sold to *Weird Tales*, where it appeared in the March 1930 issue and for which Lovecraft received $11.00.

Then, in the remarkable week between 27 December and 4 January, Lovecraft wrote the *Fungi from Yuggoth*. The thirty-six sonnets that make up this sequence are generally regarded as his most sustained weird poetic work, and the cycle has accordingly generated a considerable body of criticism. Before studying the text itself, it may be well to consider some of the factors that may have led to this tremendous outburst of weird verse.

The most general influence, perhaps, is Clark Ashton Smith. While it is true that fiction had, by around 1921, already come at least to equal poetry as Lovecraft's major aesthetic outlet, it can also be no accident that the virtual surcease of his poetic output from 1922 to 1928 commenced at the very time he came in touch with Smith. Here was a poet who was writing dense, vigorous weird and cosmic poetry in a vibrant, vital manner as far removed as possible from the eighteenth century or even from the poetry of Poe. Lovecraft had long realized, in an abstract way, the deficiencies of his own poetry, but had rarely encountered a *living* poet doing work he could admire and even envy; now he came upon just such a poet. Lovecraft's verse during this period accordingly descends to harmless birthday odes or other occasional verse, with rare exceptions such as the powerful 'The Cats', 'Primavera', or 'Festival' (published as 'Yule Horror').

Then, around 1928, he began work on Moe's *Doorways to Poetry*. After a long period of quiescence, Lovecraft was forced to turn his attention again to the theory of poetry. The immediate influence on the *Fungi*, however, clearly seems to be Wandrei's *Sonnets of the Midnight Hours*, which Lovecraft read no later than November 1927. This cycle—in which all the poems are in the first person and all are inspired by actual dreams by Wandrei—is certainly very powerful, but does not seem to me quite as polished or as cumulatively affecting as Lovecraft's. Nevertheless, Lovecraft clearly derived the basic idea of a sonnet cycle from this work.

Winfield Townley Scott and Edmund Wilson independently believed that the *Fungi* may have been influenced by Edwin Arlington Robinson, but I cannot find any evidence that Lovecraft had read Robinson by this time, or in fact ever read him. He is not mentioned in any correspondence I have seen prior to 1935. The parallels in diction adduced by Scott seem to be of a very general sort and do not establish a sound case for any such influence.

We now come to the vexed question of what the *Fungi from Yuggoth* actually is. Is it a strictly unified poem that reveals some sort of 'continuity', or is it merely a random collection of sonnets flitting from topic to topic with little order or sequence? I remain inclined toward the latter view. No one can possibly believe that there is any actual *plot* to this work, in spite of various critics' laboured attempts to find such a thing; and other critics' claims for a kind of 'unity' based on structure or theme or imagery are similarly unconvincing because the 'unity' so discovered does not seem at all systematic or coherent. My conclusion remains that the *Fungi* sonnets provided Lovecraft with an opportunity to crystallize various conceptions, types of imagery, and fragments of dreams that could not have found creative expression in fiction—a sort of imaginative housecleaning. The fact that he so exhaustively used ideas from his commonplace book for the sonnets supports this conclusion.

Some of the sonnets seem to be reworkings of some of the dominant conceptions of previous stories. 'Nyarlathotep' is a close retelling of the prose poem of 1920; 'The Elder Pharos' speaks of a figure who 'wears a silken mask', whom we first saw in *The Dream-Quest of Unknown Kadath*; 'Alienation' seems roughly based upon 'The Strange High House in the Mist'. More significantly, some poems seem to be anticipations of stories Lovecraft would write in later years, making the *Fungi* a sort of recapitulation of what he had written before and a presage of his subsequent work.

Those who argue for the 'unity' of the *Fungi* must take account of the somewhat odd manner in which the cycle achieved its present state. 'Recapture' (now sonnet XXXIV) was written in late November, presumably as a separate poem. For years after it was written, the *Fungi* comprised only thirty-five sonnets. In 1936, when R. H. Barlow considered publishing it as a booklet, he suggested that 'Recapture' be added to the cycle; but, when he rather casually tacked it on at the end of a typescript he was preparing, Lovecraft felt that it should be placed third from the end: '"Recapture" seems somehow more *specific & localised* in spirit than either of the others named, hence would go better before them—allowing the *Fungi* to come to a close with more diffusive ideas.'[15] To my mind, this suggests no more than that Lovecraft had some rough idea that the cycle ought to be read in sequence and ought to end with a more general utterance. And yet, shortly after finishing the series he was still mentioning casually the possibility of 'grind[ing] out a dozen or so more before I consider the sequence concluded'.[16]

Certainly, Lovecraft had no compunction in allowing the individual sonnets of the *Fungi* to appear quite randomly in the widest array of publications. Ten sonnets appeared in *Weird Tales* in 1930–31 (as well as 'Recapture', published earlier); five more appeared in the *Providence Journal* in the early months of 1930; nine appeared in Walter J. Coates's *Driftwind* from 1930 to 1932; the remainder appeared later in amateur journals or fan magazines, and after Lovecraft's death many more were printed in *Weird Tales*. The cycle as a unit was not published until 1943.

It had been more than a year since Lovecraft had written any original fiction; and that tale—'The Dunwich Horror'—was itself written after more than a year's interval since its predecessor, 'The Colour out of Space'. Revision, travel, and inevitably correspondence ate up all the time Lovecraft might have had for fiction, for he stated repeatedly that he required a completely free schedule to achieve the mental clarity needed for writing stories. Now, however, at the end of 1929, a revision job came up that allowed him to exercise his fictional pen far beyond what he expected—and, frankly, beyond what was required by the job in question. But however prodigal Lovecraft may have been in the task, the result—'The Mound', ghostwritten for Zealia Bishop—was well worth the effort.

Of this story it is difficult to speak in small compass. It is, at twenty-five thousand words, the lengthiest of Lovecraft's revisions of a weird tale, and is comparable in length to 'The Whisperer in Darkness'. That it is entirely the work of Lovecraft can be gauged by Bishop's original plot-germ, as recorded by R. H. Barlow: 'There is an Indian mound near here, which is haunted by a headless ghost. Sometimes it is a woman.'[17] Lovecraft found this idea 'insufferably tame & flat'[18] and fabricated an entire novelette of underground horror, incorporating many conceptions of his evolving myth-cycle, including Cthulhu (under the variant form Tulu).

'The Mound' concerns a member of Coronado's expedition of 1541, Panfilo de Zamacona y Nuñez, who leaves the main group and conducts a solitary expedition to the mound region of what is now Oklahoma and stumbles upon the underground realm of Xinaian (which he pronounces 'K'n-yan'), occupied by approximately human denizens from outer space. These people have developed remarkable mental abilities, including telepathy and the power of dematerialization—the process of dissolving themselves and selected objects around them to their component atoms and recombining them at some other location. Zamacona initially expresses wonder at this civilization, but gradually finds that it has declined both intellectually and morally from a much higher level and has now become corrupt and decadent. He attempts to escape, but suffers a horrible fate. A manuscript that he had written of his adventures is unearthed in modern times by an archaeologist, who paraphrases his incredible tale.

This skeletonic plot outline cannot begin to convey the textural richness of the story, which—although perhaps not as carefully written as many of Lovecraft's original works—is successful in depicting vast gulfs of time and in vivifying with a great abundance of detail the underground world of K'n-yan. What should also be evident is that 'The Mound' is the first, but by no means the last, of Lovecraft's tales to utilize an alien civilization as a transparent metaphor for certain phases of human (and, more specifically, Western) civilization. Initially, K'n-yan seems a Lovecraftian utopia: the people have conquered old age, have no poverty because of their relatively few numbers and their thorough mastery of technology, use religion only as an aesthetic ornament, practise selective breeding to ensure the vigour of the 'ruling type', and pass the day largely in aesthetic and intellectual activity. But as Zamacona continues to observe the people, he begins to notice disturbing signs of decadence. Science was 'falling into decay'; history was 'more and more neglected'; and gradually religion was becoming less a matter of aesthetic ritual and more a sort of degraded superstition. The narrator concludes: 'It is evident that K'n-yan was far along in its decadence—reacting with mixed apathy and hysteria against the standardised and time-tabled life of stultifying regularity which machinery had brought it during its middle period.' These sentiments are exactly echoed in Lovecraft's letters of the period.

Rich in intellectual substance as 'The Mound' is, it is far longer a work than Lovecraft needed to write for this purpose; and this length boded ill for its publication prospects. *Weird Tales* was on increasingly shaky ground, and Farnsworth Wright had to be careful what he accepted. It is not at all surprising that he rejected the tale in early 1930.

The lingering belief that Frank Belknap Long had some hand in the writing of the story—derived from Zealia Bishop's declaration that 'Long … advised and worked with me on that short novel'[19]—has presumably been squelched by Long's own declaration in 1975 that 'I had nothing whatever to do with the writing of *The Mound*. That brooding, somber, and magnificently atmospheric story is Lovecraftian from the first page to the last.'[20] Long was at this time acting as Bishop's agent, and had in fact prepared the typescript of the tale. After its rejection by *Weird Tales*, Long proceeded to abridge it by merely omitting some sheets from the typescript and scratching out portions of others with a pen. But this version also did not sell, so the story was put aside. It was finally first published only in *Weird Tales* for November 1940, and then in a severely abridged form.

Lovecraft's travels for the spring–summer of 1930 began in late April. Charleston, South Carolina, was his goal, and he seems to have shot down to the South with scarcely a stop along the route. He reports being in Richmond on the afternoon of 27 April and spending a night in Winston-Salem, North Carolina; 28 April found him in Columbia, South Carolina. Later that day Lovecraft caught a bus that took him directly to Charleston. A postcard written to Derleth on 29 April may give some inkling of Lovecraft's sentiments:

> Revelling in the most marvellously fascinating environment —scenically, architecturally, historically, & climatically—that I've ever encountered in my life! I can't begin to convey any idea of it except by exclamation points—I'd move here in a second if my sentimental attachment to New England were less strong ... Will stay here as long as my cash holds out, even if I have to cut all the rest of my contemplated trip.[21]

Lovecraft remained in Charleston until 9 May, seeing everything there was to see; and there certainly was much to see. Charleston remains today one of the most well-preserved colonial oases on the eastern seaboard—thanks, of course, to a very vigorous restoration and preservation movement that makes it today even more attractive than it was in Lovecraft's day, when some of the colonial remains were in a state of dilapidation. Everything that Lovecraft describes in his lengthy travelogue, 'An Account of Charleston' (1930), survives, with rare exceptions.

In his travelogue Lovecraft, aside from supplying a very detailed history of the town, lays down a systematic walking tour—which he optimistically states can be covered in a single day (I did so, although it took me about seven hours and several rest-stops)— which covers all the prominent antiquities of Charleston with a minimum of backtracking. The tour leaves out some fairly pictur-esque sections that are not colonial (the western end of South Battery, for example), as well as outlying areas such as Fort Sumter, Fort Moultrie on Sullivan's Island, the Citadel, and the like, although Lovecraft probably explored these himself. He recognizes that the heart of colonial Charleston is the relatively small area south of Broad Street between Legare and East Bay, including such exquisite thoroughfares as Tradd, Church, Water, and the like; the alleys in this section—Bedon's Alley, Stolls Alley, Longitude Lane, St Michael's Alley—are worth a study all their own. Progressing northward, the section between Broad and Calhoun becomes increasingly post-Revolutionary and antebellum in architecture, although the town's centre of government and business still remains the critical intersection of Broad and Meeting. North of Calhoun there is scarcely anything of antiquarian interest.

On 9 May Lovecraft reluctantly left Charleston and proceeded to Richmond, where he remained for about ten days. On the 13th he took an excursion to Petersburg, a town about fifteen miles south of Richmond full of colonial antiquities.

Lovecraft was learning to cut expenses on the road. Wandrei tells us how he saved on cleaning bills away from home: 'He neatly laid out his trousers between the mattresses of his bed in order to renew the crease and press overnight. He detached the collar from his shirt, washed it, smoothed it between the folds of a hand towel, and weighted it with the Gideon Bible, thus preparing a fresh collar for the morning.'[22] So the Gideon Bible had some use for Lovecraft after all! He was now becoming an amateur self-barber, using a 'patent hair-cutter'[23] he had picked up—no doubt a sort of trimmer.

In Richmond Lovecraft did most of the work on another ghost job for Zealia Bishop, although he seems not to have finished it until August. She surely contributed as much (or as little) to this one as to the previous two; but in this case one is more regretful of the fact, for it means that the many flaws and absurdities in the tale must be placed solely or largely at Lovecraft's door. 'Medusa's Coil' is as confused, bombastic, and just plain silly a work as anything in Lovecraft's entire corpus. Like some of his early tales, it is ruined by a woeful excess of supernaturalism that produces complete chaos at the end, as well as a lack of subtlety in characterization that (as in 'The Last Test') cripples a tale based fundamentally on a conflict of characters. The tale concerns one Denis de Russy, a young man who falls in love with a mysterious French woman named Marceline Bedard and brings her back to his family estate in Missouri, where she has a tense relationship with Denis's father (the narrator of the bulk of the story) and with Denis's friend, the painter Frank Marsh. In the end it transpires that, aside from possessing various supernatural powers, Marceline was, 'though in deceitfully slight proportion ... a negress'.

The overriding problem with this tale—beyond the luridly pulpish plot and the crudely racist conclusion—is that the characters are so wooden and stereotyped that they never come to life. Lovecraft well knew that he had both a very limited understanding of and very limited interest in human beings. He contrived his own fiction such that the human figures were not the focus of action; but in a revision—where, presumably, he had to follow at least the skeleton of the plot provided by his client—he was not always able to evade the need for vivid characterization, and it is precisely those revisions where such characterization is absent that rank the poorest.

It is, certainly, not the tale's lack of quality that prevented its publication in a pulp market, for much worse stories were published with great regularity; but for whatever reason (and excessive length may again have had something to do with it), 'Medusa's Coil' was rejected by *Weird Tales*. It finally appeared in the issue for January 1939. Both 'The Mound' and 'Medusa's Coil' were heavily altered and rewritten by Derleth for their magazine appearances, and he continued to reprint the adulterated texts in book form up to his death. The corrected texts did not see print until 1989.

Back in New York on 20 May, Lovecraft was excited to read one interesting piece of forwarded mail—a letter from Clifton P. Fadiman of Simon & Schuster encouraging Lovecraft to submit a novel. He immediately responded by saying that, although he might write a novel later (clearly *The Case of Charles Dexter Ward* was not even considered as a submission), he would like to submit a collection of short stories. A few days later Lovecraft's enthusiasm waned considerably: he discovered that the letter was merely a mimeographed form-letter sent to everyone who had appeared on the 'Honor Roll' of the O'Brien short story annuals; moreover, Fadiman had responded by saying: 'I am afraid that you are right in that our interest in a collection of short stories would not be very vivid. I hope, however, that you will buckle down & do that novel you speak of. If it is good, its subject matter will be a help rather than a hindrance.'[24] It is interesting to note that mainstream publishers' now inveterate reluctance to publish weird short story collections was already evident in 1930.

Otherwise the two weeks spent in New York included additional museum-going (Metropolitan, Brooklyn, and also the newly opened Nicholas Roerich Museum) as well as the usual round of catching up on old friendships. One unexpected acquaintance whom Lovecraft met was Hart Crane, who came to Loveman's apartment on the evening of 24 May when Lovecraft was there. *The Bridge* had been published that spring, making him 'one of the most celebrated & talked-of figures of contemporary American letters'. Lovecraft's portrait of him is simultaneously admiring and pitying:

> Poor devil—he has 'arrived' at last as a standard American poet seriously regarded by all reviewers & critics; yet at the very crest of his fame he is on the verge of psychological, physical, & financial disintegration, & with no certainty of ever having the inspiration to write a major work of literature again. After about three hours of acute & intelligent argument poor Crane left—to hunt up a new supply of whiskey & banish reality for the rest of the night![25]

Lovecraft was sadly correct in his prediction, for Crane would commit suicide two years later.

Lovecraft's return home on 13 or 14 June ended another record-breaking sojourn, but it was by no means the end of his year's travels. On 3–5 July he decided to take in the NAPA convention in Boston—only the second national amateur convention he had ever attended, the other being the NAPA convention of 1921. But even this was not the end of his travels. On 30 August we find him boarding a train north—to Quebec. It would be his first and last time out of the United States, aside from two further visits there in later years. Lovecraft had come upon a remarkably cheap $12.00 excursion fare to Quebec, and could not pass up the chance to see a place of whose antiquarian marvels he had so long heard. The sight of the Canadian countryside—with its quaint old farmhouses built in the French manner and small rustic villages with picturesque church steeples—was pleasing enough, but as he approached the goal on the train he knew he was about to experience something remarkable. And he did:

> Never have I seen another place like it! All my former standards of urban beauty must be abandoned after my sight of Quebec! It hardly belongs to the world of prosaic reality at all—it is a dream of city walls, fortress-crowned cliffs, silver spires, narrow, winding, perpendicular streets, magnificent vistas, & the mellow, leisurely civilisation of an elder world … Horse vehicles still abound, & the atmosphere is altogether of the past. It is a perfectly preserved bit of old royalist France, transplanted to the New World with very little loss of atmosphere.[26]

He stayed only three days, but by keeping constantly on the move saw almost everything there was to see—City Hall Square, Montmorency Park, Notre Dame des Victoires, Chateau Frontenac, the Ursuline Convent, and much more. A side trip to the falls of the Montmorency River capped the visit.

The travels of 1930 had again surpassed their predecessors, and were highlighted by two transcendent sites—Charleston and Quebec. In later years Lovecraft returned to both these havens of antiquity as often as his meagre funds would allow. In the meantime he could at least write about them, both in rapturous letters and postcards to his friends and in formal travelogues; and he did just that. 'An Account of Charleston', which I have already discussed, is undated, but was probably written in the fall. But Quebec impelled an even more heroic work, which occupied much of the fall and winter. *A Description of the Town of Quebeck* was the longest single work Lovecraft would ever write. After a very comprehensive history of the region, there is a study of Quebec architecture (with appropriate drawings of distinctive features of roofs, windows, and the like), a detailed hand-drawn map of the principal sites, and a detailed walking tour of both the town itself and 'suburban pilgrimages'. That Lovecraft could have absorbed enough of the town in three days to have written even the travelogue portion (the historical section was clearly learned later through much reading) is a sufficient indication of what those three crowded days must have been like.

The Quebec travelogue also lay in manuscript until long after Lovecraft's death, and was not published until 1976.

But beginning early in the year and continuing all through the spring, summer, and early autumn, Lovecraft was at work on a document that was actually designed to be read by the general public: 'The Whisperer in Darkness'. Although this would be among the most difficult in its composition of any of his major stories, this 25,000-word novelette—the longest of his fictions up to that time aside from his two 'practice' novels—conjures up the hoary grandeur of the New England countryside even more poignantly than any of his previous works, even if it suffers from some flaws of conception and motivation.

The tale focuses on the correspondence that develops between Albert N. Wilmarth, a professor of literature at Miskatonic University, and a Vermont recluse named Henry Wentworth Akeley, who soberly reports the existence of a colony of extraterrestrials from the planet Yuggoth dwelling in the region, who, by means of a complicated mechanical device, can remove the brains of human beings from their bodies and to take them on fantastic cosmic voyagings. Wilmarth is naturally sceptical of Akeley's tale, but subsequent events—including the aliens' attacks on Akeley—appear to confirm it. Wilmarth is then invited up to Vermont by Akeley, although the letter written by the recluse sounds peculiar and uncharacteristic. Nevertheless, Wilmarth makes the journey, where he meets an Akeley who seems both physically and psychologically changed. Akeley is now reconciled to the prospect of his brain being removed and taken to Yuggoth and beyond, for he will thereby acquire cosmic knowledge made available only to a handful of human beings since the beginning of civilization. Numbed with astonishment, Wilmarth retires to bed, but hears a disturbing colloquy in Akeley's room with several of the buzzing voices and other, human voices. But what makes him flee from the place is a very simple thing he sees as he sneaks down to Akeley's room late at night: 'For the things in the chair, perfect to the last, subtle detail of microscopic resemblance—or identity—were the face and hands of Henry Wentworth Akeley.'

Without the necessity of stating it, Lovecraft makes clear the true state of affairs: the last, reassuring letter by 'Akeley' was in fact a forgery by the alien entities, written as a means of getting Wilmarth to come up to Vermont with all the evidence of his relations with Akeley; the speaker in the chair was not Akeley—whose brain had already been removed from his body and placed in one of the machines—but one of the aliens, perhaps Nyarlathotep himself, whom they worship.

The genesis of the tale is nearly as interesting as the tale itself; Steven J. Mariconda has studied the matter in detail, and in large part I am echoing his conclusions.[27] The Vermont background of the tale is clearly derived from Lovecraft's visits of 1927 and 1928; indeed, whole passages of 'Vermont—A First Impression' have been bodily inserted into the text, but they have been subtly altered in such a way as to emphasize both the terror and the fascination of the rustic landscape. It is also evident that Henry Wentworth Akeley is based in part on the rustic Bert G. Akley whom Lovecraft met on the 1928 trip. Akeley's secluded farmhouse seems to be a commingling of the Orton residence in Brattleboro and Goodenough's home farther to the north. And, of course, Lovecraft has ingeniously incorporated the discovery of the planet Pluto (announced in the *New York Times* for 14 March), identifying it with his mythical Yuggoth.

The actual writing of the tale was, however, very difficult and unusually prolonged, extending from February to September. The story was 'provisionally finished' in Charleston, but underwent significant revisions after various suggestions were made by Frank Long and Bernard Dwyer. The nature of these revisions is not entirely known, but it appears that Dwyer recommended that Wilmarth be made a less gullible figure. Lovecraft did not make much headway on this point: although random details were inserted to heighten Wilmarth's scepticism, he still seems very naive in proceeding blithely up to Vermont with all the documentary evidence he has received from Akeley. And yet, Wilmarth exhibits in extreme form something we have seen in many of Lovecraft's characters: a difficulty in believing that a supernatural or supernormal event has occurred.

But 'The Whisperer in Darkness' suffers from a somewhat more severe flaw, one that we have already seen in 'The Dunwich Horror'. Once again, in violation of Lovecraft's stated wish to discard conventional morality in regard to his extraterrestrials, he has endowed his aliens with common—and rather petty—human flaws and motivations. They are guilty of cheap forgery on two occasions; and on the first occasion they are so inept as to misspell Akeley's name, in spite of the fact that, as they themselves maintain, 'Their brain-capacity exceeds that of any other surviving life-form.' Their gun-battles with Akeley take on unintentionally comic overtones, reminiscent of shoot-outs in cheap western movies.

But whereas such flaws of conception and execution cripple 'The Dunwich Horror', here they are only minor blemishes in an otherwise magnificent tale. 'The Whisperer in Darkness' remains a monument in Lovecraft's work for its throbbingly vital evocation of New England landscape, its air of documentary verisimilitude, its insidiously subtle atmosphere of cumulative horror, and its breathtaking intimations of the cosmic.

'The Whisperer in Darkness', being one of the longest stories Lovecraft actually bothered to type and submit to a publisher, brought corresponding proceeds. It was readily accepted by Farnsworth Wright, who paid Lovecraft $350.00 for it—the largest cheque he had ever received and, indeed, ever would receive for a single work of fiction. Wright planned to run it as a two-part serial;

but early in 1931 *Weird Tales* was forced into publication every two months for about half a year, so that the story appeared complete in the August 1931 issue.

The period from 1928 to 1930 saw Lovecraft write only two original weird tales (the severely flawed 'The Dunwich Horror' and the somewhat flawed but otherwise monumental 'The Whisperer in Darkness') along with three revisions for Zealia Bishop: one highly significant ('The Mound'), another fair to middling ('The Curse of Yig'), and one totally forgettable ('Medusa's Coil'). But to measure Lovecraft solely on his weird output would be an injustice both to the man and to the writer. His travels to Vermont, Virginia, Charleston, Quebec, and other antiquarian oases provided much imaginative nourishment, and his accounts of his journeys, both in letters and in travel essays, are among his most heartwarming pieces. His correspondence continued to increase as he gained new acquaintances, and their differing views—as well as his constant absorption of new information and new perspectives through books and through observation of the world around him—allowed him considerably to refine his philosophical thought. By 1930 he had resolved many issues to his satisfaction, and in later years only his political and economic views would undergo extensive revision. It is, then, appropriate to examine his thought before proceeding to the examination of the subsequent literary work based upon it.

CHAPTER SIXTEEN
Non-supernatural Cosmic Art
(1930–31)

By the early 1930s Lovecraft had resolved many of the philosophical issues that had concerned him in prior years; in particular, he had come to terms with the Einstein theory and managed to incorporate it into what was still a dominantly materialistic system. In so doing, he evolved a system of thought not unlike that of his later philosophical mentors, Bertrand Russell and George Santayana.

It appears that Lovecraft first read both these thinkers between 1927 and 1929. He clearly found Russell's reliance on science and his secular ethics to his liking, although Russell was not exactly an atheist. In 1927 Russell encapsulated his philosophical outlook in terms Lovecraft would have welcomed:

> I still believe that the major processes of the universe proceed according to the laws of physics; that they have no reference to our wishes, and are likely to involve the extinction of life on this planet; that there is no good reason for expecting life after death; and that good and evil are ideas which throw no light upon the nonhuman world.[1]

What Lovecraft had come to realize about the Einstein theory—in particular, its bearing on the three principles of materialism emphasized by Hugh Elliot (the uniformity of law, the denial of teleology, and the denial of substances not envisaged by physics and chemistry)—is that Newtonian laws of physics still work entirely adequately in the immediate universe around us: 'The given area *isn't big enough* to let relativity get in its major effects— *hence we can rely on the never-failing laws of earth to give absolutely reliable results in the nearer heavens.'.*[2] This allows Lovecraft to preserve at least the first of Elliot's principles. As for the second:

> All we can say of [the cosmos], is that it contains no visible central principle so like the physical brains of terrestrial mammals that we may reasonably attribute to it the purely

terrestrial and biological phaenomenon call'd *conscious purpose*; and that we form, even allowing for the most radical conceptions of the relativist, so insignificant and temporary a part of it ... that all notions of special relationships and names and destinies expressed in human conduct must necessarily be vestigial myths..[3]

This passage reveals how intimately the denial of teleology is, for Lovecraft, connected with the idea of human insignificance: each really entails the other. If human beings are insignificant, there is no reason why some cosmic force (whether we identify it with God or not) should be leading the universe in any given direction for the benefit of humanity; conversely, the evident absence of conscious purpose in the universe at large is one more—and perhaps the most important—indication of the triviality and evanescence of the human species.

Lovecraft is still more emphatic on the third point (denial of spirit):

The truth is, that the discovery of matter's identity with energy—and of its consequent lack of vital intrinsic difference from empty space—is *an absolute coup de grace to the primitive and irresponsible myth of 'spirit'. For matter, it appears, really is exactly what 'spirit' was always supposed to be. Thus it is proved that wandering energy always has a detectable form*—that if it doesn't take the form of waves or electron-streams, *it becomes matter itself*; and that the absence of matter or any other detectable energy-form indicates *not the presence of spirit, but the absence of anything whatever.*[4]

This entire letter must be read to appreciate Lovecraft's admirable reconciliation of Einstein and materialism. I have no doubt that he derived much of his data from contemporary literature on the subject—perhaps in the form of magazine or newspaper articles—but the vigour of his writing argues for a reasoned synthesis that is surely his own.

Lovecraft had a little more difficulty with quantum theory, which affects Elliot's first principle, and which Lovecraft seems to have absorbed around this time. Quantum theory asserts that the action of certain sub-atomic particles is inherently random, so that we can only establish statistical averages of how a given reaction will turn out. Lovecraft addresses quantum theory significantly, to my knowledge, only once in his correspondence—in a letter to Long in late 1930:

What most physicists take the quantum theory, at present, to mean, is *not that any cosmic uncertainty exists* as to which of several courses a given reaction will take; but that in certain instances *no conceivable channel of information can ever tell human beings which courses will be taken*, or by what exact course a certain observed result came about.[5]

It is clear from this that Lovecraft is merely repeating the views of experts. The point he is trying to establish is that the 'uncertainty' of quantum theory is not *ontological* but *epistemological*; that it is only our inability (an inherent inability, not merely some deficiency in our sense-perception or general reasoning capacity) to predict the behaviour of sub-atomic particles that results in uncertainty. This conclusion—although accepted by Einstein in his celebrated dictum 'God does not play dice with the cosmos'—appears to be wrong. Bertrand Russell has declared that the 'absence of complete determinism is not due to any incompleteness in the theory, but is a genuine characteristic of small-scale occurrences';[6] although he goes on to say that atomic and molecular reactions are still largely deterministic.

And yet, in the late 1920s and early 1930s quantum theory was hailed as shattering the first of Elliot's materialistic principles—the uniformity of law—just as relativity was thought to have shattered, or at least qualified, the second and third. We now know—in so far as we really know the ultimate ramifications of quantum theory— that the uniformity of law is itself only qualified, and perhaps not even in a way that has any philosophical significance. The relation between quantum theory and, say, the possibility of free will is anything but clear, and there is as yet no reason to carry the effects of quantum theory into the behaviour of macrocosmic phenomena.

Some of the most bracing pages in Lovecraft's letters of this period deal with his emphatic assertion of atheism against those of his colleagues (especially Frank Long) who felt that the 'uncertainty' revealed by modern astrophysics left room for the recrudescence of conventional religious belief. Lovecraft was well aware that he was living in a time of both social and intellectual ferment; but he had nothing but contempt for those thinkers who were using the relativity and quantum theories to resurrect old-time belief:

Although these new turns of science don't really mean a thing in relation to the myth of cosmic consciousness and teleology, a new brood of despairing and horrified moderns is seizing on the doubt of all positive knowledge which they imply; and is deducing therefrom that, *since nothing is true*, therefore *anything can be true* ... whence one may invent or revive any sort of mythology that fancy or nostalgia or desperation may dictate, and defy anyone to prove that it isn't 'emotionally' true—whatever that means. This sickly, decadent neomysticism—a protest not only against machine materialism but against pure science with its destruction of the mystery and dignity of human emotion and experience —will be the dominant creed of middle twentieth centuries aesthetes.[7]

Lovecraft's later ethics is in many ways a direct outgrowth of his metaphysics, and it is also intimately connected with his evolving social and political views. The question for Lovecraft was: how to conduct oneself with the realization that the human race was an insignificant atom in the vast realms of the cosmos? One solution was to adopt the perspective of a sort of bland cosmic spectator upon the human race. But this is not a very useful yardstick for actual behaviour, and Lovecraft had to devise some system of conduct, at least for himself, that might be consistent with cosmicism. It is only at this time that he came to espouse an aesthetic retention of *tradition* as a bulwark against the potential nihilism of his metaphysics. This view had no doubt been evolving unconsciously for many years, but it becomes explicit only now; but in so doing, Lovecraft leaves himself open to criticism at several points.

Throughout his life Lovecraft wavered between (validly) recommending tradition *for himself* and (invalidly) recommending it *for everyone*. In 1928 he had properly asserted the relativity of values (the only thing possible in a universe that has no governing deity): 'Value is wholly relative, and the very idea of such a thing as meaning postulates a symmetrical relation to something else. No one thing, cosmically speaking, can be either good or evil, beautiful or unbeautiful; for entity is simply entity.'[8]

All this is unexceptionable, and yet it gradually gives way to a much less defensible view: that, given the relativity of values, the only true anchor of fixity is tradition—specifically the racial and cultural tradition out of which each person grows. The matter crops up in a discussion with Morton, who appears to have questioned why Lovecraft was so passionately concerned about the preservation of Western civilization when he believed in a purposeless cosmos:

It is *because* the cosmos is meaningless that we must secure our individual illusions of values, direction, and interest by upholding the artificial streams which gave us such worlds of salutary illusion. That is—since nothing means anything in itself, we must preserve the proximate and arbitrary background which makes things around us seem as if they did mean something. In other words, we are either Englishmen or nothing whatever.[9]

That 'we' is very ominous. Lovecraft seems unaware that it is only those, like himself, in whom the sense of tradition has been strongly ingrained who will clutch at tradition—racial, cultural, political, and aesthetic—as the only bulwark against nihilism.

It should now be clear not only why Lovecraft clung to tradition so firmly but why he so ardently sought to preserve his civilization against onslaughts from all sides—from foreigners, from the rising tide of mechanization, and even from radical aesthetic movements. As the 1920s progressed, Lovecraft began to sense that the greatest foe to tradition was the machine culture. His views on the subject are by no means original to him, but his remarks are both incisive and compelling. Two books powerfully affected Lovecraft's thinking on these matters, although he could say with justice that he had arrived at least nebulously at the same fundamental conceptions prior to reading them. They were Oswald Spengler's *The Decline of the West* (*Der Untergang des Abendlandes* (1918–22); translated in two volumes in 1926 and 1928) and Joseph Wood Krutch's *The Modern Temper* (1929). Lovecraft read the first volume of Spengler (he never read the second, so far as I can tell) in the spring of 1927, and seems to have read Krutch no later than the fall of 1929.

Lovecraft had long been inclined to accept Spengler's basic thesis of the successive rise and fall of civilizations as each passes through a period of youth, adulthood, and old age. He later expressed reservations, as many others did, on the degree to which this biological analogy could be pressed; but otherwise he accepted Spengler enthusiastically, coming to believe that one particular phase of Western culture was coming to an end—the agrarian and early industrial phase, from the Renaissance to the early twentieth century, that had in his view seen the greatest flowering of Western culture. Whatever the future held in store, it would no longer be a part of his culture, but some other, alien culture with which he could not possibly identify.

Lovecraft's reading of Krutch's *The Modern Temper* made him face the situation of art and culture in the modern world. Krutch's book is a lugubrious but chillingly compelling work that particularly addresses itself to the question of what intellectual and aesthetic possibilities remain in an age in which so many illusions—in particular the illusions of our importance in the cosmos and of the 'sanctity' or even validity of our emotional life—have been shattered by science. This is a theme on which Lovecraft had been expatiating since at least 1922, with 'Lord Dunsany and His Work'. Indeed, I believe Krutch's work was instrumental in helping Lovecraft to effect a further evolution of his aesthetic theory. He had already passed from classicism to Decadence to a sort of antiquarian regionalism. But he knew that the past—that is, prior modes of behaviour, thought, and aesthetic expression—could be preserved only up to a point. The new realities revealed by modern science had to be faced. Around this time he began some further ruminations on art and its place in society, in particular weird art; and in so doing he produced a radical change in his theory of weird fiction that would affect much of what he would subsequently write.

Frank Long was again, somehow, the catalyst for the expression of these views. Long was lamenting the rapid rate of cultural change and was advocating a return to 'splendid and traditional ways of life'—a view Lovecraft rightly regarded as somewhat sophomoric in someone who did not know much about what these traditional ways actually were. In an immense letter written in late February 1931, Lovecraft begins by repeating Krutch's argument that much of prior literature has ceased to be vital to us because we can no longer share, and in some cases can only remotely understand, the values that produced it; he then writes: 'Some former art attitudes—like sentimental romance, loud heroics, ethical didacticism, &c.—are so patently hollow as to be visibly absurd & non-usable from the start.' Some attitudes, however, may still be viable:

> Fantastic literature cannot be treated as a single unit, because it is a composite resting on widely divergent bases. I really agree that 'Yog-Sothoth' is a basically immature conception, & unfitted for really serious literature. The fact is, I have never approached serious literature as yet ... The only permanently artistic use of Yog-Sothothery, I think, is in symbolic or assocative phantasy of the frankly poetic type; in which fixed dream-patterns of the natural organism are given an embodiment & crystallisation. The reasonable permanence of this phase of poetic phantasy as a *possible* art

form (whether or not favoured by current fashion) seems to me a highly strong probability.

I do not know what exactly Lovecraft means by 'Yog-Sothothery' here. My feeling is that it may refer to Dunsany's prodigal invention of gods in *The Gods of Pegāna*, which we have already seen Lovecraft to have repudiated as far as his own creative expression is concerned; indeed, he says here of this type of material that 'I hardly expect to produce anything even remotely approaching it myself'. He continues:

> But there is another phase of cosmic phantasy (which may or may not include frank Yog-Sothothery) whose foundations appear to me as better grounded than those of ordinary oneiroscopy; personal limitation regarding the *sense of out-sideness*. I refer to the aesthetic crystallisation of that burning & inextinguishable feeling of mixed wonder & oppression which the sensitive imagination experiences upon scaling itself & its restrictions against the vast & provocative abyss of the unknown. This has always been the chief emotion in my psychology; & whilst it obviously figures less in the psychology of the majority, it is clearly a well-defined & permanent factor from which very few sensitive persons are wholly free.

Now we are getting more to the crux of the matter: Lovecraft is beginning to provide a rationale for the type of weird fiction he has been writing for the past few years, which is a fundamentally realistic approach to the 'sense of outsideness' by the suggestion of the vast gulfs of space and time—in short, cosmicism. There is nothing here that is different from prior utterances of this idea; but Lovecraft now continues:

> The time has come when the normal revolt against time, space, & matter must assume a form not overtly incompati-ble with what is known of reality—when it must be gratified by images forming *supplements* rather than *contradictions* of the visible & mensurable universe. And what, if not a form of *non-supernatural cosmic art*, is to pacify this sense of revolt —as well as gratify the cognate sense of curiosity?[10]

This renunciation of the supernatural, as well as the need to offer supplements rather than contradictions to known phenomena, make it clear that Lovecraft was now consciously moving toward a union of weird fiction and science fiction (although perhaps not the science fiction published in the pulp magazines). Indeed, in formal terms nearly all his work subsequent to 'The Call of Cthulhu' is science fiction, in that it supplies a *scientific justification* for the purportedly 'supernatural' events; it is only in his manifest wish to *terrify* that his work remains on the borderline of science fiction rather than being wholly within its parameters. Lovecraft's work had been inexorably moving in this direction since at least the writing of 'The Shunned House', and such things as *At the Mountains of Madness* (1931) and 'The Shadow out of Time' (1934–35) are only the pinnacles in this development.

At the Mountains of Madness, written in early 1931 (the autograph manuscript declares it to have been begun on 24 February and completed on 22 March), is Lovecraft's most ambitious attempt at 'non-supernatural cosmic art'; it is a triumph in almost every way. At forty thousand words it is his longest work of fiction save *The Case of Charles Dexter Ward*. Just as his other two novels represent apotheoses of earlier phases of his career—*The Dream-Quest of Unknown Kadath* the culmination of Dunsanianism, *Ward* the pinnacle of pure supernaturalism—so is *At the Mountains of Madness* the greatest of his attempts to fuse weird fiction and science fiction.

The basic plot of the novel—the discovery by the Miskatonic Antarctic Expedition of 1930–31 of the frozen remains of bizarre barrel-shaped entities from the depths of space, and their even more terrifying 'slaves', the shoggoths, who ultimately overwhelmed their masters—is elementary; but no synopsis can even begin to convey the rich, detailed, and utterly convincing scientific erudition that creates the sense of verisimilitude so necessary in a tale so otherwise outré. We have already seen how Lovecraft's fascination with the Antarctic dated to as early as his tenth year; indeed, as Jason C. Eckhardt has demonstrated,[11] the early parts of Lovecraft's tale clearly show the influence of Admiral Byrd's expedition of 1928–30, as well as other contemporary expeditions. And, of course, Lovecraft's sight of the spectacular paintings of the Himalayas by Nicholas Roerich—mentioned a total of six times in the novel—played a role in the genesis of the work.

The real focal point of *At the Mountains of Madness* is the civilization of the alien entities, which are referred to as the Old Ones. The narrator, William Dyer, studying their history as depicted on the bas-reliefs of their immense city, gradually comes to realize the profound bonds human beings share with them, and which neither share with the loathsome, primitive, virtually mindless shoggoths. The most significant way in which the Old Ones are identified with human beings is in the historical digression Dyer provides, specifically in regard to the Old Ones' social and economic organization. In many ways they represent a utopia toward which Lovecraft clearly hopes humanity itself will one day move. The single sentence 'Government was evidently complex and probably socialistic' establishes that Lovecraft had himself by this time converted to moderate socialism.

In terms of the Lovecraft's mythos, *At the Mountains of Madness* makes explicit what has been evident all along—that most of the 'gods' of the mythos are mere extraterrestrials, and that their followers (including the authors of the books of occult lore to which reference is so frequently made by Lovecraft and others) are mistaken as to their true nature. Robert M. Price, who first noted this 'demythologizing' feature in Lovecraft,[12] has in later articles gone on to point out that *At the Mountains of Madness* does not make any radical break in this pattern, but it does emphasize the point more clearly than elsewhere. The critical passage occurs in the middle of the novel, when Dyer finally acknowledges that the titanic city in which he has been wandering must have been built by the Old Ones: 'They were the makers and enslavers of [earth] life, and above all doubt the originals of the fiendish elder myths which things like the Pnakotic Manuscripts and the *Necronomicon* affrightedly hint about.' The content of the *Necronomicon* has now been reduced to 'myth'.

The casually made claim that the novel is a 'sequel' to Poe's *Narrative of Arthur Gordon Pym* deserves some analysis. In my view, the novel is not a true sequel at all—it picks up on very little of Poe's enigmatic work except for the cry 'Tekeli-li!', as unexplained in Poe as in Lovecraft—and the various references to *Pym* throughout the story end up being more in the manner of in-jokes. It is not clear that *Pym* even influenced the work in any significant way. A recent scholar, Jules Zanger, has aptly noted that *At the Mountains of Madness* 'is, of course, no completion [of *Pym*] at all: it might be better described as a parallel text, the two tales coexisting in a shared context of allusion'.[13]

Lovecraft declared that *At the Mountains of Madness* was 'capable of a major serial division in the exact middle'[14] (after Chapter VI), leading one to think that, at least subconsciously, he envisioned the

work as a two-part serial in *Weird Tales*. But, although he delayed
his spring travels till early May in order to undertake what was for
him the herculean task of typing the text (it came to 115 pages), he
was shattered to learn in mid-June that Farnsworth Wright had
rejected it. Lovecraft wrote bitterly in early August:

> Yes—Wright 'explained' his rejection of the 'Mountains of
> Madness' in almost the same language as that with which he
> 'explained' other rejections to Long & Derleth. It was 'too
> long', 'not easily divisible into parts', 'not convincing'—& so
> on. Just what he has said of other things of mine (except for
> length)—some of which he has ultimately accepted after
> many hesitations.[15]

It was not only Wright's adverse reaction that affected Lovecraft;
several colleagues to whom he had circulated the text also seemed
less than enthusiastic. One of the unkindest cuts of all may have
come from W. Paul Cook, the very man who had chiefly been
responsible for Lovecraft's resumption of weird fiction in 1917 but
who markedly disliked his later trend toward scientific realism.

Was Wright justified in rejecting the tale? In later years Lovecraft
frequently complained that Wright would accept long and mediocre serials by Otis Adelbert Kline, Edmond Hamilton, and other
clearly inferior writers while rejecting his own lengthy work; but
some defence of Wright might perhaps be made. The serials in
Weird Tales may indeed have been, from an abstract literary perspective, mediocre; but Wright knew that they were critical in im-
pelling readers to continue buying the magazine. As a result, they
were by and large geared toward the lowest level of the readership,
full of sensationalized action, readily identifiable human characters,
and a simple (if not simple-minded) prose style. *At the Mountains of
Madness* could not be said to have any of these characteristics. Some
of Wright's cavils, as recorded by Lovecraft, were indeed unjust; in
particular, the comment 'not convincing' cannot possibly be said to
apply to this work. But Lovecraft himself knew that Wright had
come to use this phrase as a sort of rubber-stamp whenever he did
not care for a work.

It is possible, however, that the rejection affected Lovecraft so
badly because it coincided with yet another rejection—that of a
collection of his tales by G. P. Putnam's Sons. In the spring of 1931
Winfield Shiras, an editor at Putnam's, had asked to see some of
Lovecraft's stories for possible book publication. Lovecraft sent

thirty tales—nearly all the manuscripts or tearsheets he had in the house at the time—and, in spite of his characteristic predictions that nothing would come of it, he may well have held out a hope that he might see his name on a hardcover book. Putnam's had, after all, come to him, and not as a matter of form as Simon & Schuster had done the year before. But by mid-July the dismal news came: the collection was rejected.

The Putnam's rejection may in fact have been more staggering than that of *At the Mountains of Madness*:

> The grounds for rejection were twofold—first, that some of the tales are not subtle enough ... too obvious & well-explained—(admitted! That ass Wright got me into the habit of obvious writing with his never-ending complaints against the indefiniteness of my early stuff.) & secondly, that all the tales are uniformly macabre in mood to stand collected publication. This second reason is sheer bull—for as a matter of fact unity of mood is a positive asset in a fictional collection. But I suppose the herd must have their comic relief![16]

I think Lovecraft is quite right on both points here. His later tales do not, perhaps, leave enough to the imagination, and in part this may indeed be a result of subconsciously writing with *Weird Tales'* market demands in mind; but in part this is precisely because of the tendency of this work to gravitate more toward science fiction. Lovecraft was in the position of being a pioneer in the fusion of weird and science fiction, but the short-term result was that his work was found unsatisfactory both to pulp magazines and to commercial publishers that were locked in their stereotypical conventions.

A third rejection occurred at the hands of Harry Bates. Bates had been appointed editor of *Strange Tales*, a magazine launched in 1931 by the William Clayton Company. Word about the magazine must have gone out by spring (although the first issue was dated September), for in April Lovecraft sent along five old stories (all rejected by Wright); all were turned down. Lovecraft should not have been much surprised at this: not only were these on the whole inferior stories, but the Clayton firm was long known as preferring fast-paced action to atmosphere.

Strange Tales seemed at first to be a serious rival to *Weird Tales*: it paid 2 cents per word on acceptance, and it formed a significant market for such writers as Clark Ashton Smith, Henry S. Whitehead, August Derleth, and Hugh B. Cave who could mould their styles to suit Bates's requirements. Wright must have been greatly alarmed at the emergence of this magazine, for it meant that some of his best writers would submit their tales to it first and send material only to *Weird Tales* that had been rejected by *Strange Tales*. But the magazine lasted for only seven issues, folding in January 1933.

The whole issue of Lovecraft's sensitivity to rejection, or to bad opinions of his work generally, deserves consideration. Recall the *In Defence of Dagon* essays of 1921: 'There are probably seven persons, in all, who really like my work; and they are enough. I should write even if I were the only patient reader, for my aim is merely self-expression.' Admittedly, this statement was made well before his work had become more widely available in the pulp magazines, but 'self-expression' remained the cornerstone of his aesthetic to the end. Lovecraft was aware of the apparent contradiction, for the issue came up in discussions with Derleth. Lovecraft had already told Derleth that 'I have a sort of dislike of sending in anything which has been once rejected',[17] an attitude that Derleth—who in his hard-boiled way sometimes submitted a single story to *Weird Tales* up to a dozen times before it was finally accepted by Wright—must have found nearly incomprehensible. Now, in early 1932, Lovecraft expanded on the idea:

> I can see why you consider my anti-rejection policy a stub-
> bornly foolish & needlessly short-sighted one, & am not
> prepared to offer any defence other than the mere fact that
> repeated rejections do work in a certain way on my psycho-
> logy—rationally or not—& that their effect is to cause in me
> a certain literary lockjaw which absolutely prevents further
> fictional composition despite my most arduous efforts. I
> would be the last to say that they *ought* to produce such an
> effect, or that they would—even in a slight degree—upon a
> psychology of 100% toughness & balance. But unfortun-
> ately my nervous equilibrium has always been a rather
> uncertain quantity, & it is now in one of its more ragged
> phases.[18]

Lovecraft had always been modest about his own achievements— excessively so, as we look back upon it; now, rejections by Wright, Bates, and Putnam's, and the cool reactions of colleagues to whom he had sent stories in manuscript, nearly shattered whatever confidence he may have had in his own work. He spent the few remaining years of his life trying to regain that confidence, and he never seems to have done so except in fleeting moments. We can see the effect of this state of mind in his very next story.

'The Shadow over Innsmouth' was written in November and December of 1931. Lovecraft reports that his revisiting of the decaying seaport of Newburyport, Massachusetts (which he had first seen in 1923), led him to conduct a sort of 'laboratory experimentation'[19] to see which style or manner was best suited to the theme. Four drafts (whether complete or not is not clear) were written and discarded, and finally Lovecraft simply wrote the story in his accustomed manner, producing a twenty-five-thousand-word novelette whose extraordinary richness of atmosphere scarcely betrays the almost agonizing difficulty he experienced in its writing.

Once again, the plot of the story is relatively elementary. The narrator, Robert Olmstead (never mentioned by name in the story, but identified in the surviving notes), in the midst of a genealogical and antiquarian tour, comes to the decaying New England seaport of Innsmouth by accident, finding an undercurrent of the sinister there. Encountering an aged denizen, Zadok Allen, he learns the incredible history of the town: in the middle nineteenth century Obed Marsh had come upon bizarre fish-frog hybrids in the Pacific who promised him great riches if they could be allowed to mate with the residents of Innsmouth. The resulting miscegenation produces hideous physical and psychological aberrations. Later, Olmstead's snooping is detected and he is forced to flee precipitately from the hotel in which he is lodged. He escapes, but some time later he discovers that he himself is related to the Innsmouth people: he finds himself developing the 'Innsmouth look'. He makes the fateful decision not to kill himself but to return to Innsmouth and join his hybrid relations.

'The Shadow over Innsmouth' is Lovecraft's greatest tale of degeneration; but the causes for that degeneration here are quite different from what we have seen earlier. This is clearly a cautionary tale on the ill effects of *miscegenation*, or the sexual union of different races, and as such may well be considered a vast expansion and subtilization of the plot of 'Facts concerning the Late Arthur Jermyn and His Family' (1920). It is, accordingly, difficult to deny a suggestion of racism running all through the story. All through the tale the narrator expresses—and expects us to share—

his revulsion at the physical grotesqueness of the Innsmouth people, just as in his own life Lovecraft frequently comments on the 'peculiar' appearance of all races but his own.

An examination of the literary influences upon the story can clarify how Lovecraft has vastly enriched a conception that was by no means his own invention. The use of hybrid fishlike entities was derived from at least two prior works for which Lovecraft always retained a fondness: Irvin S. Cobb's 'Fishhead' (which Lovecraft read in the *Cavalier* in 1913 and praised in a letter to the editor) and Robert W. Chambers's 'The Harbor-Master', a short story later included as the first five chapters of the episodic novel *In Search of the Unknown* (1904). But in both these stories we are dealing with a *single* case of hybridism, not an entire community or civilization. This latter conception is at work in Algernon Blackwood's 'Ancient Sorceries' (in *John Silence—Physician Extraordinary* (1908)), where a traveller coming to a small town in France discovers that the townspeople all turn into cats at night. This story, therefore, is probably a more dominant literary influence than those by Cobb or Chambers, in spite of the latter's superficial similarity in motif.

The narrator, Olmstead, proves to be one of Lovecraft's most carefully etched characters. The many mundane details that lend substance and reality to his personality are in large part derived from Lovecraft's own temperament and, especially, from his habits as a frugal antiquarian traveller. Olmstead always 'seek[s] the cheapest possible route', and this is usually—for Olmstead as for Lovecraft—by bus. His reading up on Innsmouth in the library, and his systematic exploration of the town, parallel Lovecraft's own thorough researches into the history and topography of the places he wished to visit and his frequent trips to libraries, chambers of commerce, and elsewhere for maps, guidebooks, and historical background.

Lovecraft was, incredibly, profoundly dissatisfied with the story. A week after finishing it on 3 December, he wrote lugubriously to Derleth: 'I don't think the experimenting came to very much. The result, 68 pages long, has all the defects I deplore—especially in point of style, where hackneyed phrases & rhythms have crept in despite all precautions ... No—I don't intend to offer "The Shadow over Innsmouth" for publication, for it would stand no chance of acceptance.'[20] That Lovecraft meant what he said is revealed by his extraordinarily snide response to Farnsworth Wright's request to send in new work:

Sorry to say I haven't anything new which you would be likely to care for. Lately my tales have run to studies in geographical atmosphere requiring greater length than the popular editorial fancy relishes—my new 'Shadow over Innsmouth' is three typed pages longer than 'Whisperer in Darkness', and conventional magazine standards would undoubtedly rate it 'intolerably slow', 'not conveniently divisible', or something of the sort.[21]

Lovecraft is consciously throwing back into Wright's face the remarks Wright had made about *At the Mountains of Madness*.

But if Lovecraft himself refused to submit 'The Shadow over Innsmouth' to *Weird Tales*, Derleth was not so reticent. Without Lovecraft's permission or knowledge, he sent to Wright a carbon of the story in early 1933; but Wright's verdict was perhaps to be expected: 'I have read Lovecraft's story, THE SHADOW OVER INNSMOUTH, and must confess that it fascinates me. But I don't know just what I can do with it. It is hard to break a story of this kind into two parts, and it is too long to run complete in one part.'[22] Lovecraft must have eventually found out about this surreptitious submission, for by 1934 he is speaking of its rejection by Wright. Lovecraft himself, it should be pointed out, submitted only one story to Wright in the five and a half years following the rejection of *At the Mountains of Madness*.

In the summer of 1930, Lovecraft came in touch with one of the most distinctive figures in the pulp fiction of his time: Robert Ervin Howard (1906–36). Howard is a writer about whom it is difficult to be impartial. Like Lovecraft, he has attracted a fanatical cadre of supporters who both claim significant literary status for at least some of his work and take great offence at those who do not acknowledge its merits. I fear, however, that after repeated readings of his fiction I fail to be impressed with very much of it. The bulk of Howard's fiction is subliterary hackwork that does not even begin to approach genuine literature.

Howard himself is in many ways more interesting than his stories. Born in the small town of Peaster, Texas, about twenty miles west of Fort Worth, he spent the bulk of his short life in Cross Plains. His ancestors were among the earliest settlers of this 'post oaks' region of central Texas, and his father, Dr I. M. Howard, was one of the pioneer physicians in the area. Howard was more hampered by his lack of formal education than Lovecraft—he briefly attended Howard Payne College in Brownwood, but only to take bookkeeping courses—because of the lack of libraries in his town; his learning was, accordingly, very uneven, and he was quick to take strong and dogmatic opinions on subjects about which he knew little.

As an adolescent Howard was introverted and bookish; as a result, he was bullied by his peers, and to protect himself he undertook a vigorous course of body-building that made him, as an adult of five feet eleven inches and 200 pounds, a formidable physical specimen. He took to writing early, however, and it became his only career aside from the odd jobs at which he occasionally worked. A taste for adventure, fantasy, and horror—he was an ardent devotee of Jack London—and a talent for writing allowed him to break into *Weird Tales* in July 1925 with 'Spear and Fang'. Although Howard later published in a wide variety of other pulp magazines, from *Cowboy Stories* to *Argosy*, *Weird Tales* remained his chief market and published his most representative work.

That work runs the gamut from westerns to sports stories to 'Orientales' to weird fiction. Many of his tales fall into loose cycles revolving around recurring characters, including Bran Mak Morn (a Celtic chieftain in Roman Britain), King Kull (a warrior-king of the mythical prehistoric realm of Valusia, in central Europe), Solomon Kane (an English Puritan of the seventeenth century), and, most famously, Conan, a barbarian chieftain of the mythical land of Cimmeria. Howard was keenly drawn to the period of the prehistoric barbarians—perhaps because that age dimly reflected the conditions of pioneer Texas that he learnt and admired from his elders.

One does not, of course, wish to deny all literary value to Howard's work. He is certainly to be credited with the founding of the subgenre of 'sword-and-sorcery', although Fritz Leiber would later significantly refine the form; and, although many of Howard's stories were written purely for the sake of cash, his own views do emerge clearly from them. The simple fact is, however, that these views are not of any great substance or profundity and that Howard's style is crude, slipshod, and unwieldy. It is all just pulp— although, perhaps, a somewhat superior grade of pulp than the average.

Howard's letters, as Lovecraft rightly maintained, deserve to be classed as literature far more than does his fiction. It might well be imagined that the letters of two writers so antipodally different in temperament as Lovecraft and Howard would at the very least be provocative, and sure enough their six-year correspondence not only ranges widely in subject matter but also becomes, at times, somewhat testy as each man expresses his views with vigour and determination. Howard was clearly intimidated by Lovecraft's learning and felt hopelessly inferior academically; but he also felt that he had a better grasp of the realities of life than the sheltered Lovecraft, so that he was not about to back down on some of his cherished beliefs. In some instances, as in his frequent descriptions of the violent conditions of the frontier with fights, shootouts, and the like, one almost feels as if Howard is subtly teasing Lovecraft or attempting to shock him; some of Howard's accounts of these matters may, in fact, have been invented.

In his tales of the 1930s Howard started dropping references to Lovecraft's pseudomythology, and he did so in exactly the spirit Lovecraft intended—as fleeting background allusions to create a sense of unholy presences behind the surface of life. Very few of Howard's stories seem to me to owe much to Lovecraft's own tales or conceptions, and there are almost no actual pastiches. The *Necronomicon* is cited any number of times; Cthulhu, R'lyeh, and Yog-Sothoth come in for mention on occasion; but that is all.

Meanwhile Clark Ashton Smith was getting into the act. Smith's allusions to Lovecraft's pseudomythology are, like Howard's, very fleeting; indeed, it is highly misleading to think that Smith was somehow 'contributing' to Lovecraft's mythos, since from the beginning he felt that he was devising his own parallel mythology. Smith's chief invention is the god Tsathoggua, first created in 'The Tale of Satampra Zeiros'. Written in the fall of 1929, this story evoked raptures from Lovecraft. He was so taken with the invention of Tsathoggua that he cited the god immediately in 'The Mound' (1929–30) and 'The Whisperer in Darkness'; and, since the latter tale was printed in *Weird Tales* for August 1931, three months before 'The Tale of Satampra Zeiros', Lovecraft beat Smith into print with the mention of the god.

Nevertheless, Lovecraft was fully aware that he was borrowing from Smith. Smith himself, noting a few years later how many other writers had borrowed the elements he had invented, remarked to Derleth: 'It would seem that I am starting a mythology.'[23] Smith of course returned the favour and cited Lovecraft's inventions in later tales.

Toward the end of 1930 Lovecraft heard from Henry St Clair Whitehead (1882–1932), an established pulp writer who published voluminously in *Adventure, Weird Tales, Strange Tales,* and elsewhere. Whitehead was a native of New Jersey who attended Harvard and Columbia, was a reporter for a time, and in 1913 was ordained as an Anglican priest. In the late 1920s he was archdeacon in the Virgin Islands, where he gained the local colour for many of his weird tales. By 1930 he was established in a rectory in Dunedin, Florida.

Whitehead's urbane, erudite weird fiction is one of the few literary high spots of *Weird Tales,* although its lack of intensity and the relative conventionality of its supernaturalism have not won it many followers in recent years. Still, his two collections, *Jumbee and Other Uncanny Tales* (1944) and *West India Lights* (1946), contain some fine work. There is some little mystery as to what has become of Lovecraft's correspondence with Whitehead; it appears to have been inadvertently destroyed. There are also no surviving letters by Whitehead to Lovecraft. Nevertheless, it is evident that the two men became fast friends and had great respect for each other, both as writers and as human beings. Whitehead's early death was one of a succession of tragedies that would darken Lovecraft's later years.

Another significant correspondent was Joseph Vernon Shea (1912–81). Shea wrote to Lovecraft in 1931, sending a letter to *Weird Tales* for forwarding; there rapidly developed a warm and extensive correspondence—in many senses one of the most interesting of Lovecraft's later letter-cycles, even if some of the material is embarrassingly racist and militarist in content. Shea was blunt and, in youth, a trifle cocksure in the expression of his opinions, and he inspired Lovecraft to some vivid and piquant rebuttals.

Another young colleague who came into Lovecraft's horizon in 1931 was Robert Hayward Barlow (1918–51). Lovecraft had no knowledge, when first receiving a letter from Barlow, that his new correspondent was thirteen years old; for Barlow was then already a surprisingly mature individual whose chief hobby was, indeed, the somewhat juvenile one of collecting pulp fiction, but who was quite well read in weird fiction and enthusiastically embraced a myriad of other interests. Barlow was born in Kansas City, Missouri, and spent much of his youth at Fort Benning, Georgia, where his father, Col. E. D. Barlow, was stationed; around 1932 Col. Barlow received a medical discharge and settled his family in the small town of De Land, in central Florida. Family difficulties later forced Barlow to move to Washington, D.C., and Kansas.

Lovecraft was taken with Barlow, although their correspondence was rather perfunctory for the first year or so. He recognized the youth's zeal and incipient brilliance, and nurtured his youthful attempts at writing weird fiction. Barlow was more interested in pure fantasy than in supernatural horror, and the models for his early work are Lord Dunsany and Clark Ashton Smith; he was so fond of Smith that he bestowed upon the closet where he stored his choicest collectibles the name 'The Vaults of Yoh-Vombis'. This collecting mania—which extended to manuscripts as well as published material—would prove a godsend in later years.

By the time he got to know Barlow well, Lovecraft regarded him as a child prodigy on the order of Alfred Galpin; and in this he may not have been far wrong. It is true that Barlow sometimes spread himself too thin and had difficulty focusing on any single project, with the result that his actual accomplishments prior to Lovecraft's death seem somewhat meagre; but in his later years he distinguished himself in an entirely different field—Mexican anthropology—and his early death deprived the world of a fine poet and scholar. Lovecraft did not err in appointing Barlow his literary executor.

One may as well give some consideration now to Lovecraft's correspondence, for it would only grow in later years as he became the focal point of the fantasy fandom movement of the 1930s. In late 1931 he estimated that his regular correspondents numbered between fifty and seventy-five.[24] But numbers do not tell the entire story. It certainly does seem as if Lovecraft—perhaps under the incentive of his own developing philosophical thought—was engaging in increasingly lengthy arguments with a variety of colleagues. He wrote a seventy-page letter to Woodburn Harris in early 1929; a letter to Long in early 1931 may have been nearly as long. His letters are always of consuming interest, but on occasion one feels as if Lovecraft is having some difficulty shutting up.

Many have complained about the amount of time Lovecraft spent (some have termed it 'wasted') on his correspondence, whining that he could have written more fiction instead. Certainly, his array of original fiction (exclusive of revisions) over the last several years was not numerically large: one story in 1928, none in 1929, one in 1930, and two in 1931. Numbers again, however, are deceiving. Almost any one of these five stories would be in itself sufficient to give Lovecraft a place in weird fiction. Moreover, it is by no means certain that Lovecraft would have written more fiction even had he the leisure, for his fiction-writing was always dependent upon the proper mood and the proper gestation of a fictional conception; sometimes such a conception took years to develop.

But the overriding injustice in this whole matter is the belief that Lovecraft should have lived his life for us and not for himself. If he had written no stories but only letters, it would have been our loss but his prerogative. Lovecraft did indeed justify his letter-writing in a letter to Long:

> an isolated person requires correspondence as a means of seeing his ideas as others see them, and thus guarding against the dogmatisms and extravagances of solitary and uncorrected speculation. No man can learn to reason and appraise from a mere perusal of the writing of others. If he live not in the world, where he can observe the publick at first-hand and be directed toward solid reality by the force of conversation and spoken debate, then he must sharpen his discrimination and regulate his perceptive balance by an equivalent exchange of ideas in epistolary form.[25]

There is certainly much truth in this, and anyone can tell the difference between the cocksure Lovecraft of 1914 and the mature Lovecraft of 1930. What he does not say here, however, is that one of the chief motivations for his correspondence was simple courtesy. Lovecraft answered almost every letter he ever received, and he usually answered it within a few days. He felt it was his obligation as a gentleman to do so. This is how he established strong bonds of friendship with far-flung associates, many of whom never met him; it is why he became, both during and after his lifetime, a revered figure in the little worlds of amateur journalism and weird fiction.

CHAPTER SEVENTEEN
Mental Greed (1931–33)

The year 1931 was, of course, not an entire disaster for Lovecraft, even though the rejections of some of his best work stung him. His now customary late spring and summer travels reached the widest extent they would ever achieve in his lifetime, and he returned home with a fund of new impressions that well offset his literary misfortunes.

Lovecraft began his travels on Saturday, 2 May, the day after he finished the back-breaking work of typing *At the Mountains of Madness*. His customary stop in New York was very brief, and he caught a bus for Charleston via Washington, D.C., Richmond, Winston-Salem and Charlotte, North Carolina, and Columbia, South Carolina. The total time of this bus ride was thirty-six hours.

Lovecraft found Charleston pretty much the same as the year before. On the 6th Lovecraft took a bus for Savannah, and from there caught another bus for Jacksonville (saving a night's hotel or YMCA bill), arriving at 6 a.m. on the 7th. Jacksonville was a modern town and hence had no appeal for Lovecraft; it was only a way station to a more archaic place—nothing less than the oldest continuously inhabited city in the United States, St Augustine, Florida.

In the two weeks Lovecraft spent in St Augustine he absorbed all the antiquities the town had to offer. The mere fact of being in such an ancient place delighted him, although the town, with its predominantly Hispanic background, did not strike so deep a chord as a town of British origin such as Charleston did. Nevertheless, he was marvellously invigorated by St Augustine—both spiritually and physically, since the genuine tropicality of the town endowed him with reserves of strength unknown in the chilly North. He stayed at the Rio Vista Hotel on Bay Street for $4.00 a week.

Lovecraft canvassed the entire town—including the Post Office (housed in a 1591 mansion), Fort San Marcos, the Fountain of Youth, the Bridge of Lions, the Franciscan monastery, and what is presumed to be the oldest house in the United States, built in 1565

—as well as nearby Anastasia Island, which offers a spectacular view of the archaic skyline.

Lovecraft finally did break away around 21 May, as his new correspondent Henry S. Whitehead insisted that he come and visit for an extended period in Dunedin, a small town on a peninsula north of St Petersburg and Clearwater. We do not know much about this visit, but Lovecraft found both the environment and his host delightful. Lovecraft and Whitehead were of almost exactly the same build, and the latter lent Lovecraft a white tropical suit to wear during especially hot days, later making a present of it.

Either while at Dunedin or when he returned home a month or two later, Lovecraft assisted Whitehead on the writing of a story, 'The Trap'. He notes in one letter that he 'revised & totally recast'[1] the tale, and in another letter says that he 'suppl[ied] the central part myself'.[2] My feeling is that the latter three-fourths of the story is Lovecraft's. 'The Trap' is an entertaining if insubstantial account of an anomalous mirror that sucks hapless individuals into a strange realm where colours are altered and where objects, both animate and inanimate, have a sort of intangible, dreamlike exist-ence. Whitehead's and Lovecraft's styles do not seem to me to meld very well, and the urbanely conversational style of Whitehead's beginning gives way abruptly to Lovecraft's long paragraphs of dense exposition. The tale was published in the March 1932 issue of *Strange Tales*, under Whitehead's name only, Lovecraft having refused a collaborative byline.

By early June Lovecraft was ready to return north, but two timely revision cheques allowed him to prolong the trip to its ultimate destination, Key West. This was the farthest south Lovecraft would ever reach, although on this and several other occasions he yearned to hop on a boat and get to Havana, but never had quite enough money to make the plunge.

Key West, the most remote of the Florida Keys, was reached by a succession of ferries and bus rides, since the Depression had not allowed the state to construct the continuous series of causeways that now connects all the Keys. Lovecraft wished to explore this place not only because of its remoteness but because of its genuine antiquity: it had been settled in the early nineteenth century by Spaniards, who called it Caja Huesco (Bone Key); later the name was corrupted by Americans to Key West. Lovecraft spent only a few days in Key West, but he canvassed the place thoroughly.

By 16 June he was back in St Augustine. He gradually moved

north, exploring Charleston, Richmond, Fredericksburg, and Philadelphia. After a week in New York and a weekend with the Longs
at the seaside resort of Asbury Park, New Jersey, Lovecraft accepted
Talman's offer to spend a week in his large Flatbush apartment. On
6 July a gang meeting at Talman's featured, as a special guest,
Seabury Quinn, the *Weird Tales* hack. Lovecraft, although taking a
dim view of his endless array of clichéd stories (most revolving
around the psychic detective Jules de Grandin), found him
'exceedingly tasteful & intelligent',[3] although more a businessman
than an aesthete. Lovecraft finally returned home on 20 July.

Random travels in New England occupied him in October and
early November, but the increasing cold curtailed any further
outings that required extensive outdoor travel.

Lovecraft's financial situation was not getting any better, although
for the moment it was not getting any worse. The publication of
'The Whisperer in Darkness' in the August 1931 *Weird Tales* enriched him by $350.00—a sum that, given his boast that he had
now reduced his expenses to $15.00 per week, could have lasted
him for more than five months. Here is how he did it:

> $15.00 per week will float any man of sense in a very
> tolerable way—lodging him in a cultivated neighbourhood if
> he knows how to look for rooms, (this one rule, though,
> breaks down in really megalopolitan centres like New York
> —but it will work in Providence, Richmond, or Charleston,
> & would probably work in most of the moderate-sized cities
> of the northwest) keeping him dressed in soberly conser-
> vative neatness if he knows how to choose quiet designs &
> durable fabrics among cheap suits, & feeding him amply &
> palatably if he is not an epicurean crank, & if he does not
> attempt to depend upon restaurants. One must have a
> kitchen-alcove & obtain provisions at grocery & delicatessen
> prices rather than pay cafes & cafeterias the additional price
> they demand for mere service.[4]

Of course, this is predicated on Lovecraft's habit of eating only two
(very frugal) meals a day. He actually maintained that 'my digestion raises hell if I try to eat oftener than once in 7 hours'.[5]

But original fiction—especially now that he was writing work
that was not meeting the plebeian criteria of pulp editors—was not
going to help much in making ends meet. Reprints brought in very

little: he received $12.25 from Selwyn & Blount in mid-1931 (probably for 'The Rats in the Walls' in Christine Campbell Thomson's *Switch On the Light* (1931)), and another $25.00 for 'The Music of Erich Zann' in Dashiell Hammett's *Creeps by Night* (1931); but, aside from 'The Whisperer in Darkness' and $55.00 for 'The Strange High House in the Mist' from *Weird Tales*, that may have been all for original fiction sold for the year. Of course, after his double rejections of the summer, Lovecraft was in no spirit to hawk his work about. In the fall Lovecraft sent Derleth several stories he had asked to see, including 'In the Vault'. On his own initiative Derleth retyped the story (Lovecraft's typescript was becoming tattered to the point of disintegration), and then badgered Lovecraft into resubmitting it to Wright; Lovecraft did so, and the tale was accepted in early 1932 for $55.00.

Of course, a book would have been a real means to both financial gain and literary recognition. In March 1932 such a prospect emerged for the third time, but once again it collapsed. Arthur Leeds had spoken about Lovecraft to a friend of his who was an editor at Vanguard. Vanguard queried Lovecraft, saying they wanted a novel, but Lovecraft (having already repudiated *The Dream-Quest of Unknown Kadath* and *The Case of Charles Dexter Ward* and evidently not considering *At the Mountains of Madness* a true novel) said he had none at hand. Nevertheless, the firm did ask to see some of his short stories, so Lovecraft sent them 'Pickman's Model', 'The Dunwich Horror', 'The Rats in the Walls', and 'The Call of Cthulhu'. The stories eventually came back.

How was revision faring? Not especially well. After the work done for Zealia Bishop and Adolphe de Castro, no new would-be weird writers were appearing on the horizon. Of course, the revision of weird fiction was a relatively small facet of his revisory work, which centred on more mundane matter—textbooks, poetry, and the like. But the departure of David Van Bush as a regular client, along with Lovecraft's unwillingness or lack of success in advertising his services, made this work very irregular.

The prospect of a regular position emerged some time in 1931, but again came to naught. The Stephen Daye Press of Brattleboro, Vermont (managed by Vrest Orton), gave him the job of revising and proofreading Leon Burr Richardson's *History of Dartmouth College* (1932). Although Lovecraft received only $50.00 plus expenses for his work on the book, he thought that it 'may prove the opening wedge for a good deal of work from the Stephen Daye';[6] but, again, this did not happen. Lovecraft's revision on the Dartmouth College history really amounted to mere copyediting, for I cannot detect much actual Lovecraft prose in the treatise.

One very curious job Lovecraft had around this time was that of a ticket-seller in a movie theatre. A professor at Brown University, Robert Kenny (1902–83), maintained that he saw Lovecraft go downtown in the evening (he worked the night shift) and sit in a booth in one of the theatres, reading a book whenever he was not actually dispensing tickets. I asked Harry K. Brobst about the story, and he confirmed it, stating that Lovecraft admitted to him that he held such a job and saying that he actually liked it at the start, but that it did not last very long. Brobst does not know when Lovecraft held the position, but he believes it to have been in the early days of the depression, perhaps 1929–30.

Somehow or other, in spite of rejections and the precarious status of his revision work, Lovecraft managed to write another tale in February 1932, 'The Dreams in the Witch House'. Its working title—'The Dreams of Walter Gilman'—tells the whole story. A mathematics student at Miskatonic University named Walter Gilman who lives in a peculiarly angled room in the old Witch House in Arkham begins experiencing bizarre dreams filled with sights, sounds, and shapes of an utterly indescribable cast; other dreams, much more realistic in nature, reveal a huge rat with human hands named Brown Jenkin, who appears to be the familiar of the witch Keziah Mason, who once dwelt in the Witch House. In the end he is killed by Brown Jenkin, although not before he has prevented Keziah from performing some kind of sacrificial offering involving a kidnapped baby.

One can agree wholeheartedly with Steven J. Mariconda's labelling this story 'Lovecraft's Magnificent Failure'.[7] In a sense, 'The Dreams in the Witch House' is the most cosmic story Lovecraft ever wrote: he has made a genuine, and very provocative, attempt actually to visualize the fourth dimension, largely through the use of geometric imagery. The imaginative scope of the novelette is almost unbearably vast; but it is utterly confounded by slipshod writing and a complete confusion as to where the story is going. Lovecraft here lapses into hackneyed and overblown purple prose that sounds almost like a parody of his own style.

'The Dreams in the Witch House' is Lovecraft's ultimate modernization of a conventional myth (witchcraft) by means of modern science. Fritz Leiber, who has written a perspicacious essay on the tale, notes that it is 'Lovecraft's most carefully worked out story of hyperspace-travel. Here (1) a rational foundation for such travel is set up; (2) hyperspace is visualized; and (3) a trigger for such travel is devised.'[8] Leiber elaborates keenly on these points, noting that the absence of any mechanical device for such travel is vital to the tale, for otherwise it would be impossible to imagine how a 'witch' of the seventeenth century could have managed the trick; in effect, Keziah simply applied advanced mathematics and 'thought' herself into hyperspace.

Lovecraft was unsure about the merits of the tale, so it is not surprising that he refused to submit it to any magazine and merely let it gather dust. A year or so later August Derleth, although thinking it a poor story, nevertheless surreptitiously submitted it to Farnsworth Wright, who accepted it readily and paid Lovecraft $140.00 for it. It appeared in the July 1933 issue of *Weird Tales*.

Around this time still more fans, colleagues, and writers were coming into Lovecraft's horizon. One was a very strange individual from Buffalo, New York, named William Lumley. Lumley was one of several who had become intrigued with Lovecraft's evolving pseudomythology; most of these correspondents drifted away after a few weeks or months, but Lumley persisted.

A rather more level-headed person was Harry Kern Brobst (b. 1909). He had become interested in weird and science fiction as a youth, being especially fond of the work of Poe, Verne, Dunsany, Clark Ashton Smith, and Lovecraft. Writing to Farnsworth Wright of *Weird Tales*, he acquired Lovecraft's address and began a correspondence, probably in the autumn of 1931. Not long thereafter, however, a fortunate circumstance brought him into much closer touch with his new colleague.

After graduating from high school, Brobst decided to enter the field of psychiatric nursing, and he secured entry into the medical programme at Butler Hospital in Providence. Brobst arrived in Providence in February 1932. A few weeks later he came to visit Lovecraft, and his impressions both of the man and his humble residence at 10 Barnes Street are affecting:

> He was a tall man, of sallow complexion, very animated ..., with dark, sparkling eyes. I don't know if this description makes much sense, but that was the impression he made—a very vital person. We were friends immediately...

> Now at 10 Barnes Street I believe he was on the ground
> floor ... when you went into the room that he occupied
> there were no windows—it was completely cut off, and he
> just lived by artificial light. I remember going in there one
> time and it was in the colder time of the year ... The room
> was stuffy, very dusty (he wouldn't allow anybody to dust it,
> especially the books); his bedding was quite (I hate to say
> this) dirty ... And he had nothing to eat excepting a piece of
> cheese.[9]

How will Lovecraft ever live down the ignominy of dirty sheets! He
who was so meticulous about his personal tidiness appears to have
been less scrupulous about his surroundings.

Brobst would be in very close contact with Lovecraft for the next
five years, visiting him several times a week, going with him to
museums, having meals with him in restaurants, and welcoming
Lovecraft's out-of-town visitors as they came to visit him. Few
knew Lovecraft better at this period, on a personal level, than Harry
Brobst.

On 18 May Lovecraft left for New York, spending a week there in
the usual flurry of social calls on the New York gang. He finally
managed to pull away on 25 May, reaching Natchez, Mississippi, a
few days later. In Natchez Lovecraft was stimulated both by the
spectacular natural landscape (200-foot bluffs above the Mississippi,
invigorating tropical climate and vegetation) and the antiquities of
the two-hundred-year-old town itself. He then proceeded still
further south to his ultimate destination—New Orleans. It did not
take long for him to feel the charm of this distinctive city: having
arrived in late May, he was ready to declare by 6 June that the three
towns of Charleston, Quebec, and New Orleans 'stand out as the most
thoroughly ancient & exotic urban centres of North America'.[10]
Naturally the French Quarter—the Vieux Carré—with its unique
conjoining of French and Spanish architectural styles appealed to
him most, although he found even the newer parts with their long
shady streets and stately homes appealing.

An interesting social call occurred toward the end of Lovecraft's
New Orleans stay. He had written of his trip to Robert E. Howard,
who bitterly regretted his inability to travel there himself and meet
his much-admired correspondent; but Howard telegraphed his friend
E. Hoffmann Price, who had a room in the French Quarter, and told
him of Lovecraft's presence. Price accordingly met Lovecraft on

Sunday, 12 June, conducting a call that lasted 25½ hours, till midnight on Monday.

Edgar Hoffmann Price (1898–1989) was certainly an unusual individual. A man of many talents—he knew Arabic and he also knew how to fence—he wrote some fine stories for *Weird Tales* and other pulps in the early 1920s, including the superb 'Stranger from Kurdistan' (*Weird Tales*, July 1925). But the depression hurt Price in more than one way: in May 1932 he was laid off from the well-paying job he had held with the Prestolite Company, and he decided to try his hand at making a living by writing. He felt he could do so only by writing exactly what the editors wanted, so he began catering quite coldbloodedly to market requirements in many different realms of pulp fiction—weird, 'Oriental', 'weird menace', and the like. The result was that throughout the 1930s and 1940s Price landed a flood of very slick but literarily valueless material in such magazines, spelling his aesthetic damnation and relegating the vast majority of his work to the oblivion it deserves.

Price has an affecting account of his first meeting with Lovecraft:

> he carried himself with enough of a slouch to make me underestimate his height as well as the breadth of his shoulders. His face was thin and narrow, longish, with long chin and jaw. He walked with a quick stride. His speech was quick and inclined to jerkiness. It was as though his body was hard put to it to keep up with the agility of his mind ...
>
> Twenty-eight hours we gabbled, swapping ideas, kicking fancies back and forth, topping each other's whimsies. He had an enormous enthusiasm for new experience: of sight, of sound, of word pattern, of idea pattern. I have met in all my time only one or two others who approached him in what I call 'mental greed.' A glutton for words, ideas, thoughts. He elaborated, combined, distilled, and at a machine gun tempo.[11]

As if it were not evident in so many other ways, this first encounter with Price goes far in showing how Lovecraft had matured as a human being over the past fifteen years.

One curious myth that has somehow developed from Lovecraft's New Orleans trip is the belief that Price took Lovecraft to a whorehouse where the women proved to be avid readers of *Weird Tales* and were especially fond of Lovecraft's stories. In fact, this story actually applies to Seabury Quinn (assuming it is not entirely apocryphal); it appears that the women offered Quinn 'one on the house' in honour of his illustrious status. Price explicitly and rather drily remarks in his memoir that, out of deference to Lovecraft's sensibilities, 'I skipped concubines entirely.'

From New Orleans Lovecraft finally moved on to Mobile, Alabama, then to Montgomery and Atlanta, although the latter city was modern and had no attractions for him. He then proceeded up the Carolinas to Richmond, which he reached toward the end of June. After canvassing the usual sites relating to Poe and the Confederacy, Lovecraft stopped briefly at Fredericksburg, Annapolis, and Philadelphia, finally ending up back in New York around 25 June. This time he stayed in an apartment a few doors away from Loveman in Brooklyn Heights. He expected to linger in the city for more than a week, but a telegram from Annie on 1 July called him suddenly home.

Lillian was critically ill and not expected to survive. Lovecraft caught the first train to Providence, arriving late on the 1st. He found Lillian in a semi-coma, from which she would not awaken until her death on 3 July. She was seventy-six years old. The cause of death was given on her death certificate as atrophic arthritis. Lovecraft had spoken over the years of her various ailments—chiefly neuritis and lumbago—the general effect of which was to limit her mobility severely and render her largely housebound. These various maladies now finally caught up with her.

Lovecraft was not given to expressing extreme emotions in his correspondence, and that was his right; but his remarks to friends about Lillian's passing scarcely mask the deep grief he felt:

> The suddenness of the event is both bewildering and merciful—the latter because we cannot yet realise, *subjectively*, that it has actually occurred at all. It would, for example, seem incredibly unnatural to disturb the pillows now arranged for my aunt in the rocker beside my centre-table—her accustomed reading-place each evening.[12]

In August Lovecraft received a small augmentation to his self-esteem. Harold S. Farnese (1885–1945), a composer who was then Assistant Director of the Institute of Musical Art at Los Angeles, wished to set two of Lovecraft's *Fungi from Yuggoth* sonnets, 'Mirage' and 'The Elder Pharos' (both in *Weird Tales* for February–March 1931) to music. Having done so shortly thereafter, Farnese then proposed that Lovecraft write the libretto of an entire opera or music drama based generally on his work; but Lovecraft declined the offer, citing his complete lack of experience in dramatic composition (evidently his 1918 squib *Alfredo* did not qualify). It is difficult to imagine what such a work would have been like.

Lovecraft's travels for 1932 were by no means over. On 30 August he went to Boston to spend time with Cook. The next day the two of them went to Newburyport to see the total solar eclipse, and were rewarded with a fine sight. From there Lovecraft proceeded to Montreal and Quebec, spending four full days in the two towns (2–6 September). Lovecraft tried to persuade Cook to come along, but Cook did not relish the ascetic manner in which his friend travelled (sleeping on trains or buses, scant meals, nonstop sightseeing, etc.). Cook did, however, see Lovecraft on his return, and his portrait is as vivid a reflection of Lovecraft's manic travelling habits as one could ask for:

> Early the following Tuesday morning, before I had gone to work, Howard arrived back from Quebec. I have never before nor since seen such a sight. Folds of skin hanging from a skeleton. Eyes sunk in sockets like burnt holes in a blanket. Those delicate, sensitive artist's hands and fingers nothing but claws. The man was dead except for his nerves, on which he was functioning … I was scared. Because I was scared I was angry. Possibly my anger was largely at myself for letting him go alone on that trip. But whatever its real cause, it was genuine anger that I took out on him. He needed a brake; well, he'd have the brake applied right now.[13]

Cook immediately took Lovecraft to a Waldorf restaurant and made him have a plentiful meal, then took him back to his rooming house so that he could rest. Cook, returning from work at five, forced Lovecraft to have another meal before letting him go. How Lovecraft could actually derive enjoyment from the places he visited, functioning on pure nervous energy and with so little food and rest, it is difficult to imagine; and yet, he did so again and again.

Sometime in the spring or summer of 1932 a promising new revision client emerged—promising not because she showed any talent or inclination to become a writer in her own right but because she gave Lovecraft regular work. She was Hazel Heald

(1896–1961), a woman about whom I know almost nothing. She was born and apparently spent most of her life in Somerville, Massachusetts, and so far as I know published nothing aside from the five stories Lovecraft revised or ghostwrote for her. Unlike Zealia Bishop, she wrote no memoir of Lovecraft, so that it is not clear how she came in touch with him and what their professional or personal relations were like.

There is good reason to believe that several, of not all five, of the stories Lovecraft revised for Heald were written in 1932 or 1933, even though the last of them did not appear in print until 1937. The first of them appears to have been 'The Man of Stone' (*Wonder Stories*, October 1932). Heald told Derleth that Lovecraft merely touched up an existing manuscript,[14] but to me the tale's prose reads like Lovecraft throughout. He must have worked on the story by the summer of 1932 at the latest in order for it to have appeared in the October *Wonder Stories*. It is in the end a conventional story about Daniel 'Mad Dan' Morris, who finds in his ancestral copy of the *Book of Eibon* a formula to turn any living creature into a stone statue, and attempts to do so to both his wife and a man he suspects of dallying with his wife, but in the end is turned to stone himself.

The next tale, 'Winged Death', is not much of an improvement. This preposterous story tells of an insect called the 'devil-fly' that purportedly takes over the soul or personality of its victim. Sure enough, a scientist is bitten by the creature, and his soul enters its body; absurdly enough, he writes a message on the ceiling of his room by dipping his insect body in ink and walking across the ceiling. This grotesque and unintentionally comical conclusion— which Lovecraft admitted was his own invention—is clearly intended to be the acme of horror, but ends up being merely bathetic.

Lovecraft submitted the story to *Strange Tales*, but it was rejected because, incredibly enough, another just-accepted tale had already utilized this insect-writing idea! I do not know what immortal masterwork of literature beat Lovecraft to the punch; but the note about the tale's submission to *Strange Tales* is of some interest. I think it quite plausible that the earlier Heald tales were written with that better-paying market in view. There is no evidence that the other tales were submitted there; they could well have been, as all but one of them were written prior to the magazine's folding at the end of the year. Lovecraft submitted 'Winged Death' to Farnsworth Wright, but the latter must have delayed in accepting the tale, for it was published only in *Weird Tales* for March 1934.

I fervently hope that 'The Horror in the Museum' is a conscious parody—in this case, a parody of Lovecraft's own myth-cycle. Here we are introduced to a new 'god', Rhan-Tegoth, which the curator of a waxworks museum, George Rogers, claims to have found on an expedition to Alaska. Indeed, the story could be read as a parody of both 'Pickman's Model' and 'The Call of Cthulhu'. Consider the absurdity of the scenario: it is not a mere representation of a god that is secreted in a crate in the cellar of the museum, but *the actual god itself*!

The story is mentioned in a letter of October 1932: 'My latest revisory job comes so near to pure fictional ghost-writing that I am up against all the plot-devising problems of my bygone auctorial days.'[15] This story seems to have been readily accepted by Wright, for it appeared in *Weird Tales* for July 1933, in the same issue as 'The Dreams in the Witch House'.

'Out of the Æons'—which Lovecraft was working on in early August 1933—is perhaps the only genuinely successful Heald revision, although it too contains elements of extravagance that border on self-parody. This tale concerns an ancient mummy housed in a museum and an accompanying scroll in indecipherable characters. The scroll eventually yields up its secrets, telling the tale of a man who encounters the god Ghatanothoa 175,000 years ago; of course, the mummy is the man in question, whose body is petrified but whose brain still lives.

It is manifestly obvious that Heald's sole contribution to this tale is the core notion of a mummy with a living brain; all the rest is Lovecraft's. He admits as much when he says: 'Regarding the scheduled "Out of the Æons"—I should say I *did* have a hand in it … I *wrote* the damn thing!'[16] The tale is substantial, but it too is written with a certain flamboyance and lack of polish that bar it from taking its place with Lovecraft's own best tales. It appeared in *Weird Tales* for April 1935.

'The Horror in the Burying-Ground', on the other hand, returns us to earth very emphatically. Here we are in some unspecified rustic locale where the village undertaker, Henry Thorndike, has devised a peculiar chemical compound that, when injected into a living person, will simulate death even though the person is alive and conscious. Lovecraft never mentions this revision in any correspondence I have seen, so I do not know when it was written; it did not appear in *Weird Tales* until May 1937.

Lovecraft no doubt was paid regularly by Heald, even though it took years for her stories to be published; at least, he makes no complaints about dilatory payments as he did for Zealia Bishop. Although Lovecraft is still speaking of her in the present tense as a revision client as late as the summer of 1935, it does not seem as if he did much work for her after the summer of 1933.

Another revision or collaboration in which Lovecraft became unwillingly involved in the fall of 1932 was 'Through the Gates of the Silver Key'. E. Hoffmann Price had become so enamoured of 'The Silver Key' that, during Lovecraft's visit with him in New Orleans in June, he 'suggested a sequel to account for Randolph Carter's doings after his disappearance'.[17] There is no recorded response on Lovecraft's part to this suggestion, although it cannot have been very enthusiastic. On his own initiative, therefore, Price wrote his own sequel, 'The Lord of Illusion'—an appallingly awful piece of work that unwittingly parodies the story of which it claims to be an homage. And yet, Lovecraft felt some sort of obligation to try to make something of it. He rightly concluded: 'Hell, but it'll be a tough nut to crack!'[18] The rush of other work prevented him from working on it for months, and he did not finish the job until early April.

The result cannot by any means be called satisfactory. Whereas 'The Silver Key' is a poignant reflection of some of Lovecraft's innermost sentiments and beliefs, 'Through the Gates of the Silver Key' is nothing more than a fantastic adventure story with awkward and laboured mathematical and philosophical interludes. Price has remarked that 'I estimated that [Lovecraft] had left unchanged fewer than fifty of my original words',[19] a comment that has led many to believe that the finished version of 'Through the Gates of the Silver Key' is radically different from Price's original; but Lovecraft in fact adhered to the basic framework of Price's tale as best he could. Price submitted the story to *Weird Tales* on 19 June, but Farnsworth Wright turned it down. True to his contrary ways, however, he later accepted it. It appeared in the issue for July 1934.

Late in 1932 Lovecraft was pained by the death on 23 November of Henry S. Whitehead, who finally succumbed to the gastric ailment that had enfeebled him for years. Lovecraft pays unaffected tribute to him in a letter to E. Hoffmann Price.[20]

I have already mentioned Lovecraft's revision of Whitehead's 'The Trap'. There are two other stories on which he gave some assistance, although it is my belief that he contributed no actual prose to either of them. One is 'Cassius', which is clearly based upon an entry in Lovecraft's commonplace book about a man who has a miniature Siamese twin. Whitehead has followed the details of this entry fairly closely in his tale (*Strange Tales*, November 1931), except that he transfers it to his customary West Indian locale. Lovecraft later admitted that his own development of the idea would have been very different from Whitehead's.[21]

The other story on which Lovecraft had been assisting White-head was called 'The Bruise', but he was uncertain whether it had ever been completed. This matter first comes up in April 1932, when Lovecraft notes that 'I'm now helping Whitehead prepare a new ending and background for a story Bates had rejected'. The story involves a man who suffers a bruise to the head and—in Lovecraft's version—'excite[s] cells of hereditary memory causing the man to hear the destruction and sinking of fabulous Mu 20,000 years ago!'[22] Some have believed that Lovecraft may have actually written or revised this story, but from internal evidence it seems to me that none of the writing is Lovecraft's, although he does appear to have provided a synopsis of some sort. The story was not published until it appeared in Whitehead's second Arkham House volume, *West India Lights* (1946).

Lovecraft wrote a two-page obituary of Whitehead and sent it to Farnsworth Wright, urging that it be used as a quarry for an announcement in *Weird Tales*. Wright ran the piece as a separate unsigned article—'In Memoriam: Henry St. Clair Whitehead'—in the March 1933 issue, but used only about a quarter of what Love-craft had sent him, and, since Lovecraft kept no copy of his original, the full text has now been lost.

One very strange piece of writing Lovecraft did at this time was 'European Glimpses', dated on the manuscript to 19 December 1932. This is a very conventionalized travelogue of the principal tourist sites in western Europe (chiefly in Germany, France, and England), and is nothing less than a ghostwriting job for Sonia, although Lovecraft—on the few occasions when he spoke of the assignment to correspondents—went out of his way to conceal the fact. Sonia remarks in her memoir:

> In 1932 I went to Europe. I was almost tempted to invite him along but I knew that since I was no longer his wife he would not have accepted. However, I wrote to him from England, Germany and France, sending him books and pic-tures of every conceivable scene that I thought might

interest him … I sent a travelogue to H. P. which he revised for me.[23]

'European Glimpses' itself is by far the least interesting of Lovecraft's travelogues—if, indeed, it can even be called such—on account of its very hackneyed descriptions of very hackneyed tourist sites that no bourgeois traveller ever fails to visit. Perhaps its only interesting feature is its record of Sonia's glimpse of Hitler in the flesh in Wiesbaden.

At the very end of 1932 Lovecraft instituted what would become another travelling ritual, as he spent the week or so after Christmas in New York with the Longs. Naturally, he spent Christmas with Annie in Providence, but the very next day he caught a bus for New York and arrived at 230 West 97th Street for a visit of seven or eight days. Loveman and Kirk were dumbfounded to see Lovecraft in the city, but Morton proved to be away from his museum for more than a week, so that no meeting could be arranged. Lovecraft stayed in the city until 3 January.

Lovecraft's own writing career was, as noted, not progressing very well: only a single story ('The Dreams in the Witch House') was written in 1932, and none in the first half of 1933 (excluding the collaboration 'Through the Gates of the Silver Key'). Lovecraft remarks to Donald Wandrei that in mid-February 1933 'my aunt & I had a desperate colloquy on family finances',[24] with the result that Lovecraft would move from 10 Barnes Street and Annie would move from 61 Slater Avenue and unite to form a single household. That Lovecraft and Annie could not afford even the meagre rent they were no doubt paying (Lovecraft's was $10 per week, Annie's probably similar) speaks volumes for the utter penury in which both of them existed.

But luck was, on this occasion, with them. Lovecraft and Annie found a delightful house at 66 College Street, on the very crest of the hill, directly behind the John Hay Library. The house was actually owned by the university and was leased out as two large apartments, one on each of the two floors. The top floor—five rooms plus two attic storerooms—had suddenly become vacant, and Lovecraft and Annie seized on it once they heard of its rent— $10 per week total, presumably half the combined rent for their two separate apartments. Best of all, from Lovecraft's perspective, was that the house was built in the colonial style; it dates to about 1825. The place fell vacant on 1 May, and Lovecraft moved in on 15

May; Annie moved in two weeks later. Lovecraft was unable to believe his good fortune, and hoped only to be able to keep the place for a significant length of time. As it happened, he would remain there for the four years remaining in his life.

CHAPTER EIGHTEEN
In My Own Handwriting
(1933–35)

The house is a square wooden edifice of the 1800 period ...
The fine colonial doorway is like my bookplate come to life,
though of a slightly later period with side lights & fan
carving instead of a fanlight. In the rear is a picturesque,
village-like garden at a higher level than the front of the
house. The upper flat we have taken contains 5 rooms
besides bath & kitchenette nook on the main (2nd) floor,
plus 2 attic storerooms—one of which is so attractive that I
wish I could have it for an extra den! My quarters—a large
study & a small adjoining bedroom—are on the south side,
with my working desk under a west window affording a
splendid view of the lower town's outspread roofs & of the
mystical sunsets that flame behind them. The interior is as
fascinating as the exterior—with colonial fireplaces, mantels,
& chimney cupboards, curving Georgian staircase, wide floor-
boards, old-fashioned latches, small-paned windows, six-
panel doors, rear wing with floor at a different level (3 steps
down), quaint attic stairs, &c.—just like the old houses open
as museums. After admiring such all my life, I find something magical & dreamlike in the experience of actually
living in one ... I keep half-expecting a museum guard to
come around & kick me out at 5 o'clock closing time![1]

A passage like this can be found in nearly every letter Lovecraft
wrote during this period, and testifies to the miraculous stroke of
luck whereby a move made for purely economic reasons—and
after Lovecraft had come to feel so at home at 10 Barnes after seven
years' residence there—resulted in his landing in a colonial-style
house he had always longed for. Even his birthplace, 454 Angell
Street, was not colonial, although of course it remained dear to his
heart for other reasons.

Across the back garden from 66 College Street was a boarding-house, at which Annie customarily ate both her meals; Lovecraft would eat there occasionally, but he preferred either to go downtown to some cheaper eatery or to make his own humble meals out of cans or from groceries purchased at delicatessens or grocery stores such as the Weybosset Food Basket (still in operation).

One of the most engaging features of the place was a shed next to the boarding-house, whose flat roof supplied an excellent sunning place for the several cats in the area. It was not long before Lovecraft began to make friends with these cats. Since he was living on what was then Brown University's fraternity row, Lovecraft christened this group of felines the Kappa Alpha Tau (K.A.T.), which he claimed stood for *Kompson Ailouron Taxis* (Band of Elegant Cats). Their comings and goings would provide Lovecraft much pleasure, and some heartache, over the years.

A few months before he moved to 66 College, around 11 March, Lovecraft had taken a trip to Hartford, Connecticut—on what he tells one correspondent was 'a job of research which a client was conducting at the library there'.[2] Again Lovecraft has prevaricated, and again the reason is connected with his ex-wife; for this was the last time he and Sonia saw each other face to face. After she returned from her European tour, Sonia took a trip to the Hartford suburbs of Farmington and Wethersfield; she was so captivated with the colonial antiquities in these towns that she wrote to Lovecraft and asked him to join her. He did so, spending a day and a night there.

That evening, before they parted for the night, Sonia said, 'Howard, won't you kiss me goodnight?' Lovecraft replied, 'No, it is better not to.' The next morning they explored Hartford itself, and that evening, as they bade each other adieu, Sonia did not ask for a kiss.[3] They never saw each other again nor, so far as I can tell, corresponded.

The new household at 66 College got off, literally, on the wrong foot when, on 14 June, Annie fell down the stairs and broke her ankle. She remained in Rhode Island Hospital for three weeks in a cast and returned home on 5 July, essentially bedridden and with a nurse in attendance; the cast was removed on 3 August, but Annie had to continue using crutches until well into the fall. All this could not have helped the finances of the household, and in an unguarded moment Lovecraft makes note of the 'financial strain utterly ruinous to us at the present juncture!'[4]

There was some relief, however. On 30 June the peripatetic E. Hoffmann Price paid Lovecraft a four-day call in Providence in the course of an automobile tour across the country in a 1928 Ford that Lovecraft deemed the Juggernaut. This handy vehicle allowed Lovecraft to see parts of his own state that he had never visited before, in particular the so-called Narragansett Country or South County—the stretch of countryside on the western and southern side of Narragansett Bay, where in the colonial period actual plantations resembling those in the South had existed.

Harry Brobst joined in some of the festivities. On one occasion, when Price was preparing a feast of Indian curry, Brobst made the faux pas of bringing a six-pack of beer. Lovecraft had apparently never seen such a quantity of alcoholic beverages before. Let Price again tell the story:

> 'And what,' he asked, out of scientific curiosity, 'are you going to do with so *much* of it?'
>
> 'Drink it,' said Brobst. 'Only three bottles a-piece.'
>
> I'll never forget HPL's look of utter incredulity ... And he watched us with unconcealed curiosity, and with a touch of apprehension, as we drank three bottles a-piece. I'm sure he made a detailed entry in his journal to record this, to him, unusual feat.[5]

Lovecraft's third and last trip to Quebec occurred in early September, when Annie gave Lovecraft a belated birthday present of a week's vacation from nursing. He prefaced the trip by visiting Cook in Boston on 2 September, then crammed as much into the next four days as possible, seeing all the sights he had seen on his two previous visits. Lovecraft also managed one day in Montreal, which he found appealing if entirely modern.

In late summer 1933 Samuel Loveman spoke with an editor at Alfred A. Knopf, Allen G. Ullman, about Lovecraft's stories. On Ullman's request, Lovecraft sent in a total of twenty-five stories—nearly all the work he had not repudiated.

Sympathetic as I generally am to Lovecraft's relentlessly uncommercial stance, I have difficulty refraining from a strong inclination to kick him in the seat of the pants for the letter he wrote to Ullman accompanying these stories. Throughout the letter Lovecraft repeatedly denigrates his own work out of what he fancies to be gentlemanly humility but which Ullman probably took to be lack of confidence in his own work. For example: 'The Tomb' is 'stiff in diction'; 'The Temple' is 'nothing remarkable'; 'The Outsider' is 'rather bombastic in style & mechanical in climax'; and on and on.[6] For some reason, perhaps because they were not published, Lovecraft did not send *At the Mountains of Madness* or 'The Shadow over Innsmouth', two of his strongest works.

It is scarcely a surprise that Ullman ultimately rejected the collection, sending Lovecraft on another round of self-recrimination. And yet, in this case the rejection was not entirely the fault of Lovecraft's lack of salesmanship. Ullman had asked Farnsworth Wright of *Weird Tales* whether he could dispose of a thousand copies of a proposed collection of Lovecraft's stories through the magazine; Wright said he could not guarantee such a sale, and Ullman promptly turned down the stories.

The Knopf deal is probably the closest Lovecraft ever came to having a book published in his lifetime by a mainstream publisher. If he had done so, the rest of his career—and, it is not too much to say, the entire subsequent history of American weird fiction— might have been very different. But, after this fourth failure at book publication (following *Weird Tales*, Putnam's, and Vanguard), the last three and a half years of Lovecraft's life were increasingly filled with doubt, diffidence, and depression about his work, until toward the end he came to believe that he had entirely failed as a fiction writer.

In September 1933 *The Fantasy Fan* began publication. This is, canonically, the first 'fan' magazine in the domain of weird/ fantastic fiction, and it inaugurated a very rich, complex, and somewhat unruly tradition—still flourishing today—of fan activity in this realm.

It is an anomaly beyond my powers of explanation that the fields of fantasy, horror, and science fiction have attracted legions of fans who are not content to read and collect the literature but must write about it and its authors, and publish—often at considerable expense—small magazines or books devoted to the subject. There is no analogous fan network in the fields of detective fiction or the western, even though the first of these fields certainly attracts a far larger body of fans than does weird fiction. Nor is this fan activity entirely to be despised: many of today's leading critics of weird fiction emerged from the realm of fandom and still retain connections with it. Fandom is perhaps most charitably seen as a training ground that permits young writers and critics (most individuals become fans as teenagers) to hone their nascent abilities; but the field has gained well-deserved contempt because so many of its participants never seem to advance beyond its essentially juvenile level.

The Fantasy Fan was edited by Charles D. Hornig (b. 1916) of Elizabeth, New Jersey, who was scarcely seventeen when the magazine was launched. Celebrated as it is, it operated at a loss during its entire run: it had a pitifully small circulation in its day—only sixty subscribers and a print run probably not exceeding three hundred—and looks very crude and amateurish today. But it attracted immediate attention throughout the world of weird fiction, not only among fans but among its leading authors. Lovecraft saw in it a chance to land (without pay, of course) his oft-rejected tales. He urged Clark Ashton Smith, Robert E. Howard, and even the relentlessly professional August Derleth to send original stories to it, and the appearance of stories by these and other writers has made *The Fantasy Fan* a choice collectible commanding high prices.

Hornig made, however, one mistake in judgment by instituting, in the very first issue, a write-in column called 'The Boiling Point' in which controversial and polemical opinions were deliberately sought out. As a result, a nasty letter-feud broke out between Forrest J Ackerman (b. 1916)—who had harshly criticized a Clark Ashton Smith story—and Lovecraft, Smith, Barlow, and others. By February 1934 Hornig decided that 'The Boiling Point' had served its purpose and had in fact aroused too much ill-feeling to be productive. And yet, bitter, vituperative controversies of this sort have remained common in fandom and continue to this day.

Hornig made a wiser decision when he accepted Lovecraft's offer of preparing a new edition of 'Supernatural Horror in Literature' for serialization in the magazine. Lovecraft evidently revised the essay all at once, not piecemeal over the course of the serialization (October 1933 to February 1935); indeed, he seems simply to have sent Hornig an annotated copy of *The Recluse*, with separate typed (or even handwritten) sheets for the major additions. The serialization progressed very slowly, as the magazine could accommodate only a small portion of text in each issue; when the magazine folded in February 1935, it had published the text only up to the middle of Chapter VIII. For the rest of the two years of his life Lovecraft sought in vain to find some fan publisher to continue the serialization. The complete, revised text of 'Supernatural Horror in Literature' did not appear until *The Outsider and Others* (1939).

Another individual who established—or attempted to establish —various journals wavering uncertainly between the fan and semi-professional levels was William L. Crawford (1911–84), with whom Lovecraft came in touch in the fall of 1933. Lovecraft would, with a certain good-natured maliciousness, poke fun at Crawford's lack of culture by referring to him as Hill-Billy, presumably alluding both to Crawford's residence in Everett, Pennsylvania (in the Alleghanies) and to his stolid insensitivity to highbrow literature. But Crawford meant well. Initially he proposed a non-paying weird magazine titled *Unusual Stories* but almost immediately ran into difficulties, even though he accepted Lovecraft's 'Celephaïs' and 'The Doom that Came to Sarnath' for the magazine. By early 1934 he proposed a second journal, *Marvel Tales*, either as a companion to *Unusual* or as a replacement for it. 'Celephaïs' appeared in the first issue (May 1934) of *Marvel*, while 'The Doom that Came to Sarnath' finally appeared in the March–April 1935 issue. Two issues of *Unusual Stories* did emerge in 1935 (prefaced by a queer 'advance issue' in the spring of 1934), but contained no work by Lovecraft.

But Crawford's bumbling attempts deserve commendation for at least one good result. In the fall of 1933 he asked Lovecraft for a nine-hundred-word autobiography for *Unusual*, evidently the first of a series. Lovecraft had great difficulty condensing his life and opinions into nine hundred words, so on 23 November he wrote a longer version of about three thousand words and somehow managed to trim this down to the requisite size. The shortened version, now lost, never appeared; but providentially Lovecraft sent the longer version to Barlow for preservation, and this is how we have the piece entitled 'Some Notes on a Nonentity'—easily Lovecraft's finest autobiographical essay.

The revision of 'Supernatural Horror in Literature' coincided with an extensive course of rereading and analysing the weird classics in an attempt to revive what Lovecraft believed to be his flagging creative powers. Rejections were still affecting him keenly, and he was beginning to feel written out. Perhaps he needed a break from fiction as he had had in 1908–17; or perhaps a renewed critical reading of the landmarks in the field might rejuvenate him. Whatever the case, Lovecraft produced several interesting documents as a result of this work. Probably the most significant is

'Notes on Writing Weird Fiction', Lovecraft's canonical statement of his own goals for weird writing, as well as a schematic outline of how he himself wrote his own stories.

And yet, this research does not seem to have helped Lovecraft much in the short term, for the first actual story he wrote at this time—'The Thing on the Doorstep', scribbled frenetically in pencil from 21 to 24 August 1933—is, like 'The Dreams in the Witch House', one of his poorest later efforts.

The tale, narrated in the first person by Daniel Upton, tells of Upton's young friend Edward Derby, who in his thirties becomes attracted to and marries a young Innsmouth woman named Asenath Waite. It turns out that Asenath—who has anomalous hypnotic powers—is capable of thrusting her mind into the body of another person; the ousted mind then occupies her own body. Moreover, Asenath herself is in fact the mind of her father Ephraim: as his own death approached, he switched minds with his own daughter. Derby, a weak-willed individual, initially succumbs to this body-switching, but ultimately rebels by killing Asenath. But her mind is strong enough to retain life, and she again exchanges personalities with Edward, thrusting his mind into the decaying corpse of her own body. Edward, exercising superhuman strength, emerges from the grave and becomes the 'thing on the doorstep'— approaching his friend Upton and, by way of a letter, urging him to kill the person that is occupying his own body.

'The Thing on the Doorstep' has many flaws: first, the obvious- ness of the basic scenario and the utter lack of subtlety in its execution; and second, poor writing, laden (as with 'The Dreams in the Witch House') with hyperbole, stale idioms, and dragging verbosity. The story was clearly influenced by H. B. Drake's *The Shadowy Thing* (1928; first published in England in 1925 as *The Remedy*), a poorly written but strangely compelling novel about a man named Booth who displays anomalous powers of hypnosis and mind-transference. Lovecraft has amended this plot by introducing the notion of *mind-exchange*: whereas Drake does not clarify what happens to the ousted mind when it is taken over by the mind of Booth, Lovecraft envisages an exact transference whereby the ousted mind occupies the body of its possessor. The notion of mind-transference between a man and a woman may have been borrowed by Barry Pain's outstanding short novel *An Exchange of Souls* (1911), which Lovecraft is known to have read.

The fact that the mind-exchange occurs between husband and

wife gives the story some small interest, if only from a biographical perspective. Various features of Edward Derby's life supply a twisted version of Lovecraft's own childhood; but other features seem drawn from the lives of some of Lovecraft's closest associates, notably Alfred Galpin and Frank Belknap Long.[7] Derby's marriage to Asenath Waite, of course, brings certain aspects of Lovecraft's marriage to Sonia manifestly to mind. Sonia was clearly the more strong-willed member of the couple. On one occasion Frank Belknap Long told me that Sonia was a 'domineering' woman, a description very applicable to Asenath Waite. Aside from these points of biographical interest, however, 'The Thing on the Doorstep' is crude, obvious, lacking in subtlety of execution or depth of conception, and histrionically written.

Lovecraft was becoming the hub of an increasingly complex network of fans and writers in the field of weird and science fiction; and in the last four years of his life he attracted a vast number of young people (mostly boys) who looked upon him as a living legend. I have already noted that R. H. Barlow first came in touch with Lovecraft at the age of thirteen in 1931; now other teenagers came to the fore.

The most promising of them—or, rather, the one who in the end amounted to the most—was Robert Bloch (1917–94), who first wrote to Lovecraft in the spring of 1933. Bloch, born in Chicago but at this time a resident of Milwaukee, had just turned sixteen, and had been reading *Weird Tales* since 1927. To the end of his life Bloch remained grateful to Lovecraft for his lengthy reply to his fan letter and for continuing to write to him over the next four years. Lovecraft lent unstinting assistance to Bloch, meticulously criticizing his early stories and urging him to restrain the overcolouring and stylistic excesses that marred his tales (flaws that Lovecraft knew all too well from his own early work). The advice paid off in a hurry, for in July 1934 Bloch landed his first story in *Weird Tales*. From this point on he rapidly became a regular in the magazine, and—although this occurred chiefly after Lovecraft's death—branched out into the mystery and science fiction fields as well.

Richard F. Searight (1902–75) was not exactly a teenage fan when he began corresponding with Lovecraft in late summer of 1933; indeed, he had had one collaborative story in an early issue of *Weird Tales* ('The Brain in the Jar' in November 1924). A native of Michigan, Searight worked as a telegraph operator for many years.

By the early 1930s he decided to return to literature, writing a series of tales and poems which he wished Lovecraft to revise and help him to place professionally. Lovecraft felt that he could not help Searight in a revisory capacity but encouraged him to reconceive his work along less conventional lines. Searight attempted to follow Lovecraft's advice and did manage to land some tales in *Wonder Stories* and other science fiction pulps, although many remained unpublished. In one such story, 'The Sealed Casket' (*Weird Tales*, March 1935), Searight came up with a new 'book' to add to Lovecraft's pseudomythology, the Eltdown Shards; Lovecraft would cite it himself in a few later stories.

Helen V. Sully (1904–97) met Lovecraft in person before corresponding with him. The daughter of Genevieve K. Sully, a married woman in Auburn, California, with whom Clark Ashton Smith carried on a long-time affair, Sully decided to explore the eastern seaboard in the summer of 1933, and Smith urged her to look up Lovecraft in Providence. She did so, arriving in the city in early July and being shown all the sites in Providence as well as Newport, Newburyport, and elsewhere. Lovecraft paid for all of Sully's expenses—meals, trips, lodging at the boarding house across the street from 66 College—while he was her host; she could not have known what a severe burden this must have placed upon his own perilous financial condition. One evening Lovecraft took her to one of his favourite haunts, the hidden churchyard of St John's Episcopal Church:

> It was dark, and he began to tell me strange, weird stories in a sepulchral tone and, despite the fact that I am a very matter-of-fact person, something about his manner, the darkness, and a sort of eerie light that seemed to hover over the gravestones got me so wrought up that I began to run out of the cemetery with him close at my heels, with the one thought that I must get up to the street before he, or whatever it was, grabbed me. I reached a street lamp, trembling, panting, and almost in tears, and he had the strangest look on his face, almost of triumph. Nothing was said.[8]

What a ladies' man! It should be noted that Sully was indeed an exceptionally attractive woman. When she went to New York after visiting Lovecraft, she bowled over the entire weird fiction crowd there: Lovecraft drily reports having to keep Frank Long and Donald Wandrei from fighting a duel over her.

Herman C. Koenig (1893–1959) was, like Searight, well beyond his teen years when he wrote to Lovecraft in the fall of 1933. An employee of the Electrical Testing Laboratories in New York City, Koenig had an impressive private collection of rare books, and he had asked Lovecraft about the *Necronomicon* and how it could be procured. Lovecraft, disillusioning Koenig about the reality of the volume, nevertheless continued to stay in touch with him, and Koenig would lend him a significant number of weird books that would affect Lovecraft strongly over the next several years. In particular, in the summer of 1934, Koenig began circulating around the Lovecraft circle copies of the forgotten work of William Hope Hodgson, whose novels and tales—particularly *The House on the Borderland* (1908) and *The Night Land* (1912)—are prodigious feats of the imagination. August Derleth would later reprint much of Hodgson's work with Arkham House.

The post-Christmas season of 1933–34 again found Lovecraft in New York, and this time he ended up meeting an unusual number of colleagues old and new, among them Desmond Hall (associate editor of *Astounding Stories*) and Donald Wandrei's superlatively talented brother, the weird artist Howard Wandrei.

On the 31st Lovecraft saw the old year out at Samuel Loveman's flat in Brooklyn Heights, where he renewed his acquaintance with Hart Crane's mother, whom he had met in Cleveland in 1922. Crane, of course, had committed suicide in 1932. It was on this occasion, evidently—if Loveman's word can be trusted—that Loveman's roommate Patrick McGrath spiked Lovecraft's drink, causing him to talk even more animatedly than he usually did.[9] Lovecraft gives no indication of any such thing, and one would imagine that someone so sensitive to alcohol (its mere smell was nearly a purgative) would have detected the ruse. I am half inclined to doubt this anecdote, engaging as it is.

The rest of the winter and early spring of 1934 passed uneventfully, until in mid-March R. H. Barlow made a momentous announcement: he invited Lovecraft for an indefinite visit to his family's home in De Land, Florida. Lovecraft, whose last trip to Florida and its energizing heat had been in 1931, was anxious to accept the invitation, and the only obstacle was money. But the money does seem to have come in, for by mid-April Lovecraft was making definite plans to head south.

The trip began around 17 April, and after the usual few days in

New York he reached Charleston on the 24th, where he spent almost a week. Finally he boarded a bus and arrived at De Land just after noon on 2 May. Barlow and his family actually lived a good eighteen miles southwest of that city along what is now State Road 44; the residence was probably closer to the small town of Cassia than to De Land. There was a lake on the property, and the nearest neighbour was three miles away.[10]

We do not know a great deal about what Lovecraft actually did in the more than six weeks he spent with Barlow. Barlow had by this time himself become perhaps his closest, and certainly one of his most voluminous and intimate, correspondents, far more so than Derleth or Wandrei or Howard; in the sudden absence of letters to Barlow we are left to reconstruct the particulars of the visit from a variety of other documents, including Barlow's journal of the period and his later memoir, 'The Wind that Is in the Grass' (1944). In that memoir he gives an impressionistic account of the visit: 'We rowed on the lake, and played with the cats, or walked on the highway with these cats as the unbelievable sun went down among pines and cypresses ... Above all, we talked, chiefly of the fantastic tales which he wrote and which I was trying to write. At breakfast he told us his dreams.'[11]

Antiquity was not in very great supply in this region of Florida, but Lovecraft and Barlow did manage to get to a Spanish sugar-mill at De Leon Springs constructed before 1763, and other sites at nearby New Smyrna, including a Franciscan mission built in 1696. In early June Lovecraft was taken to Silver Springs, about forty-five miles northwest of De Land. He desperately hoped to get to Havana, but simply did not have the cash.

Of course, the Barlows fed and housed him at their expense, and were so abundantly hospitable that they continually vetoed any suggestion that he move on. No doubt Barlow's parents perceived that their son and Lovecraft, in spite of the almost thirty-year difference in their ages, had become fast friends. Perhaps Barlow had a lonely existence, with his much older brother Wayne (born in 1908) in the army and not around to aid in his maturation. Barlow, of course, kept himself busy with all manner of literary, artistic, and publishing projects. One of these involved W. Paul Cook's edition of *The Shunned House*, the sheets of which had been knocking about from pillar to post in the wake of Cook's nervous and financial breakdown. Although Barlow obtained about 265 of the sheets, he was at that time caught up in such a whirlwind of activities that he ultimately did little distribution of them, beyond binding about eight copies in 1934–35, one in natural leather for Lovecraft.

One literary project actually did materialize—the spoof known as 'The Battle that Ended the Century'. Barlow was clearly the originator of this squib, as typescripts prepared by him survive, one with extensive revisions in pen by Lovecraft. The idea was to make joking mention of as many of the authors' mutual colleagues as possible in the course of the document, which purported to report the heavyweight fight between Two-Gun Bob, the Terror of the Plains (Robert E. Howard) and Knockout Bernie, the Wild Wolf of West Shokan (Bernard Austin Dwyer). More than thirty individuals are mentioned. Barlow had initially cited them by their actual names, but Lovecraft felt that this was not very interesting, so he devised parodic or punning names for them: instead of Frank Belknap Long, one reads of Frank Chimesleep Short. All this is good if harmless fun, but what is more amusing is conspiratorial tones in which Lovecraft speaks of the matter in letters to Barlow. Note his comment when he hears of Frank Long receiving the mimeographed item:

> Note the signature—Chimesleep Short—which indicates that our spoof has gone out & that he at least thinks I've seen the thing. Remember that if you didn't know anything about it, you'd consider it merely a whimsical trick of his own—& that if you'd merely seen the circular, you wouldn't think it worth commenting on. I'm ignoring the matter in my reply.[12]

Lovecraft pushed on to St Augustine on 21 June, remaining there till the 28th. He then spent two days in Charleston, one in Richmond, one in Fredericksburg, two in Washington (where he looked up Elizabeth Toldridge), and one in Philadelphia. When he reached New York he found that the Longs were about to leave for the beach resorts of Asbury Park and Ocean Grove, in New Jersey, and he tagged along for the weekend. He finally returned home on 10 July, nearly three months after he had set out.

But all this proved merely the preliminary for a trip of relatively short distance but powerful imaginative stimulus. The island of Nantucket lay only 90 miles from Lovecraft's doorstep (six hours by combined bus and ferry), but he never visited it until the very end of August 1934. What a world of antiquity he stumbled upon:

> Whole networks of cobblestoned streets with nothing but colonial houses on either side—narrow, garden-bordered lanes—ancient belfries—picturesque waterfront—*everything* that the antiquarian could ask! ... I've explored old houses, the 1746 windmill, the Hist. Soc. Museum, the whaling museum, etc.—and am doing every inch of the quaint streets and alleys on foot.[13]

Returning home, Lovecraft found the legion of cats called the Kappa Alpha Tau flourishing in customary state. But tragedy was in the offing. A cat Lovecraft had named Sam Perkins, born only in June of 1934, was found dead in the shrubbery on 10 September. Lovecraft immediately wrote a touching elegy, now titled 'Little Sam Perkins'.

R. H. Barlow and Robert Bloch were not the only young boys who showered Lovecraft with their halting if promising works of fiction; another one who did so, almost from the beginning of his association with Lovecraft, was Duane W. Rimel (1915–96), a young fan and budding writer from Idaho. In May 1934, when he was in Florida, Lovecraft examined a story by Rimel entitled 'The Tree on the Hill', on which he 'tried a bit of strengthening toward the end'.[14] For some reason the story did not see print until it appeared in the fan magazine *Polaris* for September 1940. It becomes clear that Lovecraft supplied the entire third section of the story, as well as a citation from a mythical volume—the *Chronicle of Nath* by Rudolf Yergler—in the second.

Rimel falls into one of two classes of revision clients for whom Lovecraft was willing to work for no charge: 'genuine *beginners* who need a start' and 'certain *old or handicapped people* who are pathetically in need of some cheering influence—these, even when I recognise them as incapable of improvement'.[15] Even in his professional revision work, Lovecraft adopted a weird sort of altruism:

> When I revised the kindergarten pap and idiot-asylum slop of other fishes, I was, in a microscopic way, putting just the faintest bit of order, coherence, direction, and comprehensible language into something whose Neanderthaloid ineptitude was already mapped out. My work, ignominious as it was, was at least in the right direction—making that which was utterly amorphous and drooling just the minutest trifle less close to the protozoan stage.[16]

More free work was being dumped on Lovecraft's shoulders at this time, especially for the NAPA. Lovecraft ended up writing at least part of the Bureau of Critics columns in the *National Amateur* for the following issues: December 1931; December 1932; March, June, and December 1933; June, September, and December 1934; March, June, and December 1935. These articles are in essence similar to the old 'Department of Public Criticism' columns for the *United Amateur* of 1914–19, but much briefer and incorporating the quite radical shifts in Lovecraft's aesthetic sensibility that had clearly occurred in the interval.

Around July Lovecraft wrote an essay, 'Homes and Shrines of Poe', for Hyman Bradofsky's *Californian*. Bradofsky (b. 1906) quickly became one of the significant figures in the NAPA during the mid-1930s; for although he was himself an undistinguished writer, his *Californian* offered unprecedented space for writers of articles and prose fiction. During the next several years he continually asked Lovecraft for pieces of substantial length, and in this case Bradofsky wanted a two-thousand-word article for the winter 1934 issue. Lovecraft decided to write an account of all known Poe residences in America, but the resulting article is a little too mechanical and condensed to be effective.

Another essay that appeared in Bradofsky's *Californian* (in the winter 1935 issue) is 'Some Notes on Interplanetary Fiction'; but this piece had been composed around July 1934 for one of William L. Crawford's magazines although, like 'Some Notes on a Nonentity', it never appeared there. In this essay Lovecraft copies whole passages from 'Notes on Writing Weird Fiction', and in the end does not see a very promising future for science fiction unless certain significant changes in outlook are made by its writers:

> Insincerity, conventionality, triteness, artificiality, false emotion, and puerile extravagance reign triumphant throughout this overcrowded genre, so that none but its rarest products can possibly claim a truly adult status. And the spectacle of such persistent hollowness has led many to ask whether, indeed, any fabric of real literature can ever grow out of the given subject-matter.

Although his low opinion of the field is clearly derived from a sporadic reading of the science fiction pulps, Lovecraft does not think that 'the idea of space-travel and other worlds is inherently unsuited to literary use'; such ideas must, however, be presented with much more seriousness and emotional preparation than had been done heretofore.

The Christmas season of 1934 was an unusually festive one at 66 College Street. Lovecraft and Annie had a tree for the first time in a quarter-century, and Lovecraft takes naive delight in describing its decoration: 'All my old-time ornaments were of course long dispersed, but I laid in a new & inexpensive stock at my old friend Frank Winfield Woolworth's. The finished product—with tinsel star, baubles, & tinsel draped from the boughs like Spanish moss— is certainly something to take the eye!'[17]

The New Year's season of 1934–35 once more found Lovecraft in the New York area. R. H. Barlow was in town, and Lovecraft met him frequently. On New Year's night Lovecraft had stayed up till 3 a.m. with Barlow revising a story of his—' "Till A' the Seas"' (*Californian*, summer 1935). This fairly conventional 'last man' story is of interest only because Barlow's typescript, with Lovecraft's revisions in pen, survives, so that the exact degree of the latter's authorship can be ascertained. Lovecraft has made no significant structural changes, merely making a number of cosmetic alterations in style and diction; but he has written the bulk of the concluding section, especially the purportedly cosmic reflections when the last man on earth finally meets his ironic death. It's all pretty routine stuff—but Lovecraft was at this very time in the midst of writing something on somewhat the same theme but in a much more compelling way.

By the fall of 1934 Lovecraft had not written a work of original fiction for more than a year. His confidence in his own powers as a fiction writer were clearly at a low ebb. As the months dragged on, Lovecraft's colleagues began to wonder whether any new story would ever emerge from his pen. In October E. Hoffmann Price urged Lovecraft to write another story about Randolph Carter, but Lovecraft declined.

Given all the difficulties Lovecraft was experiencing in capturing his ideas in fiction, it is not surprising that the writing of his next tale, 'The Shadow out of Time', took more than three months (10 November 1934 to 22 February 1935, as dated on the autograph manuscript) and went through two or perhaps three entire drafts. Moreover, the genesis of the story can be traced back at least four years before its actual composition. Before examining the painful birth of the story, let us gain some idea of its basic plot.

The story deals with Nathaniel Wingate Peaslee, a professor at Miskatonic University who suffers a five-year amnesia (1908–13). Regaining his memory, he gradually learns that his type of amnesia is analogous to that of a very small number of people throughout history who believe they have been psychically possessed by the Great Race, a group of entities shaped like ten-foot-high rugose cones who have perfected the technique of mind-exchange over time, and who cast their minds back and forth across time into the bodies of many different species in order to learn the secrets of the universe. On an expedition to Australia, Peaslee learns in a most poignant way that the Great Race actually existed: he discovers the manuscript he must have written (for it is 'in my own handwriting') millions of years ago as a captive mind of the cone-shaped creatures.

The cosmic scope of this work—second only to *At the Mountains of Madness* in this regard—allows 'The Shadow out of Time' to attain a very high place in Lovecraft's fictional work; and the wealth of circumstantial detail in the history, biology, and civilization of the Great Race is as convincing as in *At the Mountains of Madness* but perhaps still better integrated into the story. Indeed, the Great Race become the centrepiece of the story, in such a way that they—like the Old Ones of *At the Mountains of Madness*—come to seem like the 'heroes' of the tale.

The basic mind-exchange scenario of the tale has been taken from at least three sources. First, of course, is H. B. Drake's *The Shadowy Thing*, which we have already seen as an influence on 'The Thing on the Doorstep'. Second, there is Henri Béraud's obscure novel *Lazarus* (1925), which Lovecraft had in his library and which he read in 1928.[18] This novel presents a man, Jean Mourin, who remains in a hospital for sixteen years while suffering a long amnesia; during this time he develops a personality very different from that of his usual self. A third dominant influence is not a literary work but a film: *Berkeley Square* (1933), which enraptured Lovecraft by its portrayal of a man whose mind somehow drifts back into the body of his ancestor in the eighteenth century. He saw the film four times, and was clearly much captivated by it.

Two other literary influences can be noted if only to be dismissed. It has frequently been assumed that 'The Shadow out of Time' is simply an extrapolation upon Wells's *The Time Machine*; but there is really very little resemblance between the two works. Lovecraft did read Wells's novel in 1925, but there is little in it that might be thought to have a direct bearing on his story. Olaf Staple-don's *Last and First Men* (1930) has been suggested as an influence on the enormous stretches of time reflected in the story, but Lovecraft did not read this work until August 1935, months after his tale's completion.[19]

The core of the plot had already been conceived as early as 1930, emerging out of a discussion between Lovecraft and Clark Ashton Smith regarding the plausibility of stories involving time-travel. By March 1932 Lovecraft had devised the basic idea of mind-exchange over time, as outlined in another letter to Smith.[20] It is important to cite this letter in order to show that the conception of mind-exchange over time had been devised *before* Lovecraft saw *Berkeley Square*, the only other work that might conceivably have influenced this point.

Lovecraft began the actual writing of 'The Shadow out of Time' in late 1934. He announces in November: 'I developed that story *mistily and allusively* in 16 pages, but it was no go. Thin and unconvincing, with the climactic revelation wholly unjustified by the hash of visions preceding it.'[21] What this sixteen-page version could possibly have been like is almost beyond conjecture. The disquisition about the Great Race must have been radically compressed, and this is what clearly dissatisfied Lovecraft about this version; for he came to realize that this passage, far from being an irrelevant digression, was really the heart of the story. Lovecraft finally wrote a second (and perhaps even a third) draft, completing it by late February 1935. Clearly this tale was one of the most difficult in genesis of any of Lovecraft's tales. And yet, in many ways it is the culmination of his fictional career and by no means an unfitting capstone to a twenty-year attempt to capture the sense of wonder and awe he felt at the boundless reaches of space and time. Although Lovecraft would write one more original tale and work on several additional revisions and collaborations with colleagues, his life as a fiction writer ends, and ends fittingly, with 'The Shadow out of Time'.

CHAPTER NINETEEN
Caring about the Civilization (1929–37)

In the summer of 1936 Lovecraft made an interesting admission:

> I used to be a hide-bound Tory simply for traditional and antiquarian reasons—and because I had never done any real *thinking* on civics and industry and the future. The depression —and its concomitant publicisation of industrial, financial, and governmental problems—jolted me out of my lethargy and led me to reëxamine the facts of history in the light of unsentimental scientific analysis; and it was not long before I realised what an ass I had been.[1]

This is one of the few times Lovecraft explicitly mentions the Depression as signalling a radical change in his beliefs on politics, economics, and society; but perhaps he need not have made such an admission, for his letters from 1930 onward return again and again to these subjects.

There was little in Lovecraft's *personal* circumstances that led him to the adoption of a moderate socialism; he did not—as many impoverished individuals did—become attracted to political or economic radicalism merely because he found himself destitute. First, he was never truly destitute—at least, not in comparison with many others in the Depression (including some of his own friends), who lost all their money and belongings and had no job and no roof over their heads; second, he scorned Communism as unworkable and culturally devastating, recommending an economic system considerably to the left of what the United States actually adopted under Roosevelt but nevertheless supporting the New Deal as the only plan of action that had any chance of being carried out.

And yet, Lovecraft's conversion to socialism was not entirely surprising, first because socialism as a political theory and as a concrete alternative to capitalism was experiencing a resurgence during the 1930s, and second because Lovecraft's brand of socialism still retained many of the aristocratic features that had shaped his earlier political thought. The latter point I shall take up presently; the former is worth elaborating briefly.

The United States has never been an especially fertile soil for socialism or Communism, but there have been occasions when they have been a little less unpopular than usual. Socialism had done reasonably well in the first two decades of the century: the I.W.W. (Industrial Workers of the World), founded in 1905, was gaining influence in its support of strikes by a variety of labour unions, and Eugene V. Debs won nearly a million votes in 1912 as a third-party candidate. But in the period immediately after the First World War, with its 'Red Scare' and virulent suppression of all radical groups, socialism was forced underground for nearly a decade.

The depression led to a resurgence in which socialists teamed with labour to demand reforms in working conditions. The socialist presidential candidate Norman Thomas polled a little less than 900,000 votes in 1932—not a very large figure, but a larger one than he achieved during any of his other campaigns. A wide array of intellectuals were also in support of socialism (of either a moderate or a Marxist variety) or outright Communism.

And yet, the shift for Lovecraft was in many ways very slow, even grudging at the outset. It seems jointly to have been the result of observation of the increasingly desperate state of affairs engendered by the Depression and of more searching thought on what could be done about it. President Hoover's staunch belief in voluntarism had made him unwilling to permit the government to give direct relief to the unemployed. Even Roosevelt was only just radical enough to advocate policies that kept the country from total economic collapse, and it was really the Second World War that pulled the United States and the world out of the depression.

What really concerned Lovecraft is not the welfare of the general populace but the civilization-ending revolution this populace could cause if it is not appeased. For after all, 'All that I care about is *the civilisation*':

> *The maintenance of* [a] *high cultural standard is the only social or political enthusiasm I possess* ... In effect, I venerate the principle of aristocracy without being especially interested in aristocrats as persons. I don't care who has the dominance, so long as that dominance remains a *certain kind* of dominance, intellectually and aesthetically considered.[2]

Up to the last few years of his life, Lovecraft believed that only a socially recognized aristocracy could ensure such a condition—either through actual patronage of the arts or through a general climate of refined civilization that would axiomatically be regarded as a condition toward which all society would aspire. Revolution of any kind was the last thing he wanted, and this is why he loathed Bolshevik Russia to the end of his days—because it had fostered a *cultural* destruction that was in no way necessary to the *economic* reform that its leaders were claiming as their paramount goals. It would take some years for Lovecraft to modify his position on aristocracy, but that modification was finally articulated in 1936:

> what I used to respect *was not really aristocracy, but a set of personal qualities which aristocracy then developed better than any other system ... a set of qualities, however, whose merit lay only in a psychology of non-calculative, non-competitive disinterestedness, truthfulness, courage, and generosity fostered by good education, minimum economic stress, and assumed position,* AND JUST AS ACHIEVABLE THROUGH SOCIALISM AS THROUGH ARISTOCRACY.[3]

During the early years of the Depression Lovecraft actually fancied that the plutocracy—now about the only thing equivalent to an aristocracy in the United States—might itself adopt the mores of a true aristocracy. But in the course of time he saw the error of his ways and discarded this approach to the solution of the problem.

There were probably no specific events that led Lovecraft to the shift, but rather an accumulation of many. One significant factor, perhaps, was the so-called Technocracy survey of 1932. The term technocracy was coined by an inventor, William H. Smith, to mean rule by technologists. Elaborated by Howard Scott, an economist and intellectual, the notion led to Lovecraft's most important conclusion about the economic state of the nation: that technology had made full employment impossible even in principle because machines that required only a few workers to tend them were now doing the work previously done by many individuals, and this tendency would only increase as more and more sophisticated machines were developed. Any sensible and realistic economic and political system must then be based on this premise.

The election of 1932 was of course a landmark. Roosevelt won in one of the largest landslides in American history; but his inauguration would not occur until 4 March 1933, and on 22 February

Lovecraft wrote one of his most concentrated and impassioned pleas for political and economic reform—the essay 'Some Repetitions on the Times'.

In this essay—which he apparently made no effort to prepare for publication, or even to show to his colleagues—Lovecraft advocated the following economic proposals: (1) Governmental control of large accumulations of resources (including utilities) and their operation not on a basis of profit but strictly on need; (2) Fewer working hours (but at higher pay) so that all who were capable of working could work at a livable wage; (3) Unemployment insurance and old age pensions. None of these ideas was, of course, Lovecraft's original contribution—they had been talked about for years or decades, and the very title of Lovecraft's essay makes it clear that he is simply echoing what others had said over and over again. Let us consider the history of these proposals in greater detail.

The least problematical was the last. Old age pensions had been instituted in Germany as early as 1889, in Australia in 1903, and in England tentatively in 1908 and definitively by 1925. In 1911–14 unemployment insurance came to England. In the United States, the Social Security Act was signed by Roosevelt on 14 August 1935, although disbursement of money did not begun until 1940.

Government control of large accumulations of wealth has always been a pipe-dream in America, but government control (or at least supervision) of utilities and other institutions was by no means a radical conception in the 1930s. The Roosevelt administration did not undertake such an action until 1934, when the Federal Communications Commission (FCC) was formed to regulate interstate telephone and telegraph rates. By 1935 the Federal Power Commission was governing interstate sale of electric power (natural gas came under control in 1938), the Public Utility Holding Company Act had authorized the Securities and Exchange Commission (SEC) to curb abuses by holding companies (specifically those governing utilities), banks came under federal regulation, and higher taxes were imposed on the wealthy. This was certainly not socialism—although reactionary politicians and businessmen constantly bandied that word about to frighten the electorate and to preserve their own wealth—but it was at least a step in that direction. Of course, many foreign countries exercised actual governmental ownership of public utilities, whereas the United States continues to this day to settle only for governmental supervision.

The most striking of Lovecraft's proposals is the limitation of working hours so that all who were capable of working could work. This idea enjoyed a brief popularity among political theorists and reformers, but in the end the rabid opposition of business doomed it. In April 1933 Senator Hugo Black of Alabama and William Connery, chairman of the House Labor Committee, proposed a bill for a thirty-hour week so that more people could be employed. Roosevelt did not favour it and countered with the NIRA (National Industrial Recovery Act), which ultimately led to the NRA (National Recovery Administration). This established a minimum wage of $12 a week for a forty-hour week. But, although hailed initially as a landmark in co-operation between government, labour, and business, the NRA quickly ran into trouble because its director, General Hugh Samuel Johnson, believed that businesses would of their own accord adopt codes of fair competition and fair labour practice, something that naturally did not happen. The NRA became the object of criticism from all sides, especially among labour unions and small businesses. Less than two years after it was enacted, on 27 May 1935, it was struck down by the Supreme Court as unconstitutional, and was officially abolished on 1 January 1936. Many of its labour provisions, however, were ultimately re-established by other legislation.

Although the movement for shorter working hours continued to the end of the Depression, it never regained the momentum it had had in the early 1930s, prior to its co-opting by the NRA. The forty-hour work week has now been enshrined as a sacrosanct tenet of business, and there is not much likelihood that a move to shorter hours—the chief component of Lovecraft's (and others') plans for full employment—will ever be carried out.

Roosevelt, of course, realized that unemployment was the major problem to be dealt with in the short term (at least twelve million were unemployed in 1932—nearly a quarter of the work force), and one of the first things he did upon gaining office was to establish various emergency measures in an attempt to relieve it. Among these was the CCC (Civilian Conservation Corps), which would enlist young men from the ages of seventeen to twenty-four for the reforestation of parks, flood control, power development, and the like.

Some have wondered why Lovecraft himself never made an attempt to sign on to some such programme. But he was never strictly speaking unemployed: he always had revision work and very sporadic sales of original fiction, and perhaps he feared that he would lose even these modest sources of income if he joined a government-sponsored work programme. What of the WPA (Works Progress Administration), instituted in the summer of 1935? This mostly generated blue-collar construction jobs obviously unsuited for Lovecraft, but the Federal Writers' Project was an important subdivision of the WPA and resulted in the production of a number of significant works of art and scholarship. Lovecraft could perhaps have worked on the guide to Rhode Island published in 1937, but he never made any effort to do so.

One perhaps unintended effect of the economic crisis was to deflect Lovecraft's attention from other social evils. The 18th Amendment was repealed on 6 December 1933. A year and a half earlier Lovecraft had already announced that his enthusiasm for prohibition was a thing of the past,[4] but he made it clear that this was only because he realized that the law against liquor was essentially unenforceable. Lovecraft was surely not pleased at the repeal, but his reference to alcoholism as a 'relatively insignificant rat'[5] certainly contrasts with his fulminations against drinking a decade and a half earlier.

Where Lovecraft departed most radically from the Roosevelt administration itself as well as from the main stream of American opinion was in his suggestions for political reform. He saw economics and politics as quite separate phenomena requiring separate solutions. While proposing the spreading of economic wealth to the many, he concurrently advocated the restricting of political power to the few. This should come as no surprise, given Lovecraft's early (and romanticized) support for the English aristocracy and monarchy, his later readings in Nietzsche, and his own intellectual superiority. And yet, because Lovecraft enunciated his view somewhat misleadingly—or, perhaps, in a deliberately provocative way—he has taken some criticism from later commentators.

In the first place, Lovecraft's 'oligarchy of intelligence and education' (as he terms it in 'Some Repetitions on the Times') is not actually an aristocracy or even an oligarchy in the strictest sense. It is indeed a democracy—but merely a democracy that recognizes the ill effects of universal suffrage if the electorate consists (as in fact it does today) largely of the uneducated or the politically naive. Lovecraft's argument is a very simple one, and is again an outgrowth of his realization of the socioeconomic complexities brought on by the machine age: governmental decisions are now too complex for anyone other than a sophisticated specialist to understand. He discusses the matter cynically with Robert E. Howard:

> Democracy—as distinguished from universal opportunity and good treatment—is today a fallacy and impossibility so great that any serious attempt to apply it cannot be considered as other than a mockery and a jest ... Government 'by popular vote' means merely the nomination of doubtfully qualified men by doubtfully authorised and seldom competent cliques of professional politicians representing hidden interests, followed by a sardonic farce of emotional persuasion in which the orators with the glibbest tongues and flashiest catch-words herd on their side a numerical majority of blindly impressionable dolts and gulls who have for the most part no idea of what the whole circus is about.[6]

How little things have changed.

The first thing that should be done about this situation, in Lovecraft's view, is to restrict the vote 'to those able to pass rigorous educational examinations (emphasising civic and economic subjects) and scientific intelligence tests' ('Some Repetitions on the Times'). It need not be assumed that Lovecraft automatically included himself in this number; in 'Some Repetitions on the Times' he declares himself a 'rank layman' and goes on to say: 'No non-technician, be he artist, philosopher, or scientist, can even begin to judge the labyrinthine governmental problems with which these administrators must deal.' Lovecraft does not seem entirely aware of the difficulty of ensuring that these tests be fair to all, but he maintained that such a restriction of the vote would indeed be fair because—as we shall see presently—educational opportunities would be vastly broadened under his political scheme.

It is unfortunate that Lovecraft occasionally used the term 'fascism' to denote this conception; it does not help much that he says on one occasion, 'Do not judge the sort of fascism I advocate by any form now existing.'[7] Lovecraft never actually renounced Mussolini, but his support of him in the 1930s does not seem quite as ardent as it was when Mussolini first rose to power in 1922. The problem is, however, that by the 1930s the term 'fascism' connoted not only Mussolini but various English and United States extremists with whom Lovecraft had no intention of aligning himself. The

American fascists of the middle to late 1930s were, in Lovecraft's view, not so much dangerous radicals as mere buffoons who could do little harm to the political fabric. They were not by any means a co-ordinated group, but even individually they represented threats to the government with which both the administration and political thinkers (even armchair ones like Lovecraft) had to come to terms.

The first was the redoubtable Senator Huey P. Long of Louisiana. Elected governor in 1928, Long quickly achieved popularity by appealing for a radical redistribution of wealth. Then, in 1934, as a senator he formed the Share Our Wealth Society in an attempt to put his theories into practice. If it be thought that Long's political vision was actually similar to Lovecraft's in its union of economic socialism and political fascism, it should be made clear that Long was not by any means a socialist—he did not believe in collectivism but instead yearned nostalgically for a small-town America in which everyone would be an individualistic small business person—and his fascism was of a ruthless sort that rode roughshod over his opponents and in the end led to his being shot by an assassin on 8 September 1935; he died two days later.

Then there was the Reverend Charles E. Coughlin, who in his weekly radio programme ('The Golden Hour of the Little Flower') had, since 1930, fulminated against both Communism and capitalism, attacking bankers specifically. In late 1934 he conceived of a wealth distribution scheme by forming the National Union for Social Justice.

Lovecraft took frequent note of Long and Coughlin, and in the end he finally repudiated them—not for their economic policies (with which he was more in agreement than otherwise), but for their genuinely fascistic political tactics. But he never regarded them as serious threats. He writes airily in early 1937 that 'I doubt whether the growing Catholic–fascist movement will make much headway in America'[8] (an explicit reference to Coughlin) and later remarks, in regard to a broad group of pro-Nazi organizations in the United States:

> Granting the scant possibility of a Franco-like revolt of the Hoovers and Mellons and polite bankers, and conceding that —despite Coughlinism, the Black Legion, the Silver Shirts, and the K.K.K.—the soil of America is hardly very fertile for any variant of Nazism, it seems likely that the day of free and easy plutocracy in the United States is over.[9]

He might have been less sanguine had he seen how Coughlin—who was already becoming increasingly anti-Semitic by 1936—sloughed off his social justice pretence in 1938 and came out forthrightly as a pro-Nazi, attracting millions in the process.

Lovecraft knew that Roosevelt was trying to steer a middle course between right- and left-wing extremism; and on the whole he approved that course. Just after the 1932 election he remarks that a vote for the socialist Norman Thomas 'would have been simply thrown away'.[10] Nevertheless, although he yearned for Roosevelt to progress still farther and faster with reform, it quickly became obvious to him that the New Deal was the only series of measures that had any real hope of actually passing, given the violent resistance on both sides of the political spectrum. He referred to Coughlin, Long, and other radicals as 'salutary irritants'[11] who would help push Roosevelt more to the left (something that in fact happened following the midterm elections of 1934, which gave Congress a more liberal slant). But in early 1935 he was announcing that he wanted something 'considerably to the left of the New Deal',[12] although he did not think it was practicable; and by the summer of 1936 he expressed a naive irritation that the administration was 'too subservient to capitalism'[13]—as if Roosevelt had any intention of ushering in real socialism (even of a liberal, non-Marxist variety) instead of merely shoring up capitalism!

The death-knell of capitalism was indeed being rung by many political thinkers of the day, as was entirely natural in the wake of the Depression, capitalism's most signal disaster. John Dewey's thunderous declaration—'Capitalism must be destroyed'—is prototypical. Some of Lovecraft's younger colleagues—Frank Long, R. H. Barlow, Kenneth Sterling—were wholeheartedly espousing Communism, to the point that at the very end of his life Lovecraft expostulated in mock horror, 'Damme, but are all you kids going bolshevik on grandpa?'[14]

And yet, as time went on Lovecraft increasingly lost patience with the social and political conservatism of the middle-class milieu in which he found himself. He came to understand the *temperament* that led fiery youths like Long and Barlow to Communism without being himself entirely inclined in that direction. He knew that this leftward swing on the part of youths was a natural response to the increasing stodginess and reactionary tendencies of the other side:

As for the Republicans—how can one regard seriously a frightened, greedy, nostalgic huddle of tradesmen and lucky idlers who shut their eyes to history and science, steel their emotions against decent human sympathy, cling to sordid and provincial ideals exalting sheer acquisitiveness and condoning artificial hardship for the non-materially-shrewd, dwell smugly and sentimentally in a distorted dream-cosmos of outmoded phrases and principles and attitudes based on the bygone agricultural-handicraft world, and revel in (consciously or unconsciously) mendacious assumptions (such as the notion that *real liberty* is synonymous with the single detail of *unrestricted economic license*, or that a rational planning of resource-distribution would contravene some vague and mystical 'American heritage' ...) utterly contrary to fact and without the slightest foundation in human experience? Intellectually, the Republican idea deserves the tolerance and respect one gives to the dead.[15]

How little things have changed.

When the election actually occurred—with another landslide for Roosevelt against the hapless Alf Landon and a third-party candidate, William Lemke, a stooge of Coughlin and Francis E. Townsend, the proponent of old age pensions—Lovecraft was of course delighted. His last few months were perhaps spent in satisfaction, with the thought that Roosevelt could now continue his reforms and achieve a genuine moderate socialist state; it must have been a comforting thought as he lay dying.

As the 1930s advanced Lovecraft became more and more concerned with the place of art in modern society. As he matured he became convinced that art could not retreat unthinkingly into the past but must—as he himself had done on an intellectual level—come to some sort of terms with the machine age if it were to survive and remain a living force in society.

The central issue Lovecraft was facing was how to steer a middle course between 'high' culture, which in its radicalism was consciously being addressed to an increasingly small coterie of devotees, and 'popular' culture—notably the pulps—which was adhering to false, superficial, and outmoded standards through the inevitable moral conservatism such forms of culture have always displayed. This may be the primary reason for Lovecraft's lack of commercial success in his lifetime: his work was not conventional enough for the pulps but not daring enough (or daring enough in the right way) for the modernists. Lovecraft correctly recognized that capitalism and democracy gave rise to this split in the nineteenth century:

> Bourgeois capitalism gave artistic excellence and sincerity a death-blow by enthroning cheap *amusement-value* at the expense of that *intrinsic excellence* which only cultivated, non-acquisitive persons of assumed position can enjoy. The determinant market for written ... and other heretofore aesthetic material ceased to be a small circle of truly educated persons, but became a substantially larger ... crcle of mixed origin numerically dominated by crude, half-educated clods whose systematically perverted ideals ... prevented them from ever achieving the tastes and perspectives of the gentlefolk whose dress and speech and external manners they so assiduously mimicked. This herd of acquisitive boors brought up from the shop and the counting-house a complete set of artificial attitudes, oversimplifications, and mawkish sentimentalities which no sincere art or literature could gratify—and they so outnumbered the remaining educated gentlefolk that most of the purveying agencies became at once reoriented to them. Literature and art lost most of their market; and writing, painting, drama, etc. became engulfed more and more in the domain of *amusement enterprises.*[16]

The principal foe, again, is capitalism, in that it inculcates values that are actively hostile to artistic creation:

> in the past did capitalism award its highest benefits to such admittedly superior persons as Poe, Spinoza, Baudelaire, Shakespeare, Keats, and so on? Or is it just possible that the real beneficiaries of capitalism are *not* the truly superior, but merely *those who choose to devote their superiority to the single process of personal acquisition rather than to social service or to creative intellectual or aesthetic effort* ... those, and the lucky parasites who share or inherit the fruits of their narrowly canalised superiority?[17]

But what then is to be done? Even if economic reform is effected, how does one change a society's *attitude* in regard to the relative value of money as opposed to the development of personality? The solution was simple: education. The shorter working hours proposed in Lovecraft's economic scheme would allow for a radically increased leisure time for all citizens, which could be utilized profitably in education and aesthetic appreciation. As he states in 'Some Repetitions on the Times': 'Education ... will require amplification in order to meet the needs of a radically increased leisure among all classes of society. It is probable that the number of persons possessing a sound general culture will be greatly increased, with correspondingly good results to the civilisation.' This was a common proposal—or dream—among the more idealistic social reformers and intellectuals. Did Lovecraft really fancy that such a utopia of a broadly educated populace that was willing or able to enjoy the aesthetic fruits of civilization would actually come about? It certainly seems so; and yet, we cannot hold Lovecraft responsible for failing to predict either the spectacular recrudescence of capitalism in the generations following his own or the equally spectacular collapse of education that has produced a mass audience whose highest aesthetic experiences are pornography, television miniseries, and sporting events.

The interesting thing about Lovecraft's speculations of the 1930s is that they gradually enter into his fiction as well as his letters and essays. We have seen that 'The Mound' (1929–30) contains searching parallels between the political and cultural state of the underground mound denizens and Western civilization; and in *At the Mountains of Madness* (1931) there is a fleeting mention that the government of the Old Ones was probably socialistic. These tentative political discussions reach their culmination with 'The Shadow out of Time'. The Great Race is a true utopia, and in his description of its political and economic framework Lovecraft is manifestly offering his view as to the future of mankind:

> The Great Race seemed to form a single, loosely knit nation or league, with major institutions in common, though there were four definite divisions. The political and economic system of each unit was a sort of fascistic socialism, with major resources rationally distributed, and power delegated to a small governing board elected by the votes of all able to pass certain educational and psychological tests ...
>
> Industry, highly mechanised, demanded but little time from each citizen; and the abundant leisure was filled with intellectual and aesthetic activities of various sorts.

This and other passages can be seen as virtually identical to those in Lovecraft's later letters on the subject and with 'Some Repetitions on the Times'. The note about 'highly mechanised' industry is important in showing that Lovecraft has at last—as he had not done when he wrote 'The Mound' (1929–30) and even *At the Mountains of Madness*—fully accepted mechanization as an ineradicable aspect of modern society, and has devised a social system that will accommodate it.

The one area of Lovecraft's thought that has—justifiably—aroused the greatest outrage among later commentators is his attitude on race. My contention is, however, both that Lovecraft has been criticized for the wrong reasons and that, even though he clearly espoused views that are illiberal, intolerant, or plain wrong scientifically, his racism is at least logically separable from the rest of his philosophical and even political thought.

Lovecraft retained to the end of his days a belief in the biological inferiority of blacks and also of Australian aborigines, although it is not clear why he singled out this latter group. In any event, Lovecraft advocated an absolutely rigid colour line against intermarriage between blacks and whites, so as to guard against 'miscegenation'. This view was by no means uncommon in the 1920s, and many leading American biologists and psychologists wrote forebodingly about the possibility that racial intermixture could lead to biological abnormalities. Of course, laws against interracial marriage survived in the United States until an embarrassingly recent time.

But Lovecraft in the course of time was forced to back down increasingly from his claims to the superiority of the Aryan (or Nordic or Teuton) over other groups aside from blacks and aborigines. How, then, can he continue to defend segregation? He does so simply by asserting—from an illegitimate generalization of his own prejudices—a wildly exaggerated degree of incompatibility and hostility amongst different cultural groups. And there is a subtle but profound hypocrisy here also: Lovecraft trumpets 'Aryan' conquests over other races (European conquest of the American continent, to name only one example) as justified by the inherent strength and prowess of the race, but, when other 'races' or cultures—the French-Canadians in Woonsocket, the Italians and Portuguese in Providence, the Jews in New York—make analogous incursions into 'Aryan' territory, Lovecraft sees it as somehow contrary to Nature. He is backed into this corner by his claim that the Nordic is *'a master in the art of orderly living and group preservation'*[18]—and he therefore cannot account for the increasing heterogeneity of 'Nordic' culture.

Lovecraft is, of course, entirely at liberty to feel personally uncomfortable in the presence of aliens; he is even, I believe, at liberty to wish for a culturally and racially homogeneous society. This wish is in itself not pernicious, just as the wish for a racially and culturally diverse society—such as the United States has now become—is not in itself self-evidently virtuous. Each has its own advantages and drawbacks, and Lovecraft clearly preferred the advantages of homogeneity (cultural unanimity and continuity, respect for tradition) to its drawbacks (prejudice, cultural isolationism, fossilization). Where Lovecraft goes astray philosophically is in attributing his own sentiments to his 'race' or culture at large.

In my view, Lovecraft leaves himself most open to criticism on the issue of race not by the mere espousal of such views but by his lack of openmindedness on the issue, and more particularly his resolute unwillingness to study the most up-to-date findings on the subject from biologists, anthropologists, and other scientists of unquestioned authority who were, through the early decades of the century, systematically destroying each and every pseudo-scientific 'proof' of racialist theories. In every other aspect of his thought—metaphysics, ethics, aesthetics, politics—Lovecraft was constantly digesting new information (even if only through news-paper reports, magazine articles, and other informal sources) and readjusting his views accordingly. Only on the issue of race did his thinking remain relatively static. He never realized that his beliefs had been largely shaped by parental and societal influence, early reading, and outmoded late nineteenth-century science. The mere fact that he had to defend his views so vigorously and argumentatively in letters—especially to younger correspondents like Frank Long and J. Vernon Shea—should have encouraged him to rethink his position; but he never did so in any significant way.

The brute fact is that by 1930 every 'scientific' justification for racism had been demolished. The spearhead of the scientific opposition to racism was the anthropologist Franz Boas (1857–1942), but I find virtually no mention of him in any of Lovecraft's letters or essays. The intelligentsia—among whom Lovecraft surely would have wished to number himself—had also largely repudiated racist assumptions in their political and social thought. Indeed, such things as the classification of skulls by size or shape—which Lovecraft and Robert E. Howard waste much time debating in their letters of the 1930s—had been shown to be preposterous and unscientific even by the late nineteenth century.

And yet, ugly and unfortunate as Lovecraft's racial views are, they do not materially affect the validity of the rest of his philosophical thought. They may well enter into a significant proportion of his fiction (miscegenation and fear of aliens are clearly at the centre of such tales as 'The Lurking Fear', 'The Horror at Red Hook', and 'The Shadow over Innsmouth'), but I cannot see that they affect his metaphysical, ethical, aesthetic, or even his late political views in any meaningful way. These views do not stand or fall on racialist assumptions. I certainly have no desire to brush Lovecraft's racism under the rug, but I do not think that the many compelling positions he advocated as a thinker should be dismissed because of his clearly erroneous views on race.

If Lovecraft's racism is the one aspect of his thought that has been subject to the greatest censure, then within that aspect it is his qualified support of Hitler and his corresponding suspicion of Jewish influence in America that has—again justifiably—caused even greater outrage. He argued the matter at length with J. Vernon Shea in the early 1930s, and the late date of this discussion emphatically refutes the claims of many of Lovecraft's apologists that he somehow 'reformed' at the end of his life and shed many of the beliefs he had spouted so carelessly in his *Conservative* essays twenty years before. Some of his comments are acutely embarrassing:

> [Hitler's] vision is of course romantic & immature, & coloured with a fact-ignoring emotionalism ... There surely is an actual Hitler peril—yet that cannot blind us to the honest rightness of the man's basic urge ... I repeat that there is a great & pressing need behind every one of the major planks of Hitlerism—racial-cultural continuity, conservative cultural ideals, & an escape from the absurdities of Versailles. The crazy thing is not what Adolf wants, but the way he sees it & starts out to get it. I know he's a clown, but by God, I *like* the boy![19]

These points are elaborated at great length in this and other letters. According to Lovecraft, Hitler is right to suppress Jewish influence in German culture, since 'no settled & homogeneous nation ought (a) to admit enough of a decidedly alien race-stock to bring about an actual alteration in the dominant ethnic composition, or (b) tolerate the dilution of the culture-stream with emotional & intellectual elements alien to the original cultural impulse'. Hitler is,

Lovecraft believes, wrong in the extremism of his hostility toward anyone with even a small amount of Jewish blood, since it is culture rather than blood that should be the determining criterion.

The whole question of American and British support for Hitler is one that has received surprisingly little scholarly study. Certainly, Lovecraft was not alone among the intellectual classes prior to 1937 in expressing some approbation of Hitler; and just as certainly, Lovecraft cannot possibly be thought to be of the same stripe as the American pro-Nazi groups in the United States, much less such organizations as the Friends of the New Germany or the German-American Bund, who generally attracted a small number of disaffected German-Americans and were even operated for the most part by German Nazis. Lovecraft cannot even be lumped indiscriminately with the common run of American anti-Semites of the 1930s, most of whom were extreme political conservatives who sought to equate Jewishness with Bolshevism. My feeling is that Lovecraft came by his overall economic and political views, as well as his racial stance, by independent thought on the state of the nation and the world. His beliefs are so clearly and integrally an outgrowth of his previous thinking on these issues that the search for some single intellectual influence seems misguided.

Harry Brobst provides some evidence of Lovecraft's awareness of the horrors of Hitler's Germany toward the very end of his life. He recalls that a Mrs Shepherd (the downstairs neighbour of Lovecraft and Annie Gamwell at 66 College) was a German native and wished to return for a time to Germany. She did so, but (in Brobst's words) 'it was at that time that Nazism was beginning to flower, and she saw the Jews beaten, and she was so horrified, upset, distraught that she just left Germany and came back to Providence. And she told Mrs. Gamwell and Lovecraft about her experiences, and they were both very incensed about this.'[20] Lovecraft indeed remarks about the departure of Mrs Alice Shepherd in late July 1936. I find, however, no mention in any letters of her abrupt return, nor any expression of horror at any revelations she may have conveyed. But references to Hitler do indeed drop off radically in the last year of Lovecraft's life, so it is conceivable that Lovecraft, having heard accounts from Mrs Shepherd, simply shut up about the matter in the realization that he had been wrong. It would be a comforting thought.

Lovecraft's point about Jewish domination of German culture leads directly to his assessment of what he feels is happening in the

United States, specifically in its literary and publishing capital, New York:

> As for New York—there is no question but that its overwhelming Semitism has totally removed it from the American stream. Regarding its influence on literary & dramatic expression—it is not so much that the country is flooded directly with Jewish authors, as that Jewish publishers determine just which of our Aryan writers shall achieve print & position. That means that those of us who least express our own people have the preference. Taste is insidiously moulded along non-Aryan lines—so that, no matter how intrinsically good the resulting body of literature may be, it is a special, rootless literature which does not represent us.[21]

Lovecraft goes on to mention Sherwood Anderson and William Faulkner as writers who, 'delving in certain restricted strata, seldom touch on any chord to which the reader personally responds'. If this is not a case of generalizing from personal experience, I don't know what is! Newspaper reporting in New York also angers him:

> not a paper in New York dares to call its soul its own in dealing with the Jews & with social & political questions affecting them. The whole press is absolutely enslaved in that direction, so that on the whole length & breadth of the city *it is impossible to secure any public American utterance—any frank expression of the typical mind & opinions of the actual American people—on a fairly wide & potentially important range of topics* ... Gawd knows I have no wish to injure any race under the sun, but I *do* think that something ought to be done to free American expression from the control of *any* element which seeks to curtail it, distort it, or remodel it in any direction other than its natural course.[22]

But what *is* the 'natural course' of American expression? And why does Lovecraft axiomatically believe that he and people like him are the 'actual American people' (which means that others who do not share his views are necessarily 'un-American')? Lovecraft is again being haunted by the spectre of change: Faulkner and Sherwood Anderson don't write the way the more conservative novelists write or used to write, so they are deemed 'unnatural' or unrepresentative.

What Lovecraft wanted was simply *familiarity*—the familiarity of the milieu in a racially and culturally homogeneous Providence that he had experienced in youth. In stating that even art must satisfy our 'homesickness … for the things we have known' ('Heritage or Modernism'), Lovecraft is testifying to the homesickness he himself felt when, as an 'unassimilated alien'[23] in New York or even in latter-day Providence, he witnessed the increasing urbanization and racial heterogeneity of his region and his country. Racialism was for him a bulwark against acknowledging that his ideal of a purely Anglo-Saxon America no longer had any relevance and could never be recaptured.

More generally, the increasing racial and cultural heterogeneity of his society was for Lovecraft the chief symbol of *change*—change that was happening too fast for him to accept. The frequency with which, in his later years, he harps on this subject—'change is intrinsically undesirable';[24] 'Change is the enemy of everything really worth cherishing'[25]—speaks eloquently of Lovecraft's frantic desire for social stability and his quite sincere belief (one, indeed, that has something to recommend it) that such stability is a necessary precondition of a vital and profound culture.

Lovecraft's final years were characterised both by much hardship (painful rejections of his best tales and concomitant depression over the merit of his work; increasing poverty; and, toward the very end, the onset of his terminal illness) and by moments of joy (travels all along the eastern seaboard; the intellectual stimulus of correspondence with a variety of distinctive colleagues; increasing adulation in the tiny worlds of amateur journalism and fantasy fandom). But to the end, Lovecraft continued to wrestle, mostly in letters, with the fundamental issues of politics, economics, society, and culture, with a breadth of learning, acuity of logic, and a deep humanity born of wide observation and experience that could not have been conceived by the 'eccentric recluse' who had so timidly emerged from self-imposed hermitry in 1914. That his largely private discussions did not have any influence on the intellectual temper of the age is unfortunate; but his unceasing intellectual vigour, even as he was descending into the final stages of cancer, is as poignant a testimonial to his courage and his devotion to the life of the mind as anyone could wish. Lovecraft himself, at any rate, certainly did not think the effort wasted.

CHAPTER TWENTY

The End of One's Life (1935–37)

For the time being 'The Shadow out of Time' remained in manuscript; Lovecraft was so unsure of its quality that he didn't know whether to type it up or tear it up. Finally, in a kind of despair, he sent the notebook containing the handwritten draft to August Derleth at the end of February 1935—as if he no longer wished to look at it. Meanwhile the fifth proposal by a publisher to issue a collection of Lovecraft's stories emerged in mid-February—this time through the intercession of Derleth—but ended in a rejection, as Loring & Mussey declined on a collection of tales in July.

Lovecraft went to see Edward H. Cole in Boston on 3–5 May, and in spite of the unusually cold weather managed at least to get to beloved Marblehead. On 25 May Charles D. Hornig, the erstwhile editor of the *Fantasy Fan*, visited Lovecraft in Providence. By this time, however, he was already in the midst of planning for another grand southern tour—the last, as it happened, he would ever take. For in early May Barlow had invited him down to Florida for another stay of indefinite length. Lovecraft was naturally inclined to accept, and only money stood in the way; but by 29 May Lovecraft concluded optimistically, 'Counting sestertii, & I think I can make it!'[1]

Once again we do not know much of Lovecraft's activities during his unprecedently long stay with Barlow (9 June to 18 August). Correspondence to others is our sole guide, and this time we do not even have the supplements of any memoirs by Barlow himself. In a postcard to Donald and Howard Wandrei written in July, Lovecraft gives some idea of his activities:

> Programme much the same as last year ... Bob has built a cabin in an oak grove across the lake from the house, & is busy there with various printing projects—of some of which you'll hear later on ... Last month we explored a marvellous tropical river near the Barlow place. It is called Black Water Creek, & is lined on both sides by a cypress jungle with festoons of Spanish moss. Twisted roots claw at the water's

edge, & palms lean precariously on every hand. Vines & creepers—sunken logs—snakes & alligators—all the colour of the Congo or Amazon.[2]

Of the printing projects Lovecraft mentions, we know one in particular—an edition of Long's collected poetry written subsequent to *The Man from Genoa* (1926), entitled *The Goblin Tower*. Lovecraft helped to set type on this very slim pamphlet, which Barlow managed to print and bind by late October. Lovecraft took occasion to correct Long's faulty metre in some of the poems. Barlow was bursting with ideas for other projects, chiefly a collection of Clark Ashton Smith's poems entitled *Incantations*; but, as with so many other of his ambitious endeavours, this venture hung fire for years before finally coming to nothing.

One other idea Barlow had evolved at about this time was a volume of C. L. Moore's best stories. Catherine Lucile Moore (1911–87) first appeared in *Weird Tales* in November 1933 with the striking fantasy 'Shambleau'. She went on to publish several more stories in *Weird Tales* that evocatively combined exotic romance, even sexuality, with otherworldly fantasy. Barlow had Lovecraft get in touch with Moore about the proposed volume, and a very substantive correspondence ensued, Lovecraft continually beseeching Moore not to kowtow to pulp standards and to preserve her aesthetic independence, even if it meant economic losses in the short term. Had he lived longer, he would have taken heart in her subsequent career, for she became one of the most distinctive and respected voices in the next generation of science fiction and fantasy writers.

But perhaps the most important function that Barlow performed was not printing but typing. By mid-July Derleth had still given no report on the autograph manuscript of 'The Shadow out of Time'; and, as Barlow was enthusiastic about seeing it, Lovecraft asked Derleth to send it down to Florida. By early August Lovecraft was expressing a certain irritation that Barlow was apparently not making much of an effort to read the thing; but very shortly he was forced, delightedly, to eat his words. For in fact Barlow was surreptitiously preparing a typescript of the story.

Lovecraft was completely bowled over by Barlow's diligence and generosity in this undertaking. Although he generously wrote that Barlow's transcript was 'accurately typed',[3] he later admitted that there were a number of errors in it. Nevertheless, Lovecraft sent the typescript on the usual round of readers.

Lovecraft finally moved along on 18 August, spending some time in St Augustine, Charleston, Richmond, and other points before reaching New York on the 2nd. He finally reached home on 14 September.

One thing Lovecraft did in Charleston and Richmond was finish what he called a 'composite story'—a round-robin weird tale entitled 'The Challenge from Beyond'. This was the brainchild of Julius Schwartz, who wanted two round-robin stories of the same title, one weird and one science fiction, for the third anniversary issue of *Fantasy Magazine* (September 1935). The weird item was written successively by C. L. Moore, A. Merritt, Lovecraft, Robert E. Howard, and Frank Belknap Long. Lovecraft's segment is the only one that actually advances the plot; and in so doing he has cannibalized his own (as yet unpublished) 'Shadow out of Time' by introducing the notion of mind-exchange between human beings and some alien entities. The resulting tale is merely a literary curiosity, although the science fiction version is still worse.

Another story on which Lovecraft worked around this time— Duane W. Rimel's 'The Disinterment'—is, however, a very different proposition. This tale—very similar in atmosphere to some of Lovecraft's early macabre stories, especially 'The Outsider'—is to my mind either wholly written by Lovecraft or a remarkably faithful imitation of Lovecraft's style and manner. Rimel has emphatically maintained that the story is largely his, Lovecraft acting only as a polisher; and correspondence between the two men— especially Lovecraft's enthusiastic initial response to the story— seems to support this claim. In a letter to Rimel of 28 September 1935, Lovecraft does speak of making 'slight verbal changes' in the manuscript; but in the absence of the manuscript or typescript, it is difficult to know what this means. In the story Rimel (or Lovecraft) has taken the hackneyed 'mad doctor' trope and shorn it of its triteness and absurdity by a very restrained portrayal, one that suggests far more than it states. 'The Disinterment' was published in *Weird Tales* for January 1937.

In mid-October 1935 Lovecraft broke his self-imposed rule against collaboration by revising a story by William Lumley entitled 'The Diary of Alonzo Typer'. Lumley had produced a hopelessly illiterate draft of the tale—set in an abandoned house near Lumley's hometown of Buffalo—and sent it to Lovecraft, who, feeling sorry for the old codger, rewrote the story wholesale while still preserving as much of Lumley's conceptions and even his prose as possible. The result, however, is still a dismal failure. Lovecraft feels the need to supply a suitably cataclysmic ending, so he depicts the narrator coming upon the locus of horror in the basement of the house, only to be seized by a monster at the end while hero-ically (or absurdly) writing in his diary: 'Too late—cannot help self—black paws materialise—am dragged away toward the cellar.' Undeterred, Lumley enterprisingly sent the story to Farnsworth Wright, who accepted it in early December for $70.00; Lovecraft magnanimously let Lumley keep the entire sum. The story was not published in *Weird Tales*, however, until February 1938.

Lovecraft may have been in a generous mood at this time because of some remarkable financial developments of his own. Probably during his stay in New York in early September, Julius Schwartz had come to a gathering of the weird fiction gang at Donald Wandrei's apartment. Schwartz, who was attempting to establish himself as an agent in the weird and science fiction fields, had been in touch with F. Orlin Tremaine, editor of *Astounding*, who wished to broaden the scope of the magazine to include some weird or weird/science material. Schwartz asked Lovecraft whether he had any tales that might fit into this purview, and Lovecraft replied that *At the Mountains of Madness* had been rejected by Wright and had not been submitted elsewhere. Schwartz eventually took the story to Tremaine, probably in late October. Here is his account of what occurred:

> The next time I went up to Tremaine, I said, roughly, 'I have in my hands a 35,000 word story by H. P. Lovecraft.' So he smiled and said roughly to the equivalent, 'You'll get a check on Friday.' Or 'It's sold!' …
>
> Now I'm fairly convinced that Tremaine never read the story. Or if he tried to, he gave up.[4]

What this shows is that Lovecraft was by this time sufficiently well known in the weird/science fiction pulp field that Tremaine did not even need to read the story to accept it; Lovecraft's name on a major work—whose length would require it to be serialized over several issues—was felt to be a sufficient drawing card. Tremaine was true to his word: he paid Schwartz $350.00; after keeping his $35.00 agent's fee, Schwartz sent the rest to Lovecraft.

Lovecraft was of course pleased at this turn of events, but in less than a week he would have reason to be still more pleased. In early November he learned that Donald Wandrei had submitted 'The

Shadow out of Time'—which presumably had found its way to him on Lovecraft's circulation list—to Tremaine, and that story was also accepted, for $280.00. In all likelihood Tremaine scarcely read this tale either.

The financial boon for Lovecraft was certainly marked: he puts it in graphic terms when he writes, 'I was never closer to the bread-line than this year.'[5] Aside from $105 for 'Through the Gates of the Silver Key' and $32.50 from the London agency Curtis Brown for a proposed reprinting of 'The Music of Erich Zann' that never came to pass, Lovecraft had had no sales of original fiction in 1934 or 1935. We shall shortly see that even these two welcome cheques from Street & Smith could scarcely save Lovecraft and Annie from severe economies in the coming spring.

Lovecraft's jubilation at the *Astounding* sales would later turn sour when he saw the actual stories in print; but that was months in the future. Just as a rejection—or even an unfavourable report from an associate—would plunge Lovecraft into depression and self-doubt about his abilities as a writer, so this double acceptance directly stimulated him into renewed composition. On 5–9 November he reeled off a new tale, 'The Haunter of the Dark'.

This last original story by Lovecraft came about almost as a whim. Robert Bloch had written a story, 'The Shambler from the Stars', in the spring of 1935, in which a character—never named, but clearly meant to be Lovecraft—is killed off. Lovecraft was taken with the story, and, when it was published in *Weird Tales* (September 1935), a reader, B. M. Reynolds, praised it and had a suggestion to make: 'Contrary to previous criticism, Robert Bloch deserves plenty of praise for *The Shambler from the Stars*. Now why doesn't Mr. Lovecraft return the compliment, and dedicate a story to the author?'[6] Lovecraft took up the offer, and his story tells of one Robert Blake who ends up a glassy-eyed corpse staring out his study window.

But the flippancy of the genesis of 'The Haunter of the Dark' should not deceive us; it is one of Lovecraft's more substantial tales. It tells of Robert Blake, a young writer of weird fiction, who comes to Providence for a period of writing, but who becomes fascinated with an abandoned church in the Italian district known as Federal Hill. Entering the place, Blake finds a curious object—a metal box containing a curious gem or mineral—as well as the decaying skeleton of an old newspaper reporter whose notes Blake reads. These notes speak of the ill-regarded Starry Wisdom church, and a 'Shining Trapezohedron' and a 'Haunter of the Dark' that cannot exist in light. Blake concludes that the object on the pillar is the Shining Trapezohedron. Suddenly terrified, he closes the lid of the object and flees the place. This action unwittingly releases a monster confined in the belfry of the church; and this creature—an avatar of Nyarlathotep—escapes fleetingly from its confinement during a black-out, but perishes just at the moment when it fuses its mind with that of Blake, who is staring at it out of his window. Blake dies also.

Many of the surface details of the plot were taken directly from Hanns Heinz Ewers's 'The Spider', which Lovecraft read in Dashiell Hammett's *Creeps by Night* (1931). This story involves a man who becomes fascinated with a strange woman he sees through his window in a building across from his own, until finally he seems to lose hold of his own personality.

A great proportion of the landmarks described in the story are based upon actual sites. The view from Blake's study, as is well known, is nothing more than a poignant description of what Lovecraft saw out of his own study at 66 College Street. The church that figures so prominently in the tale is (or, rather, was) also real: it is St John's Catholic Church on Atwell's Avenue in Federal Hill, destroyed in 1992. It was, in Lovecraft's day, very much a going concern, being the principal Catholic church in the area. The description of the interior and belfry of the church is quite accurate. Lovecraft heard that the steeple had been destroyed by lightning in late June of 1935 (he was not there at the time, being in Florida visiting Barlow); and instead of rebuilding the steeple, the church authorities decided merely to put a conical cap on the brick tower. This incident no doubt started his imagination working.

The end of 1935 saw Lovecraft's fourth—and last—Christmas visit to Frank Long and the rest of the New York gang. Amid the usual round of socializing with old friends, he met some new figures. He met Seabury Quinn for the first time since 1931, and attended a dinner of the American Fiction Guild, an organization that Hugh B. Cave had for years been trying to get him to join. On two occasions Lovecraft went to the new Hayden Planetarium of the American Museum of Natural History. Barlow surprised him with a unique Christmas gift—a forty-two-copy printing of *The Cats of Ulthar*.

Another booklet that seems to have emerged at this time is *Charleston*. This is a mimeographed pamphlet that exists in two 'editions', if such they can be called. H. C. Koenig was planning a trip to Charleston in early 1936 and asked Lovecraft for a brief description of some of the highlights of the place. Lovecraft wrote a long letter on 12 January that combined a potted history of Charleston with a specific walking tour. This letter merely paraphrases and abridges Lovecraft's superb unpublished 1930 travelogue, 'An Account of Charleston', leaving out the archaic usages and also some of the more interesting but idiosyncratic personal asides. Koenig was so taken with this letter that he typed it up and mimeographed it, running off probably fewer than twenty-five copies. When Lovecraft received the item, he found a number of mistranscriptions which he wished to correct; meanwhile Koenig had asked Lovecraft to rewrite the beginning and ending so as to transform the piece from a letter into an essay. After these corrections and changes were made, Koenig ran off about thirty to fifty copies of the new version, 'binding' it (as he had done with the first version) in a cardboard folder.

Not long after returning from New York, Lovecraft—although overwhelmed by revision work, a growing feud in the NAPA, and (ominously) a severe case of what he called 'grippe'—still managed to find time to lapse into one more collaborative fiction venture— this time with Kenneth Sterling (1920–95), a young fan who had introduced himself to Lovecraft in March 1935. The result is the interesting if insubstantial science fiction tale 'In the Walls of Eryx'.

Sterling has stated that the idea of the invisible maze was his, and that this core idea was adapted from Edmond Hamilton's celebrated story (which Lovecraft liked), 'The Monster-God of Mamurth' (*Weird Tales*, August 1926), which concerns an invisible building in the Sahara Desert. Sterling wrote a draft of six to eight thousand words; Lovecraft entirely rewrote the story ('in very short order', Sterling declares), making it about twelve thousand words in the process.[7] Sterling's account suggests that the version as we have it is entirely Lovecraft's prose, and indeed it reads as such; but one suspects (Sterling's original draft is not extant) that, as with the collaborated tales with Price and Lumley, Lovecraft tried to preserve as much of Sterling's own prose, and certainly his ideas, as possible.

The authors have made the tale amusing by devising nasty in-jokes on certain mutual colleagues (e.g., farnoth-flies = Farnsworth Wright of *Weird Tales*; effjay weeds and wriggling akmans = Forrest J Ackerman); I suspect these are Lovecraft's jokes. The narrative, however, turns into a *conte cruel* when the hapless protagonist, trapped in the invisible maze whose opening he can no longer locate, reveals his deteriorating mental and physical condition in the diary he writes as he vainly seeks to escape.

The story was apparently submitted to *Astounding Stories*, *Blue Book*, *Argosy*, *Wonder Stories*, and perhaps *Amazing Stories*. Finally it was published in *Weird Tales* for October 1939.

Less than a month after Lovecraft recovered from his bout of 'grippe', he reported to his correspondents that his aunt Annie was stricken with a much severer case, one that ultimately involved hospitalization (beginning 17 March), then a two-week stay at a private convalescent home (7–21 April). Here is one more of the relatively few occasions in which Lovecraft is guilty of deceit, but in this case it is entirely understandable. In fact, Annie Gamwell was suffering from breast cancer, and her hospital stay involved a mastectomy. It is not a subject someone like Lovecraft would wish to discuss openly even to close associates.

The result for Lovecraft was a complete disruption of his schedule. At one point he states rather harrowingly: 'My own programme is totally shot to pieces, & I am about on the edge of a nervous breakdown. I have so little power of concentration that it takes me about an hour to do what I can ordinarily do in five minutes—& my eyesight is acting like the devil.'[8]

The one thing Annie's illness and hospital stay brought out was the severe state of the family finances—something made graphically real by one of the saddest documents ever written by Lovecraft, a diary that he kept while Annie was away and which he would bring to her every few days in order to give an account of his activities.[9] Here we receive an unvarnished account of the severe economies—especially in food—which Lovecraft was compelled to practise at this time.

On 20 March we learn that Lovecraft had gone back to a bad habit of Clinton Street days—eating canned food cold—for we now hear of his 'experiment[ing] with *heating*' a can of chile con carne. It gets worse. On March 22 some twenty-minute eggs plus half a can of baked beans make 'a sumptuous repast'. Around 24 March Lovecraft feels the necessity to use canned goods that had been lying around for at least three years, since they had been brought over from Barnes Street. On 29 March he begins using up some old Chase & Sanborn coffee that would otherwise go bad, even though he likes Postum better. Dinner on 30 March was cold hot dogs, biscuits, and mayonnaise.

On 10 April Lovecraft began experimenting with a tin of ten-year-old Rich's Cocoa and found that it had 'acquired an earthy taste': 'However, I shall use it up somehow.' He was true to his word: over the next three days he mixed it with condensed milk and resolutely drank it. Afterward he found a tin of Hershey's Cocoa, a nearly full container of salt from Barnes Street, and a can of diced carrots on the top shelf of a kitchen cabinet and set these down for eventual use, also beginning to eat some old canned brown bread, which seemed all right.

The entire effect of all this economizing and eating of old and possibly spoiled food can only be conjectured. Is it any wonder that on 4 April Lovecraft admits to feeling so tired during the middle of the day that he had to rest instead of going out, and that on 13 April he finds, after a nap, that 'I was too weak & drowsy to do anything'? It should, of course, be emphasized that the meals prepared during this period did not represent his normal eating habits, although these were ascetic enough. I shall have more to say about this later.

At exactly this point, Lovecraft was distracted by another debacle that nearly drove him to give up writing altogether. In mid-February he had seen the first instalment of *At the Mountains of Madness* in the February 1936 *Astounding* and professed to like it; in particular, he had words of praise for the interior illustrations by Howard Brown. But the attractiveness of the illustrations soon soured when Lovecraft actually studied the text.

When he consulted the third and last instalment (April 1936), he discovered the serious tampering that the *Astounding* editors had performed on the story, particularly the last segment. Lovecraft went into a towering rage:

> But hell & damnation! ... In brief, that goddamn'd dung of a hyaena Orlin Tremaine has given the 'Mts.' the worst hashing-up any piece of mine ever received—in or out of Tryout! I'll be hanged if I can consider the story as published at all—the last instalment is a joke, with whole passages missing ...
>
> I pass over certain affected changes in sentence-structure, but see red again when I think of the *paragraphing*. Venom of Tsathoggua! Have you seen the damn thing? *All my paragraphs cut up into little chunks* like the juvenile stuff the other pulp hacks write. Rhythm, emotional modulations, & minor climactic effects thereby destroyed ... Tremaine has tried to

make 'snappy action' stuff out of old-fashioned leisurely prose ...

But the *supremely* intolerable thing is the way the text is cut in the last instalment—to get an old serial out of the way quickly. Whole passages ... are left out—the result being to decrease vitality & colour, & make the action mechanical. So many important details & impressions & touches of sensation are missing from the concluding parts that the effect is that of a flat ending. After all the adventure & detail *before* the encounter with the shoggoth in the abyss, the characters are shot up to the surface without any of the gradual experiences & emotions which make the reader *feel* their return to the world of man from the nighted aeon-old world of the Others. All sense of the *duration & difficulty* of the exhausted climb is lost when it is dismissed objectively in only a few words, with no hint of the fugitives' reactions to the scenes through which they pass.[10]

What this passage shows is how conscious Lovecraft was of the emotional and psychological effect of prose and the need (in serious literature as opposed to pulp hackwork) to ground a weird or wonder tale in the most careful realism both of scene and of mood. Perhaps Lovecraft was trying to have his cake and eat it too in writing a story containing very advanced philosophical and scientific conceptions in 'old-fashioned leisurely prose' and then expecting it to appear intact in a science fiction pulp magazine.

What Lovecraft therefore did was to purchase three copies of each instalment and laboriously correct the text, either by writing in the missing portions and connecting the paragraphs together by pencil or by eliminating the excess punctuation by scratching it out with a penknife. This whole procedure took the better part of four days in early June. All this may seem somewhat anal-retentive, but Lovecraft wished to lend these three copies to colleagues who had not seen the typescript and would otherwise be reading only the adulterated *Astounding* text.

On top of this, the story itself was received relatively poorly by the readers of the magazine. This negative response has perhaps been exaggerated by later critics, but certainly there were a sufficient number of readers who failed to understand the point of the tale or felt it inappropriate for *Astounding*. Robert Thompson lays in with pungent sarcasm: 'I am glad to see the conclusion to *At the Mountains of Madness* for reasons that would not be pleasant to Mr.

Lovecraft.' But Cleveland C. Soper, Jr, is the most devastating: 'why in the name of science-fiction did you ever print such a story as *At the Mountains of Madness* by Lovecraft? Are you in such dire straits that you *must* print this kind of drivel? … If such stories as this … are what is to constitute the future yarns of Astounding Stories, then heaven help the cause of science-fiction!'

'The Shadow out of Time' appeared in the June 1936 issue of *Astounding*. Lovecraft incredibly says that 'It doesn't seem even nearly as badly mangled as the Mts.',[11] and the one surviving annotated copy of the issue bears relatively few corrections; but the recently unearthed autograph manuscript makes it abundantly clear that this story suffered the same reparagraphing that *At the Mountains of Madness* received. Other errors are apparently due to Barlow's inability to read Lovecraft's handwriting when he prepared the typescript. It is a mystery why Lovecraft did not complain more vociferously about the corruption of this text, even though no actual passages were omitted. My feeling is that he may have felt so indebted to both Barlow (for typing the story) and Wandrei (for submitting it) that any complaints might have struck him as a sign of ingratitude. In any event, in a very short time other matters would distract him from such a relatively harmless matter.

'The Shadow out of Time' was received much more unfavourably than *At the Mountains of Madness* by readers. The August 1936 issue (the only one that contains any significant comment on the story) contains a barrage of criticism. Some individuals, however, either came to Lovecraft's defence in regard to the attacks received by *At the Mountains of Madness* or had generous praise for the new story. These latter comments negate the claim that Lovecraft's work was universally panned in *Astounding*.

Lovecraft, however, had little time to bother with the reaction of his work in the magazine: he knew that he was not likely to write very much more that would find favour with *Astounding*. In any case, other events closer to home were occupying his attention.

The only viable amateur organization, the NAPA, was reaching unheard-of levels of spite and vindictiveness. The locus of this new feuding was Hyman Bradofsky (b. 1906), whose *Californian* offered unprecedented space for lengthy prose contributions and whom Lovecraft had supported in his successful bid for the presidency of the NAPA for the 1935–36 term.

I am not entirely clear why Bradofsky created so much hostility among other members. He was evidently accused of being high-handed in various procedural matters relating to the NAPA constitution, and he himself apparently responded to criticism in a somewhat testy manner. Whether Bradofsky's being Jewish had anything to do with it is similarly unclear; I suspect that this was a factor, although Lovecraft never acknowledges it. In any case, it is certainly to Lovecraft's credit that he came to Bradofsky's defence, since by all accounts many of the attacks upon him were highly unjust, capricious, and snide.

Lovecraft's chief response was an essay written on 4 June, entitled 'Some Current Motives and Practices'. In it Lovecraft censures Bradofsky's opponents—or, rather, the thoroughly despicable tactics they are using against him—refutes the attacks by vindicating Bradofsky's conduct, and in general pleads for a return to civilized standards in amateurdom. Lovecraft arranged with Barlow to mimeograph the essay, which would be sent to all NAPA members. Barlow must have distributed the item by the end of June. I cannot sense that it had any particular effect.

In early June Robert E. Howard wrote to his friend Thurston Tolbert: 'My mother is very low. I fear she has not many days to live.'[12] He was correct: on the morning of 11 June, Hester Jane Ervin Howard fell into a coma from which her doctors said she would never emerge. Howard got into his car and shot himself in the head with a gun. He died eight hours later; his mother died the next day, leaving Howard's aged father, Dr I. M. Howard, doubly bereaved. Robert E. Howard was thirty years old.

At a time when telephones were not as common as now, the news spread relatively slowly. Lovecraft heard of it only around 19 June, when he received a postcard written three days earlier by C. L. Moore. He got the full story a few days later from Dr Howard. Lovecraft was overwhelmed with shock and grief:

> Damnation, what a loss! ... I can't understand the tragedy—for although R E H had a moody side expressed in his resentment against civilisation (the basis of our perennial and voluminous epistolary controversy), I always thought that this was a more or less impersonal sentiment ... He himself seemed to me pretty well adjusted—in an environment he loved, with plenty of congenial souls ... to talk and travel with, and with parents whom he obviously idolised. His mother's pleural illness imposed a great strain upon both him and his father, yet I cannot think that this would be

sufficient to drive his tough-fibred nervous system to self-destructive extremes.[13]

In the short term Lovecraft assisted Dr Howard as best he could, by sending various items—including his letters from Howard—to a memorial collection at Howard Payne College in Brownwood, Texas. Lovecraft's own letters to Howard met a more unfortunate fate, and appear to have been inadvertently destroyed by Dr Howard some time in the late 1940s. But very large—perhaps nearly complete—extracts of them had been transcribed under August Derleth's direction; a relatively small proportion of them was actually published in the *Selected Letters*. A joint Lovecraft–Howard correspondence would be very illuminating.

Almost immediately Lovecraft wrote a poignant memoir and brief critical appraisal, 'In Memoriam: Robert Ervin Howard', that appeared in *Fantasy Magazine* for September 1936. R. H. Barlow wrote a touching sonnet, 'R. E. H.', that formed his first and last appearance in *Weird Tales* (October 1936). That issue contained a wealth of tributes to Howard in the letters column, one of which was of course from Lovecraft.

Various outings in spring and summer and visits by a number of friends old and new during the latter half of the year made 1936 not quite the disaster it had been up to then. The heat of summer was anomalously late in arriving, but the week of 8 July finally brought temperatures in the 90s and saved Lovecraft 'from some sort of general breakdown'.[14] On 11 July he took a boat trip to Newport, doing considerable writing on the lofty cliffs overlooking the ocean.

As for guests, first on the agenda was Maurice W. Moe, who had not seen Lovecraft since the latter's fat days of 1923. Moe came with his son Robert for a visit on 18–19 July, and, since Robert had come in his car, they had convenient transport for all manner of sightseeing. They went to the old fishing village of Pawtuxet (then already absorbed into the Providence city limits), drove through Roger Williams Park, and visited the Warren–Bristol area that Robert and Lovecraft had seen in March of the previous year. At Warren they had an all-ice-cream dinner.

On 28 July no less important a guest arrived than R. H. Barlow, who was forced to leave his Florida home because of family disruptions that ultimately sent him to live with relatives in Leavenworth, Kansas. Barlow stayed more than a month in Providence, taking up quarters at the boarding-house behind 66 College and not leaving until 1 September. During this time he was quite unremitting in his demands on Lovecraft's time, but the latter felt obliged to humour him in light of the superabundant hospitality he himself had received in Florida in 1934 and 1935.

Still another visitor descended upon Providence on 5 August—Adolphe de Castro, who had just been to Boston to scatter his wife's ashes in the sea. By now a broken man—in his seventies, with no money, and his beloved wife dead—de Castro was still trying to foist various unrealistic projects upon Lovecraft. Trying to cheer the old boy up, Lovecraft and Barlow took him on 8 August to St John's Churchyard in Benefit Street, where the spectral atmosphere—and the fact that Poe had been there courting Sarah Helen Whitman ninety years before—impelled the three men to write acrostic 'sonnets' on the name Edgar Allan Poe. (These were, of course, one line shorter than an actual sonnet.) Of these three Barlow's may well be the best. But de Castro was the canniest of the bunch, for he later revised his poem and submitted it to *Weird Tales*, where it was quickly accepted. When Lovecraft and Barlow learnt this, they too submitted their poems—but Farnsworth Wright wanted to use only one. Lovecraft and Barlow were forced to dump their pieces on a fan magazine, the *Science-Fantasy Correspondent*, where they appeared in the March–April 1937 issue.

Another literary project on which Lovecraft and Barlow probably worked during his stay in Providence was 'The Night Ocean'. We are now in a position to gauge the precise degree of Lovecraft's contribution to this tale, as the manuscript has recently resurfaced. It shows that Lovecraft only touched up the prose here and there, making substantial improvements but basically merely 'copy editing' the text; as it stands, the story is at least 90 per cent Barlow's. Barlow had been progressing remarkably as a writer: his 'A Dim-Remembered Story' (*Californian*, summer 1936) is a superbly crafted tale but one that does not seem to bear any revisory hand by Lovecraft at all. Lovecraft waxed enthusiastic about it when he read it in manuscript. 'The Night Ocean'—published in the winter 1936 *Californian*—is an even finer work. Of all the tales written by Lovecraft's colleagues, it comes the closest to capturing the essential spirit of the weird tale, as Lovecraft wrote of some of Blackwood's works in 'Supernatural Horror in Literature': 'Here art and restraint in narrative reach their very highest development, and an impression of lasting poignancy is produced without a single strained passage or a single false note ... Plot is everywhere negligible, and atmosphere reigns untrammelled.'

Lovecraft's old amateur colleague Anne Tillery Renshaw, who had gone from being a professor to running her own school, The Renshaw School of Speech, in Washington, D.C., resurfaced at this time. In early 1936 she wished him to do revision and editing on a booklet she was writing entitled *Well Bred Speech*, designed for her adult education classes. Lovecraft was eager to work on the project, not only because it would be intrinsically interesting but because it would presumably bring in revenue at a time when revision work was fairly lean and sporadic.

Lovecraft received at least a partial draft of the text by mid-February, and came to realize that 'the job is somewhat ampler than I had expected—involving the furnishing of original elements as well as the revision of a specific text'; but—in spite of his aunt's illness at this time—he was willing to undertake the task if he received clear instructions on how much expansion he should do. He breezily adds, 'Rates can be discussed later—I fancy that any figure you would quote (with current precedent in mind) would be satisfactory.'[15] Later, after all the work was finished, he felt that Renshaw would be a cheapskate if she paid him anything less than $200. In the end, he received only $100, but this seems to have been his own fault, since his own final price was $150, which he reduced to $100 because of his tardiness.

Lovecraft initially tried to meet Renshaw's deadline of 1 May, but with all his troubles of the spring and summer this became quite unfeasible. Faced with a new deadline of 1 October, Lovecraft worked for *sixty hours without a break* in mid-September and somehow managed to get the thing done.

Much of both Renshaw's and Lovecraft's work on *Well Bred Speech* survives in manuscript, and allows us to gauge precisely how much each contributed to most parts of the text. The result is, however, a mediocre work, even with Lovecraft's additions. He has added most significantly to chapters I (The Background of Speech), III (Words Frequently Mispronounced), VI (Bromides Must Go [on clichés]), and X (What Shall I Read?). But much of this material was excised in the published version. The final chapter (published posthumously as 'Suggestions for a Reading Guide') has been gutted, in particular the last section—covering recent books on the sciences.

The chapter as a whole (as Lovecraft wrote it) is a fairly sound beginner's guide to both literature and scholarship up to his day.

In his final year Lovecraft continued to attract new—and mostly young—correspondents who, unaware of his increasing ill health, were thrilled to receive actual letters from this giant of weird fiction. Most of them continued to reach him through *Weird Tales*, but several got in touch through the increasingly complex network of the science fiction and fantasy fan circuit.

Among the most promising of these was Henry Kuttner (1915–58). A friend of Robert Bloch's, he had published only a single poem in *Weird Tales* before writing to Lovecraft early in 1936. Several colleagues thought that Lovecraft had either ghostwritten or extensively revised Kuttner's 'The Graveyard Rats' (*Weird Tales*, March 1936), but this story had already been accepted before Lovecraft heard from Kuttner. Kuttner had, however, by this time already written a tale whose first draft—rejected by *Weird Tales*—may have been consciously Lovecraftian. In his second letter to Kuttner, on 12 March, Lovecraft offers a lengthy criticism of 'The Salem Horror'; and it is clear that Kuttner made major changes in the story based upon these comments. Kuttner's geographical, historical, and architectural knowledge of Salem was all wrong, and Lovecraft set about correcting it; his letter is full of drawings of representative Salem houses, a map of the city, and even sketches of various types of headstones found in the older cemeteries. Other parts of Lovecraft's letter suggest that significant overhauling to the basic plot and incidents of the story was also done.

One small detail in Lovecraft's letters to Kuttner proved to be of great moment in the subsequent history of weird, fantasy, and science fiction. In May he casually asked Kuttner to pass on some photographs of Salem and Marblehead to C. L. Moore once Kuttner himself had finished with them; and it was in this way that Moore and Kuttner became acquainted. Marrying in 1940, the couple jointly wrote some of the most distinguished work of the 'Golden Age' of science fiction.

One of the most distinctive of Lovecraft's late associates—not so much for what he accomplished at the time as for what he did later—was Willis Conover, Jr (1921–96). In the spring of 1936, as a fifteen-year-old boy living in the small town of Cambridge, Maryland, Conover had conceived the idea of a magazine, the *Science-Fantasy Correspondent*. In addition to publishing the work of fans,

Conover wished to lend prestige to his magazine by soliciting minor pieces from professionals. He got in touch with Lovecraft in July, and later expressed regret that the *Fantasy Fan* serialization of 'Supernatural Horror in Literature' had ended so abruptly. Lovecraft casually suggested that Conover continue the serialization in his own magazine from the point where it had left off (the middle of chapter eight); Conover jumped at the idea. This item could not be accommodated in the first issue of the *Science-Fantasy Correspondent* (November–December 1936), but by September Lovecraft had already sent Conover the same annotated copy of the *Recluse* (with additions written on separate sheets) that he had lent to (and received back from) Hornig.

Shortly after this time, however, Conover took over Julius Schwartz's *Fantasy Magazine*, since Schwartz wished to abandon fan editing to become a full-time agent in the science fiction field. Conover then decided to reprint 'Supernatural Horror in Literature' from the beginning. The second issue of the *Science-Fantasy Correspondent* was dated January–February 1937, but did not contain any segment of the essay. No more issues of the magazine appeared; but some of the material was later transferred to Stickney's *Amateur Correspondent*, including 'Notes on Writing Weird Fiction'.

We know so much about the relationship between Conover and Lovecraft—which is, in all frankness, a fairly minor one in the totality of Lovecraft's life, although clearly it was significant to Conover—not only because Lovecraft's letters to him survive but because of the volume Conover published in 1975 entitled *Lovecraft at Last*. This book is not only one of the finest examples of modern book design, but a poignant, even wrenching testimonial to the friendship between a middle-aged—and dying—man and a young boy who idolized him.

Two other fan editors with whom Lovecraft exchanged a few letters were James Blish (1921–75) and William Miller, Jr (b. 1921), two youths living in East Orange, New Jersey. Blish went on to become one of the most important science fiction writers of his generation. Lovecraft's influence on him cannot be said to be especially significant, but Blish seems to have remembered his brief association for the whole of his own sadly abbreviated life.

In addition to writers, editors, and publishers, Lovecraft also heard from weird artists. Chief among these was Virgil Finlay (1914–71), whose work in *Weird Tales* Lovecraft had admired for several months prior to coming in touch with him. Finlay is indeed now recognized as perhaps the greatest pictorial artist to emerge from the pulps, and his stunning pen-and-ink work is unmistakable in its precision and imaginative scope. Lovecraft first heard from him in September 1936, and their correspondence was cordial even though Lovecraft in the end wrote only five letters and one postcard to him. Willis Conover had secretly arranged for Finlay to draw the celebrated portrait of Lovecraft as an eighteenth-century gentleman to head the first instalment of 'Supernatural Horror in Literature' in the *Science-Fantasy Correspondent*, a portrait that, after the demise of that fanzine, appeared on the cover of *Amateur Correspondent* for April–May 1937.

In November 1936 Lovecraft heard from an individual whom he correctly identified as 'a genuine find'.[16] Fritz Leiber, Jr (1910–92) was the son of the celebrated Shakespearian actor Fritz Leiber, Sr, whom Lovecraft had seen around 1912 playing in Robert Mantell's company when it came to the Providence Opera House. The son was also interested in drama, but was increasingly turning toward literature. He had been reading the weird and science fiction pulps from an early age, and later he testified that 'The Colour out of Space' in the September 1927 *Amazing* 'gave me the gloomy creeps for weeks'.[17] Then, when *At the Mountains of Madness* and 'The Shadow out of Time' appeared in *Astounding*, Leiber's interest in Lovecraft was renewed and augmented—perhaps because these works probed that borderline between horror and science fiction which Leiber himself would later explore in his own work. And yet, he himself was too diffident to write to Lovecraft, so his wife Jonquil did so via *Weird Tales*; for a time Lovecraft was corresponding quasi-separately to both of them.

In mid-December Leiber sent Lovecraft a novella or short novel, 'Adept's Gambit'. The work profoundly impressed Lovecraft. This was the first tale of Fafhrd and the Gray Mouser—two swashbuckling characters (modelled upon Leiber himself and his friend Harry O. Fischer, with whom Lovecraft also briefly corresponded) who roamed some nebulous fantastic realm in search of adventure—and Lovecraft wrote a long letter commenting in detail about it and praising it effusively. The published version of the story (in Leiber's collection, *Night's Black Agents*, 1947) apparently differs somewhat from the version Lovecraft saw, hence Leiber presumably revised it substantially along the lines Lovecraft recommended.

Leiber has testified frequently and eloquently to the importance of his brief but intense relationship with Lovecraft. Writing in 1958, he confessed: 'Lovecraft is sometimes thought of as having been a lonely man. He made my life far less lonely, not only during the brief half year of our correspondence but during the twenty years after.'[18] Leiber's subsequent career—with such landmark works of fantasy and science fiction as *Gather, Darkness!* (1950), *Conjure Wife* (1953), *The Big Time* (1958), *A Specter Is Haunting Texas* (1969), *Our Lady of Darkness* (1977), and dozens of Fafhrd and Gray Mouser stories—is as distinguished as that of any writer in these fields during the past half-century. He learned much from Lovecraft, but, like the best of Lovecraft's associates and disciples, he became his own man and his own writer.

Late in 1936 Lovecraft finally saw something he never thought he would see—a published book bearing his name. But predictably, the entire venture was, from first to last, an error-riddled debacle. It is little consolation that *The Shadow over Innsmouth* has, by virtue of its being the only actual book published and released in Lovecraft's lifetime, become a valued collectors' item.

William L. Crawford had a variety of plans for issuing either *At the Mountains of Madness* or 'The Shadow over Innsmouth' or both as a booklet. He was proposing all manner of schemes for the two stories, including prior serialization in either *Marvel Tales* or *Unusual Stories* before their book appearance. Finally—presumably after learning of the acceptance of *Mountains* by *Astounding*—Crawford focused on 'Innsmouth'. The process began in early 1936, and the book was typeset by the *Saxton Herald*, the local paper in Everett, Pennsylvania. Lovecraft began reading proofs later that spring, finding them full of mistakes but laboriously correcting them as best he could; some pages were apparently so bad that they had to be reset virtually from scratch.

It was Lovecraft who, in late January or early February, had urged Crawford to use Frank Utpatel as an artist for the book. Utpatel executed four woodcuts, one of which—a spectacularly hallucinatory depiction of Innsmouth's decaying roofs and spires, rather suggestive of El Greco—was also used for the jacket illustration. Lovecraft was delighted with the illustrations, even though the bearded Zadok Allen was portrayed as clean-shaven.

The illustrations, in the end, proved to be perhaps the only worthy item in the book, for certainly the text itself was seriously mangled. Lovecraft did not receive a copy of the book until November—a point worth noting, since book's copyright page gives the date of April 1936. Lovecraft claimed to have found thirty-three misprints in the book, but other readers found still more. He managed to persuade Crawford to print an errata sheet—whose first version was itself so misprinted as to be virtually worthless—and also found the time and effort to correct many copies of the book manually.

Although four hundred copies of the sheets were printed, Crawford had the money to bind only about two hundred. Lovecraft declares that Crawford had actually borrowed money from his father for the entire enterprise.[19] The book—although advertised in both *Weird Tales* and some of the fan journals—sold slowly (it was priced at $1.00), and shortly after its publication Crawford was forced to give up printing and publishing for seven years; at some point during this time the remaining unbound sheets were destroyed. So much for Lovecraft's 'first book'.

Lovecraft's own career as a practising fiction-writer was certainly not going very well. In late June Julius Schwartz, evidently intent on following up the success of placing *At the Mountains of Madness* with *Astounding*, had proposed what Lovecraft considered a wild and impractical idea of placing some of his stories in England. Lovecraft sent him 'a lot of manuscripts'[20] (leading one to think that Schwartz may have intended to approach book publishers), and, in order to exhaust the American market for as-yet unpublished stories, Lovecraft finally submitted 'The Thing on the Doorstep' and 'The Haunter of the Dark' to *Weird Tales*—the first stories he had personally submitted since he sent in 'In the Vault' in 1932. Lovecraft claimed to be surprised that Farnsworth Wright accepted these stories immediately, but he should not have been. Readers of the magazine had been clamouring for his work for years, and had to be satisfied with reprints.

In fact, Lovecraft had reached a psychological state that made both the marketing and the writing of fiction nearly impossible. As early as February 1936—three months after the writing of his last original tale, 'The Haunter of the Dark', and several months before the contretemps over his stories in *Astounding*—he was already admitting:

> [*At the Mountains of Madness*] was written in 1931—and its hostile reception by Wright and others to whom it was shewn probably did more than anything else to end my effective fictional career. The feeling that I had failed to crystallise the mood I was trying to crystallise robbed me in

some subtle fashion of the ability to approach this kind of problem in the same way—or with the same degree of confidence and fertility.[21]

Lovecraft is already speaking of his fictional career in the past tense.

It is difficult to know exactly when Lovecraft realized that he was dying. The summer of 1936 finally brought the temperature up to a level where he could actually enjoy being outdoors and have the energy to accomplish his work. The fall saw him still taking long walks, resulting in his seeing several sections of his native city he had never before seen in his life. One expedition—on 20 and 21 October—took him to the east shore of Narragansett Bay, in an area called the Squantum Woods. On 28 October Lovecraft went to an area of the Neutaconkanut woods three miles northwest of College Hill.

Christmas was a festive occasion. Lovecraft and Annie had a tree, and the two of them had dinner at the boarding-house next door. Lovecraft received a gift which he certainly did not expect but which he professed to find delightful: a long-interred human skull, found in an Indian graveyard and sent to him by Willis Conover. Conover has received much criticism for sending this item at this time, but of course he could not have known of the state of Lovecraft's health; and Lovecraft's pleasure at receiving this mortuary relic seems quite sincere. The entire winter was unusually warm, allowing Lovecraft to continue neighbourhood walks into December and even January. Various letters of this time certainly bespeak no intimations of mortality.

In early January, however, Lovecraft admitted to feeling poorly—'grippe' and bad digestion, as he put it. By the end of the month he was typing his letters—always a bad sign. Then, in mid-February, he told Derleth that he had had an offer (of which nothing is known) for a revised version of some old astronomical articles (presumably the *Asheville Gazette-News* series), which caused him to unearth his old astronomy books and explore new ones. He added at the end of this letter: 'Funny how early interests crop up again toward the end of one's life.'[22]

Lovecraft was at this time finally receiving the attention of a doctor, who prescribed three separate medications. On 28 February he made a feeble response to Talman's continued queries about a book deal from William Morrow: 'Am in constant pain, take only liquid food, and so bloated with gas that I can't lie down. Spend all time in chair propped with pillows, and can read or write only a few minutes at a time.'[23] Two days later Harry Brobst, who was much on the scene during this time, wrote to Barlow: 'Our old friend is quite ill—and so I am writing this letter for him. He has seemed to grow progressively weaker the last few days.'[24] On a postcard sent to Willis Conover on 9 March, Lovecraft writes in pencil: 'Am very ill & likely to be so for a long time.'[25]

The nature of Lovecraft's various illnesses is not well understood, at least in terms of their aetiology. This may be because Lovecraft waited so long to have them examined by a competent medical authority. On his death certificate the principal cause of death was given as 'Carcinoma of small intestine'; a contributory cause was 'chronic nephritis', or kidney disease.

Cancer of the small intestine is relatively rare, colon cancer being much more common; as a result, this cancer frequently goes undetected for years, even when patients are examined. Lovecraft, of course, was never examined until a month before his death, at which time it was too late to do anything except relieve his pain—and even massive doses of morphine seemed to offer little alleviation. It can be hypothesized why Lovecraft did not go to a doctor earlier, since he first experienced a serious bout of what he called indigestion as early as October 1934.[26] Lovecraft's habitual term for this condition—'grippe'—is simply an antiquated layman's term for the flu, although it is quite clear (and was probably clear to Lovecraft) that that is not what he had. But Lovecraft's phobia of doctors and hospitals may have been of very long standing. Recall that his mother's death was caused by a gall bladder operation from which she was unable to recover. Although it was probably Susie's general physical and psychological debilitation that led to her death, rather than any medical malfeasance, perhaps Lovecraft gained a fear and suspicion of doctors from this point onward.

The causes of intestinal cancer are various. Chief among them is diet: a high-fat, low-fibre diet results in the greater absorption of animal proteins in the digestive tract, and cancer can result in this manner. Interestingly enough, in view of the amount of canned food Lovecraft ate, studies have shown that modern food additives and preservatives may actually inhibit intestinal cancer.[27] It is not that the preservatives in the canned food Lovecraft ate caused his cancer, but that their possible absence may have done so.

It is a difficult question whether Lovecraft's kidney problems were related to or actually produced by his cancer or were a separate phenomenon entirely; the latter seems quite possible. Chronic nephritis is a now antiquated term for a variety of kidney ailments. In all likelihood, Lovecraft had chronic glomerulonephritis (formerly known as Bright's disease)—the inflammation of the renal glomeruli (small bulbs of blood capillaries in the kidney). If unrelated to the cancer, the cause of this ailment is not entirely clear. In some cases it is a function of a breakdown of the immune system; in other cases, poor nutrition may be a factor.[28] In other words, poor diet may have caused or contributed to both his cancer and his renal failure.

At this point we may as well study Lovecraft's anomalous sensitivity to cold, although what relation—if any—it had to his worsening cancer is impossible to determine. It has been thought that Lovecraft suffered from a supposed ailment called poikilothermia. This is, however, not a disease but merely a physiological property of certain animals, whereby their body temperature varies with the external environment; in other words, this property applies to cold-blooded animals such as reptiles. Mammals are all homeo-thermic, or capable of maintaining a constant body temperature (within narrow limits) regardless of the external environment.

Now there is no explicit evidence that Lovecraft's actual body temperature decreased during the cold, although it could have; since he was never hospitalized when suffering from exposure to cold, no tests exist on what his body temperature was in such a state. We only have various anecdotes as to his symptoms on such occasions: disturbed cardiovascular and/or respiratory functions; swelling of feet (customarily an indication of poor blood circulation); difficulty in the manipulation of hands; headache and nausea, sometimes leading to vomiting; and in extreme cases (perhaps three or four times in his life) actual unconsciousness. I have no idea what this concatenation of symptoms signifies.

What could have caused this condition? There does not seem to be any actual illness coinciding with these symptoms, but one hypothesis can perhaps be made. Body temperature is, in mammals, almost certainly regulated by the central nervous system. Experi-ments with animals have shown that a lesion in the caudal section of the hypothalamus can result in homeothermic animals becom-ing quasi-poikilothermic: they do not sweat in hot weather, nor do they shiver in cold weather.[29] Lovecraft, of course, *did* admit to sweating profusely in hot weather, but claimed nevertheless that he had nearly unbounded energy on these occasions. Nevertheless, I believe it is at least possible that some sort of damage to the hypothalamus—which does not affect intellectual or aesthetic capacity in any way—caused Lovecraft's sensitivity to cold.

And yet, Lovecraft makes it abundantly clear that his 'grippe' really did improve whenever the weather warmed up. This, at any rate, was the case during the winter of 1935–36. This fact may have led Lovecraft to believe that his digestive problems were some by-product of his sensitivity to cold, which he apparently believed to be non-treatable; if so, it could have contributed to his failure to see a doctor until the very end.

Lovecraft's last month of life is agonizing merely to read about; what it must have been like to experience can scarcely be imagined. This period has been made suddenly more vivid by a diary of his condition that Lovecraft kept until he could scarcely hold a pen.[30] Lovecraft began keeping the diary at the very beginning of 1937. He notes lingering digestive trouble throughout the first three weeks of January. Dr Cecil Calvert Dustin was brought in on 16 February. According to his recollections, he could tell immediately that Lovecraft was suffering from terminal cancer, so that he prescribed a variety of painkillers. Lovecraft's condition did not improve, and the medications did not even appear to alleviate his pain. He took to sleeping propped up in the morris-chair, since he could not lie down comfortably. Also, there was enormous distension in his abdomen. This is an oedema in the peritoneal cavity caused by his kidney disease.

On 27 February Annie told Dr Dustin that Lovecraft was much worse. When Dustin came over, he claims to have notified Lovecraft that his condition was terminal. Lovecraft, of course, kept up a good front to his colleagues, saying merely that he would be out of commission for an indefinite period. On 1 March Annie asked Dustin to call in a specialist in internal medicine. Dustin contacted Dr William Leet, but clearly not much could be done at this stage. The diary entry for 2 March tells the story: 'pain—drowse—intense pain—rest—great pain'. On 3 and 4 March Harry Brobst and his wife paid a visit; Brobst, with his medical know-ledge, must have immediately known of the nature of Lovecraft's condition, although he too put up a good front when writing to mutual colleagues.

On 6 March Dr Leet came over and found Lovecraft in the bath: immersions in hot water appeared to alleviate the pain somewhat. On this day Lovecraft suffered 'hideous pain'. By 9 March Lovecraft was unable to take any food or drink. Leet called the next day and advised that Lovecraft check into Jane Brown Memorial Hospital. He was taken there that day in an ambulance. Lovecraft's diary ends on 11 March; presumably he was unable to hold a pen thereafter.

For the next several days Lovecraft had to be fed intravenously, as he continued vomiting up all nourishment, even liquids. On 12 March Annie wrote to Barlow:

> I have intended to write you a gay little letter, long since, but now I am writing a sad little letter telling you that Howard is so pitifully ill & weak ... the dear fellow grows weaker & weaker—nothing can be retained in his stomach ...
>
> Needless to say he has been pathetically patient & philosophical through it all ... .[31]

On 13 March Harry Brobst and his wife came to visit Lovecraft in the hospital. Brobst asked Lovecraft how he felt; Lovecraft responded, 'Sometimes the pain is unbearable.' Brobst, in parting, told Lovecraft to remember the ancient philosophers—a reference, presumably, to their stoicism in facing death. Lovecraft smiled—the only response Brobst received.[32]

On 14 March Lovecraft's oedema was so severe that a stomach tap drained six and three-fourths quarts of fluid. That day Barlow, having received Annie's letter, telegraphed her from Leavenworth, Kansas: 'WOULD LIKE TO COME AND HELP YOU IF AGREEABLE ANSWER LEAVENWORTH TONIGHT.'[33]

Howard Phillips Lovecraft died early in the morning of March 15, 1937. He was pronounced dead at 7.15 a.m. That evening Annie telegraphed a reply to Barlow:[34]

HOWARD DIED THIS MORNING NOTHING TO DO THANKS

Thou Art Not Gone

On the evening of 15 March the *Providence Evening Bulletin* ran an obituary, full of errors large and small; but it made mention of the 'clinical notes' Lovecraft kept of his condition while in the hospital—notes that 'ended only when he could no longer hold a pencil'. This feature was picked up by the wire services, and a brief obituary appeared in the *New York Times* on 16 March. Frank Long, Lovecraft's best friend, learnt of his death from reading this obituary.

A funeral service was held on 18 March at the chapel of Horace B. Knowles's Sons at 187 Benefit Street. Only a small number of friends and relatives were there—Annie, Harry Brobst and his wife, and Annie's friend Edna Lewis. These individuals then attended the actual burial at Swan Point Cemetery, where they were joined by Edward H. Cole and his wife and Ethel Phillips Morrish, Lovecraft's second cousin. The Eddys had planned to come but arrived after the gravesite ceremony was over. Lovecraft's name was inscribed only on the central shaft of the Phillips plot, below those of his father and mother: 'their son / HOWARD P. LOVECRAFT / 1890–1937'. It took forty years for Lovecraft and his mother to receive separate headstones.

The outpouring of grief from both the weird fiction and the amateur press was instantaneous and overwhelming. The June 1937 issue of *Weird Tales* contained only the first wave of letters from colleagues and fans alike. It is remarkable how perfect strangers such as Robert Leonard Russell, who knew Lovecraft only from his work, could write: 'I feel, as will many other readers of *Weird Tales*, that I have lost a real friend.' Many real friends—from Hazel Heald to Robert Bloch to Kenneth Sterling to Clark Ashton Smith to Henry Kuttner—also wrote moving letters. Jacques Bergier, in the September 1937 issue, concluded: 'The passing of Lovecraft seems to me to mark an end of an epoch in the history of American imaginative fiction.'

One of the most remarkable phenomena about Lovecraft's passing is the number of poetic tributes it inspired. Henry Kuttner,

Richard Ely Morse, Frank Belknap Long, August Derleth, Emil Petaja, and many others wrote fine elegies; but the best without question is Clark Ashton Smith's 'To Howard Phillips Lovecraft', written on 31 March 1937 and published in *Weird Tales* for July. Its conclusion can only be quoted:

> And yet thou art not gone
> Nor given wholly unto dream and dust:
> For, even upon
> This lonely western hill of Averoigne
> Thy flesh had never visited,
> I meet some wise and sentient wraith of thee,
> Some undeparting presence, gracious and august.
> More luminous for thee the vernal grass,
> More magically dark the Druid stone
> And in the mind thou art for ever shown
> As in a wizard glass;
> And from the spirit's page thy runes can never pass.[1]

It is beyond the scope of this volume to trace the subsequent history of the appreciation of Lovecraft and his work; in any event, this information has now been more exhaustively chronicled elsewhere. A few points, however, may be touched upon here, in order to provide some hints of how an obscure writer who died with no book issued by a major publisher has now achieved worldwide renown as the leading author of supernatural fiction in the twentieth century.

An unsung hero in this transformation is R. H. Barlow, who was named Lovecraft's literary executor in a document written by Lovecraft toward the end of his life, 'Instructions in Case of Decease'. Barlow came to Providence shortly after Lovecraft's death and eventually donated most of his manuscripts and some printed matter to the John Hay Library of Brown University. This act allowed for the eventual correction of Lovecraft's texts based upon consultation of manuscript and early printed sources.

August Derleth and Donald Wandrei teamed up to establish Arkham House, a firm initially designed solely to preserve Lovecraft's work in hard covers. Arkham House quickly broadened its range to publish the work of other weird and science fiction writers, and today it retains its place as a leading small press publisher in this realm. Largely through Wandrei's influence, Arkham House issued five substantial volumes of Lovecraft's *Selected Letters* (1965–

76), thereby revealing Lovecraft's greatness as an epistolarian and the complex philosophical thought that underlay his creative work.

Paperback editions of Lovecraft emerged as early as the 1940s, and Ballantine Books began its fruitful paperback publications in the late 1960s, continuing to the present day. Ballantine, however, has not consistently used the corrected texts of Lovecraft's work published by Arkham House under my editorship in four volumes (1984–89); but Penguin has begun issuing these corrected texts in annotated editions beginning with *The Call of Cthulhu and Other Weird Stories* (1999).

Criticism of Lovecraft—initially fed through 'fan' circles (including such noted critics as Fritz Leiber, George T. Wetzel, and Matthew H. Onderdonk)—had to fight off vicious and clumsy attacks on his work by professional critics insensitive to weird fiction (chiefly Edmund Wilson's notorious review-article, 'Tales of the Marvellous and the Ridiculous', published in the *New Yorker* for 24 November 1945), but eventually this work bore fruit with the emergence of more scholarly criticism in the 1970s, led initially by Dirk W. Mosig and carried on by such critics as Donald R. Burleson, Peter Cannon, David E. Schultz, Robert H. Waugh, Robert M. Price, and myself. The scholarly journal *Lovecraft Studies* was established in 1979 and has published much sound criticism of Lovecraft.

Many of Lovecraft's colleagues wrote memoirs of Lovecraft, chiefly at the urging of August Derleth, who published them in various volumes of Lovecraft miscellany published by Arkham House over the years. These have now been gathered in Peter Cannon's noteworthy volume, *Lovecraft Remembered* (1998). L. Sprague de Camp's *Lovecraft: A Biography* appeared in 1975, but was widely criticized for lack of sympathy with its subject and an inadequate discussion of Lovecraft's work and thought.

Media adaptations of Lovecraft were somewhat slow in appearing, and to this day their quality is very variable. Lovecraft's work was heard on radio as early as the late 1940s; some film versions appeared in the 1960s (*The Haunted Palace*, 1964; *Die, Monster, Die!*, 1965; *The Dunwich Horror*, 1970), but they were both unfaithful and mediocre. Stuart Gordon's series of films, beginning with *Re-Animator* (1985), are over-the-top, self-parodic adaptations of some of Lovecraft's worst tales, but they were nevertheless intermittently successful in their campy manner, and have brought new fans to Lovecraft. His work has been adapted for comic books, role-playing games (most famously, *The Call of Cthulhu*, published by Chaosium), interactive computer games, and the like. But Lovecraft's dense prose and slow-moving action has proved very difficult to translate into other media, and it cannot be said that any of these adaptations is, from an aesthetic point of view, entirely successful.

The widespread imitation of what came to be called the 'Cthulhu Mythos' is difficult to discuss objectively. Through the urging of August Derleth, who seemed to have a kind of mania about the Mythos, many horror and science fiction writers tried their hands at imitating Lovecraft, but with almost uniformly poor results. Perhaps only Colin Wilson (*The Mind Parasites*, 1967) and a very few others, who used Lovecraft as springboards for their own conceptions, have produced sound work in this vein. Ramsey Campbell began his career at a very early age by writing a volume of Lovecraft imitations, published by Arkham House in 1964, but very quickly found his own voice and has now become the finest writer in the field, although he lacks the popularity of some of his best-selling colleagues.

Lovecraft has now been dead for more than sixty years, and his work commands a far wider, and far more diverse, audience than it ever did in his own lifetime. His tales have been translated into more than a dozen languages and have elicited a library of learned commentary, his letters, essays, and poems have been published, his life has become the stuff of legend, and he himself has emerged as a dark but compelling icon of popular culture. Lovecraft is one of those few authors whose work appeals to college professors as well as to teenagers, to hippies as well as to businessmen, to highbrow novelists as well as to lowbrow film producers.

As for Lovecraft's life, perhaps it is sufficient to say that, in large part, he lived it very much as he wished. We all wish that he could have secured a greater modicum of commercial success during his own lifetime; but he was willing to make sacrifices in personal comfort so as to preserve the purity of his art, and the endurance and increasing popularity of his work show that he made the right decision. So perhaps it is time to honour a man whose devotion to his work, generosity to his friends, and sensitivity of imagination knew virtually no bounds. His life is over now, and only his work remains.

Notes

Abbreviations used in the notes: AHT = Arkham House transcripts ofLovecraft's letters; JHL = John Hay Library, Brown University (Providence, RI); SHSW = State Historical Society of Wisconsin (Madison, WI); SL = *Selected Letters* (1965–76; 5 vols.).

Chapter One

1. The 1850 U.S. census, probably enumerated in June 1850, gives George Lovecraft's age as thirty-one. See Kenneth W. Faig, Jr, 'Lovecraft's Ancestors', *Crypt of Cthulhu* No. 57 (St John's Eve 1988): 19.

2. HPL spells his maternal grandmother's first name as 'Rhoby', but Robie is given on the central shaft of the Phillips plot at Swan Point Cemetery in Providence.

3. HPL to Frank Belknap Long, 26 October 1926 (SL II.88).

4. HPL to F. Lee Baldwin, 13 January 1934 (SL IV.344).

5. See Kenneth W. Faig, Jr, 'Whipple V. Phillips and the Owyhee Land and Irrigation Company', *Owyhee Outpost* No. 19 (May 1988): 21–30.

6. HPL to F. Lee Baldwin, 31 January 1934 (SL IV.351).

7. HPL to Maurice W. Moe, 1 January 1915 (SL I.6).

8. HPL to Rheinhart Kleiner, 16 November 1916 (SL I.29).

9. SL I.33–34 (note 8).

10. Clara Hess in August Derleth, 'Lovecraft's Sensitivity' (1949); rpt in *Lovecraft Remembered*, ed. Peter Cannon (Sauk City, WI: Arkham House, 1998), p. 32.

11. Ibid., pp. 34–35.

12. See Richard D. Squires, *Stern Fathers 'neath the Mould: The Lovecraft Family in Rochester* (West Warwick, RI: Necronomicon Press, 1995).

13. Sonia H. Davis, *The Private Life of H. P. Lovecraft*, ed. S. T. Joshi (West Warwick, RI: Necronomicon Press, rev. ed. 1992), p. 7.

14. HPL to Edwin Baird, 3 February 1924 (SL I.296).

Chapter Two

1. HPL to Annie E. P. Gamwell, 19 August 1921 (SL I.147).

2. HPL to J. Vernon Shea, 4 February 1934 (SL IV.354).

3. HPL to Bernard Austin Dwyer, 3 March 1927 (SL II.107).

4. HPL to Rheinhart Kleiner, 16 November 1916 (SL I.32).

5. Henry G. Fairbanks, *Louise Imogen Guiney: Laureate of the Lost* (Albany, NY: Magi Books, 1972), p. 2.

6. SL I.32 (note 4).

7. HPL to August Derleth, [January 1930] (SL III.100).

8. SL I.33 (note 4).

9. HPL to Rheinhart Kleiner, 16 November 1916 (AHT; not in SL).

10. HPL to Edwin Baird, 3 February 1924 (SL I.296).

11. HPL to Maurice W. Moe, 1 January 1915 (SL I.6).

12. Quoted by Kenneth W. Faig, Jr, *The Parents of Howard Phillips Lovecraft* (West Warwick, RI: Necronomicon Press, 1990), p. 11.

13. M. Eileen McNamara, M.D., 'Winfield Scott Lovecraft's Final Illness', *Lovecraft Studies* No. 24 (Fall 1991): 14.

14. Winfield Townley Scott, 'His Own Most Fantastic Creation: Howard Phillips Lovecraft' in *Lovecraft Remembered*, p. 16. Sarah Susan Lovecraft's medical records no longer survive, but Scott consulted them around 1944.

15. SL I.6 (note 11).

16. HPL to J. Vernon Shea, 29 May 1933 (SL IV.191).

17. HPL to Maurice W. Moe, 5 April 1931 (SL III.362).

18. SL I.34 (note 4).

19. Scott, 'His Own Most Fantastic Creation', p. 11.

20. SL IV.355 (note 2). The same anecdote is found in HPL to Rheinhart Kleiner, 16 November 1916 (AHT).

21. SL III.362 (note 17).

22. Faig, *Parents*, p. 7.

23. SL I.33 (note 4).

24. HPL to Robert E. Howard, 16 January 1932 (SL IV.8).

25. HPL to Robert E. Howard, 16 January 1932 (AHT).

26. HPL to J. Vernon Shea, 8 November 1933 (ms., JHL).

27. SL I.34–35 (note 4).

28. HPL to Virgil Finlay, 24 October 1936 (SL V.335).

29. HPL to August Derleth, 9 September 1931 (SL IV.407).

30. SL I.7 (note 11).

31. SL I.33 (note 4).

32. SL I.7 (note 11).

33. SL II.108 (note 3).

34. SL I.36 (note 4).

35. SL II.109 (note 3).

Chapter Three

1. HPL to R. H. Barlow, 25 June 1931 (ms., JHL).

2. HPL to J. Vernon Shea, 19–31 July 1931 (ms., JHL).

3. HPL to J. Vernon Shea, 4 February 1934 (SL IV.354).

4. Edmund Pearson, *Dime Novels* (Boston: Little, Brown, 1929), pp. 4f.

5. L. Sprague de Camp, *Lovecraft: A Biography* (Garden City, NY: Doubleday, 1975), p. 33.

6. HPL to Rheinhart Kleiner, 7 March 1920 (SL I.110).

7. HPL to Rheinhart Kleiner, 16 November 1916 (SL I.37).

8. W. Paul Cook, *In Memoriam: Howard Phillips Lovecraft* (1941), in *Lovecraft Remembered*, p. 112.

9. SL IV.355–56 (note 3).

10. HPL to Maurice W. Moe, 1 January 1915 (SL I.8).

11. HPL to Robert E. Howard, 25–29 March 1933 (SL IV.172).

12. HPL to August Derleth, 4 March 1932 (SL IV.26).

13. HPL to Maurice W. Moe, 5 April 1931 (SL III.368).

14. HPL to Richard F. Searight, 5 March 1935; *Letters to Richard F. Searight* (West Warwick, RI: Necronomicon Press, 1992), p. 51.

15. J. Vernon Shea, 'Did Lovecraft Suffer from Chorea?', *Outré* No. 5 (May 1977): 30–31.

16. Scott, 'His Own Most Fantastic Creation', p. 12.

17. SL III.367 (note 13).

18. Davis, *Private Life*, p. 8.

19. See frontispiece to SL II.

20. SL I.32 (note 7).

21. Frontispiece to *Something about Cats and Other Pieces* (1949).

22. R. H. Barlow, *On Lovecraft and Life* (West Warwick, RI: Necronomicon Press, 1992), p. 18.

23. Ms., JHL.

24. SL I.35 (note 7).

25. SL I.29–30 (note 7).

26. HPL to Elizabeth Toldridge, 29 May 1929 (SL II.348).

27. SL I.35 (note 7).

28. Interview of Ethel Phillips Morrish by Paul R. Michaud, August 1977.

29. HPL to J. Vernon Shea, 8 November 1933 (ms., JHL).

30. HPL to J. Vernon Shea, 10 February 1935 (SL V.104).

31. SL I.36 (note 7).

32. SL I.37 (note 7).

33. See HPL to Maurice W. Moe, 18 September 1932 (SL IV.67) for titles; HPL to Marion F. Bonner, 26 April 1936 (SL V.237) for dates. In this latter letter the title of the second treatise is given as *Ross's Explorations*.

34. C. L. Moore to HPL, 6 October 1936 (ms., JHL): 'Thank you for the privilege of reading that early publication of the Royal Atlas Company, "Wilks' Exploration" [*sic*] … I am returning "Wilks' Exploration" with a sigh …' The Royal Atlas Company must have been yet another of Lovecraft's juvenile imprints.

Chapter Four

1. I am grateful to Sam Moskowitz for information on the hectograph.

2. 'Autobiography of Howard Phillips Lovecraft' (written in 1934), *Boys' Herald* 71, No. 1 (October 1941): 7.

3. HPL to Rheinhart Kleiner, 16 November 1916 (SL I.38).

4. HPL to Duane W. Rimel, 29 March 1934 (SL IV.398).

5. HPL to Rheinhart Kleiner, 20 January 1916 (SL I.19).

6. SL I.39 (note 3).

7. HPL to Helen Sully, 4 December 1935 (ms., JHL).

8. HPL to Rheinhart Kleiner, 16 November 1916 (AHT).

9. HPL to Rheinhart Kleiner, 2 February 1916 (SL I.20).

10. HPL to the Gallomo, [January] 1920 (SL I.104–5).

11. HPL to August Derleth, 31 December 1930 (SL III.246).

12. Stuart J. Coleman to Winfield Townley Scott, 30 December [1943] (ms., JHL).

13. Clara Hess in August Derleth, 'Lovecraft's Sensitivity'; quoted in *Lovecraft Remembered*, p. 34.

14. HPL to J. Vernon Shea, 4 February 1934 (SL IV.357).

15. Kenneth W. Faig, Jr, 'Howard Phillips Lovecraft: The Early Years 1890–1914', *Nyctalops* 2, No. 1 (April 1973): 14n.16, citing probate records.

16. SL IV.358–59 (note 14).

17. SL I.39 (note 3).

18. HPL to Robert E. Howard, 25–29 March 1933 (SL IV.172).

19. SL I.30 (note 3).

20. HPL to J. Vernon Shea, 8 November 1933 (ms., JHL).

21. *The Rhode Island Journal of Astronomy*, 30 July 1905.

22. HPL to Alfred Galpin, 29 August 1918 (ms., JHL; published in part in SL I.75).

23. HPL to Maurice W. Moe, 15 May 1918 (SL I.60).

24. HPL to Annie E. P. Gamwell, 19 August 1921 (SL I.146).

25. Ibid.

26. See note 20.

27. See *The Rhode Island Journal of Astronomy*, April 1907; HPL to Samuel Loveman, [c. 5 January 1924]; *Letters to Samuel Loveman and Vincent Starrett* (West Warwick, RI: Necronomicon Press, 1994), p. 23.

28. SL I.39 (note 3).

29. SL I.38 (note 3).

30. HPL to Rheinhart Kleiner, 16 November 1916 (AHT).

31. See note 20.

32. SL IV.360 (note 14).

33. SL IV.170 (note 18).

34. HPL to Maurice W. Moe, 5 April 1931 (SL III.367).

35. HPL to R. H. Barlow, 10 April 1934 (ms., JHL).

36. HPL to Maurice W. Moe, [6 April 1935] (SL V.140).

37. HPL to Robert Bloch, 1 June 1933; *Letters to Robert Bloch* (West

Warwick, RI: Necronomicon Press, 1993), p. 15.

38. HPL to Lillian D. Clark, 14–19 November 1925 (ms., JHL).

39. SL I.40 (note 3).

40. SL V.141 (note 36).

41. HPL to Rheinhart Kleiner, 7 March 1920 (SL I.110–11).

42. HPL to Alfred Galpin, 21 August 1918 (SL I.70).

Chapter Five

1. HPL to Maurice W. Moe, 1 January 1915 (SL I.9).

2. HPL to Rheinhart Kleiner, 16 November 1916 (SL I.40–41).

3. HPL to Bernard Austin Dwyer, 3 March 1927 (SL II.110).

4. HPL to Helen Sully, 4 December 1935 (ms., JHL).

5. Will Murray, 'An Interview with Harry Brobst', *Lovecraft Studies* Nos 22/23 (fall 1990): 34.

6. Harold W. Munro, 'Lovecraft, My Childhood Friend' (1983), in *Lovecraft Remembered*, pp. 70–71.

7. HPL to Robert E. Howard, 25–29 March 1933 (SL IV.172).

8. R. Alain Everts, 'Howard Phillips Lovecraft and Sex', *Nyctalops* 2, No. 2 (July 1974): 19.

9. SL I.9 (note 1).

10. SL I.31 (note 2).

11. HPL to Alfred Galpin, 19 August 1918 (SL I.75).

12. David H. Keller, 'Lovecraft's Astronomical Notebook', *Lovecraft Collector* No. 3 (October 1949): 1–4.

13. Keller has transcribed 'Providence Evening Journal', but this is evidently his error.

14. HPL to Jonquil Leiber, 29 November 1936 (SL V.363).

15. Scott, 'His Own Most Fantastic Creation', p. 15.

16. HPL to Maurice W. Moe, 5 April 1931 (SL III.367).

17. Faig, *Parents*, p. 28.

18. Quoted in Derleth, 'Lovecraft's Sensitivity', in *Lovecraft Remembered*, pp. 32, 34.

19. HPL to Duane W. Rimel, 13 April 1934 (ms., JHL).

20. HPL to Sarah Susan Lovecraft, 24 February 1921 (SL I.123).

21. Sonia H. Davis, 'Memories of Lovecraft: I' (1969), in *Lovecraft Remembered*, p. 276.

22. *Lovecraft Remembered*, p. 34.

23. *Lovecraft Remembered*, p. 71.

24. See the photograph published with Kenneth W. Faig, Jr, 'The Early Years': 11.

25. HPL to Rheinhart Kleiner, 4 December 1918 (SL I.78).

26. HPL to R. H. Barlow, 23 July 1936 (SL V.282).

27. HPL to Frank Belknap Long, 8 February 1922 (AHT).

28. Scott, p. 13.

29. SL I.41 (note 2).

30. SL II.110 (note 3).

31. SL I.41 (note 2).

32. HPL to R. H. Barlow, 31 March 1932 (ms., JHL).

33. HPL to R. H. Barlow, 14 April 1932 (ms., JHL).

34. HPL to James F. Morton, 23 February 1936 (SL V.227).

35. All letters by and about HPL in the *Argosy* and *All-Story* are now collected in *H. P. Lovecraft in the Argosy* (West Warwick, RI: Necronomicon Press, 1994).

36. SL I.42 (note 2).

Chapter Six

1. HPL to J. Vernon Shea, 27 October 1932 (SL IV.97).

2. L. Sprague de Camp, 'Young Man Lovecraft' (1975), in *The Necronomicon*, ed. George Hay (London: Corgi, 1980), pp. 143–44.

3. *Science versus Charlatanry: Essays on Astrology* (Madison, WI: Strange Co., 1979), p. xiv. See this edition, passim, for all articles in the Lovecraft–Hartmann controversy.

4. HPL to Maurice W. Moe, 8 December 1914 (SL I.3–4).

5. HPL to Elizabeth Toldridge, 8 March 1929 (SL II.314–15).

6. HPL to Maurice W. Moe, 5 April 1931 (SL III.369–70).

7. HPL to Rheinhart Kleiner, 13 May 1921 (SL I.132).

8. Steven J. Mariconda, 'On Lovecraft's "Amissa Minerva"', *Etchings and Odysseys* No. 9 [1986]: 97–103.

9. HPL to Rheinhart Kleiner, 23 August 1916 (SL I.24).

10. Thomas Henry Huxley, *Man's Place in Nature* (1894), p. 233.

11. De Camp, *Lovecraft*, pp. 95–99.

12. Thomas F. Gossett, *Race: The History of an Idea in America* (Dallas: Southern Methodist University Press, 1963), p. 348.

13. HPL to R. H. Barlow, 13 June 1936 (SL V.266).

14. HPL to the Gallomo, 30 September 1919 (SL I.89).

15. James F. Morton, '"Conservatism" Gone Mad', *In a Minor Key* No. 2 [1915]: [15–16].

16. HPL to Rheinhart Kleiner, 23 May 1917 (SL I.45–46).

17. HPL to Rheinhart Kleiner, 27 August 1917 (SL I.49).

18. See note 16.

19. HPL to Rheinhart Kleiner, 22 June 1917 (SL I.48).

20. HPL to John T. Dunn, 6 July 1917 (ms., JHL).

21. Samuel Eliot Morison et al., *The Growth of the American Republic*, 7th ed. (New York: Oxford University Press, 1980), 2:285.

22. HPL to Zealia Bishop, 13 February 1928 (SL II.229).

23. HPL to J. Vernon Shea, 10 November 1931 (SL III.434).

24. HPL to Maurice W. Moe, 15 May 1918 (SL I.64).

25. SL III.370 (note 6).

26. HPL to J. Vernon Shea, 4 February 1934 (SL IV.355).

27. HPL to Rheinhart Kleiner, 6 December 1915 (SL I.18).

28. HPL to Rheinhart Kleiner, 30 September 1915 (SL I.14).

29. 'Extracts from the Letters to G. W. Macauley' (1938), *Lovecraft Studies* 1, No. 3 (fall 1980): 14.

Chapter Seven

1. HPL to Richard Ely Morse, 30 August [1932] (ms., JHL).

2. HPL to Elizabeth Toldridge, 8 March 1929 (SL II.315).

3. HPL to the Gallomo, [January 1920] (AHT).

4. HPL to Maurice W. Moe, 15 May 1918 (SL I.62).

5. See note 3.

6. HPL to Rheinhart Kleiner, 8 November 1917 (SL I.51).

7. HPL to Rheinhart Kleiner, 23 December 1917 (SL I.52).

8. Samuel Eliot Morison et al., *The Growth of the American Republic*, 2:112.

9. Cook, *In Memoriam*, in *Lovecraft Remembered*, pp. 110–11.

10. HPL to Rheinhart Kleiner, 24 September 1917 (SL I.49).

11. Rheinhart Kleiner, 'A Memoir of Lovecraft' (1949), in *Lovecraft Remembered*, p. 195.

12. HPL to Winifred Virginia Jackson, 7 June 1921 (SL I.138).

13. HPL to Rheinhart Kleiner, 21 September 1921 (SL I.152–33).

14. Samuel Loveman, 'Howard Phillips Lovecraft' (1949), in *Lovecraft Remembered*, p. 204.

15. HPL to Rheinhart Kleiner, 23 April 1921 (SL I.128).

16. L. Sprague de Camp, 'Young Man Lovecraft', p. 144.

17. HPL to Alfred Galpin, 27 May 1918 (ms., JHL).

18. HPL to John T. Dunn, 14 October 1916 (ms., JHL).

19. Clara Hess in August Derleth, 'Lovecraft's Sensitivity', in *Lovecraft Remembered*, p. 35.

20. HPL to Rheinhart Kleiner, 23 May 1917 (SL I.46).

21. Faig, *Parents*, p. 29.

22. HPL to Rheinhart Kleiner, 18 January 1919 (SL I.78).

23. HPL to Rheinhart Kleiner, 19 March 1919 (SL I.80).

24. See note 19.

25. HPL to Arthur Harris, 23 August 1915 (ms., JHL).

26. George Julian Houtain, 'Lovecraft' (1921), in *Lovecraft Remembered*, p. 87.

27. HPL to Frank Belknap Long, 26 January 1921 (SL I.122).

Chapter Eight

1. HPL to Rheinhart Kleiner, 19 March 1919 (SL I.81).

2. Scott, p. 16.

3. *Epgephi*, Sept. 1920, pp. 6, 21.

4. HPL to Rheinhart Kleiner, 10 September 1920; 'By Post from Providence', *Californian* 5, No. 1 (Summer 1937): 20.

5. HPL to Rheinhart Kleiner, 27 September 1919 (SL I.88).

6. See George T. Wetzel and R. Alain Everts, *Winifred Virginia Jackson— Lovecraft's Lost Romance* ([Madison, WI: Strange Co.,] 1976).

7. Ibid.

8. HPL to Rheinhart Kleiner, 14 September 1919 (SL I.87).

9. HPL to Rheinhart Kleiner, 7 March 1920 (SL I.112).

10. Ibid. (SL I.111–12).

11. Oscar Wilde, 'Preface' to *The Picture of Dorian Gray* (1891).

12. HPL to Clark Ashton Smith, 14 April 1929 (SL II.328).

13. HPL to Richard Ely Morse, 28 July 1932 (ms.).

14. See note 12.

15. *Tryout* 5, No. 12 (December 1919): 12.

16. HPL to Frank Belknap Long, 3 June 1923 (SL I.234).

17. HPL to Frank Belknap Long, 19 November 1920 (AHT).

18. HPL to Rheinhart Kleiner, 7 March 1920 (SL I.110).

19. HPL to Rheinhart Kleiner, 3 December 1919 (SL I.93).

20. Lord Dunsany, Letter to August Derleth (28 March 1952), quoted in *Lovecraft Studies* No. 14 (spring 1987): 38.

21. HPL to Edwin Baird, [c. October 1923]; *Weird Tales*, March 1924.

22. Will Murray, 'Behind the Mask of Nyarlathotep', *Lovecraft Studies* No. 25 (fall 1991): 25–29.

23. Donald R. Burleson, 'On Lovecraft's Themes: Touching the Glass', in *An Epicure in the Terrible: A Centennial Anthology of Essays in Honor of H. P. Lovecraft*, ed. David E. Schultz and S. T. Joshi (Rutherford, NJ: Fairleigh Dickinson University Press, 1991), p.135.

24. HPL to J. Vernon Shea, 19 June 1931 (SL III.379).

Chapter Nine

1. Scott, 'His Own Most Fantastic Creation', p. 17.

2. HPL to Anne Tillery Renshaw, 1 June 1921 (SL I.133).

3. Faig, *Parents*, p. 40.

4. HPL to Maurice W. Moe, 5 April 1931 (SL III.370).

5. HPL to Maurice W. Moe, 15 June 1925 (ms., JHL).

6. Rheinhart Kleiner, 'A Memoir of Lovecraft', in *Lovecraft Remembered*, p. 197.

7. Alfred Galpin, 'Memories of a Friendship' (1959), in *Lovecraft Remembered*, p. 170.

8. Davis, *Private Life*, p. 15.

9. HPL to the Gallomo, 21 August 1921 (AHT).

10. Davis, *Private Life*, p. 24.

11. HPL to Anne Tillery Renshaw, 14 June 1922 (SL I.185–86).

12. HPL to Lillian D. Clark, 29 September 1922 (SL I.199).

13. HPL to Anne Tillery Renshaw, 3 October 1921 (SL I.154).

14. HPL to Frank Belknap Long, 8 October 1921 (SL I.158).

15. HPL to Rheinhart Kleiner, 17 June 1922 (SL I.188).

16. HPL to Samuel Loveman, 17 November [1922]; *Letters to Samuel Loveman and Vincent Starrett*, pp. 9–10.

17. HPL to Maurice W. Moe, 18 May 1922 (SL I.176).

18. Davis, *Private Life*, p. 16.

19. SL I.180 (note 17).

20. Davis, *Private Life*, p. 17.

21. Sonia H. Davis to Winfield Townley Scott, 11 December 1948 (ms., JHL).

22. Davis, *Private Life*, p. 19.

23. HPL to Lillian D. Clark, 9 August 1922 (ms., JHL).

24. Ibid.

25. HPL to Lillian D. Clark, 29 September 1922 (SL I.198).

26. HPL to Robert E. Howard, 25–29 March 1933 (SL IV.170).

27. HPL to Rheinhart Kleiner, 11 January 1923 (SL I.204).

28. HPL to James F. Morton, 12 March 1930 (SL III.126–27).

29. HPL to James F. Morton, 19 October 1929 (SL III.31).

Chapter Ten

1. HPL to Lillian D. Clark, 27 July 1925 (ms., JHL).

2. HPL to Rheinhart Kleiner, 29 April 192[3] (SL I.131). The letter is misdated to 1921 in SL.

3. Davis, *Private Life*, p. 18.

4. Cole, 'Ave atque Vale!' (1940), in *Lovecraft Remembered*, p. 101.

5. See Robert E. Weinberg, *The Weird Tales Story* (West Linn, OR: FAX Collector's Editions, 1977), p. 3.

6. HPL to the Gallomo, [January] 1920 (AHT).

7. HPL to Bernard Austin Dwyer, [1932] (SL IV.4).

8. Steven J. Mariconda, '*Curious Myths of the Middle Ages* and "The Rats in the Walls"', *On the Emergence of 'Cthulhu' and Other Observations* (West Warwick, RI: Necronomicon Press, 1995), pp. 53–56.

9. HPL to J. Vernon Shea, 8–22 November 1933 (ms., JHL).

10. HPL to Frank Belknap Long, 8 November 1923 (SL I.259).

11. HPL to Robert E. Howard, 2–5 November 1933 (SL IV.297).

12. Muriel E. Eddy, *The Gentleman from Angell Street* ([Providence: Privately printed,] 1961), p. 2.

13. HPL to Frank Belknap Long, 7 October 1923 (SL I.254).

14. HPL to James F. Morton, 28 October 1923 (SL I.257).

15. HPL to August Derleth, [1929] (ms., SHSW).

16. 'In the Editor's Study', *Conservative*, July 1923.

17. T. S. Eliot, 'The Metaphysical Poets' (1921), *Selected Essays* (New York: Harcourt, Brace, 1950), p. 248.

18. HPL to Frank Belknap Long, 13 May 1923 (SL I.229).

19. HPL to Frank Belknap Long, 20 February 1924 (SL I.315).

20. HPL to J. Vernon Shea, 24 March 1933 (SL IV.159).

21. Barton L. St Armand and John H. Stanley, 'H. P. Lovecraft's *Waste Paper*: A Facsimile and Transcript of the Original Draft', *Books at Brown* 26 (1978): 40.

22. HPL to Clark Ashton Smith, 17 October 1930 (SL III.195).

23. HPL to Myrta Alice Little, 17 May 1921; *Lovecraft Studies* No. 26 (Spring 1992): 28.

24. HPL to Clark Ashton Smith, 16 November 1926 (SL II.90).

25. HPL to James F. Morton, 26 May 1923 (SL I.231).

26. HPL to James F. Morton, 10 February 1923 (SL I.207).

27. *Twilight of the Idols* [1888], in *Twilight of the Idols and The Anti-Christ*, tr. R. J. Hollingdale (Harmondsworth: Penguin, 1968), p.93.

28. SL I.208 (note 26).

29. HPL to Samuel Loveman, [5 January 1924] (SL I.277).

Chapter Eleven

1. Kleiner, 'A Memoir of Lovecraft', in *Lovecraft Remembered*, pp. 197–98.

2. HPL to Lillian D. Clark, 9 March 1924 (SL I.319–22).

3. Davis, *Private Life*, p. 18.

4. Ibid.

5. Sonia H. Greene to Lillian D. Clark, 9 February 1924 (AHT).

6. HPL to James F. Morton, 12 March 1924 (SL I.325).

7. Note to Sonia H. Davis, 'The Psychic Phenominon of Love' (ms., JHL).

8. 'Lovecraft on Love', *Arkham Collector* No. 8 (Winter 1971): 244.

9. HPL to Lillian D. Clark, 22–23 December 1924 (ms., JHL).

10. HPL to Frank Belknap Long, 21 March 1924 (SL I.332).

11. HPL to Frank Belknap Long, 7 February 1924 (SL I.304).

12. Weinberg, *The Weird Tales Story*, p. 4.

13. Sonia H. Davis, ['Autobiography'] (ms., JHL).

14. HPL to Lillian D. Clark, [10 March 1924] (postcard) (ms., JHL).

15. HPL to Lillian D. Clark, 1 August 1924 (SL I.337).

16. Ibid.

17. SL I.338 (note 15).

18. Letter of application, 1924 (SL I.xxvii–xxviii).

19. Kleiner, 'A Memoir of Lovecraft', pp. 201–02.

20. HPL to Lillian D. Clark, 29–30 September 1924 (ms., JHL).

21. Frank Belknap Long, *Howard Phillips Lovecraft: Dreamer on the Nightside* (Sauk City, WI: Arkham House, 1975), pp. 80–82.

22. See note 20.

23. HPL to Lillian D. Clark, 4–6 November 1924 (ms., JHL).

24. R. Alain Everts, 'Howard Phillips Lovecraft and Sex; or, The Sex Life of a Gentleman', *Nyctalops* 2, No. 2 (July 1974): 19.

25. Sonia H. Davis, 'Memories of Lovecraft: I', in *Lovecraft Remembered*, p. 275.

26. Ibid., pp. 275–76.

27. See note 24.

28. Davis, *Private Life*, p. 13.

29. See note 25.

30. HPL to Maurice W. Moe, 15 June 1925 (SL II.19).

31. Davis, *Private Life*, p. 12.

32. HPL to August Derleth, 16 January 1931 (SL III.262).

33. HPL to James F. Morton, 6 May 1924 (SL I.337).

34. Mara Kirk Hart, 'Walkers in the City: George Willard Kirk and Howard Phillips Lovecraft in New York City, 1924–1926' (1993), in *Lovecraft Remembered*, p. 224.

35. Long, *Dreamer on the Nightside*, pp. 157–58.

36. Davis, *Private Life*, pp. 18–19.

37. Wilfred B. Talman, 'The Normal Lovecraft' (1973), in *Lovecraft Remembered*, p. 220.

38. HPL to Lillian D. Clark, 1 August 1924 (AHT).

39. See note 20.

40. Hart Crane, Letter to Grace Hart Crane and Elizabeth Belden Hart (14 September 1924), *Letters of Hart Crane and His Family*, ed. Thomas S. W. Lewis (New York: Columbia University Press, 1974), pp. 342–43.

41. Kleiner, 'A Memoir of Lovecraft', p. 200.

42. See note 23.

Chapter Twelve

1. Sonia H. Davis, Letter to Samuel Loveman (1 January 1948), quoted in Gerry de la Ree, 'When Sonia Sizzled', in Wilfred B. Talman et al., *The Normal Lovecraft* (Saddle River, NJ: Gerry de la Ree, 1973), p. 29.

2. Hart, 'Walkers in the City', p. 233.

3. HPL to Maurice W. Moe, 15 June 1925 (SL II.18–19).

4. HPL to Lillian D. Clark, 2 April 1925 (ms., JHL).

5. HPL to Lillian D. Clark, 11 April 1925 (ms., JHL).

6. HPL to Lillian D. Clark, 24–27 October 1925 (ms., JHL).

7. See note 5.

8. HPL to Lillian D. Clark, 28 May 1925 (SL II.11–12).

9. HPL to Lillian D. Clark, 14–15 October 1925 (ms., JHL).

10. HPL to Lillian D. Clark, 24–27 October 1925 (ms., JHL).

11. HPL to Lillian D. Clark, 21 April 1925 (ms., JHL).

12. HPL to Frank Belknap Long, 2 August 1925 (SL II.20).

13. Davis, *Private Life*, p. 12.

14. HPL to Lillian D. Clark, 27 July 1925 (ms., JHL).

15. HPL to August Derleth, 26 November 1926 (ms., SHSW).

16. Davis, *Private Life*, p. 11.

17. Ibid., p. 20.
18. Ibid., pp. 26–27.
19. HPL to Lillian D. Clark, 11 January 1926 (ms., JHL).
20. See Elaine Schechter, *Perry Street—Then and Now* (New York: Privately printed, 1972).
21. HPL to Lillian D. Clark, 13 August 1925 (ms., JHL).
22. HPL to Lillian D. Clark, 8 August 1925 (ms., JHL).
23. HPL to Lillian D. Clark, 2 December 1925 (ms., JHL).
24. HPL to Lillian D. Clark, 28–30 September 1925 (ms., JHL).
25. Ibid.
26. HPL to Lillian D. Clark, 14–19 November 1925 (ms., JHL).
27. HPL to Lillian D. Clark, 12–13 April 1926 (ms., JHL).
28. HPL to Lillian D. Clark, 29–30 September 1924 (ms., JHL).
29. HPL to J. Vernon Shea, 5 February 1932 (SL IV.15).
30. HPL to Lillian D. Clark, 6 January 1926 (postcard) (ms., JHL).
31. HPL to Lillian D. Clark, 11 January 1926 (ms., JHL).
32. HPL to Henry Kuttner, 29 July 1936; *Letters to Henry Kuttner* (West Warwick, RI: Necronomicon Press, 1990), p. 21.
33. HPL to Lillian D. Clark, 6 March 1926 (ms., JHL).
34. HPL to Lillian D. Clark, 27 March 1926 (ms., JHL).

Chapter Thirteen

1. HPL to Lillian D. Clark, 2 April 1925 (ms., JHL).
2. HPL to Lillian D. Clark, 14–19 November 1925 (ms., JHL).
3. HPL to Lillian D. Clark, 8 August 1925 (ms., JHL).
4. Scott, p. 18. The essay first appeared in *Marginalia* (1944). In his copy of the book (now owned by Kenneth W. Faig, Jr), Benjamin Crocker Clough, a reviewer for the *Providence Journal*, has written: 'So he [Loveman] told me, and I told WTS. "Phial" I'm not sure of.'
5. HPL to Lillian D. Clark, 22–23 December 1925 (ms., JHL).
6. Scott, 'His Own Most Fantastic Creation', p. 18.
7. Long, *Dreamer on the Nightside*, p. 167.
8. HPL to Lillian D. Clark, 29 March 1926 (ms., JHL).
9. HPL to Lillian D. Clark, 1 April 1926 (ms., JHL).
10. Davis, *Private Life*, pp. 14, 20.
11. HPL to Maurice W. Moe, [2 July] 1929 (SL III.5, 8).
12. Davis, *Private Life*, p. 11.
13. HPL to Frank Belknap Long, 1 May 1926 (SL II.46–47).
14. Cook, *In Memoriam*, in *Lovecraft Remembered*, p. 116.
15. Cook, *In Memoriam*, pp. 116–17.
16. HPL to James F. Morton, 16 May 1926 (SL II.50).
17. Steven J. Mariconda, 'On the Emergence of "Cthulhu"', in *On the Emergence of 'Cthulhu'*, p. 59 (citing the *New York Times*, 1 March 1925).
18. HPL to Lillian D. Clark, 14–19 November 1925 (ms., JHL).

19. HPL to August Derleth, 16 May 1931 (ms., SHSW).

20. HPL to Farnsworth Wright, 5 July 1927 (SL II.150).

21. See David E. Schultz, 'The Origin of Lovecraft's "Black Magic" Quote', *Crypt of Cthulhu* No. 48 (St John's Eve 1987): 9–13.

22. See David E. Schultz, 'From Microcosm to Macrocosm: The Growth of Lovecraft's Cosmic Vision', in Schultz and Joshi, *An Epicure in the Terrible*.

23. John Milton, *Paradise Lost*, 1.26.

24. Kenneth W. Faig, Jr, '"The Silver Key" and Lovecraft's Childhood', *Crypt of Cthulhu* No. 81 (St John's Eve 1992): 11–47.

25. HPL to Frank Belknap Long, 6 September 1927 (SL II.164).

26. HPL to August Derleth, [early December 1926] (SL II.94).

Chapter Fourteen

1. HPL to Wilfred B. Talman, 19 December 1926 (SL II.95).

2. HPL to Clark Ashton Smith, 7 November 1930 (SL III.212).

3. HPL to Frank Belknap Long, [February 1927] (SL II.100).

4. HPL to Lillian D. Clark, 24 August 1925 (ms., JHL).

5. See M. Eileen McNamara and S. T. Joshi, 'Who Was the Real Charles Dexter Ward?', *Lovecraft Studies* No 19/20 (fall 1989): 40–41, 48. Most of the information in this article is derived from discussions with Mauran's widow, Grace Mauran.

6. HPL to R. H. Barlow, [19 March 1934] (ms., JHL).

7. HPL to Clark Ashton Smith, 24 March 1927 (SL II.114).

8. HPL to Richard Ely Morse, 13 October 1935 (ms., JHL).

9. HPL to J. Vernon Shea, [30 October 1931] (SL III.429).

10. HPL to Farnsworth Wright, 5 July 1927 (SL II.151).

11. M. R. James, 'An M. R. James Letter' [to Nicholas Llewelyn Davies, 12 January 1928], *Ghosts & Scholars* 8 (1986): 28–33. I am grateful to Hubert Van Calenbergh for bringing this item to my attention.

12. Donald Wandrei to HPL, 27 September 1928 (ms., JHL).

13. HPL to Lillian D. Clark, [17 July 1927] (ms., JHL).

14. HPL to Maurice W. Moe, 30 July 1927 (SL II.157).

15. Ibid.

16. HPL to Farnsworth Wright, 22 December 1927 (AHT).

17. HPL to Donald Wandrei, [20 January 1928] (ms., JHL).

18. HPL to Frank Belknap Long, [December 1927] (SL II.207).

19. Ibid.

20. Zealia Bishop, 'H. P. Lovecraft: A Pupil's View' (1953), in *Lovecraft Remembered*, p. 267.

21. HPL to August Derleth, 6 October [1929] (ms., SHSW).

22. HPL to Zealia Bishop, 1 May 1928 (SL II.238).

Chapter Fifteen

1. Davis, *Private Life*, p. 21.

2. HPL to James F. Morton, 10 May 1928 (SL II.239).

3. Davis, *Private Life*, p. 21.

4. HPL to Lillian D. Clark, [12 June 1928] (postcard) (ms., JHL).

5. 'Literary Persons Meet in Guilford', *Brattleboro Daily Reformer* (18 June 1928): 1.

6. HPL to Lillian D. Clark, 24 June 1924 (postcard) (ms., JHL).

7. HPL to August Derleth, [1928] (ms., SHSW).

8. HPL to Elizabeth Toldridge, 1 July [1929] (ms., JHL).

9. HPL to Donald Wandrei, 12 September 1929 (ms., JHL).

10. Davis, *Private Life*, p. 21.

11. Arthur S. Koki, 'H. P. Lovecraft: An Introduction to His Life and Writings' (M.A. thesis: Columbia University, 1962), pp. 209–10.

12. See Nelson Manfred Blake, *The Road to Reno: A History of Divorce in the United States* (New York: Macmillan, 1962), pp. 189–202.

13. HPL to Lillian D. Clark, [17 August 1929] (postcard) (ms., JHL).

14. Winfield Townley Scott, 'A Parenthesis on Lovecraft as Poet' (1945), in *H. P. Lovecraft: Four Decades of Criticism*, ed. S. T. Joshi (Athens: Ohio University Press, 1980), p. 213.

15. HPL to R. H. Barlow, 13 June 1936 (ms., JHL).

16. HPL to Elizabeth Toldridge, [January 1930] (SL III.116).

17. R. H. Barlow, ms. note on the T.Ms. of 'The Mound' (JHL).

18. HPL to Elizabeth Toldridge, 20 December 1929 (SL III.97).

19. Zealia Bishop, 'H. P. Lovecraft: A Pupil's View', in *Lovecraft Remembered*, p. 271.

20. Long, *Dreamer on the Nightside*, pp. xiii–xiv.

21. HPL to August Derleth, [29 April 1930] (postcard) (ms., JHL).

22. Wandrei, 'Lovecraft in Providence' (1959), in *Lovecraft Remembered*, p. 309.

23. HPL to Lillian D. Clark, 13–14 May 1930 (ms., JHL).

24. Cited in HPL to Lillian D. Clark, 24–26 May 1930 (ms., JHL).

25. HPL to Lillian D. Clark, 20–21 May 1930 (ms., JHL).

26. HPL to Elizabeth Toldridge, [c. 3 September 1930] (SLIII. 164).

27. Steven J. Mariconda, 'Tightening the Coil: The Revision of "The Whisperer in Darkness"', *Lovecraft Studies* No. 32 (spring 1995): 12–17.

Chapter Sixteen

1. Quoted in Russell's *Why I Am Not a Christian* (New York: Simon & Schuster, 1957), p. 104.

2. HPL to Frank Belknap Long, 20 February 1929 (SL II.265).

3. SL II.261 (note 2).

4. SL II.266–67 (note 2).

5. HPL to Frank Belknap Long, 22 November 1930 (SL III.228).

6. Bertrand Russell, *Human Knowledge: Its Scope and Limits* (New York: Simon & Schuster, 1948), p. 23.

7. HPL to James F. Morton, 30 October 1929 (SL III.53).

8. HPL to Frank Belknap Long, [April 1928] (SL II.234).

9. HPL to James F. Morton, 6 November 1930 (SL III.208).

10. HPL to Frank Belknap Long, 22 February 1931 (SL III.293–96).

11. 'Behind the Mountains of Madness: Lovecraft and the Antarctic in 1930', *Lovecraft Studies* No. 14 (Spring 1987): 31–38.

12. Robert M. Price, 'Demythologizing Cthulhu', in *H. P. Lovecraft and the Cthulhu Mythos* (Mercer Island, WA: Starmont House, 1990).

13. Jules Zanger, 'Poe's Endless Voyage: *The Narrative of Arthur Gordon Pym*', *Papers on Language and Literature* 22 (Summer 1986): 282.

14. HPL to August Derleth, 24 March [1931] (ms., SHSW).

15. HPL to J. Vernon Shea, 7 August 1931 (SL III.395).

16. SL III.395–96 (note 15).

17. HPL to August Derleth, [1929] (ms., SHSW).

18. HPL to August Derleth, 4 March 1932 (ms., SHSW).

19. HPL to Clark Ashton Smith, [20 November 1931] (SL III. 435).

20. HPL to August Derleth, 10 December 1931 (ms., SHSW).

21. HPL to Farnsworth Wright, 18 February 1932 (SL IV.17).

22. Farnsworth Wright to August Derleth, 17 January 1933 (ms., SHSW).

23. Clark Ashton Smith to August Derleth, 24 December 1932 (ms., SHSW).

24. HPL to J. Vernon Shea, 28 August 1931 (AHT).

25. HPL to Frank Belknap Long, 3 November 1930 (SL III.205–6).

Chapter Seventeen

1. HPL to August Derleth, 23 December 1931 (ms., SHSW).

2. HPL to R. H. Barlow, 25 February 1932 (ms., JHL).

3. HPL to Lillian D. Clark, 8–10 July 1931 (ms., JHL).

4. HPL to August Derleth, 16 January 1931 (ms., SHSW).

5. HPL to Robert E. Howard, 7 November 1932 (SL IV.104).

6. HPL to August Derleth, 9 October 1931 (ms., SHSW).

7. 'Lovecraft's Cosmic Imagery', in Schultz and Joshi, *An Epicure in the Terrible*, p. 192.

8. See Fritz Leiber, 'Through Hyperspace with Brown Jenkin: Lovecraft's Contribution to Speculative Fiction', in Lovecraft's *The Dark Brotherhood and Other Pieces* (Sauk City, WI: Arkham House, 1966), pp. 171–73.

9. 'An Interview with Harry K. Brobst', *Lovecraft Studies* Nos 22/23 (fall 1990): 24–26.

10. HPL to August Derleth, 6 June 1932 (ms., SHSW).

11. E. Hoffmann Price, 'The Man Who Was Lovecraft' (1949), in *Love-craft Remembered*, pp. 288–90.

12. HPL to James F. Morton, 5 July 1932 (SL IV.47).

13. Cook, *In Memoriam*, in *Lovecraft Remembered*, p. 131.

14. Hazel Heald to August Derleth, 30 September 1944; quoted in a footnote in *The Horror in the Museum and Other Revisions* (1970 ed.), p. 27.

15. HPL to E. Hoffmann Price, 20 October 1932 (ms., JHL).

16. HPL to Clark Ashton Smith, 26 March 1935 (SL V.130).

17. Price, 'The Man Who Was Lovecraft', p. 291.

18. HPL to J. Vernon Shea, 24 March 1933 (SL IV.158).

19. 'The Man Who Was Lovecraft', p. 291.

20. HPL to E. Hoffmann Price, 7 December 1932 (SL IV.116–17).

21. HPL to Duane W. Rimel, 12 September 1934 (SL V..33).

22. HPL to Clark Ashton Smith, 4 April 1932 (SL IV.37).

23. Davis, *Private Life*, p. 17.

24. HPL to Donald Wandrei, 21 February 1933 (ms., JHL).

Chapter Eighteen

1. HPL to Carl F. Strauch, 31 May 1933 (ms., JHL).

2. HPL to Carl F. Strauch, 18 March 1933 (ms., JHL).

3. Davis, *Private Life*, pp. 22–23.

4. HPL to Alfred Galpin, 24 June 1933 (SL IV.215).

5. Price, 'The Man Who Was Lovecraft', p. 293.

6. HPL to Allen G. Ullman, 16 August 1933 (ms., JHL).

7. See my essay, 'Autobiography in Lovecraft', *Lovecraft Studies* No. 1 (fall 1979): 7–19.

8. Helen V. Sully, 'Memories of Lovecraft: II' (1969), in *Lovecraft Remembered*, p. 278.

9. Samuel Loveman, 'Lovecraft as a Conversationalist' (1958), in *Love-craft Remembered*, pp. 210–11.

10. For a comprehensive discussion of Lovecraft's three trips to Florida (1931, 1934, and 1935), see Stephen J. Jordan, 'H. P. Lovecraft in Florida', *Lovecraft Studies* Nos 42/43 (forthcoming).

11. Barlow, 'The Wind that Is in the Grass', in *Lovecraft Remembered*, p. 358.

12. HPL to R. H. Barlow, 29 June 1934 (ms., JHL).

13. HPL to E. Hoffmann Price, 31 August 1934 (SL V.24–25).

14. HPL to Duane W. Rimel, 13 May 1934 (ms., JHL).

15 HPL to R. H. Barlow, 25 September 1934 (ms., JHL).

16. HPL to Kenneth Sterling, 14 December 1935; cited in Sterling's 'Caverns Measureless to Man' (1975), in *Lovecraft Remembered*, p. 376.

17. HPL to August Derleth, 30 December 1934 (ms., SHSW).

18. HPL to August Derleth, [February 1928] (ms., SHSW).

19. HPL to August Derleth, 7 August 1935 (ms., SHSW).

20. HPL to Clark Ashton Smith, [11 November 1930] (SL III.217); HPL to Clark Ashton Smith, [2 March 1932] (SL IV.25–26).

21. HPL to E. Hoffmann Price, 18 November 1934 (SL V.71).

Chapter Nineteen

1. HPL to Jennie K. Plaisier, 8 July 1936 (SL V.279).

2. HPL to Woodburn Harris, 25 February–1 March 1929 (SL II. 290,308).

3. HPL to C. L. Moore, [c. mid-October 1936] (SL V.321).

4. HPL to Robert E. Howard, 25 July 1932 (SL IV.51).

5. HPL to R. H. Barlow, [17 December 1933] (ms., JHL).

6. HPL to Robert E. Howard, 7 November 1932 (SL IV.106–07).

7. HPL to James F. Morton, [3 February 1932] (SL IV.13).

8. HPL to Henry George Weiss, 3 February 1937 (SL V.392).

9. HPL to C. L. Moore, [7 February 1937] (SL V.402).

10. HPL to Elizabeth Toldridge, 22 December 1932 (SL IV.124).

11. HPL to J. Vernon Shea, 13 March 1935 (SL V.122).

12. HPL to J. Vernon Shea, 10 February 1935 (ms., JHL).

13. HPL to C. L. Moore, [August 1936] (SL V.297).

14. HPL to R. H. Barlow, 27 December 1936 (ms., JHL).

15. SL V.293–94 (note 13).

16. SL V.397–98 (note 9).

17. SL V.329 (note 3).

18. HPL to J. Vernon Shea, 25 September 1933 (SL IV.253).

19. HPL to J. Vernon Shea, 25 September 1933 (SL IV.257).

20. 'An Interview with Harry Brobst', p. 29.

21. HPL to J. Vernon Shea, 30 July 1933 (SL IV.230–31).

22. HPL to J. Vernon Shea, 8–11 November 1933 (SL IV.307).

23. HPL to Clark Ashton Smith, 15 October 1927 (SL II.176).

24. HPL to J. Vernon Shea, 8–11 November 1933 (ms.).

25. HPL to Helen V. Sully, 28 October 1934 (SL V.50).

Chapter Twenty

1. HPL to R. H. Barlow, [24–29 May 1935] (ms., JHL).

2. HPL to Donald and Howard Wandrei, [July 1935] (postcard) (ms., JHL).

3. HPL to August Derleth, 19 August 1935 (ms., SHSW).

4. See Will Murray's interview, 'Julius Schwartz on Lovecraft', *Crypt of Cthulhu* No. 76 (Hallowmass 1990): 14–18.

5. HPL to J. Vernon Shea, 5 December 1935 (SL V.210).

6. *Weird Tales* 36, No. 5 (November 1935): 652.

7. Sterling, 'Caverns Measureless to Man', pp. 375–76.

8. HPL to R. H. Barlow, 11 March 1936 (ms., JHL).

9. The untitled diary is in JHL.

10. HPL to R. H. Barlow, 4 June 1936 (ms., JHL).

11. Ibid.

12. Robert E. Howard, *Selected Letters 1931–1936* (West Warwick, RI: Necronomicon Press, 1991), p. 79.

13. HPL to E. Hoffmann Price, 20 June 1936 (SL V.272–73).

14. HPL to R. H. Barlow, 23 July 1936 (ms., JHL).

15. HPL to Anne Tillery Renshaw, 24 February 1936 (ms., JHL).

16. HPL to R. H. Barlow, 11 December 1936 (ms., JHL).

17. Fritz Leiber, 'Through Hyperspace with Brown Jenkin', p.170.

18. Fritz Leiber, 'My Correspondence with Lovecraft' (1958), in *Lovecraft Remembered*, p. 301.

19. HPL to Donald Wandrei, 8 November 1936 (ms., JHL).

20. HPL to Farnsworth Wright, 1 July 1936 (SL V.274).

21. HPL to E. Hoffmann Price, [12 February 1936] (SL V.223–24).

22. HPL to August Derleth, 17 February 1937 (SL V.412).

23. HPL to Wilfred B. Talman, 28 February 1937 (SL V.419).

24. 'The Last Days of H. P. Lovecraft: Four Documents', *Lovecraft Studies* No. 28 (spring 1993): 36.

25. Willis Conover, *Lovecraft at Last* (Arlington, VA: Carrollton-Clark, 1975), p. 245.

26. HPL to Duane W. Rimel, 8 October 1934 (ms., JHL).

27. Thomas J. Slaga, 'Food Additives and Contaminants as Modifying Factors in Cancer Induction', in *Nutrition and Cancer: Etiology and Treatment*, ed. Guy R. Newell and Neil M. Ellison (New York: Raven Press, 1981), pp. 279–80.

28. Stewart Cameron, *Kidney Disease: The Facts*, 2nd ed. (Oxford: Oxford University Press, 1986), ch. 8.

29. See John Bligh, *Temperature Regulation in Mammals and Other Vertebrates* (Amsterdam: North-Holland Publishing Co., 1973).

30. See, in general, R. Alain Everts, *The Death of a Gentleman: The Last Days of Howard Phillips Lovecraft* (Madison, WI: Strange Co., 1987). The 'death diary' is transcribed on pp. 25–28.

31. 'The Last Days of H. P. Lovecraft', p. 36.

32. 'An Interview with Harry K. Brobst', p. 32.

33. 'The Last Days of H. P. Lovecraft', p. 36.

34. Ibid.

Epilogue

1. Smith, *Selected Poems* (Sauk City, WI: Arkham House, 1971), pp. 287–88.

Index